Writing between the Lines
Portraits of Canadian Anglophone Translators

Writing between the Lines
Portraits of Canadian Anglophone Translators

edited with an introduction by
AGNES WHITFIELD

Wilfrid Laurier University Press

Wilfrid Laurier University Press acknowledges the support of the Canada Council for the Arts for our publishing program. We acknowledge the financial support of the Government of Canada through the Book Publishing Industry Development Program for our publishing activities. This work was supported by the Research Support Fund.

Library and Archives Canada Cataloguing in Publication

Writing between the lines : portraits of Canadian anglophone translators / edited with an introduction by Agnes Whitfield.

Includes bibliographical references.
Issued in print and electronic formats.
ISBN 978-1-55458-616-5 (paperback).—ISBN 978-0-88920-908-4 (pdf)

1. Canadian literature (French)—20th century—Translations into English—History and criticism. 2. Translators—Canada—Biography. I. Whitfield, Agnes, 1951–

P306.9.W75 2006   C840.9'0054   C2005-906968-6

Cover design by P.J. Woodland, using an image courtesy of Patricia Claxton.
Text design by Catharine Bonas-Taylor.

© 2006 Wilfrid Laurier University Press
Waterloo, Ontario, Canada
www.wlupress.wlu.ca

Every reasonable effort has been made to acquire permission for copyright material used in this text, and to acknowledge all such indebtedness accurately. Any errors and omissions called to the publisher's attention will be corrected in future printings.

No part of this publication may be reproduced, stored in a retrieval system, or transmitted, in any form or by any means, without the prior written consent of the publisher or a licence from the Canadian Copyright Licensing Agency (Access Copyright). For an Access Copyright licence, visit http://www.accesscopyright.ca or call toll free to 1-800-893-5777.

Contents

Introduction / 1
Agnes Whitfield

1 William Hume Blake, or the Translator as Amateur Ethnologist / 19
Sherry Simon

2 Glassco Virtuoso / 37
Patricia Godbout

3 Joyce Marshall, or the Accidental Translator / 53
Jane Everett

4 Philip Stratford: The Comparatist as Smuggler / 75
Gillian Lane-Mercier

5 On D.G. Jones and Translating Outside / 107
Stephanie Nutting

6 Patricia Claxton: A Civil Translator / 139
Agnes Whitfield

7 Sheila Fischman: The Consummate Professional / 169
Pamela Grant

8 Transformations of Barbara Godard / 203
Kathy Mezei

9 Ray Ellenwood: The Translator as Activist / 225
   Barbara Kerslake

10 Susanne de Lotbinière-Harwood: Totally Between / 245
   Agnès Conacher

11 John Van Burek: Bringing Tremblay to Toronto / 267
   Jane Koustas

12 Linda Gaboriau: Playing with Performance / 287
   Robert Wallace

   List of Contributors / 309

Introduction

AGNES WHITFIELD

The motivation for this book grew out of a desire to explore the individual experience of some of Canada's most eminent contemporary anglophone literary translators, to delve beneath biography in order to capture the intercultural spirit writing between the lines. The translators profiled here will be immediately recognized by readers of Canadian literature and by Canadian theatregoers. These translators have won prestigious awards in Canada and abroad. Their names appear on the covers of the books they translate, contributing in no small measure to the success of the new works. In tandem with their authors, they criss-cross Canada for public readings and literary festivals.

Despite their increasing public presence, however, we know amazingly little about these generous yet discreet advocates of communication between our francophone and anglophone solitudes. Translation remains an invisible, unfamiliar, even mysterious profession. Who are these translators? How have they learned their craft? What motivated them to become the purveyors of their cultural "other"? What kind of challenges do they face when translating a text? How do they view their role within the Canadian and Québec literary institutions, and more generally, within the Canadian cultural domain? By drawing together the individual answers to these and other questions, and by giving particular priority to what our translators say about their craft, this book offers the first comprehensive, inside view of the practice of anglophone literary translation in Canada.

Early Experiences

As the portraits in this book demonstrate, the paths towards an engagement with literary translation from French into English in Canada are deeply personal. Early exposure to French is not necessarily a prerequisite. Feminist translator Susanne de Lotbinière-Harwood grew up in a bilingual home in Montréal, learning early to separate her mother and father tongues. John Glassco and Joyce Marshall, known for their own writing as well as their translations, were also born in Montréal, and learned French in primary school. However, for the other translators profiled here, French was far from being an obvious interest. Award-winning poet and translator D.G. Jones spent his childhood in Bancroft, Ontario, and admits to almost failing French in high school. Linda Gaboriau and John Van Burek, whose translations of Québec playwrights have travelled the world, lived a significant part (Van Burek) if not all (Gaboriau) of their youth in the United States. Patricia Claxton, whose translation of *A Sunday at the Pool in Kigali* by Gil Courtemanche is being read in England and Australia, was raised in northern India and spent her summers in Kashmir; nor was she particularly interested in learning French when she returned to Kingston as a high-school student. Sheila Fischman, one of Canada's best-known translators, and Philip Stratford, one of the founding figures of comparative literature in Canada, both grew up in small anglophone towns in Ontario. How could one predict that Toronto-born and -bred Barbara Godard would come to translate Québec lesbian feminist writer Nicole Brossard, or that Ray Ellenwood, schooled in south Edmonton, Alberta, would become an enthusiastic advocate of Québec surrealist writer Claude Gauvreau?

There is, nonetheless, in the early days of almost all these diverse lives, a discernable presence of otherness that cannot be unrelated to their eventual commitment to translation and its role in the facilitation of intercultural communication. Interestingly, for Gaboriau, Van Burek, Ellenwood, and Fischman, cultural difference was an experience first encountered not between two languages, but within English itself. For Gaboriau and Van Burek, living as children in the United States, it was their Canadian roots (Gaboriau's mother was from Saskatchewan, and Van Burek was born in Toronto). For Fischman, it was being raised in the only Jewish family in Elgin, Ontario. For Ellenwood, it was listening to the Geordie accent of his mother, who came to Canada from England. Otherness also surfaces through a family heritage of interlinguistic difference. Marshall's roots go back to Scotland, Norway, England, and Wales. Fischman's paternal and maternal grandfathers were born outside Canada, in Russia and Poland, respectively.

De Lotbinière-Harwood's double heritage is inscribed in her very name, the result of a marriage in 1823 between the daughter of a French nobleman, Louise-Josephte de Lotbinière, and a newly arrived Yorkshire businessman, Robert Unwin Harwood.

A complex mixture of predisposition and circumstance channelled this general sensitivity to difference into a desire to learn French and to acquire a better understanding of Québec's distinct culture. For some, the passage was mediated by France. Philip Stratford's decision to study in Bordeaux may reflect his desire to render homage to his three uncles killed in France in the First World War. He was also following in the footsteps of a francophile father who himself held a doctorate from the Université de Lyon. Glassco, in contrast, confesses that Paris was his grand escape from a painful and repressive childhood. Godard was caught up as a graduate student in the May 1968 intellectual effervescence of the French capital. Ellenwood's initial attraction to European francophone culture stemmed in part from his appreciation for modern French art, but France also offered the practical possibility of a teaching assistantship. Van Burek, too, first came to learn and love French in France.

For others, Québec was the source of their inspiration from the beginning. Gaboriau came to Montréal precisely to learn French. Like Jones, Glassco, Claxton, and Marshall, she studied at McGill University. For Fischman, French came alive with a Canadian accent in a Toronto high-school classroom, thanks to a Franco-Ontarian teacher to whom she would dedicate her first translation. From the age of twelve, Blake left Toronto to spend his summers at the family's country home in Murray Bay, Charlevoix; hearing and speaking Québécois became indelibly associated for him with the natural beauty of the Laurentians and the pleasures of fishing and hiking in the region.

For some of Blake's successors, however, living the duality of Québec was not an unproblematic experience. Marshall, the first woman editor of the *McGill Daily* and winner of the English department's language and literature medal, chose to leave Québec, after graduation in 1935, for economic and political reasons. Despite her fluency in French, she did not feel that she could find a place, as a non-francophone, non-Catholic woman, in Québec under a Duplessis government. Many years later, Claxton would be struck by the physical and cultural separation of the solitudes in Montréal, the Boulevard Saint-Laurent dividing the two, francophones to the east, and anglophones to the west. Her forays with the McGill fencing team across the "border" and her discomfort with unilingual anglophone insensibility would prove strong motivators in her decision to perfect her spoken French and become a translator. For de Lotbinière-Harwood, growing up astride the barrier would lead to many social and personal confrontations. The constant sense of having to choose one or the other of her languages and cultures would spark an intense internal revolt and incite her to formulate a radical form of translation bilingualism.

Translation as Social Practice

In a country where English and French have always, as Hugh MacLennan has written, "live[d] their separate legends, side by side,"[1] literary translation is only beginning to be recognized as a specific activity in its own right. Translation did not present itself to any of the well-known translators whose work is analyzed in this volume as a professional choice. None of them grew up with the ambition to become a translator. Like many of their historical counterparts, most of the translators in the present volume have juggled more than one career. Blake was a lawyer. Glassco delivered the mail in the Eastern Townships, where he was also the mayor of Foster, his small community. Jones, Ellenwood, and Godard are academics, as was Stratford. Van Burek is a theatre director and co-founder of Toronto's Tarragon Theatre. Gaboriau and Marshall began their careers in broadcasting and journalism. De Lotbinière-Harwood started as a freelance critic for the entertainment section of the now-defunct *Montreal Star*. Claxton's first real job was as an investment analyst for an insurance company, Sun Life. After studying chemistry and anthropology at the University of Toronto, Fischman took an office job at the CBC, before writing reviews for the *Globe and Mail* and working in the promotion department of the University of Toronto Press. For only three, Claxton, Fischman, and Gaboriau, was translation to become their principal professional activity.

Rather than being extraneous to their work as translators, these other activities have served to inform and nurture the practice of those profiled here. For translation inevitably includes a variety of tasks that go beyond understanding the original text and finding the words in the target language to re-express it. Historically, translators have created alphabets, set up their own printing presses, identified (through their own travels or other professional activities) the texts that should be translated, and negotiated with secular and religious powers the right to translate and the conditions under which they have worked.

Although the precise nature of these activities has changed, the translators in this volume are no different in their exercise of what can be called the social practice of translation. Far from being passive reproducers of texts, they have often, themselves, though their other professional or personal interests, identified the texts they felt were important to bring to the attention of Canadian anglophone readers or theatre audiences, and then set about translating them. Blake's travels to Charlevoix awoke his interest in language and his desire to share his knowledge of the region with his fellow anglophones. Van Burek's first goal was to bring Québec and French theatre to Toronto. Jones saw translating Québec poetry as a way of enriching the range of poems available to anglophone readers. In their roles as professors of comparative literature, Stratford and Jones both discovered that their teaching goals were hampered by the lack of Québec literary texts accessible in English translation. Fellow academics Ellenwood and Godard wanted to bring into English the important contributions Québec writers were making to specific aesthetic and intellectual debates: surrealism for Ellenwood, feminism for Godard. As a freelance journalist, de Lotbinière-Harwood wrote an article on Québec singer/poet Lucien Francoeur for the *Montreal Star* and, lacking an English translation of his lyrics, penned the English versions herself.

The connections between translation and professional or personal interests can take other forms as well. Swept up in the politically charged Québec of the 1960s and 1970s, both Fischman and Claxton undertook their first translations as personal and political exercises to improve their French skills in order to demonstrate their openness to francophone culture. Fischman started with a short story by her neighbour, writer Roch Carrier, and went on to translate his novel *La Guerre, Yes Sir!* Claxton applied herself to a controversial political essay by a young Québec intellectual who would become prime minister of Canada, Pierre Elliot Trudeau. Their translations in hand, both undertook the arduous task of finding a publisher for the work. For Gaboriau and Marshall, their involvement in broadcasting opened the door to translation: Marshall was asked, since she knew French, to translate a short story by Gabrielle Roy for CBC radio; Gaboriau "fell into translating for the theatre,"[2] as she puts it, through her personal contacts with the Québec French-speaking theatre community as theatre critic at the Montréal newspaper, the *Gazette*, and as broadcaster for *Québec Now*, a CBC national network show. Similarly, Glassco was introduced to the first text he would translate, Québec poet Saint Denys-Garneau's *Journal*, by friend, fellow poet, and cultural *animateur* Frank Scott.

In a complementary fashion, all these translators have put their personal and professional skills to use in the service of their translation work. Fischman's knowledge of how the Canadian publishing industry operates, gained through her early experience with the University of Toronto Press, has enabled her to lobby adroitly on behalf of her authors and promote their work. Claxton has used her sense of the business and insurance world, and the importance of contractual obligations, in her efforts to obtain codified recognition of copyright for translators in Canadian law. As academics, Ellenwood, Godard, Jones, and Stratford have written numerous articles on their authors, stimulating English-Canadian reception of the translated works. Marshall was an important contributor of texts on francophone writers to the *Oxford Companion to Canadian Literature*. Glassco published an anthology entitled *The Poetry of French Canada in Translation*. Jones founded a bilingual review of poetry, *ellipse*. De Lotbinière-Harwood has brought together her strategies for feminization in a book, both practical and theoretical, *Re-belle et infidèle / The Body Bilingual*, which can be used by other translators. Almost all have spoken out in public discussions or published texts on the process of translation, and they have contributed their personal expertise to the advancement and recognition of literary translation as a profession. In short, they have helped create the very conditions that would facilitate the publication, reading, and intercultural understanding of the Québec literary works they translate.

Towards a Canadian Tradition of Anglophone Literary Translation

This book offers an overview of anglophone translation in Canada at a distinctive period in its development. With the exception of Blake, whose translations were done in the 1920s, all the translators presented here belong to the generation of dedicated individuals whose efforts, from the late 1950s to the 1970s, were instrumental in setting up the institutional structures that would establish a vital anglophone tradition of literary translation in Canada. To put their achievements in perspective, it is important to realize how few literary translations were published in Canada before the 1970s. As John O'Connor observes in the *Oxford Companion to Canadian Literature*, "from 1900 to the start of the Quiet Revolution, 67 literary translations were published—an average of little more than one book a year."[3] Or to quote Joyce Marshall when Marshall translated her first short story by Gabrielle Roy around 1959, "nobody much was translating then."

These were, of course, momentous years for the arts in Canada and Québec generally, and more particularly, for the institutional recognition of both English-Canadian and Québec literature. The lives of the translators profiled here were marked in one way or another by this broader tapestry of events and in turn they left their own mark on it. What is perhaps most striking is how intricately the flowering of translation during this period is connected to the warp and weft of other dimensions of literary life in Canada, both chronologically and institutionally.

In the 1950s, the growing national interest in culture was reflected in the report of the Royal Commission on National Development in the Arts, Letters, and Sciences, otherwise known as the Massey Commission Report. Filed in 1951, it led to the creation of the Canada Council for the Arts by an act of the Canadian Parliament on March 28, 1957. While writers' conferences may be commonplace today, the first Canadian Writers' Conference to bring together participants from across the country was held in Kingston, Ontario, in July 1955. Both Marshall and Jones attended. Nor was this kind of professional brainstorming get-together unique to English Canada. Jones also participated in the Rencontre des poètes, a Québec writers' retreat held in 1958 at Morin Heights in the Laurentians. Spurred on by the enthusiasm of Montréal anglophone poets A.J.M. Smith and Frank Scott, Glassco would organize his own informal conference of poets in Foster, Québec, in 1963; it was, he writes, "no sterile love-feast, no singsong or genteel eisteddfod. There was a constant sense of clash and conflict...sharply differing conceptions of the role of the poet in society and even of the nature of poetry itself."[4] For Marshall, Jones, and Glassco, whose work as translators was fundamentally grounded in their practice as writers, these lively encounters and exchanges played a crucial role in their motivation and opportunities for translation. Their careers show the different ways in which they negotiated the tensions between their two creative activities, as part of an important, but intermittent, tradition of anglophone writers translating.[5]

Throughout the 1960s, the interest in translations from Québec would grow as much for political as aesthetic reasons. As Claxton puts it, "Big changes were happening in Québec and English-speaking Canadians needed to understand what they were about." Significantly, it was during these years of not-so-Quiet Revolution, artistic ebullience, and Front de libération du Québec bombings that Jones, Stratford, Gaboriau, and Fischman all arrived in Québec. Understandably, it is also during this decade that it became intolerably evident that, if literary translation in Canada were to finally develop after over two hundred years of French-English co-existence, appropriate institutional structures needed to be put in place. Starting in 1959, the Canada Council funded translations on an ad hoc basis, but, as Claxton pointed out in 1967 in her urgent call to action, "Culture Vulture," such aid would be to no avail if the translations were of poor quality. She called for professional training for translators, prizes to recognize their work, and a professional association to ensure quality. A year later, Stratford would sound a different alarm. Pointing out that "non-literary works, history, geography, economics," were taking "the biggest part of the [council's] pie," he decried the dearth of literary translations in Canada: "The brute reality…is that public interest is small, or nascent at best, that publishers are reluctant to run the risk of large scale promotion," not to mention the "lack of competent translators…[and] weak incentives for those that are, since rates for literary translation are so inferior to commercial rates."[6]

The move towards increased professional recognition of literary translation in the 1970s was one response to these practical challenges. The Literary Translators' Association of Canada, with Claxton as president and Stratford as secretary, was officially voted into being on May 17, 1975, at the Bonaventure Hotel in Montréal. By enabling them to share information and experience, the association helped translators in their contractual negotiations with publishers and lent a specific professional identity to the practice of literary translation. At the same time, the creation of the association was very much in keeping with other, similar, professional regroupings of the time. The Writers' Union of Canada held its first meeting in Ottawa on November 3, 1973; the Québec equivalent, the Union des écrivaines et écrivains québécois, was founded in March 1977 in Montréal. All three groups would be concerned about changes to Canada's copyright laws, although not necessarily for the same reasons. The 1970s was also a period of identification of shared Canadian research interests within academic circles, which sought to contribute to an increased understanding between anglophone and francophone cultures in Canada, although their precise impact on literary translation is yet to be examined: the Association for Canadian Studies was founded in Kingston, Ontario, in 1973; the Association for Canadian and Québec Literatures in Toronto, in 1974.

However, the most important impetus in this period for improving the professional status of literary translation between English and French was undoubtedly the creation of the Canada Council Translation Grants Program in 1972. A year later, the council would inaugurate its annual prizes for literary translation, renamed in 1986 the Governor General's Awards. Although the fee structure was conservative, to say the least, in terms of commercial rates, the program did ensure steady funding for literary translation, and thus the number of texts that were translated increased considerably. As John O'Connor points out, "approximately ninety percent of all French-to-English literary translations in Canada have appeared in the quarter-century since the Canada Council inaugurated its program of financial support for literary translation."[7]

The portraits that follow illuminate the seminal role of particular individuals within a complex interweaving of institutional structures. In the 1950s and 1960s, CBC program organizer and producer Robert Weaver and Frank Scott, himself an award-winning translator,[8] were important forces in generating translation opportunities. It was Weaver who launched Marshall's career as a translator; he wanted to include a short story by Gabrielle Roy in his new radio series *Anthology*.[9] As editor of the *Tamarack Review*, founded in Toronto in 1956, he published Marshall's translations of Naïm Kattan's "Montreal Letters." Despite probable opposition from other members of the editorial board, he also included Glassco's translations of Saint-Denys Garneau in the review. Scott's exchange of letters with Anne Hébert over his translation of her poetry, published in 1970 under the title *Dialogue sur la traduction*, with a preface by Northrop Frye, was an inspirational text for contemporary Canadian and Québec literary translators. As these portraits demonstrate, Scott also played a generous role as literary matchmaker, encouraging Glassco to translate Saint-Denys-Garneau's *Journal*, sending Jones to the Rencontre des poètes that would change his destiny as poet, and generally stimulating, along with fellow Montréal poet, A.J.M. Smith, intercultural and intracultural literary exchange.

For Jones, Ellenwood, and Godard, it is clear that involvement with a literary review or press was crucial in facilitating their translation work.[10] The bilingual poetry review *ellipse*, founded by Jones in 1969, served as a key publisher for both English-Canadian and Québécois poets, in the original and in translation, and the review stimulated valuable discussion on the translation process. Ellenwood published many of his translations in the review *Exile* (founded in 1971), or at Exile Press (created in 1976), both directed by York University colleague Barry Callaghan; in her portrait of Ellenwood, Barbara Kerslake describes Callaghan as Ellenwood's veritable translation "pipeline." Similarly, much of the initial incentive for Barbara Godard's early translations came from her involvement with *Open Letter*, a journal of experimental writing and criticism founded by Frank Davey, with whom she directed the Coach House Press Québec Translation Series from 1975 to 1985. In the 1980s, Godard's involvement in the feminist review *Tessera* provided her with opportunities to develop her translation and translation-related activities, notably through a special issue, *La traduction au féminin/Translating Women*, published in 1989.

De Lotbinière-Harwood, Van Burek, and Gaboriau found equivalent support in their participation in other artistic milieux. Through her position as a member and the co-ordinator of Powerhouse Gallery in the early 1980s, de Lotbinière-Harwood made a connection with Montréal feminist writers and artists that informed her future practice of translation. Van Burek's and Gaboriau's translation activity is grounded in their involvement with the Toronto and Montréal theatre milieu.

For Stratford, Claxton, and Fischman, the situation is somewhat more complex. While Stratford's status as an academic gave him access to scholarly reviews for publishing his reflections on the state of literary translation in Canada, including editing a special issue of the *Canadian Review of Comparative Literature* in 1979, this did not necessarily open publishers' doors for his own literary translations. Revealingly, it is in the portraits of these three translators that one catches something of the nitty-gritty work involved in actually getting a translation published. To quote Stratford's comments in the portrait below, the translator "really does get thickly covered in dust from the market place." Claxton and Fischman's cultivated, ongoing relationships with publishers are in some ways their equivalent to the more specific community of interests to which other translators are connected. Fischman, in particular, negotiates these relationships, as Pamela Grant points out, through a sense of loyalty to her authors, in much the same way that an art gallery cultivates and promotes a stable of artists. The portraits point to the particular efforts of a small number of presses—Oberon, Exile, Coach House, Talonbooks, House of Anansi, Simon and Pierre, Lester and Orpen Dennys, and McClelland and Stewart—who rose to the specific challenges involved in editing, printing, and promoting translated texts.

These interconnected networks shed a certain light on what might at first glance appear to be an unexpected, if not paradoxical, effect of the Canada Council Translation Grants program. Set up "in the hope that making the best writing in French or English available in the other language would foster mutual understanding and cultural exchange,"[11] the program has indeed contributed substantially to an increase in literary translation. It has also drawn attention to the vast number of important books that still remain untranslated. By 1997, as John O'Connor points out, Canadian anglophones had acquired access to only a small part of Québec literary works: "approximately 300 works of fiction, 100 books of poetry, and more than 50 plays, as well as numerous other works" including "anthologies in various genres; journals and travel accounts; autobiography and literary criticism; folklore and folksongs; and children's books."[12] Other studies by contemporary translation scholars lend weight to the criticism Stratford voiced in 1977: "The fact is we lag behind most Western nations in this field....There never has been any systematic attempt to translate major works of the cultural other."[13] There are considerable discrepancies between the range of Québec works chosen for translation into English, and the works that Québec writers, critics, and scholars themselves would identify as their canonical texts.[14]

The relationships between translators and publishers that surface throughout these portraits demonstrate in concrete terms how tensions between economic and literary values have been articulated within the practice of literary translation in Canada. The patterns of how texts are chosen, tend to be, for better or for worse, a somewhat random affair based on encounters between writers, individual publisher interests, and translators' affinities. Within this haphazard context, particularly with the increased professional recognition of translation since the 1970s, translators have responded in two ways. Some, such as Ellenwood, Godard, and to a lesser degree de Lotbinière-Harwood, have been part of what one might call strategic alliances with publishers around specific aesthetic and/or political values, thus facilitating publication of works that espouse these values. Others, including in particular Gaboriau, Claxton, and Fischman, for whom translation is a principal profession (this is also true of Van Burek, whose translation work is closely connected with his role as theatre director and producer), have negotiated more directly the tensions between their own affinities and the values of the marketplace, in other words, between what they would like to translate, and what the publisher or producer thinks will "play" or "sell." It is this latter model that appears to have gained momentum in the 1990s.[15]

Conceptualizing the Practice of Literary Translation

Interestingly, the translators profiled in this book have been active almost solely in professional organizations related to literature rather than in professional translators' associations. While provincial associations had long been in existence (the Association of Translators and Interpreters of Ontario was founded in 1921 and the Société des traducteurs du Québec in 1940), and were themselves active in the 1970s in the pursuit of increased professional recognition and accreditation, these were not the professional affiliations of choice within official literary translation circles. Claxton, one of the few well-known translators to be an active member of a professional order of translators, points out that tensions between literary translators and those who specialized in non-literary texts were already present when the Literary Translators' Association of Canada (LTAC) was created: "certain Québec professional translators' circles, having succeeded in unifying disparate groups, regarded [the] initiative as a betrayal."[16] Similarly, while the Canadian Association of Schools of Translation was founded in 1973, and the 1970s marked an important expansion in the number of Canadian university translation programs, this evidence of increasing professionalization does not appear to have led to any form of consistent, institutionalized contact between LTAC members and the university community involved in training professional translators.[17]

This division can be related to a persistent cultural perception, widely held but empirically difficult to justify, that there is an inherent difference between literary and pragmatic (including technical) translation.[18] The superior financial rewards for commercial translation and the demands of the marketplace have certainly influenced the conception of professional translation programs. Beyond these factors, however, the experience of our leading literary translators reveals an historical reality that bears noting: theirs is exclusively a self-learned, learn-as-you-go practice of translation. As Marshall observes, "I learned whatever I've learned about the craft of translating by doing. [When I tackled my first translation] I'd never met anyone who'd done even a single translation—in fact, there were few such people in this country at the time. I'd never (nor have I yet) taken a course in translating. (I don't think that in those days there were any such courses.)"[19]

Marshall's use of the word "craft" is also significant. Jones or Stratford might well have said "art." Both words define the view of translation that underlies more or less explicitly the way the translators profiled here conceptualize their practice. When discussing their work, all emphasize, directly or indirectly, the individual, creative dimension of translation. This is consistent with the self-directed learning process that their particular generation of literary translators has assumed. At the same time, by affirming the specificity of literary translation against the broader, and more recognizably "professional" field of commercial translation, and by under-reporting the economic constraints of their practice, they validate their "literary" status as independent, aesthetic creators. The tension between the two visions of the translator encapsulated by "literary professional" is not always disclosed in the portraits in this collection, although it may well be specific to the practice of literary translation, a dynamic component of the inevitably "in between" nature of such an activity. To this tension must also be added, as these portraits demonstrate, the active intercultural brokerage functions negotiated by the translator.

The articles in this volume trace in detail each translator's method of translating, the translators' experiences with both their authors and their publishers, and their expectations of their translations. Not surprisingly, each has his or her own approach and process. Blake can been seen "as an amateur ethnologist, fascinated by difference...in a rear-guard attempt to preserve an idealized vision of a culture." For Glassco, "translations must stand on their own, dependent on their own poetic merits, owing to their originals nothing but the inspiration that has here found a partial rebirth." Personal affinity, a sense of challenge, the "desire to promote French-Canadian literature in English Canada" and a "conception of the translator's relative freedom to choose and invent" were important factors in both Stratford's choice of books to translate and his approach to the process of translating. Joyce Marshall's memories of her lengthy, sometimes heated, and always productive discussions with author Gabrielle Roy were part of a process of negotiation to arrive at a translation that met both Roy's expectations of English, and Marshall's own demands as a writer. "I approach a translation as I would a poem," says Jones. "I work on both the same way."

For Claxton, attentiveness to the "accuracy of references to time and space are clearly part of the civil contract the translator undertakes with his or her reader." Fischman reflects, "Translating a book means, for me at any rate, becoming totally absorbed, not only in it, but by it." And Godard writes in her translation journal, "Translation is not a carrying across, but a reworking of meaning." De Lotbinière-Harwood emphasizes translation as an experience of embodied language, how she feels reading a text's words, and how her body reacts to the words she herself writes in response. In the field of theatre translation, where actors have to say the words she finds, Gaboriau works through a collective experience aimed at making "the translation play." Van Burek readily admits that his biggest challenge was finding an anglophone voice for Michel Tremblay's *joual*.

Fostering the Study of Literary Translation in Canada

When I asked the scholars who have contributed portraits to this volume to participate in the project, I little anticipated the breadth and depth of commentary about translation that would result. Nor did I expect such a wide range of motivations and metaphors to emerge. Translators as smugglers, performers, activists, virtuosos, comparatists, and ventriloquists, translators who retreat between the lines, translators who flaunt their signature, translation as news from the front, or engineering the passage—the metaphors of the translation process that emerge from the portraits in this book are as varied and numerous as the translators themselves.

Some of these captivating and evocative images extend to the role of literary translation in facilitating intercultural communication in Canada. From an early view of translation as "a bridge of sorts," Stratford gradually shifted to a more complex view of translation "as a paradoxical creative process in which author and translator enter into a 'close yet critical discipleship' based on faithfulness and betrayal, sameness and difference." Stratford also suggests the image of the parallel as way of conceptualizing the relationship between English-Canadian and Québec literature. Jones used the image of the ellipse to represent the interaction between the two linguistic groups, although he considered the Canadian reality to be "rather more fantastic, a figure generated by the interaction of language from myriad centres—something more like the older definition of God, as a circle whose centre is nowhere and whose circumference is everywhere."[20] His statement that "Our cultural reality is not a stable figure; it is a figure of transformation"[21] would resonate with more than one of his fellow translators.

Like literary translation in Canada, the discipline of translation studies is still mapping its territory.[22] Through its detailed analysis of the practice of a generation of acclaimed Canadian anglophone literary translators, this volume seeks to make a contribution not only to the study of literary translation in Canada, but also to a broader understanding of literary translation as intercultural exchange. At the crossroads between Europe and the United States, Canadian translators have participated in the international exchange of ideas about translation, sharing their own experience and profiting from the writings of literary translation scholars and practitioners from other parts of the world. Concepts from New Criticism and the American translation workshop tradition, particularly under the influence of Ezra Pound, can be seen at work in the way Jones and Ellenwood envisage the artistic integrity of the translated text.[23] Godard and de Lotbinière-Harwood have been an integral part of the international development of a feminist practice of literary translation. Throughout the portraits, other connections surface through references to editorial contacts, the distribution of translations, and public readings. At the same time, the particular intercultural context of literary translation in Canada offers new insights and leads to the formulation of concepts useful for understanding the social practice of literary translators in other countries.

This volume does not claim to represent all the major contemporary Canadian anglophone translators. A variety of factors, predominantly of a pragmatic nature, have played a role in the final choice of subjects. The relative newness of translation studies in Canada[24] has meant that the contributors to the volume come from a variety of disciplines: Québec literature, comparative literature, English-Canadian literature, critical theatre, drama studies, and translation studies. They have all taken up the challenge of the portrait framework with enthusiasm, ingenuity, and grace. The translators themselves have responded with generosity, providing up-to-date lists of their published and unpublished translations, as well as their various written texts on translation. The bibliographies included at the end of each portrait will no doubt serve as an important resource for the further study of their individual and collective practice.

Many of the translators who lobbied for the Canada Council Translation Grants Program, who founded the Literary Translators' Association of Canada in 1975, and who are still working tirelessly on behalf of literary translation and their Québécois authors, are close to retirement, if such a notion can indeed be applied to their continued devotion to translating. It is time to examine their rich heritage, to gather together the biographical and bibliographical information that can foster further research, and, through a collective analysis of their work, to lay the groundwork for a better understanding of the intercultural importance and complexity of anglophone literary translation in Canada.

NOTES

1 Hugh MacLennan, *Two Solitudes* (Toronto: Stoddart, 1993), p. 2.
2 Linda Gaboriau, "The Cultures of Theatre," in *Culture in Transit*, ed. Sherry Simon (Montréal: Vehicule Press, 1995), p. 89.
3 John J. O'Connor, "Translations: French to English," in the *Oxford Companion to Canadian Literature*, ed. Eugene Benson and William Toye (Toronto: Oxford University Press, 1997), p. 1127.
4 John Glassco, *English Poetry in Quebec: Proceedings of the Foster Poetry Conference, October 12–14, 1963.* (Montréal: McGill University Press, 1965), p. 6–7.
5 The tradition of the writer/translator is much more prominent in Québec letters than in English-Canadian literature. For a parallel volume of portraits of Canadian francophone translators see Agnes Whitfield, ed., *Le Métier du double*, Collection Nouvelles études québécoises (Montréal: Fides, 2005).
6 Philip Stratford, "French-Canadian Literature in Translation," *Méta* 13, no. 4 (Dec. 1968): 182.
7 O'Connor, "Translations," p. 1127.
8 Frank Scott has not been included in this book, since a comprehensive study of his life and work already exists. See Sandra Djwa, *The Politics of the Imagination: A Life of F.R. Scott* (Toronto: McClelland and Stewart, 1987).
9 Weaver gave one of the lectures at the First Canadian Writers' Conference in Kingston in 1955. Robert Weaver, "Broadcasting," in *Writing in Canada: Pro-*

ceedings of the Canadian Writers' Conference Held at Queen's University July 1955, ed. George Whalley (Toronto: Macmillan, 1956), p. 112.
10 For the broader context of small literary magazines in Canada, see Ken Norris, *The Little Magazine in Canada 1925–80* (Toronto: ECW Press, 1984). The report of the Royal Commission on Book Publishing, *Canadian Publishers and Canadian Publishing* (Toronto: Queen's Printer for Ontario, 1972), offers an in-depth analysis of the Canadian publishing industry in the early 1970s. More recently, Roy MacSkimming, in *The Perilous Trade: Publishing Canada's Writers* (Toronto: McClelland and Stewart, 2003) has traced the adventures of Canada's main presses. However, there is surprisingly little direct information on the practice of literary translation in any of these volumes.
11 Gérard Pelletier, quoted by Ruth Martin, "Translated Canadian Literature and Canada Council Grants 1972–1992: The Effect on Authors, Translators and Publishers," *ellipse*, no. 51 (1994): 56.
12 O'Connor, "Translations," p. 1127.
13 Philip Stratford, *Bibliography of Canadian Books in Translation: French to English and English to French / Bibliographie de livres canadiens traduits de l'anglais au français et du français à l'anglais*. (Ottawa: Humanities Research Council of Canada/Conseil de recherches sur les humanités, 1977), p. ii.
14 See, for instance, Ruth Martin, "Translated Canadian Literature," pp. 55–84; Larry Shouldice, "On the Politics of Literary Translation in Canada," in *Translation in Canadian Literature Symposium 1982*, ed. Camille R. La Bossière (Ottawa: University of Ottawa Press, 1983), pp. 73–82.
15 John O'Connor raises concerns about the effect of market factors on literary translation in Canada, particularly in view of the economic recession in the 1990s and its consequences for Canadian publishers, O'Connor, "Translations," p. 1132. See also Agnes Whitfield, "Translations, Traductions," *University of Toronto Quarterly* 72, no. 1 (2002–2003): 291–306; and "Translations, Traductions," *University of Toronto Quarterly* 73, no. 1 (2003–2004): 79–96.
16 Patricia Claxton, "Introduction: Looking Back," *Méta* 45, no. 1 (2000): 7.
17 This remains much the case today, despite the fact that the association is now housed permanently in a building belonging to Concordia University in Montréal, and that some individual members teach part-time or full-time within different university programs. In the late 1990s, an attempt was made by the LTAC executive to set up an official mentoring program, but due to lack of funds the program was not implemented.
18 As Peter Newmark has pointed out, "all sorts of false distinctions have been made between literary and technical translation" by translation theorists, "but the distinction between careful, sensitive and elegant writing…cuts across all this." Peter Newmark, *Approaches to Translation* (Oxford: Pergamon, 1981), p. 5–6.
19 Joyce Marshall, "The Writer as Translator," *Canadian Literature*, no. 117 (1988): 26.
20 D.G. Jones, "Tracing Ellipse," *ellipse*, no. 4 (1988): 21.
21 Jones, "Tracing Ellipse," p. 21.

22 For an analysis of James S. Holmes's initial mapping of the discipline, see Mary Snell-Hornby, "Translation Studies—Art, Science or Utopia," in *Translation Studies: The State of the Art*, ed. Kitty M. van Leuven-Zwart and Ton Naaijkens. (Amsterdam: Rodopi, 1991), pp. 13–24. For recent trends, see the John Benjamin's online *Translation Studies Bibliography*, ed. Yves Gambier and Luc van Doorslaer, John Benjamins Publishing <www.benjamins.com/online>.
23 See the chapter "The American Translation Workshop" in Edwin Gentzler, *Contemporary Translation Theories* (London/New York: Routledge, 1993), pp. 7–42.
24 For further bibliographical references, see the Université de Sherbrooke's online *Bibliography of Comparative Studies in Canadian, Québec and Foreign Literatures* <www.compcanlit.ca>, which includes Translation Studies.

BIBLIOGRAPHY

Bibliography of Comparative Studies in Canadian, Québec and Foreign Literatures. Université de Sherbrooke, <www.compcanlit.ca>.

Canada. Royal Commission on Book Publishing. *Canadian Publishers and Canadian Publishing.* Toronto: Queen's Printer, 1972.

Claxton, Patricia. "Culture Vulture." *Méta* 12, no. 1 (1967): 9–13.

———. "Introduction: Looking Back." *Méta* 45, no.1 (2000): 7–12.

Djwa, Sandra. *The Politics of the Imagination: A Life of F. R. Scott.* Toronto: McClelland and Stewart, 1987.

Gaboriau, Linda. "The Cultures of Theatre." In *Culture in Transit*, ed. Sherry Simon. Montréal: Vehicule Press, 1995. 83–90.

Gambier, Yves, and Luc van Doorslaer, eds. *Translation Studies Bibliography*. John Benjamins Publishing Company, <www.benjamins.com/online>.

Gentzler, Edwin. *Contemporary Translation Theories.* London and New York: Routledge, 1993.

Glassco, John. *English Poetry in Québec: Proceedings of the Foster Poetry Conference, October 12–14, 1963.* Montréal: McGill University Press, 1965.

Jones, D. G. "Tracing Ellipse." *ellipse* 4 (1988): 18–21.

MacLennan, Hugh. *Two Solitudes.* Toronto: Stoddart, 1993.

MacSkimming, Roy. *The Perilous Trade: Publishing Canada's Writers.* Toronto: McClelland and Stewart, 2003.

Marshall, Joyce. "The Writer as Translator: A Personal View." *Canadian Literature* 117 (1988): 25–29.

Martin, Ruth. "Translated Canadian Literature and Canada Council Grants 1972–1992: The Effect on Authors, Translators and Publishers." *ellipse* 51 (1994): 54–84.

Newmark, Peter. *Approaches to Translation.* Oxford: Pergamon Press, 1981.

Norris, Ken. *The Little Magazine in Canada 1925–80.* Toronto: ECW Press, 1984.

O'Connor, John J. "Translations: French to English." In *The Oxford Companion to Canadian Literature*, ed. Eugene Benson and William Toye. Toronto: Oxford University Press, 1997. 1127–1132.

Shouldice, Larry. "On the Politics of Literary Translation in Canada." In *Translation in Canadian Literature Symposium 1982*, ed. Camille R. La Bossière. Ottawa: University of Ottawa Press, 1983. 73–82.

Snell-Hornby, Mary. "Translation Studies—Art, Science or Utopia." In *Translation Studies: The State of the Art*, eds. Kitty M. van Leuven-Zwart. Amsterdam: Rodopi, 1991. 13–23.

Stratford, Philip. "French-Canadian Literature in Translation." *Méta* 13, no. 4 (1968): 180–187.

———. *Bibliography of Canadian Books in Translation: French to English and English to French/Bibliographie de livres canadiens traduits de l'anglais au français et du français à l'anglais*. Ottawa: Humanities Research Council of Canada/Conseil de recherches sur les humanités, 1977.

Weaver, Robert. "Broadcasting." In *Writing in Canada: Proceedings of the Canadian Writers' Conference Held at Queen's University July 1955*, ed. George Whalley. Toronto: MacMillan, 1956. 103–114.

Whitfield, Agnes. "Translations, traductions." *University of Toronto Quarterly* 73, no. 1 (2002–03): 291–306; 73, no. 1 (2003–04): 79–96.

———, ed. *Le Métier du double*. Collection Nouvelles études québécoises. Montréal: Fides, 2005.

William Hume Blake,
or the Translator as Amateur Ethnologist

SHERRY SIMON

Philippe Dubé's chronicle of two centuries of social life in Murray Bay, Charlevoix County, Québec, includes a photograph of William Hume Blake (1861–1924) standing by his canoe.[1] He has a pipe in one hand and a wicker basket of provisions in the other; his eyes are turned dreamily toward the sky. He is surely about to embark on one of his many expeditions into the hinterland of Charlevoix. Blake was a member of the English-Canadian patrician class that, along with its American counterpart, enjoyed the impressive landscape of Murray Bay and, by the end of the nineteenth century, had made it one of the wealthiest watering holes on the eastern seacoast. Before the arrival of the automobile or even the railway, visitors from eastern Canada and the United States took the steamship every summer to this land of lakes and cliffs overlooking the St. Lawrence River.

Blake's passion for the outdoor life was infused with the sensibilities of a linguist and writer. His affection for the rugged country of Charlevoix extended to its *habitants* and especially to their ways of speech. These interests came together in two collections of essays, *Brown Waters and Other Sketches* (1915) and *In the Fishing Country* (1922). Blake's literary activities were undertaken in parallel with his professional work as a lawyer, but he is best known for his translations of *Maria Chapdelaine* (1921), Louis Hémon's classic tale of life in early twentieth-century Québec, and *Chez Nous* (1923), a volume of sketches of country life by Québec essayist Adjutor Rivard. Although Montréal writer and medical professor Andrew Macphail produced a competing translation of *Maria Chapdelaine* the same year, Blake's version "with the subtitle *A Tale of the Lake St. John Country*, remains the standard one."[2] Important for its literary qualities and passionate attachment to the *habitants*, Blake's work nonetheless reveals the colonial relationship between English and French Canada through its focus on the traditional, folkloric aspects of French-Canadian life. Both the novel *Maria Chapdelaine* and its translation promoted a view of French Canada that, even at the time, was considered problematic by francophone critics.

M'sieu Willie: A Canadian Isaac Walton

Born in Toronto, Blake studied law at the University of Toronto. In the 1870s, when he was in his early teens, his family was one of the first to settle into the summer country house scene at Murray Bay, La Malbaie-Pointe-au-Pic. "A beautiful grassy valley on the north shore" of the St. Lawrence, downriver from Québec, Murray Bay had first become a site of steamboat excursions around 1830. The construction of a quay at Pointe-au-Pic in 1853 made it possible to open a regular steamer service between Québec and the Saguenay fjord during the summer season, and Murray Bay soon became a "fashionable destination."[3] Blake's grandfather, William Hume Blake (1809–70), and his uncle, Edward Blake (1833–1912),[4] had played important political roles in Ontario. His grandfather was solicitor-general of Upper Canada in the Baldwin-Lafontaine administration; as a representative of his constituency, he was called upon to attend the pre-Confederation Parliament, which sat periodically in Québec. This was the opportunity that led him to discover Charlevoix: "After that, the Blake family never missed a single season, though they already owned a second house on the outskirts of Toronto." Both of his sons purchased homes in Murray Bay, and the younger, William Hume Blake's father, Samuel, built a house there called "Mille Roches."[5]

Although he lived and practised law in Toronto, Blake's attachment to Charlevoix and its people was legendary. Philippe Dubé writes, "The Ontario Irishman loved the people who lived in the deep forests of Charlevoix and the *coureurs de bois* who served as guides on his many expeditions in Laurentides Park." Blake was married in the Protestant chapel at Murray Bay and chose to be buried there: "His epitaph was a paraphrase of Napoleon's: 'I wish my ashes to rest on the banks of the river amidst these people I have loved so much.'" Dubé adds a theme that will be echoed elsewhere: Blake was so attached to and knowledgeable about Charlevoix that he was the "obvious choice" to translate *Maria Chapdelaine*.[6] The first edition of his translation, published in 1921, was accompanied by a note from the publisher, a highly unusual feature. In this preface, Hugh Eayrs draws attention to the "privilege" of publishing Blake's "able translation" and to "the habit of mind and the lucidity and beauty of his literary style" that make him particularly suited to "essay the task of acquainting English-speaking Canada with this treasury of French-Canadian life and lore."[7]

Subsequent editions were also accompanied by testimonials. When the book was re-released in 1948, the preface again paid tribute to Blake's special credentials as translator. There "was no one in Canada quite so equipped to do it," Eayrs writes. "Blake knew and loved French Canada and its people and they loved him. He was a familiar figure for many years at Point-au-Pic. His family home was there and I think he knew every man, woman and child in the countryside. At fifty he was still 'M'sieu Willie' to them."[8] As Blake's college friend F.C. Wade was to state, "Is it any wonder that with such knowledge and experience he was able to give the world the exquisite translation of Maria Chapdelaine?"[9]

Blake's affection for Charlevoix seemed to be all encompassing. Not a very enthusiastic lawyer, Blake seems to have turned all his emotional and intellectual energy into his summertime activities. Every year, he mounted expeditions into the hinterland of Charlevoix. Wade recalls Blake's enthusiasm and physical energy: "With our canots mounted on charrettes we climbed the mountains of lower Québec, made many a long portage, and fished in Lac Louis, Lac Anise, Lac Long, and Lac de Baie des Rochers." Blake led the march "gaily and resolutely," while the other members of the party looked for pretexts to take a rest. In Wade's account, camping and fishing were more than a diversion for Blake, they became "a passion, a religion."[10]

This combination of religion and naturalism is clearly expressed in Blake's essays. *Brown Waters and Other Sketches* includes texts on fishing, the countryside, *habitant* families, and the survival of the native legend of the Wendigo (werewolf). *In a Fishing Country*, another series of essays on similar themes, offers a more technical treatment of trout fishing. However, Blake is especially known for his *Fishermen's Creed*. Published in 1923, the work is a short reflective essay on the importance of a personal and intellectual religion as opposed to one based on the constraints of ritual or institutions. Well received at the time, these fishing essays were considered remarkable contributions to the genre. Blake has been called "the Isaac Walton of our literature."[11] His essays, Carl Klinck notes, are appreciated for the way they contrast the busy world of "politics, stock-markets, courts, theatres, [and] clubs," with the simple natural world where "the evening and the morning are the first and every following day." Blake combines qualities of simplicity and intelligence, a "quiet intellectual approach" to the world of nature. He is able to communicate the virtues he admires: "appreciation of natural beauty, skill in fishing, the courage of the trout, the hospitality and shrewdness of the French guide." His style complements his creed: "The careful shape of his sentences, the gentle ebb and flow of the rhythm, the unpretentious yet solid structure of his paragraphs, all are marks of the good workmanship which Blake admired so much in every walk of life."[12]

More pertinent for Blake's later activities as a translator is his admiration for the language of the *habitants*. For forty years, writes Wade, he explored the Laurentian country, "and keenly studied the habitant at close range in everyday life." Language was one of the most important aspects of his research, which had none of the superficiality of dabbling. Blake wanted to know everything: why the *habitants* of Murray Bay used particular expressions like "Arc-en-ciel du matin met le mauvais temps dans le chemin," and what the origin of the names "Pointe-au-Pic, Pointe à Gaze and Pointe des Monts" was. He was just as "interested in the ancient history of the Sagas as the recent history of the golf club house at the end of the Butte de l'eau-de-vie built in 1905."[13]

In *Brown Waters*, Blake recounts how he was constantly impressed by the *habitants*' respect for correct expression. As he traveled through the region, he was attuned to "the courtesy, the hospitality, the kind inquiries and seasonable complements in well-turned phrase, which never fail among these amiable people."[14] He relates a conversation between two of his guides. Bow says to Médée, "It crossed my mind, once or twice, as we came along that this was perhaps not your first experience in a canoe." Médée replies, "It is an odd thing, but rounding the big point, the thought came to me that possibly you had handled a paddle before."[15] In his English text, Blake is of course translating; this is how he hears the decorous turns of phrases exchanged by his guides. Occasionally he reminds his readers, by using obvious Gallicisms, that his companions are speaking French. At one point his driver bids him to "regard well" and in telling a joke about how a bullet killing a moose came from the guide's rifle rather than the "monsieur's," Blake has his guide say, "One bullet hole, assuredly, yes only one, but not from the first rifle. How disappointing that Monsieur should have nothing but misses to remember; better so, but it is sacredly amusing."[16] "Regard well" and "sacredly amusing" are Blake's way of trying to convey in English the expressions he finds so eloquent in French.

Blake's use of Gallicized vocabulary and turns of phrase, both in his essays and in his translations, expresses his appreciation for French-Canadian speech. He wants this "difference" to intrude into English. He includes such words and expressions as a distinctive mark of the French-Canadian society he is representing, a society that, he is convinced, will disappear as it modernizes. Typically, landscape and people are mentioned in the same breath. They are similar objects of Blake's attention and affection. He is equally appreciative of both, treating each with the same sympathetic respect. His enthusiasm embraces all the different dimensions of the natural world, whether they be the elemental forces of wildlife, the impressive strength of the landscape, or the pristine virtues of the *habitants* themselves.

Translating *Maria Chapdelaine*

While Blake's fishing essays enjoyed success (*Brown Waters and Other Sketches* was reprinted in 1925 with a preface by Vincent Massey[17]), his translation of *Maria Chapdelaine* is the work for which he is most remembered today. Written by French-born Louis Hémon and published first in serial form in the Parisian newspaper *Le Temps*, *Maria Chapdelaine* was remarkable for its extraordinary commercial success. The novel has sold over ten million copies and has been translated into more than twenty languages. The story takes place in the farming community of the Lac Saint-Jean area, where Hémon had worked as a farmhand after his arrival in Canada in 1911, until his tragic death in a train mishap near Chapleau, Ontario, in 1913. In the book, Maria lives with her family in the wooded hilly country outside the village of Péribonka. After the death of her true love, François Paradis, she chooses to marry Eutrope Gagnon, a humble farmer, rather than desert her community for the more exciting life in the city offered to her by yet another suitor, Lorenzo Surprenant.

The novel has been traditionally interpreted as a symbolic representation of French Canada's faithfulness to tradition, whatever the hardship. However, as Nicole Deschamps has pointed out, the considerable critical literature that has grown up around *Maria Chapdelaine* since the 1920s has been monopolized by a right-wing perspective that has presented the novel as an expression of French-Canadian social conservatism in praise of the traditional way of life. Other readings of the text are possible, but have only begun to surface since 1960. Through her analysis of Hémon's representation of language, Deschamps herself "portrays Hémon as a social reformer whose novel seeks not to glorify colonized Québécois but to awaken in them a sense of their own plight."[18]

The history of the translation is somewhat unusual, as Blake was not the only English-Canadian writer to take an interest in translating Hémon's novel. Two translations of *Maria Chapdelaine* were published in 1921. The second was by Sir Andrew Macphail (1864–1938), professor of the history of medicine at McGill, editor of the *University Magazine*, and author of several volumes of fiction and essays. This double publication is an exceptional occurrence, unusual in any country, and particularly in Canada where translations were rare. In fact, Blake and Macphail initially planned to collaborate on the translation, but the two had very different ideas about how to go about their task. More specifically, as Ian Ross Robertson indicates, "they were unable to agree on stylistic matters."[19] Macphail's translation appeared a few months before Blake's. Despite its prestigious publisher, international distribution, and illustrations by Suzor-Côté, Macphail's version was overshadowed by Blake's, which has become the authoritative version.

Considering that the two translators were equally respected and established authors, and that they had clearly articulated and opposing views on translation, the nature of the differences between their versions is worth investigating. Even a quick look at the two texts reveals their divergences. Macphail remains steadfastly literal, while Blake is much bolder in rearranging sentences and adding intensifiers. Perhaps to fend off potential critics, Blake states in his preface that "the attempt in this English version has been to capture the spirit Louis Hémon has imprisoned on his page, rather than to invite its escape in a too literal rendering."[20] Blake and Macphail do agree on some points; both decide, for instance, to retain certain French terms, calling the dog "Chien," and the brothers "Tit'Bé" and "Da'Bé," and referring to maple sugar candy as "la tire." Macphail pursues this strategy more consistently than Blake, using the curse word "Blasphème" and the expression "Grands brûlés," which Blake translates to "Perdition" and "burnt lands."

Two aspects of Blake's translation are especially important: his treatment of the spoken word and his liberal approach to sentence reconstruction. His strategy with regard to spoken language is unusual: he doesn't 'lower' the vernacular to familiarity, but rather gives his characters a language of dignity, always ceremonious, which confers an aura of reverence to the whole text: "How nice it would be to live in a country where there is hardly any winter, and where the earth makes provision for man and beast. Up here man himself, by dint of work, must care for his animals and land," says Mother Chapdelaine in conversation with Eutrope Gagnon.[21]

Blake's use of greetings and names also evokes a world in which people speak to one another with respectful distance. He uses archaic modes ("she saw them not," "the morrow," "habited"), unfamiliar or invented words with French resonance ("moveless," "incult," "essayed"), and leaves characters' names in French. He occasionally throws in bits of dialogue that are simply direct reproductions of the French: "Well Mr. Larouche, do things go pretty well across the water?" "Not badly, my lads, not badly"; "It was the Demon of disobedience lured me into that. Beyond doubt it was he."[22] All these devices colour the text, reminding the reader that the reality he or she is observing is unfamiliar and distant.

The particular genius of Blake's translation is sentence rhythm. He regularly transforms and rephrases sentences in order to make them more rhetorically effective. For instance, in the particularly dramatic passage where Maria learns of the death of her lover, François Paradis, Hémon writes: "Une main s'était glissée dans sa gorge, l'étouffant, dès que le dénouement du récit tragique était devenu clair pour elle."[23] Blake's translation reads as follows: "A hand had fastened upon her throat, stifling her, as the narrative unfolded and the inevitable end came within her view."[24] The melodrama of the passage is intensified as Blake moves from "s'était glissé" to "fastened," "dénouement" to "inevitable end."

A few lines later in the original text comes a powerful representation of Maria Chapdelaine's grief:

> Vu du seuil, le monde figé dans son sommeil blanc semblait plein d'une grande sérénité; mais dès que Maria fut hors de l'abri des murs, le froid descendit sur elle comme un couperet, et la lisière lointaine du bois se rapprocha soudain, sombre façade derrière laquelle cent secrets tragiques, enfouis, appelaient et se lamentaient comme des voix.[25]

Blake writes,

> The world that lay beyond the threshold, sunk in moveless white repose, was of an immense serenity; but when Maria passed from the sheltering walls the cold smote her like the hungry blade of a sword and the forest leaped toward her in menace, its inscrutable face concealing a hundred dreadful secrets which called aloud to her in lamentable voices.[26]

By changing the order of the sentence from "Vu du seuil" to "The world that lay beyond the threshold," Blake makes the view more grandly affirmative. He then adds almost cinematographic melodrama by changing "descendit" to "smote" and by anthropomorphizing "couperet" to "the hungry blade of a sword." The forest that Hémon had made move forward suddenly now "leaped toward her in menace," showing not a "sombre façade" but an "inscrutable face."

This capacity to reshape the prose to render Maria's intense emotional response sets Blake apart from Macphail. In the following passage, Maria is under the spell of Lorenzo Surprenant, who seeks to seduce her with his descriptions of the exciting life in the city, compared to the dull life of the farmer. Hémon writes,

> Tout ce qu'il y a de merveilleux, d'énivrant, dans le spectacle et le contact des multitudes; toute la richesse fourmillante de sensations et d'idées qui est l'apanage pour lequel le citadin a troqué l'orgueil âpre de la terre, Maria pressentait tout cela confusément, comme une vie nouvelle dans un monde nouveau, une glorieuse métempsycose dont elle avait la nostalgie d'avance. Mais surtout elle avait un grand désir de s'en aller.[27]

Macphail's translation reads as follows:

> All that was strange and intoxicating in the spectacle and contact of multitudes, all the swarming wealth of sensations and ideas, which is the lot for which the city dweller has traded the eager pride of the earth—Maria envisaged all that confusedly like a new life in a new world, a glorious transformation for which she was homesick in advance. But above all she had a great desire to go away."[28]

Blake's version makes better metaphorical sense of the passage:

> Whatsoever there may be of wonder and exhilaration in the sight and touch of the crowd; the rich harvests of mind and sense for which the city dweller has bartered his rough heritage of pride in the soil, Maria was dimly conscious of as part of this other life in a new world, this

glorious re-birth for which she was already yearning. But above all else, the desire was strong upon her now to flee away, to escape.²⁹

All the awkward prosaic touches in Macphail's text—"contact of multitudes," the "eager pride of the earth," a "new life in a new world"—become stronger and more coherent in Blake's translation: "sight and touch of the crowd," "his rough heritage of pride in the soil," "this other life in a new world." Blake brings out the intensity of the images. His diction is vivid; his sentences are shaped with care.

One could quote many other examples showing the way that Blake leaves his mark on his translation, especially through his attention to rhythm and sonority. Indeed, some might even criticize Blake for playing up Hémon's rhetoric, but there is ample literary justification for the intensifiers that he introduces. All of Blake's decisions are directed towards an aesthetics of estrangement. There is no attempt, in other words, to bring the world of *Maria Chapdelaine* closer to his readers or to a more recognizable horizon of anglophone references.

In this respect, Blake's translation contrasts vividly with a more recent version by Alan Brown, done for an illustrated children's book published by Tundra Books. Looking for a more idiomatic, de-dramatized, and contemporary tone, Brown handles the painful passage of Maria's grief (quoted above) as follows:

> Seen from the threshold, the world, frozen in its snow-covered sleep, seemed still and serene, but as soon as Maria left the shelter of the walls the cold fell on her like a sharp blade, and the distant verge of the forest seemed to advance toward her, a dark façade behind which a hundred tragic secrets lay buried, crying out and lamenting, calling for help.³⁰

The continuation of this same passage demonstrates even more clearly the differences between Brown's more sober and Blake's more dramatic diction. First, the passage as Hémon wrote it:

> Elle se recula avec un gémissement, referma la porte et s'assit près du poêle, frissonnante. La stupeur première du choc commençait à se dissiper; son chagrin s'aiguisa et la main qui lui serrait le coeur se mit à inventer des pincements, des déchirures, vingt tortures rusées et cruelles.³¹

Blake's translation is vivid:

> With a little moan she drew back, and closing the door sat shivering beside the stove. Numbness was yielding, sorrow taking on an edge,

and the hand that clutched her heart set itself to devising new agonies, each one subtler and more cruel than the last.[32]

In Brown's translation, the passage is considerably shorter:

> She drew back with a moan, closed the door and sat down by the stove, shuddering. The stupor of her first shock was passing; her sorrow grew sharper and more cruel.[33]

While Blake has heightened the dramatic presentation of Maria's movements, Brown has clearly adopted a more condensed style, eliminating, in deference to his contemporary audience, the personification of the hand of death gripping Maria's heart.

The Meaning of *Chez Nous*: Blake and Adjutor Rivard

As Blake himself explains in his preface, his second translation, *Chez Nous*, was "next to a hopeless task."[34] The book is a series of vignettes of country life, written by Adjutor Rivard (1868–1945), a judge who was also a linguist. *Chez nous* is a combination of Rivard's two collections *Chez nous* (1914) and *Chez nos gens* (1918), which had been published together in French as *Chez nous* in 1919. In fact, the book is a lesson in dialectology disguised as literary sketches. Rivard was one of the founders of the Société du parler français au Canada in 1902 and the author of numerous works on the French language in Québec. *Chez nous* was awarded a prize by the Académie française in 1920.

The sketches evoke memories about an object, a person, or an event. Reminiscences about a baby's crib lead to reflections on the beginnings of the colony and the many births that have occurred since. The kitchen stove recalls the many conversations that have taken place around it, conversations with neighbours or family, or the intimate discussions of husband and wife. Character types like the "beggar" are described. Rivard evokes these vignettes in order to help conserve the collective memory and to glorify the past.[35]

The "translator's perplexities," Blake explains in his preface, "begin with the title...but they do not end with it, for words and phrases of the old dialect (or dialects), smacking of the soil, multiply on Judge Rivard's page." Rivard was heavily involved with the language debates of the time, and he wrote as a traditionalist. The real subject of Rivard's book is the collusion between language, memory, and identity, and this mix cannot be rendered in another language. Yet Blake hopes that even if "the traces of its style disappear in this alien garb, something of the intimacy and fidelity of its portraiture may survive; and those who love our country and our countrymen will find reward in the reading."[36]

Again, Blake is conscious of pursuing a rearguard action, of seeking to preserve a language "less and less frequently heard on the lips of the rising generation—levelling downwards to a dull indistinction beneath the Procrustean hand of 'education!'" These are the words of a true conservative, undoubtedly out of sync with progressive ideas at the time. Blake takes on a mandate whose terms evoke an imaginary, nostalgic world. He hopes that his translation of Adjutor Rivard's *Chez nous* will "lay bare to us the generous and kindly French-Canadian heart."[37]

From the first chapter, significantly entitled "The House," the nostalgic flavour of Rivard's text (and Blake's translation) is easily captured:

> Il y avait de plus grandes; il n'y en avait pas de plus hospitalière. Dès le petit jour, sa porte matinale laissait entrer, avec le parfum des trèfles, les premiers rayons du soleil. Et jusqu'au soir, elle offrait aux passants le sourire de ses fenêtres en fleurs, l'accueil de son perron facile, l'invitation de sa porte ouverte. De si loin que vous l'aperceviez, elle vous plaisait déjà, et, quand vous étiez tout proche, elle se faisait si attrayante que résister à son appel devenait impossible; vous entriez. Dès l'abord vous étiez chez vous. "Asseyez-vous, l'ami, et prenez du repos."[38]

Blake's translation emphasizes the sense of familiarity, warmth, and welcome:

> Others may have been larger, but surely none held a more welcoming aspect. The door, thrown wide to admit the sun's earliest ray and the scent of the clover and standing open till the fall of night, the windows smiling with flowers, the easy steps, all offered invitation. When your eye fell upon it from afar the house beckoned, and on nearer approach the summons was so imperative that you must enter. Crossing the threshold you were instantly at home.—"Friend, sit a while and rest."[39]

Blake's text is stylish and fluent, the tales cleverly told. He seems, however, to have abandoned any attempt to provide Gallic touches. Except for the title, *Chez Nous* (which is given an explicative subtitle, *Our Old Quebec Home*), there are no French words besides proper nouns or titles such as Monsieur le Curé. There is no attempt to highlight local usage, as Rivard does, by using italics. In contrast to *Maria Chapdelaine*, this collection of sketches has few literary pretensions. It is rather offered as homage to the virtues of the traditional values shown by the inhabitants of rural Québec.

An Aesthetics of Conservative Ethnography

Even for his time, Blake was a conservative. He preferred the country and its folk to the "more sophisticated town-dweller,"[40] and fought for the preservation of the old ways. He opposed the extension of the railway to Murray Bay, correctly fearing that the area would lose its quaint character. He defended the *habitants'* "simple faith," championing "the living principle that animates any religion worth having" against the prejudices of his readers and challenging them "to abandon their superior smiles and to approach Québec with a tolerant and unbigoted mind."[41]

The "superior smiles" Blake refers to might have had their origins in the work of William Henry Drummond (1854–1907), whose dialect poetry dealing with French-Canadian *habitant* life was wildly popular in English Canada at the turn of the century. Drummond's *The Habitant and Other French-Canadian Poems* was first published in 1897 with an introduction by Louis Fréchette, then republished in a Canadian edition in 1926; it was continuously used as school text in English Canada until at least the 1960s. Drummond's characters speak in broken English, a "bastard idiom" which is the source of much of the comedy in the work.[42] By the 1940s, A.M. Klein was scathing in his criticism of those who continued to recite this dialect poetry; he condemned Drummond as a "patrician patronizing the patois," portraying the *habitants* as having "homespun minds," "white natives, characters of a comical Québec, of speech neither Briton nor Breton, a fable folk, a second class of aborigines, docile, domesticate, very good employees, so meek that even their sadness made dialect for a joke."[43]

Blake's relation to French Canada is different. As Gerald Noonan observes, the "*Montreal Star* noted at the time of his death…[that] Drummond's medical practice had been mostly in Montréal, and his country experience 'was not among the French-Canadians but among the Highland Scotch.'"[44] His knowledge of the *habitant* was largely second hand. If Drummond and Blake shared the same passion for the "fabled folk" whose lives were so different from their own, they found different means of expression. Blake is closer to the people he writes about; his link with the landscape gives him a privileged access to their culture.

Publisher Hugh Eayrs's recollection of an evening he shared with Blake in the 1920s encapsulates some of the elements of Blake's intellectual and social world. Among Eayrs's cherished memories, he recounts, is that of a long weekend spent at Lac Gravel with the former United States president Taft and Sir Lomer Gouin (1861–1929), a prominent Québec politician and former premier: "I remember that we sat in front of a roaring fire, after a long day's fishing, while Blake read his translation to us. He was anxious that English-speaking Canada first, and after that the world, should have this picture of the Province which was his second home."[45] The presence of both the American president and the Québec liberal politician is evidence of Blake's wide connections. The setting is also highly suggestive: isolated at a fishing camp, in front of a fire, the dignitaries are treated to a literary work that speaks of simple peasantry, idealized rural values, and unswerving religious faith. Politics, sports, and literature combine in homage to nature and old-world values.

Blake's affection for Québec can be set in the context of the early twentieth-century search for those corners of North America where authentic culture was thought to have survived. In America, those sites were the American Southwest, traditional artists' colonies (including the Berkshires, Cape Cod, and the Maine coast), Québec, and the Maritime Provinces. Artists joined ethnographers in seeking out those surviving preindustrial rural cultures "which seemed to serve as models of resistance to the alienation of the modern order."[46] The perception of untamed Canada as a place where the harried city dweller could be spiritually refreshed is described by Edmund Wilson. In O *Canada: An American's Notes on Canadian Culture*, he recalls the men of his father's generation hunting game: "They liked to think they had been losing themselves, escaping from the trials and anxieties of a precarious commercial society...They sometimes maintained permanent camps in which they reverted to these pastimes, and had season after season the same half-breed guide, whose sayings they delighted to tell about at the family dinner table."[47]

Catholic, agrarian, preindustrial societies had great appeal for this generation of artists, which included Paul Strand and Georgia O'Keefe; many of them were disillusioned with the materialism and alienation of urban, industrial America. In this sense, Blake's nature essays can be compared to picturesque landscapes (such as O'Keefe's famous painting of a roadside cross) created by painters expressing their admiration for the restorative values of the land. Well into the 1930s and 1940s, furthermore, the primary relation of English Canadians and Americans to Charlevoix was an ethnographic one. *Charlevoix 1930*, Jori Smith's entertaining memoir of life as an artist with her husband Jan Palardy in Charlevoix during the 1930s illustrates the aesthetic and cultural riches that Charlevoix represented for the outsider.

Blake's translations can also be placed in the context of the emerging literary dialogue between English and French Canada. Commentators note that Blake's nature writing had the added virtue of "fostering mutual comprehension between French- and English-speaking Canadians."[48] His translation inaugurates a literary conversation that had only started to emerge at the time—as far as the novel was concerned—with Sir Charles G.D. Roberts's translation of Philippe Aubert de Gaspé's *Les Anciens Canadiens*. In the now-legendary introduction to his 1890 translation, Roberts frames the tradition of literary translation to come: "We, of English speech, turn naturally to French-Canadian literature for knowledge of the French-Canadian people."[49] As one of the first novels to be translated from French to English, then, *Maria Chapdelaine* came to stand for Québec society as a whole. The "myth" of *Maria Chapdelaine* in both English and French is the idea that all of Québec society can be reduced to the same simple equations provided in the novel.

Whatever its value as a representation of Québec society, Blake's translation of *Maria Chapdelaine* must be considered what Antoine Berman calls a "historic" translation, a work we read not as only as a reproduction of the original, but for what it tells us about the poetics of translation. We read it, in other words, in order to catch glimpses of the translator's vision as it drives and forms the new text. The match between Blake and Hémon is fortunate. That Blake thought of this translation as his own writing, that he considered it a major task, is evident in Hugh Eayrs's description of the weekend at Lac Gravel. What Blake read aloud in front of the fire to his illustrious friends reflected a sensibility he recognized as his own. Blake's respectful and affectionate relationship to language characterizes his work as a translator. He handles and manipulates words, holds them at a distance. His translations breathe the energy of language consciously shaped to aesthetic ends.

Blake translates in the same way that he writes, as an amateur ethnologist fascinated by difference. This difference is historically and socially framed. Blake's sense of the redemptive powers of French-Canadian culture was the result of a rearguard attempt to preserve an idealized vision of a culture. This conservatism, as much as Blake's literary skills and his familiarity with rural Québec, was surely what made him an appropriate translator for a work whose verisimilitude was challenged even by its first public. At the same time, Blake's translation captures the sense of stark otherness, of separate universes, which observers like artist Jori Smith have felt in relation to Québec rural life. Blake's adoration of French Canada expresses that long-standing desire on the part of English Canadians to understand a culture that, though geographically close, remains mysterious. Because this distance corresponded to the gap between urban modernity and rural premodernity, the mystery represented a fullness of existence that moderns felt denied.

In both his essays and his translations, Blake displayed his keen knowledge of land, people, and language, and transformed these into stylish and lyrical prose. His translation of *Maria Chapdelaine* is an elegant hybrid. On the one hand, he makes strong stylistic incursions into the text, intensifying its dramatic qualities. On the other, he also gives a strong Gallic inflection to the novel, by maintaining words in French or by introducing a vocabulary of Gallicized English words. The resulting text is graceful yet innovative. This mixture is an expression of Blake's affiliation with a shared cultural space. By accepting interference from French, his English translation suggests a sense of a shared linguistic environment. Through his gracious but occasionally strained English prose, Blake is trying to convey to his fellow English-Canadians the special qualities of rural French Canada. He is also translating himself into Charlevoix, and creating a place for himself in the landscape he loved.

NOTES

1 Philippe Dubé, *Charlevoix: Two Centuries at Murray*. Trans. Tony Martin-Sperry. (Montréal: McGill-Queen's University Press, 1990), p. 36.
2 Paul Socken, "Hémon, Louis," in the *Oxford Companion to Canadian Literature*, 2nd ed., ed. Eugene Benson and William Toye (Toronto: Oxford University Press, 1997), p. 526.
3 Dubé, *Charlevoix*, 46.
4 The entries on Blake in the *Oxford Companion to Canadian Literature and History* (1967) and the *Oxford Companion to Canadian Literature* (1983) both state that Blake was a grandson of Edward Blake. This is impossible. Edward Blake (1833–1912) would have been twenty-eight when William Hume Blake was born.
5 Dubé, *Charlevoix*, pp. 93, 94.
6 Dubé, *Charlevoix*, pp. 93, 94.
7 Hugh Eayrs, preface to *Maria Chapdelaine: A Romance of French Canada*, by Louis Hémon, trans. W.H. Blake (Toronto: Macmillan, 1921).
8 Eayrs, preface to *Maria Chapdelaine: A Romance of French Canada*, by Louis Hémon, trans. W.H. Blake (Toronto: Macmillan, 1921).
9 F.C. Wade, "William Blake," *University of Toronto Monthly*, June 1924, p. 415.
10 Wade, "William Blake," pp. 412–15.
11 Carl F. Klinck, ed., *Literary History of Canada: Canadian Literature in English*, 2nd ed., vol. 1 (Toronto: University of Toronto Press, 1967), p. 389.
12 Klinck, *Literary History of Canada*, pp. 359–60.
13 Wade, "William Blake," p. 415.
14 W.H. Blake, *Brown Waters and Other Sketches* (Toronto: Macmillan, 1915), p. 121.
15 Blake, *Brown Waters*, p. 147.

16 Blake, *Brown Waters*, p. 153.
17 Kathryn Hamer, "Blake, William Hume," in the *Oxford Companion to Canadian Literature*, ed. Eugene Benson and William Toye (Toronto: Oxford University Press, 1997), p. 127.
18 Paul Socken, "Hémon, Louis," p. 526. See also Nicole Deschamps, *Le Mythe de Maria Chapdeleine* (Montréal: Presses de l'Université de Montréal, 1980).
19 Ian Ross Robertson, "Macphail, Sir Andrew," in the *Oxford Companion to Canadian Literature*, 2nd ed., ed. Eugene Benson and William Toye (Toronto: Oxford University Press, 1997), p. 714.
20 W.H. Blake, translator's preface to *Maria Chapdelaine: A Romance of French Canada*, by Louis Hémon (Toronto: Macmillan, 1921).
21 Louis Hémon, *Maria Chapdelaine: A Romance of French Canada*, trans. W.H. Blake (Toronto: MacMillan, 1921), pp. 44–45.
22 Hémon, *Maria Chapdelaine*, trans. W.H. Blake (1921), p. 40.
23 Louis Hémon, *Maria Chapdelaine: A Romance of French Canada* (Montréal: Fides, 1975), p. 130.
24 Hémon, *Maria Chapdelaine*, trans. W.H. Blake (1921), p. 154.
25 Hémon, *Maria Chapdelaine*, (1975), p. 131.
26 Hémon, *Maria Chapdelaine*, trans. W.H. Blake (1921), p. 155.
27 Hémon, *Maria Chapdelaine*, trans. W.H. Blake (1921), p. 158.
28 Louis Hémon, *Maria Chapdelaine: A Romance of French Canada*, trans. Andrew Macphail, illus. M.A. Suzor-Côté (Montréal: A.T. Chapman, 1921), p. 155.
29 Hémon, *Maria Chapdelaine*, trans. W.H. Blake (1921), p. 190.
30 Louis Hémon, *Maria Chapdelaine: A Romance of French Canada*, trans. Alan Brown, illus. Gilles Tibo, intro. Roch Carrier (Montréal: Tundra Books, 1989), p. 56.
31 Hémon, *Maria Chapdelaine*, (1975), p. 131.
32 Hémon, *Maria Chapdelaine*, trans. W.H. Blake (1921), p. 155.
33 Hémon, *Maria Chapdelaine*, trans. Alan Brown (1989), p. 56.
34 W.H. Blake, translator's preface to *Chez Nous (Our Old Quebec Home)*, by Adjutor Rivard (Toronto: McClelland and Stewart, 1924), p. 11.
35 See Maurice Lemire, "Chez Nous," *Dictionnaire des œuvres littéraires du Québec*, vol. 2 (Montréal: Fides, 1987), p. 226.
36 Blake, translator's preface in *Chez Nous*, pp. 11, 15.
37 Blake, translator's preface in *Chez Nous*, p. 15.
38 Adjutor Rivard, *Chez nous; Chez nos gens* (Québec: Éditions de l'Action sociale catholique, 1919), p. 9–10.
39 Adjutor Rivard, *Chez Nous (Our Old Quebec Home)*, trans. W.H. Blake (Toronto: McClelland and Stewart, 1924), p. 19.
40 Blake, *Brown Water*, p. 139.
41 Blake, *Brown Water*, p. 140.
42 Translated from *La Patrie*, 15 Dec. 1901, and quoted in Gerald Noonan, "Drummond, William Henry," in the *Oxford Companion to Canadian Literature*, ed. Eugene Benson and William Toye (Toronto: Oxford University Press), p. 334.

43 A.M. Klein, "Doctor Drummond," in *Collected Poems of A.M. Klein*, vol. 2 (Toronto: University of Toronto Press, 1990), p. 655.
44 Noonan, "Drummond, William Henry," p. 333.
45 Eayrs, preface, 1948.
46 B.H. Russell, "Québec and Américanisme" (unpublished paper), Department of Art History, Concordia University, p. 2.
47 Edmund Wilson, O *Canada: An American's Notes on Canadian Culture* (New York: Farrar, Straus and Giroux, 1965), p.36.
48 Klinck, *Literary History of Canada*, p. 360.
49 Charles G.D. Roberts, introduction to *Canadians of Old* (Toronto: McClelland and Stewart, 1974), p. 5.

BIBLIOGRAPHY
I. Sources
Literary Translations
Hémon, Louis. *Maria Chapdelaine: A Romance of French Canada*. Trans. W.H. Blake. Pref. Hugh Eayrs. Toronto: Macmillan, 1921.
———. *Maria Chapdelaine: A Romance of French Canada*. Trans. W.H. Blake. Pref. Hugh Eayrs. Toronto: Macmillan, 1948.
Rivard, Adjutor. *Chez Nous (Our Old Quebec Home)*. Trans. W.H. Blake. Illus. A.Y. Jackson. Toronto: McClelland and Stewart, 1924.

Literary Works
Blake, W.H. *Brown Waters and Other Sketches*. Toronto: Macmillan 1915; 1925.
———. *In a Fishing Country*. Toronto: Macmillan, 1922.
———. *A Fisherman's Creed*. Toronto: Macmillan, 1923.

II. Secondary References
Benson, Eugene and William Toye, eds. *Oxford Companion to Canadian Literature*. 2nd ed. Toronto: Oxford University Press, 1997.
Berman, Antoine. *L'Epreuve de l'étranger*. Paris: Gallimard, 1983.
Dubé, Philippe. *Charlevoix: Two Centuries at Murray Bay*. Trans. Tony Martin-Sperry. In collaboration with the photographer Jacques Blouin. Montréal: McGill-Queen's University Press, 1990.
Eayrs, Hugh. Preface to *Maria Chapdelaine: A Romance of French Canada*, by Louis Hémon, trans. W.H. Blake. Toronto: Macmillan, 1921.
———. Preface to *Maria Chapdelaine: A Romance of French Canada*, by Louis Hémon, trans. W.H. Blake. Toronto: Macmillan, 1948.
Hamer, Kathryn. "Blake, William Hume." In the *Oxford Companion to Canadian Literature*, ed. Eugene Benson and William Toye. Toronto: Oxford University Press, 1997. 127.
Hémon, Louis. *Maria Chapdelaine: A Romance of French Canada*. Trans. Andrew Macphail. Illus. M.A. Suzor-Côté. Montréal: A.T. Chapman, 1921.

———. *Maria Chapdelaine.* Montréal: Fidès, 1975.
———. *Maria Chapdelaine: A Romance of French Canada.* Trans. Alan Brown. Illus. Gilles Tibo. Introd. Roch Carrier. Montréal: Tundra Books, 1989.
K.K.B. "W.H. Blake." *Canadian Bookman* 5, no. 11 (1923): 297.
Klein, A.M. "Doctor Drummond." In *Complete Poems of A.M. Klein*, vol. 2, Toronto: University of Toronto Press, 1990. 655–56.
Klinck, Carl F., ed. *Literary History of Canada: Canadian Literature in English.* 2nd ed. Vol. 1, Toronto: University of Toronto Press, 1976.
Lemire, Maurice, ed. *Dictionnaire des oeuvres littéraires du Québec.* Vol. 2. Montréal: Fidès, 1987.
Noonan, Gerald. "Drummond, William Henry." In the *Oxford Companion to Canadian Literature*, 2nd ed., ed. Eugene Benson and William Toye. Toronto: Oxford University Press, 1997. 334.
Rivard, Adjutor. *Chez nous; Chez nos gens.* Québec: Éditions de l'Action sociale catholique, 1919. Reprinted by Librairie Garneau, 1945.
Roberts, Charles G.D. Introduction to *The Canadians of Old*, by Philippe Aubert de Gaspé, trans. C.G.D. Roberts. Toronto: McClelland and Stewart, 1974. 3–6.
Robertson, Ian Ross. "Macphail, Sir Andrew." In the *Oxford Companion to Canadian Literature*, 2nd ed., ed. Eugene Benson and William Toye. Toronto: Oxford University Press, 1997. 713–15.
Russell, B.H. "Québec and Américanismes." Unpublished paper. Department of Art History, Concordia University, 2001.
Smith, Jori. *Charlevoix County, 1930.* Manotick, ON: Penumbra Press, 1998.
Socken, Paul. "Hémon, Louis." In the *Oxford Companion to Canadian Literature*, 2nd ed., ed. Eugene Benson and William Toye. Toronto: Oxford University Press, 1997. 526.
Story, Norah. *Oxford Companion to Canadian History and Literature.* Toronto: Oxford University Press, 1967.
Wade, F.C. "William Blake." *University of Toronto Monthly*, June 1924, 412–15.
Wilson, Edmund. *O Canada: An American's Notes on Canadian Culture.* New York: Farrar, Straus and Giroux, 1965.

2

Glassco Virtuoso

PATRICIA GODBOUT

Speaking of his friend "Buffy" Glassco on CBC radio nearly a year after Glassco's death, D.G. Jones described him as "something of an extraordinary mixture."[1] A poet and translator, Glassco (1909–81) had lived a large part of his life in the Eastern Townships and taken an active interest in his rural community. He had delivered the mail along the country roads around Knowlton and Foster, founded the Foster Horse Show, and served as mayor of Foster from 1952 to 1954. Yet, as Jones (himself an award-winning poet and translator profiled in this book) explained, the same man who knew the hills and mountains of his region by name and gave them pride of place in his poetry was also the author of several pornographic works. Part of the wave of North American expatriates living in Paris in the 1920s, he had rubbed shoulders with this turbulent bohemian milieu, which he later skillfully depicted in his *Memoirs of Montparnasse* (1970). Glassco, according to Jones, was undoubtedly a type of English Canadian more likely to be found in Québec than elsewhere in Canada.

In the same radio program, interviewer Jacques Marchand was quick to probe Jones about another paradox, namely the passionate interest by this author of erotic novellas for the austere life and works of the Québécois poet Saint-Denys Garneau (1912–43) whose *Poésies complètes* and *Journal* Glassco had translated. Jones pointed out adroitly that Glassco had explored his own relationship with religion and the Church in his pornographic writings, and that he was indeed quite familiar with Christian thinking on sin and vice in sexual matters. This same thinking, in fact, had given rise to the literature of the *poètes maudits* and the so-called Decadents (writers such as Huysmans, Pater, and Villiers). In this respect, Glassco's interest in Saint-Denys-Garneau ("a man who was more or less a libertine, particularly in his youth, and almost a puritan at the end of his life") could be seen as part of the continuum of his thinking. Like that of Saint-Denys-Garneau, Glassco's literary sensibility was formed largely by the European, and particularly the French, School. Although Saint-Denys-Garneau had probably not inhaled all the scents of the Baudelairian *"fleurs du mal,"* Jones reminded his listeners, he was nonetheless acquainted with spleen, ennui, despair, and emptiness. These were also the realities that Glassco had experienced in his own way in Paris and the Eastern Townships, and had recounted in his work and translations. As George Woodcock so rightly says of Glassco's pornographic novel, *Harriet Marwood, Governess* (1975), "behind the sadism and masochism in the text, redolent of the Victorian era, lies the central theme of dehumanization and the transformation of a character through suffering."[2]

A man of many contrasts—dandy, pony breeder, and lover of literature—Glassco was to play a not-insignificant role in Québec and Canadian letters in the second half of the twentieth century, by inspiration as much as by example. The level of virtuosity and literary style that characterize both his own writing and his translations earned him the respect of more than one generation of Canadian writers. "Glassco's essays, reviews, prefaces and introductions," writes Fraser Sutherland, "demonstrate a superb critical intelligence and make an important contribution to the aesthetics of poetry, pornography, and translation…his translations are models of coherence and lucidity, and greatly add to an understanding of Québec's literature."[3] Or, as poet and scholar Robin Skelton pungently observed, "We never knew what he would write next, what he would renew by translation."[4]

From Montréal to Montparnasse

The son of Archibald P.S. Glassco and Beatrice Rawlings, John Glassco was born in Montréal in 1909 into an affluent milieu. He attended the best private schools to obtain the kind of education his father considered essential for the scion of a good family: Selwyn House School, Bishop's College School, and Lower Canada College. In 1925, he enrolled in the Faculty of Letters at McGill, where he met the young poets Frank R. Scott, Arthur Smith, A.M. Klein, and Leo Kennedy, who would later be known as the "Montreal Group" and play a key role in modernizing English-language poetry in Canada. Glassco struck up a lifelong friendship with Scott, with whom he shared his enthusiasm for French-Canadian literature and translation.

In 1928, Glassco left university before taking a degree. Despite his father's disapproval, he preferred to round off his education in his own way. "Student life at McGill University had depressed me to a point where I could not go on," he wrote in *Memoirs of Montparnasse*. "My real problem was a combination of precocity, impatience, and inability to take in anything more from books." With his friend Graeme Taylor, he set off for Paris, the meeting place at the time for an entire English-speaking artistic colony of expatriates, including James Joyce, Gertrude Stein, and Ernest Hemingway. The two friends were united "by comradeship, a despisal of everything represented by the business world, the city of Montréal and the Canadian scene, and a desire to get away."[5] Glassco spent three years in France, before returning precipitously to Montréal. Suffering from tuberculosis, he had to undergo delicate surgery to remove one lung. It was during his stay in France that his first work appeared in print—a surrealist poem entitled "Conan's Fig," published in 1928 in the review *Transition*—and he started to write his memoirs.[6]

Until the mid-1950s, Glassco published only the occasional poem in journals. A difficult childhood at the hands of a violent, sadistic father had left its mark, and he doubted his creative powers. He was therefore particularly pleased to receive a letter from Arthur Smith in 1956 requesting permission to include his poem "Deserted Buildings under Shefford Mountain" in Smith's forthcoming anthology, *The Oxford Book of Canadian Verse*. Two years later, with the publication of *A Deficit Made Flesh* (1958), Glassco was finally able to assemble into a collection the poems he had been carrying around for years. *A Point of Sky* followed in 1964.

In quantitative terms, John Glassco wrote few books, and these are mostly slim volumes. Besides *Memoirs of Montparnasse* (1970), *The Fatal Woman* (1974), and short works published in literary reviews, his prose works include several "exercises in mannered pornography":[7] *Contes en crinoline* (1930), *The Temple of Pederasty* (1970), and *Fetish Girl* (1972). His work as a translator includes an anthology, *Poetry of French Canada in Translation* (1970), and three Québec novels: *Lot's Wife* (1975), by

Monique Bosco; *Creature of the Chase* (1979), by Jean-Yves Soucy; and a retranslation of *Les demi-civilisés*, by Jean-Charles Harvey, published after Glassco's death as *Fear's Folly* in 1982.

Glassco's preferred form of writing, as Woodcock has noted, was a particular form of literary rewriting that Gérard Genette has called palimpsest: "Glassco takes an existing text, removes part of it and rewrites new material which blends plausibly into the original, to produce a new work in its own right."[8] One example of Glassco's palimpsests, in the erotic vein, is his continuation of *Under the Hill*, an unfinished work by British writer and illustrator Aubrey Beardsley (1872–98). Glassco had read the text for the first time in the expurgated version as a student at McGill. Beardsley was known in the 1890s as the artist par excellence of *fin-de-siècle* decadence. Taking up where Beardsley had left off, Glassco provided his own ending to the incomplete erotic tale of Venus and Tannhäuser.

In 1974, when Glassco published a collection of three erotic novellas under the title *The Fatal Woman*, a journalist wrote in the *Winnipeg Free Press* that the collection "read like the translation from the fey and mannered French of a decadent turn-of-the-century aristocrat."[9] It is easy to imagine that Glassco, who knew that the best, but also the most paradoxical, compliment that can be paid to translators is to tell them that their translation reads as though it were not a translation, appreciated the comment to the full.

Saint-Denys-Garneau, a Companion

In 1957, at Frank Scott's initiative, Glassco undertook the translation of Saint-Denys Garneau's *Journal*. Scott made the suggestion in a letter dated November 3, 1957: "Since you like [Saint-Denys] Garneau, may I suggest you read his *Journal*, published by Beauchemin? There is nothing like it in Canadian literature. There's a translation for you!" At the bottom of the typed letter was the following note, in Glassco's handwriting: "This letter sparked the translation of the *Journal*. J.G."[10]

From the moment Glassco undertook the translation of the *Journal*, Saint-Denys-Garneau's work became his constant companion. To echo a few lines from the Québec poet's well-known poem "Accompagnement," Glassco was an attentive reader of Saint-Denys-Garneau and one who was much moved. Being both troubled and intrigued by "this company," he devoted much time and effort to transposing the work "par toutes sortes d'opérations, des alchimies, / Par des transfusions de sang / Des déménagements d'atomes / par des jeux d'équilibre,"[11] or in F.R. Scott's translation, "By all sorts of devices, by alchemies / By blood transfusions, / Displacement of atoms, / by balancing tricks."[12]

Patricia Whitney, in her doctoral thesis on the life and work of Glassco, evokes the difficult period Glassco was going through in his personal life at this time. His companion, Graeme Taylor, was dying, and he himself felt more dead than alive. Approaching fifty, he was profoundly demoralized by the failure he saw as his life. In Whitney's opinion, the discipline he then imposed on himself by undertaking the translation of the *Journal* helped him to recover: "The translation of the Garneau *Journal* was the disciplined task that Glassco seemed to need....It is doubtless true that the translation, at this particular time, was crucial to Glassco's regaining his creative energy."[13]

Once the idea of translating Saint-Denys-Garneau's *Journal* had formed in his mind, Glassco lost no time in getting down to work, nor Frank Scott in spreading the good news. On December 11, 1957, Robert Weaver, editor of the then-brand-new Toronto periodical *Tamarack Review*, wrote to Glassco that Scott had informed him of his plan to translate the *Journal*. He offered to publish extracts from the translation[14] in his review: "We're very anxious to include in the magazine as much writing as we can get from French Canada, and Frank has offered to give us some of his new translations of the Hexagone poets." Glassco enthusiastically accepted the proposal: "I'm very glad the *Tamarack Review* is interested in the writing of French Canada: so much of it is so very good that the rest of the country should know about it."

Over the next few months, there ensued an exchange of correspondence between the two men. Commenting on a sample of the work on May 25, 1958, Weaver wrote Glassco, "I find [the excerpts] odd, painful, very interesting, and judging almost entirely from the English versions, I'd say you have made a fine translation of very difficult material." Weaver's remark is typical of other judgements that were passed on the quality of Glassco's translation based on the readability of the English text without a comparison with the original. Excerpts of the *Journal* nonetheless appeared in the review in the summer of 1958.[15]

Curiously, the rejection letters Glassco received some time later for publication of the *Journal* in its entirety were signed by two members of Weaver's editorial committee. On April 30, 1959, Macmillan returned the submitted excerpts of the *Journal* to Glassco with the following note from Kildare Dobbs: "You have done what appears to us a fine job of translation, but…we can't believe that it would commend itself to many readers. This is not a question of our being afraid of anything literary or *avant-garde*. We fear that Garneau's *mal de siècle* [*sic*] has occurred in the wrong *siècle*, and to the reader who comes at his *Journal* without preconceptions he has neither interest nor charm."[16] The negative response from Oxford University Press, more nuanced, was based in essence on the argument that the publication of a poet's journal is justified when the author's poetry is known, which was not the case of Saint-Denys-Garneau's poetry in English Canada. "Rightly or wrongly," wrote I.M. Owen on January 8, 1960, "we don't think there is an audience for the private papers of a poet who is not known as a poet in the English-speaking world."[17]

An examination of the editorial policies of the two publishing houses at the time would no doubt reveal what further factors prompted the rejection. However, these comments on Glassco's English version of the *Journal* are sufficient to reveal the efforts required of the translator himself to bring the work to light. Glassco's task was not confined to the translation of Saint-Denys-Garneau's work; he also had to "sell" his translation to potential publishers at the risk of having to meet with tiresome, and discouraging, rejection slips. In a letter to Frank Scott dated June 18, 1959, Glassco confirmed that he had completed two-thirds of the translation and summed up the situation as follows: "If I can't find a publisher I must drop the project, though I can hardly face the prospect of this: the original book seems finer than ever to me."

Fortunately, the disheartenment that had taken hold of Glassco was short-lived, thanks to the timely intervention of Frank Scott, who promptly set about finding a publisher for his friend. "We shall help to civilize this country despite all the barriers raised by the Establishment," Scott exclaimed in a letter dated July 20, 1959. Notwithstanding a certain irony and self-deprecation, the comment also contains an element of truth and reveals Scott's determination in the service of a particular vision of the country. For Scott, there was no contradiction between politics and poetry, as is so aptly reflected in the title of Sandra Djwa's biography, *The Politics of the Imagination*.

When Glassco sent the first draft of his translation to McClelland and Stewart, the reader's report was generally favourable, although reservations were expressed about the quality of the translation. As a result, Glassco contacted Jean Le Moyne, who had a house in the country not far from his in the Eastern Townships. An essayist and close friend of the Québec poet, Jean Le Moyne was to publish an important collection of essays entitled *Convergences*, for which he won the Governor General's Award in 1961.[18] In a letter dated July 18, 1960, Glassco wrote that he wanted to consult him, "as I would like the final English version to be as close to perfection as possible."[19] It is significant that Glassco did not write "as close to the original," but rather, "as close to perfection as possible." His desire for the consummate result evokes a certain parallel with Saint-Denys-Garneau himself.

By the end of the summer of 1960, Glassco and LeMoyne had established a fruitful collaboration. As Whitney recounts, even fifteen years after Saint-Denys-Garneau's death, the sustained project was a trying emotional experience for Le Moyne: "As the intensity of the experience of reliving the memory of his beloved friend grew, Le Moyne would frequently be forced to draw his automobile to the verge of the road on the trip back to Bondville, so overcome with grief and nausea he was unable to handle his car until he had re-established his emotional equilibrium. This was the price Le Moyne was willing to pay to assist in the translation of the Journal."[20] During the sessions, which took place in English, the text of the journal was reviewed word by word.

At the same time as he was working on the translation of the *Journal*, Glassco also began to translate Saint-Denys-Garneau's poems. A few appeared in translation in the *Tamarack Review* in 1962, along with new excerpts from the *Journal*. By the time the *Complete Poems of Saint-Denys Garneau* was published in 1975, Glassco had been polishing the translations for fifteen years. In general, these early attempts are not as poetically effective as the versions published later in the *Complete Poems*. For example, in "Monde irrémédiable désert," Saint-Denys-Garneau writes, "Un grand couteau d'ombre / Passe au milieu de mes regards."[21] Glassco had initially rendered these lines as "A great knife of shadow / Cleaves the centre of my gaze."[22] More opaque and less flowing than the original, this version resorts to words, such as "to cleave" for "passer," that are less common than those of the source text. In the final version of these lines, the vocabulary is more accurate: "A great knife of darkness / Cuts across my eyes."[23] The meaning of the passage has been clarified, and the translator has imbued the poem in the target language with a spirit of its own.

Glassco, Poet Anthologist

Glassco believed that poets alone were capable of translating poets. This was the only way to ensure the quality of translations of poetry, one of his great concerns. In his anthology *The Poetry of French Canada in Translation* (1970), Glassco admitted that he had not only chosen solely poets for the translations but that he had omitted important poems that proved resistant to translation and had retained good translations of less representative texts. "In a sense," he wrote, "this is an anthology of poetical translations rather than of translations of poetry....The translations in this collection are presented as things that must stand on their own, dependent on their own poetic merits, owing to their originals nothing but the inspiration that has here found a partial rebirth."[24]

According to Glassco, translators inevitably let their presence be felt. In his introduction to the *Complete Poems of Saint Denys Garneau*, he explains his reasoning: "In translating the poems I have followed a course that was bound to result in the intrusion of my own personality. Such personal colouring, however unwelcome and however resisted, is inevitable....These renderings are faithful but not literal."[25] Glassco does not perceive translation as a derivative activity requiring little creativity. Far from being an obstacle, the fact that translation is a secondary activity is a source of interest, since the task of translation often becomes the starting point for writing.

Glassco's anthology of Québec poetry in translation is certainly one of his most important contributions to literary translation in Canada. Over two hundred texts by more than fifty Québécois poets are rendered into English by some twenty English-Canadian poets and translators. The choice of authors is broad, ranging from Marc Lescarbot to André Major. The poets who receive the most attention are Émile Nelligan, Hector de Saint-Denys-Garneau, and Anne Hébert. Glassco himself was the principal translator; he translated the texts of thirty-seven different poets (including Robert Choquette, Paul Morin, Alfred DesRochers, Sylvain Garneau, Roland Giguère, Alain Grandbois, Gilles Hénault, Rina Lasnier, Pierre Trottier, and, naturally, Saint-Denys-Garneau). He also engaged the services of well-known writers such as Louis Dudek, Ralph Gustafson, Frank Scott, and Arthur Smith.

In an article published in the journal *Méta* shortly before the publication of his anthology, Glassco quoted Sir John Denham, a seventeenth-century English poet, on the translation of poetry: according to Denham, the delicate spirit of poetry disappears in the transfusion from one language to another, "unless a new, or an original spirit is infused by the Translator himself."[26] That Glassco should take as his inspiration the poetics of translation of a seventeenth-century author imbued with the spirit of the *"belles infidèles"* is no coincidence. He also draws an important source of inspiration for his own poetry from the seventeenth and eighteenth centuries, from metaphysical poets like John Donne or representatives of neo-classicism like Alexander Pope. Sir John Denham is largely remembered in British literary history for *Cooper's Hill* (1642), which Samuel Johnson characterized as a topographical poem, i.e., verse whose theme is a defined landscape onto which historical considerations and meditative thought have been grafted. This form is also the basis of a good deal of Glassco's poetry, in which abandoned farmhouses seen in the area surrounding Foster or chance shortcuts taken on his walks are the starting point for rather sombre musings on the passage of time, the fleeting nature of life, and the permanency of death.

While preparing his anthology, Glassco was fully resolved to make use of his pen, and those of poets he respected, to reveal French-Canadian poetry to his fellow English-speaking Canadians and thereby spare French-Canadian poets the potential ill effects of poor translation. In this regard, it may be said that he accomplished what he set out to do, for none of the translations published in *The Poetry of French Canada in Translation* detracts from the original. In "The Opaque Medium," Glassco gives a great deal of importance to the first translation of a work. He speaks in this connection of a "disastrous law" which says that a bad translation drives out a good one. The translated work of art "becomes, as it were, the property of the first translator, for better or worse." This is because a first, very bad, translation nevertheless acquires a sort of right of ownership by virtue of occupying the territory ("squatters' rights") in the eyes of both reader and publisher.[27] Whether this was also how he felt about his own first published versions of Saint-Denys-Garneau's poems is not clear. However, it is interesting to recall in this respect that Glassco's ultimate stylistic composition, *Fear's Folly* (1982), was a retranslation of Jean-Charles Harvey's novel *Les demi-civilisés*, an initial English version by Lukin Barette having been published by Macmillan under the title *Sackcloth for Banner* in 1938.

The Translator of His Own Feelings

Glassco translated two other Québec novels. In Monique Bosco's novel, *La femme de Loth* (1970), translated by Glassco as *Lot's Wife* (1975), a forty-year-old woman is in the process of absorbing the shock of the breakup with her lover, a married man who has had enough of living a "double life." On the level of content, Glassco was undoubtedly sensitive to the genuine descent into pain that the novel expresses in a style that is both adroit and direct: "De temps à autre, un mot, une phrase, entendus malgré moi, me frappent comme un autre soufflet immérité."[28] Glassco translates this as "Now and then a word, a sentence heard in spite of myself, strikes me like another undeserved blow."[29] A word, a blow; making the air tremble with one's words and one's blows. The association of ideas here would have put Glassco on ground that was both familiar and tormented; he had suffered a great deal of ill-treatment in his childhood and had subsequently filled his pornographic work with scenes of masochism. Translation, in this regard, can be seen as a way of learning to redirect or deflect the words one receives.

At the heart of Monique Bosco's novel is the image of Lot's wife who, contrary to what God had enjoined her to do, looked back, and was turned into a pillar of salt. The novel poses the question: should one, can one, return to one's past through narrative? Is it not preferable to "laisser la ville en flammes se consumer. Sans se retourner," or as Glassco translates, "leave the city to perish in its flames. Without turning back"?[30] And even if one does choose to look back, how is an account of the past to be given, how is it to be told, what is to be written? "Alas, I'll never write anything but stupid stories without beginning or end, full of strange characters gnawed by obscure sufferings," as the English version of Monique Bosco's novel says.[31] Glassco echoes much the same sentiment in his *Memoirs*, observing that he had "decided to write only books utterly divorced from reality, stories where nothing happens."[32]

Glassco also translated Jean-Yves Soucy's first work, *Un dieu chasseur*. In one of the rare examples in Canadian literature of a directly reciprocal exchange between writer and translator, Soucy later translated *Memoirs of Montparnasse* into French under the title *Souvenirs de Montparnasse* (1983). *Un dieu chasseur* spotlights the tension between Nature and the human male, the latter sometimes referred to as a "two-legged dog" and a "tree-without-roots." Even after twenty-five years of living in the forest, Mathieu, the main character, still senses a "barrier between a man like him and nature." Although his experience of sexuality is limited, he nevertheless feels a sense of unease about it that he is unable to identify.

In the original French version, the novel contains a foreword in which Soucy explains that "this book contains a certain number of canadianisms, neologisms and words of English or other origin. Readers wishing to acquaint themselves with these terms will find a glossary which provides definitions at the end of the book."[33] Francophone readers are thus advised that they are dealing with a "marked" text, one they must decode, so to speak, and for which they have been provided with a special lexicographical tool. To avoid erasing this characteristic of the source text, Glassco has adopted several strategies. To preserve the Québécois flavour of the entire text, proper names are not translated. The main character of *Creatures of the Chase* is still called Mathieu and his dogs are still called Orient, Occident, and Ti-Noir. However, English words such as "trail" or "run," used in collocations such as "courir les trails" or "faire la run des pièges,"[34] no longer appear as borrowings and in the translation working-class Québécois speech such as "Toute la forêt est à moé" is translated neutrally as: "The whole forest is mine."[35] To compensate for these losses, Glassco adds a small Québécois touch here and there to the English text. For example, he translates "un flacon d'alcool" by "a bottle of whisky blanc."[36] Elsewhere, he leaves expressions or even whole sentences in French: "Salut, l'Indien."[37]

Glassco's decision to retranslate Jean-Charles Harvey's *Les demi-civilisés* at the end of his life was far from innocent. The novel had been denounced by the archdiocese of Québec a few weeks after its publication in 1934. The ban imposed included publishing, reading, keeping, selling, and passing the book on to others.[38] The novel tells the story of a man thirsting for freedom, who is guilty of loving a young woman. As John O'Connor writes in his introduction to Glassco's translation, "Harvey was determined to demonstrate that the Québec of the 1920s and 1930s was a society undergoing a radical transition among its common people, however serene and submissive it appeared to its rulers."[39]

A new translation was essential in O'Connor's view, not only because Lukin Barette's original translation, *Sackcloth for Banner*, with its numerous omissions, was "very unreliable"[40] but also because Harvey had revised his novel for a new edition published in 1966, the year before his death. As he himself points out in a short translator's note,[41] Glassco used this corrected text as the basis for *Fear's Folly*, while consulting as well both the first edition and Barette's original translation. Of the translator's final contribution to Canada's literary heritage, O'Connor writes, "Glassco has skillfully avoided the pitfalls of both slavish literalism and carefree license; in so doing, he has achieved the twin ideals of all translations: a graceful style and consistent reliability."[42]

Being Faithful to Oneself and the Other

As his anthology *The Poetry of French Canada in Translation* clearly demonstrates, Glassco's sphere of translational interest was extensive; he could translate eighteenth-century Québec authors such as Joseph Quesnel or contemporary poets like Saint-Denys-Garneau with equal ease. He surely shared Quesnel's awareness of the fact that "l'ingrat Canadien / Aux talens de l'esprit n'accorde jamais rien," or as he puts it, that "Canada, whose graceless brood / Withholds from talent, ev'n a livelihood."[43] Undaunted, Glassco nevertheless continued to work away as a diligent man of letters, ever concerned about finding the *mot d'esprit*, the *mot juste* that would be an act of fidelity, in spirit, both to himself and the other.

Glassco included his own dedication in his translation of *La femme de Loth*. While the question of who writes the dedication in a book could be considered trivial, as we are led to believe it is always the author, this is not necessarily the case. Gide, for instance, dedicated his translation of Joseph Conrad's *Typhoon* to A. Ruyters. In Gérard Genette's view, such dedications of translated works serve to obscure the notion of "authorship."[44] Certainly, both as translator and writer, Glassco challenged the limits of this notion, whether it be through his practice of palimpsest in his completion of Aubrey Beardsley's erotic story *Under the Hill*, or through his attention to the creative dimensions of translating poetry. As Fraser Sutherland observes, "He often implied that art is a collaboration of past and present, and that authorship should not be held immutably sacred."[45]

Lot's Wife is dedicated to Sheila Fischman, a renowned literary translator who has translated several novels by Anne Hébert, Jacques Poulin, Roch Carrier, Michel Tremblay, and others into English. The dedication can be seen as Glassco's attempt to make a more explicit connection between himself, an aging author and translator who knew that he was at the end of his career, and a translator at the beginning of hers whose great talent he sensed. "Buffy" wanted to establish descendants and even set his mark on a new tradition of literary translation in Canada. Significantly, the year the translation was published (1975) was also the year that the Literary Translators' Association of Canada was founded. "Glassco gave, in his life, a memorable example of purpose and persistence," writes Sutherland.[46] Following his death, in an indication of the respect and affection in which Glassco was held by his colleagues, the association established its first prize for literary translation, and appropriately named it in his honour.

NOTES

This chapter has been translated from the French by Lin Burman, an accredited member of the Literary Translators' Association of Canada.

1 The excerpts from remarks by D.G. Jones are taken from: "Les poètes québécois de langue anglaise," CBC Transcription Services, no. 6, December 24, 1982, pp. 2–4.
2 George Woodwock, "John Glassco (19 December 1909–29 January 1981)," in *Dictionary of Literary Biography*, vol. 68, *Canadian Writers* 1920–1959, 1st ser., ed. W.H. New (Detroit: Gale Research, 1988) p. 145.
3 Fraser Sutherland, *John Glassco: An Essay and Bibliography* (Downsview, ON: ECW Press, 1984), p. 43.
4 Quoted in Fraser Sutherland, *John Glassco*, p. 42.
5 John Glassco, *Memoirs of Montparnasse* (Toronto: Oxford University Press, 1970), p. 1.
6 See in this connection Michael Gnarowski's introduction to the new edition of *Memoirs of Montparnasse* (Toronto: Oxford University Press, 1995): "Fic-

tion for the Sake of Art: An Introduction to the Making of *Memoirs of Montparnasse*," pp. x–xxv.
7 George Woodcock and William Toye, "Glassco, John," in the *Oxford Companion to Canadian Literature*, 2nd ed., ed. Eugene Benson and William Toye (Don Mills, ON: Oxford University Press, 1997), p. 467.
8 George Woodcock, "Private Fantasies: Collective Myths," *Tamarack Review*, no. 65 (March 1975). Quoted in Fraser Sutherland, *John Glassco*, p. 108.
9 Perry Nodelman, "A Canadian Decadent," *Winnipeg Free Press*, December 21, 1974, p. 18. Quoted in Fraser Sutherland, *John Glassco*, p. 107.
10 The letters from which a few excerpts are quoted here were consulted in the John Glassco Collection, Rare Book Room, McGill University, Montréal.
11 Hector de Saint-Denys-Garneau, "Accompagnement," *Poésies complètes* (Montréal: Fides, 1949), p. 101.
12 Hector de Saint-Denys Garneau, "Accompaniment," trans F.R. Scott. John Glassco, *The Poetry of French Canada in Translation*, ed. J. Glassco (Toronto: Oxford University Press, 1970), p. 104.
13 Patricia Whitney, "Darkness and Delight: A Portrait of the Life and Work of John Glassco," (PhD diss., Carleton University, 1988), pp. 331–32.
14 John Glassco, "Saint-Denys Garneau: The Dimensions of Longing; Extracts from the Journals," *Tamarack Review*, no. 8 (summer 1958): 17–35. Quotations from the Weaver-Glassco correspondence are from the John Glassco Collection, Rare Book Room, McGill University, Montréal.
15 Whitney, "Darkness and Delight," pp. 331–32.
16 This excerpt from Kildare Dobbs's letter is also quoted by Patricia Whitney in "Darkness and Delight" (p. 306); in her opinion, this reply constitutes a "wrongheaded" assessment of Saint-Denys Garneau's place in English-Canadian literature.
17 Whitney, "Darkness and Delight," p. 306.
18 See Patricia Whitney, who met Jean Le Moyne several times when she was working on her dissertation, for further light on this aspect of Glassco's work.
19 Quoted in Patricia Whitney, "Darkness and Delight," p. 310.
20 Whitney, "Darkness and Delight," p. 312.
21 de Saint-Denys-Garneau, *Poésies complètes* (Montréal: Fides, 1949), p. 159
22 John Glassco, trans., "Saint-Denys Garneau: Three Poems," *Tamarack Review*, no. 22 (winter 1962): 75.
23 John Glassco, trans., *Complete Poems of Saint-Denys Garneau*, by Hector de Saint-Denys Garneau (Toronto: McClelland and Stewart, 1962), p. 123.
24 John Glassco, ed., *The Poetry of French Canada in Translation* (Toronto: Oxford University Press, 1970), p. xxiv.
25 Glassco, trans., *Complete Poems of Saint-Denys Garneau*, p. 17.
26 John Glassco, "The Opaque Medium: Remarks on the Translation of Poetry with a Special Reference to French-Canadian Verse," *Méta* 14, no. 1 (Mar. 1969): 27.
27 Glassco, "The Opaque Medium," p. 30.
28 Monique Bosco, *La femme de Loth* (Paris: Éditions Robert Laffont, 1979; Montréal: Éditions HMH, 1970), p. 13.

29 Monique Bosco, *Lot's Wife*, trans. John Glassco (Toronto: McClelland and Stewart, 1975), p. 4.
30 Bosco, *La femme de Loth*, p. 21; Bosco, *Lot's Wife*, trans. John Glassco, p. 9.
31 Bosco, *Lot's Wife*, trans. John Glassco, p. 10–11.
32 Quoted in Woodcock and Toye, "Glassco, John," p. 467.
33 Jean-Yves Soucy, *Un dieu chasseur* (Montréal: Fides, 1980), p. 4. Translation by Lin Burman.
34 Soucy, *Un dieu chasseur*, p. 16.
35 Soucy, *Un dieu chasseur*, p. 14; Jean-Yves Soucy, *Creatures of the Chase*, trans. John Glassco (Toronto: McClelland and Stewart, 1979), p. 14.
36 Soucy, *Un dieu chasseur*, p. 15; Soucy, *Creatures of the Chase*, trans. John Glassco, p. 14.
37 Soucy, *Creatures of the Chase*, trans. John Glassco, p. 15.
38 *Dictionnaire des œuvres littéraires du Québec 1900–1939* (Montréal: Fides, 1980), p. 347.
39 John O'Connor, introduction to *Fear's Folly*, by Jean-Charles Harvey, trans. John Glassco (Ottawa: Carleton University Press, 1982), p. 5.
40 O'Connor, introduction, p. 20.
41 The translator's note, to which Glassco only appended his initials, reads as follows: "This translation was made from the final edition of *Les demi-civilisés* as revised by the author and published in 1966, just prior to his death. It has been collated with the original edition of 1934, and with the translation by Lukin Barette published in 1938." After the note, under Glassco's initials, the following indications appear with regard to place and date: "Foster, Que. August 1980." Harvey, *Fear's Folly*, n. p.
42 O'Connor, introduction, pp. 20–21.
43 Quoted in Michael Gnarowski, ed. *Joseph Quesnel 1749–1809: Selected Poems and Songs after the Manuscripts in the Lande Collection/Quelques poèmes et chansons selon des manuscrits dans la collection Lande*. (Montréal: Lawrence M. Lande Foundation at the McLennan Library, McGill University, 1970), p. 57–60.
44 Gérard Genette, *Seuils* (Paris: Seuil, 1987), p. 132.
45 Sutherland, *John Glassco*, p. 12.
46 Sutherland, *John Glassco*, p. 42.

BIBLIOGRAPHY

I. Primary Sources

Translations

Bosco, Monique. *Lot's Wife*. Trans. John Glassco. Toronto: McClelland and Stewart, 1975.

Harvey, Jean-Charles. *Fear's Folly*. Trans. John Glassco. Introd. John O'Connor, Ottawa: Carleton University Press, 1982.

Quesnel, Joseph. *Épître à Généreux Labadie*. Trans. John Glassco. In *Joseph Quesnel 1749–1809: Selected Poems and Songs after the Manuscripts in the Lande Col-*

lection, ed. M. Gnarowski. Montréal: Lawrence M. Lande Foundation at the McLennan Library, McGill University, 1970.

Riel, Louis. "To Sir John A. MacDonald." [Letter from Louis Riel]. Trans. John Glassco. *Canadian Literature*, no. 37 (Summer 1968): 40–45.

Saint-Denys-Garneau, Hector de. "Saint-Denys Garneau: The Dimensions of Longing. Extracts from the Journals." *Tamarack Review*, no. 8 (Summer 1958): 17–35.

———. *The Journal of Saint-Denys-Garneau*. Trans. John Glassco. Introd. Gilles Marcotte. Toronto: McClelland and Stewart, 1962.

———. "Saint-Denys Garneau : Extracts from *The Journal*." Trans. John Glassco. *Tamarack Review*, no. 22 (Winter 1962): 54–70.

———. "Saint-Denys Garneau: Three Poems." Trans. John Glassco. *Tamarack Review*, no. 22 (Winter 1962): 71–76.

———. Hector de. *Complete Poems of Saint Denys Garneau*. Trans. And introd. John Glassco. Ottawa: Oberon Press, 1975.

Soucy, Jean-Yves. *Creatures of the Chase*. Trans. John Glassco. Toronto: McClelland and Stewart, 1979.

Von Sacher-Masoch. *Venus in Furs*. Trans. and introd. John Glassco. Burnaby, BC: Blackfish Press, 1977.

Anthologies

Glassco, John, ed. *English Poetry in Quebec: Proceedings of the Foster Poetry Conference, October 12–14, 1963*. Montréal: McGill University Press, 1965.

———, ed. *The Poetry of French Canada in Translation*. Toronto: Oxford University Press, 1970.

Literary Works

Glassco, John. *The Deficit Made Flesh*. Toronto: McClelland and Stewart, 1958.

———, and Aubrey Beardsley. *Under the Hill*. Paris: Olympia, 1959.

———. *A Point of Sky*. Toronto: Oxford University Press, 1964.

———. *The Fatal Woman*. Toronto: House of Anansi, 1974.

———. *Memoirs of Montparnasse*. Introd. Leon Edel. Toronto: Oxford University Press, 1970. Toronto: Oxford University Press, 1995. Translation *Souvenirs de Montparnasse*, Montréal. Trans. Jean-Yves Soucy. Montréal: Éditions Hurtubise HMH, 1983.

Works on Translation

Glassco, John. "The Opaque Medium: Remarks on the Translation of Poetry with a Special Reference to French-Canadian Verse." *Méta* 14, no. 1 (Mar. 1969): 27–30.

II. Secondary Sources

Bosco, Monique. *La femme de Loth*. Paris: Éditions Robert Laffont, 1970; Montréal: Éditions HMH, 1970.

Dictionnaire des œuvres littéraires du Québec 1900–1939. Montréal: Fidès, 1980.

Djwa, Sandra. *The Politics of the Imagination: A Life of F.R. Scott*. Toronto: McClelland and Stewart, 1987. Translation *F.R. Scott: Une vie*. Trans. Florence Bernard. Montréal: Éditions du Boréal, 2000.

Harvey, Jean-Charles. *Les demi-civilisés*. Montréal: Éditions du Totem, 1934. Montréal: Éditions de l'Homme, 1966.

Genette, Gérard. *Seuils*. Paris: Seuil, 1987.

Glassco, John. Fonds John-Glassco. Rare Book Room, McGill University, Montréal.

Godbout, Patricia. *Traduction littéraire et sociabilité interculturelle au Canada (1950–1960)*. Ottawa: Presses de l'Université d'Ottawa, 2004.

Gnarowski, Michael. "Fiction for the Sake of Art: An Introduction to the Making of *Memoirs of Montparnasse*." In *Memoirs of Montparnasse*, by John Glassco. Toronto: Oxford University Press, 1995. x–xxv.

Gnarowski, Michael, ed. *Joseph Quesnel 1749–1809: Selected Poems and Songs after the Manuscripts in the Lande Collection/Quelques poèmes et chansons selon des manuscrits dans la collection Lande*. Trans. of *Épitre à Généreux Labadie* by John Glassco. Montréal: Lawrence M. Lande Foundation at the McLennan Library, McGill University, 1970.

Jones, D.G. Interview by Jacques Marchand. Broadcast on Radio-Canada Dec. 24, 1982. Transcription Services, "Les poètes québécois de langue anglaise." Cahier no. 6.

O'Connor, John. Introduction to *Fear's Folly*, by Jean-Charles Harvey, trans. John Glassco. Ottawa: Carleton University Press, 1982.

Saint-Denys Garneau, Hector de. *Poésies complètes*. Introd. Robert Élie. Montréal: Fidès, 1949.

Soucy, Jean-Yves. *Un dieu chasseur*. Montréal: Éditions La Presse, 1978 (1976).

Stratford, Philip, and Maureen Newman, eds. *Bibliographie de livres canadiens traduits de l'anglais au français et du français à l'anglais*. Ottawa: CCRH, 1975.

Sutherland, Fraser. *John Glassco: An Essay and Bibliography*. Downsview, ON: ECW Press, 1984.

Whitney, Patricia. "Darkness and Delight: A Portrait of the Life and Work of John Glassco." PhD diss., Carleton University, 1988.

Woodcock, George. "Glassco, John (19 December 1909—29 January 1981." In *Dictionary of Literary Biography*, vol. 68, *Canadian Writers, 1920–1959*, 1st ser., ed. W.H. New. Detroit, MI: Gale Research, 1988. 143–148.

———, and William Toye. "John Glassco." In *Oxford Companion to Canadian Literature*, ed. Eugene Benson and William Toye, 2nd ed. Don Mills, ON: Oxford University Press, 1997. 466–67.

3

Joyce Marshall,
or the Accidental Translator

JANE EVERETT

 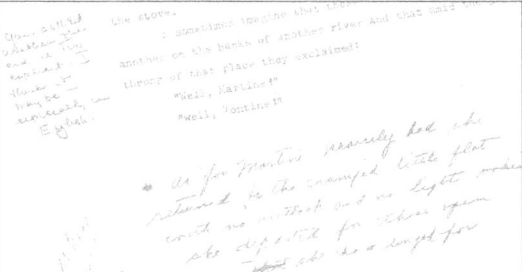

Joyce Marshall is first and foremost a writer whose professional career began in the mid-1930s. Students of Canadian literature know her as the author of two novels and many short stories, a number of which have been broadcast and published. It was not until 1959 that she began what was to become a distinguished career as a literary translator, attracting critical notice for her work on the letters of Marie de l'Incarnation and her translations of Gabrielle Roy's *The Road Past Altamont* (1966), *Windflower* (1970), and *Enchanted Summer* (1976), for which she received the 1976 Canada Council Translation Prize. Marshall never set out to become a translator, nor did she initiate any of the translation projects she eventually undertook. Moreover, she does not consider her translations, with the possible exception of her edition of Marie de l'Incarnation's letters, to be important in her body of work.[1]

Happenstance was responsible for her introduction to this unintended career: "Bob Weaver [program organizer for CBC radio's *Anthology* and an editor of *Tamarack Review*] knew I knew French," recalls Marshall, "and it started when he asked me to translate a story of Gabrielle Roy's...for the CBC. It must have been about 1959. I don't remember exactly, and nobody much was translating then."[2] The story, "Grandmother and the Doll" (1960), was part of *La Route d'Altamont*. Roy, who took an active interest in the English translations of her works, was very pleased with the result, and Marshall was asked to translate the rest of the book. "I happened to be bored with my own writing at that time," writes Marshall. "I felt that I knew what I would say before I said it since I'd been saying the same things, or at least the same sorts of things, for years. So I agreed."[3] What follows is an attempt to bring together the various strands of a career which, however accidental, has left its mark on the history of literary translation in Canada.

A Writer's Life

Born in Montréal on November 28, 1913, Joyce Marshall comes from a family that traces its roots back to Scotland, Norway, England, and Wales. Her maternal grandfather,[4] Canon W.P. Chambers, was a reporter for the *Montreal Star* before going on to study divinity at Bishop's University in Québec's Eastern Townships. His wife Alice, of Welsh descent, was "a rich girl, born in Québec City" whom he married upon his ordination as an Anglican priest. They lived for a time in the area north of the Gatineau River, then in Knowlton, before finally settling in Lachine. He resigned the ministry when he was around fifty and went to work for the *Family Herald and Weekly Star*, a newspaper with a wide rural readership; he retired, under protest, at the age of eighty-four. Joyce Marshall describes him as being the "epitome of the Victorian father, like Leslie Stephen," that is, "a sentimentalist and a bully." He and his wife had nine children, the eldest of whom was Ruth, Joyce Marshall's mother. Alice Chambers having taken to her bed, Ruth was obliged to leave school at the age of sixteen in order to care for her siblings, a responsibility she resented. She would later impress upon her daughters the importance of personal and economic independence.

Marshall's paternal great-grandfather was a sculptor who had moved from the Highlands to Edinburgh when his children were young, in order to work in the atelier of a prominent sculptor.[5] Marshall's grandfather,[6] one of his three sons, came to Canada with the army. While stationed at Québec, he met his future wife, Helena, the daughter of Norwegian immigrants Even and Rangdi Pedersen (later changed to Peterson), who lived in nearby Saint-Vallier. The young couple moved to Halifax in 1871, and then, after he left the army, to Montréal, where he worked for Macdonald Tobacco. They had seven children, the sixth of whom was Joyce Marshall's father, William Wallace, a "stocks-and-bonds dealer and an amateur singer."[7] He married Ruth Chambers in February 1913; Joyce Marshall is the eldest of their five children (they had four daughters and one son).

Marshall became fascinated with writing at a very early age and was producing stories and poems while still in primary school; some of her first stories were published in the *Family Herald and Weekly Star*, where her grandfather had worked. She attended public schools in Montréal from 1920 to 1929, and a private girls' boarding school, St. Helen's (in Dunham, Québec), from 1929 to 1932, completing her formal education with an Honours BA in English from McGill University. She published poems and stories in various university magazines and was an editor (the first woman to hold such a position) for the *McGill Daily*. Upon graduation in 1935, she was awarded the English Department's language and literature medal.[8]

Like all children in the Protestant school system at the time, Marshall started learning French in grade three; unlike many others of her generation, she continued to perfect her knowledge of the language even when it was no longer required. Despite her familiarity with French, however, she did not feel at home in Québec. As W.H. New explains, "as a non-Catholic, non-francophone female in the restrictive conservative Québec of Premier Maurice Duplessis, she felt she was denied not only economic opportunities but also a political voice. So in 1937, with Europe beyond economic reach, she moved to Toronto."[9] In addition to being "to her eyes a politically more open city," Toronto "was also a rapidly growing city, and as [it] became the center for English-language radio broadcasting in Canada...she began to find both a congenial literary medium and a literary voice."[10]

Initially supporting herself with low-paying jobs in the service sector, Marshall was eventually able to make her living (however precariously) entirely through writing or related work. She published a number of poems in the first years, as well as articles and short stories.[11] Her first novel, *Presently Tomorrow*, was published in 1946; the second, *Lovers and Strangers*, in 1957. She is perhaps best known, though, for her short stories, many of which have been read on CBC radio, or published in magazines[12] and anthologies (for both general and academic audiences). Three volumes have also appeared: *A Private Place* (1975), *Any Time At All and Other Stories* (1993), and *Blood and Bone / En chair et en os* (1995).

From 1949 to 1980,[13] Marshall was a reader-editor for CBC radio's *Canadian Short Stories* and *Anthology* programs. Her reviews and essays have appeared in the *Tamarack Review, Books in Canada,* and *Canadian Literature.* A frequent member of juries judging literary works,[14] translations, arts grant applications, and writing competitions, Marshall has also read manuscripts for McClelland and Stewart,[15] and she was general editor for *Enchantment and Sorrow,* Patricia Claxton's translation of Gabrielle Roy's *La détresse et l'enchantement.*[16] She has participated in countless public readings throughout Canada, and was writer-in-residence at Trent University in 1980–81 and writer-in-library in Vaughan in 1991.

Both in and of the English-Canadian literary institution (more precisely, of the Toronto-based part of it), Marshall has always been very aware of what is happening in the Québec literary world. Review articles she wrote in the late 1950s for the *Tamarack Review* and in 1965 for the *Montrealer* reveal her familiarity with contemporary trends and her understanding of the cultural and socio-political contexts of the day. In an article published in *Books in Canada* in 1992, she reminisces about a visit to Montréal to find stories that could be translated for *Anthology.* "It was 1965," she recalls, "bombs had exploded in mailboxes two years previously and we were all anxious to do something about our poor threatened Canadian unity. Translation, we believed, would be at the very least a start."[17]

Marshall's familiarity with Québec literature is undoubtedly one of the reasons she was asked to provide articles on Hubert Aquin, Gérard Bessette, Réjean Ducharme, Anne Hébert, Gabrielle Roy, Gilles Vigneault, and other Québec writers[18] to the *Supplement* to the 1967 *Oxford Companion to Canadian History and Literature.* Marshall contributed as well to the first edition of *The Oxford Companion to Canadian Literature* (1983), writing articles on Marie-Claire Blais (including a separate one on *La belle bête*), Gérald Godin, André Major, Marie de l'Incarnation and others. The second edition (1997) contains the same entries, updated, as well as a new article on Elizabeth Harvor. Joyce Marshall herself is the subject of entries in the *Supplement,* written by the general editor, William E. Toye, and in the 1983 and 1997 editions of the *Oxford Companion to Canadian Literature,* by Robert Weaver; she is also mentioned in these volumes in general entries dealing with the development of the novel, the short story, and literary translation.

Actively involved in professional organizations such as the Writers' Union of Canada (established in 1976), Marshall is a founding member of the Literary Translators' Association of Canada (LTAC), created in May 1975[19] "to promote literary translation and to protect the interests of its members throughout the country."[20] At the time, as Patricia Claxton recalls, "it was common practice not only to ignore a book's translator completely in reviews, publicity, catalogues, lists and bibliographies, but to omit credit to the translator even on the title page of a book and in anthologies."[21] There was no industry-wide consensus as to appropriate fees and fee scales, and even some confusion as to who should pay for the translation. In the eyes of many literary translators, one of the most pernicious expressions of this lack of awareness was editors' tendency to make changes to the translation without reference to the overall project or indeed to the translator. Marshall, says Claxton, worked actively to track these different practices and bring them to the attention of newspaper editors, magazine editors, reviewers, publicists, and publishers, among others. In 1995, in explicit recognition of Marshall's contributions to the English- and French-speaking literary institutions, as a writer and as a translator, LTAC published *Blood and Bone / En chair et en os*, a collection of seven stories by Marshall with their French translations.

The Occasional Translator

"Every book I translated I was asked to do," notes Marshall.[22] In other words, the projects came to her. This is not altogether surprising, perhaps, given her already well-established reputation as a fine writer and editor, and the quality of her translations. Her long-standing association with people occupying key positions within the emerging Toronto-based literary institution, such as Bob Weaver and Jack McClelland, presumably added to her visibility, as did her connection with Gabrielle Roy. This latter relationship, it must be emphasized, worked both ways, Marshall being a privileged intermediary between Roy and the English-Canadian literary and cultural establishment. She frequently dealt on Roy's behalf with Jack McClelland and various editors at McClelland and Stewart. She also introduced Roy to the works of contemporary Canadian writers such as Margaret Laurence and Ethel Wilson. English-speaking journalists and academics wishing to interview Roy would contact Marshall to ask her to intervene in their favour; and when CBC television produced a literary program (*The Garden and the Cage*, written by Timothy Findley and William Whitehead) on the works of Marie-Claire Blais and Roy, Joyce Marshall was hired as a consultant to ensure that the interpretation of Roy's work was accurate.[23]

Most of Marshall's translations were done in the 1960s and 1970s. After "Grandmother and the Doll" (1960), she translated a book review by Bernard Weilbrenner, "New France under the Sun King" (1965), and three articles by Naïm Kattan, "Montreal Letter" (1964), "Montreal Letter: French-Canadian Plays" (1965), and "Montreal and French-Canadian Authors: What They Mean to English-Canadian Novelists" (1966) for the *Tamarack Review*. Her translation of Gabrielle Roy's *La route d'Altamont* was published in 1966, the same year as the original. The celebrations surrounding Canada's centennial year brought two more translation projects: "The Theme Unfolded, by Gabrielle Roy," a text the latter had been commissioned to write for Montréal's 1967 World Exhibition, and *Word from New France: The Selected Letters of Marie de l'Incarnation*.[24] *No Passport: A Discovery of Canada*, Marshall's translation of Eugène Cloutier's *Le Canada sans passeport*, appeared in 1968; *Windflower*, the English version of Gabrielle Roy's novel *La rivière sans repos*, in 1970;[25] and *A Woman in a Man's World*, the translation of Thérèse F. Casgrain's *Une femme chez les hommes*, in 1972.

When *The Hidden Mountain* (1962), Harry Lorin Binsse's translation of Roy's *La montagne secrète*, was reissued in 1974 by McClelland and Stewart in their New Canadian Library collection, Marshall was asked to edit the text and make minor changes. In 1976, the same company published *The October Crisis*, Marshall's translation of Gérard Pelletier's *La crise d'octobre*, as well as her last full-length translation for Gabrielle Roy, *Enchanted Summer*, a collection of interconnected prose pieces. Marshall chose at that point to end the partnership with Gabrielle Roy as her own writing was requiring more and more of her time and mental energy. She felt, moreover, that she had learned all that was to be learned from the translation process.[26] Roy could not but be sympathetic to such reasons, however much she may have regretted losing such a valuable collaborator.

For both *The Selected Letters of Marie de l'Incarnation* and Eugène Cloutier's *No Passport*, Marshall's role as translator included a substantial editorial, almost authorial, dimension. Her edition of the letters includes a lengthy historical introduction, short texts presenting each section[27] of the letters and their context, footnotes, an index, and a bibliography. Marshall's choices reflect a well-thought out editorial project: "As my purpose was to provide a narrative of the life of the time," she notes in the introduction, "I have included very few of the wholly 'spiritual' letters.... When cuts were made, and indicated in the usual manner, it was to avoid repetition or monotony of tone."[28] The *Literary History of Canada* attests to the success of Marshall's historical project, calling the book "striking new evidence" on the "social history of New France."[29]

For *No Passport*, as she indicates in her brief translator's note, Marshall started from the same initial manuscript as the author; however, "working independently, [Cloutier] and I have not always made the same selections, and so we now have two books, one in French and one in English, which to some extent complement each other."[30] In choosing her material, Marshall "tried as much as possible to keep the leisurely quality that was so charming a feature of the original....The experiences, the responses, and the conclusions are all M. Cloutier's: only the selection is my own."[31] Again, Marshall's editorial decisions, like her translation choices, were determined primarily by "writerly" considerations.[32]

The Writer as Translator

Some years ago, reading for the first time one of Joyce Marshall's translations of a work by Gabrielle Roy—*The Road Past Altamont*, to be specific—I became aware that the voice I was hearing in my head was the same one that I hear when reading Gabrielle Roy in the original. Now one might object that such recognition is simply a by-product of my familiarity with Roy's work in French, the expectation of hearing Roy's voice in the text "adjusting" or filtering the way I hear the translation. That is no doubt partly the case, but the explanation does not account for the fact that I do not hear the voice I expect to hear—or not, at any rate, to the same extent—in translations of Roy's works done by others. Does this mean that Joyce Marshall's translation voice is closest to Gabrielle Roy's authorial voice? Not necessarily (the question is, I think, unanswerable), though it could mean that both voices have characteristics that I "hear" as similar. Marshall's comments and observations regarding the translation process offer some insights into the production of this translation voice that, to me, is Roy's.

Like Harry L. Binsse, who preceded her as Roy's translator, and Alan Brown, who succeeded her, Marshall had the advantage of being able to work closely with Roy:[33]

> We used to spend three or four days going over my translation, not once but several times....I found it a stimulating but exhausting business. I was made to turn the meaning and connotation of words (not to say my own head) up and down and sideways as I'd never had to do before. Some rare old rows took place. Gabrielle's knowledge of English grammar was no longer as complete as she believed it was and she sometimes considered me *exigeante* (fussy) in my insistence on strict English word-order and usage. I, on the other hand, benefited by her excellent ear, her sense of the nuances and subtleties as well as the sound and rhythm of language. I owe her a great deal as a writer and translator.[34]

Marshall had no formal translation training (not that there was much available when she started); in her first attempt, she "simply rendered the text baldly, more or less word for word, then struggled to turn the result into something that didn't outrage too many of the rules and taboos of English."[35] This remained for the most part her way of working thereafter, and while she acknowledges that it might have been useful to have some guidelines to which to refer,[36] the problems encountered in translation are invariably unique. Solving one type of problem in one particular text is not necessarily helpful in solving the same type of problem in another work, whether it be by the same author or not.[37] This viewpoint is consistent with Marshall's contention that translation is a craft, not an art or a form of creative endeavour (nor, one supposes, a science); and that this craft, though it is something that can be learned by doing (and by ceaselessly questioning language), ultimately resists systematization and theorization.

Some of the difficulties Marshall encountered were due to the "deceptive and (for a translator) tormenting simplicity of [Roy's] style, which by then, had become so limpid it almost seemed to disappear."[38] The first lines of "Les îles," in *Cet été qui chantait*, are fairly typical:

> Ce n'est pas par temps clair que l'on déchiffre le mieux le lointain. De chez nous, on aperçoit au large du fleuve, sous des ciels d'orage ou avant le froid vif, de petites îles que l'on ne voit pas en d'autres temps. À peine les a-t-on eues pour compagnes un ou deux jours que déjà elles partent à la dérive, dans une sorte d'existence de rêve où il arrive que l'on saisisse, pour un instant encore, le contour imprécis de l'une puis de l'autre.[39]

Trying to keep to the structure of the second and third sentences would have resulted in a choppy, tortured passage. Marshall's solution—shifting a few phrases—preserves the flow and the limpidity of the original:

> It is not in clear weather that one can best decipher the distance. Under storm clouds or just before the onset of the bitter cold, we in our part of the world can see some little islands in the open river that are never visible at other times. But when we've had them as companions for only a day or so, they drift away into a sort of dream existence where from time to time we can grasp the vague outline of first one and then another for an instant more.[40]

Marshall also had trouble on occasion finding the right equivalents for French words with "wide, rather loose meanings," and Roy would attempt to define "the fraction of this meaning she had had in mind."[41] A case in point is the adjective "désaxée," used by Roy in the novel *La rivière sans repos*. One day, the inhabitants of Fort Chimo (Kuujjuaq) are startled to hear some of their number being addressed by name, via radio, from a US reconnaissance plane flying overhead. They speculate that the person speaking is Jimmy, the runaway son of the novel's main character, Elsa. Since she herself does not hear the voice, Elsa asks people if her son seemed happy. The village priest replies, "Le Père Eugène hochait la tête. À lui, cette fanfaronnade dans le ciel avait donné l'impression d'une jeunesse devenue tôt cynique et désaxée. Elsa n'alla plus jamais solliciter ses impressions sur l'événement."[42]

Roy and Marshall discussed the problem posed by "désaxée" when they met for an intensive work session in the fall of 1969, but were unable to solve it. In a letter written shortly thereafter, Gabrielle Roy suggests that if Marshall "could find a word meaning that all his life and not only the war [in Vietnam] are responsible for the quirks of his mind, all would be well."[43] Marshall eventually chose "twisted": "Father Eugene shook his head. To him the boasting in the sky had suggested a youth become cynical and twisted. Elsa never went to ask for his impressions again."[44]

It was not always easy to reconcile Roy with English usage. Although Roy knew English well, according to Marshall, she was not as attuned as she thought to "how an English sentence is supposed to sound." As a result, "each translation I did for her brought its separate problems":[45] "With *The Road Past Altamont* it was the harmless little word 'thing'....I was triumphant when I managed to remove every 'thing' but two from *Windflower*, only to find that she'd now disapproved of sentences ending with 'it,' a structure that she stated (correctly) is never used in French and that she thought weak....When I worked on *Enchanted Summer* I did my best to avoid such sentences but now Gabrielle had another bête noire—the word 'had' and our composite verbs in general, which I had to explain and keep explaining was just one of the ways the English language went."[46] For Marshall, knowing the ways the English language "goes," how it should sound, is an important touchstone in translation, one that not only cannot be taken for granted, but must be continually reinforced. When translating, she observes, "I had to spend some time every day reading English—not the newspapers but the most immaculate English I could find. Otherwise I simply forgot, or was at least in danger of forgetting, how an English sentence was put together and why it was put together that way."[47]

This is a position Marshall has always held. In a 1958 review of three novels by Françoise Mallet-Joris, she criticized the "somewhat rickety translation," the "troubling clumsiness in the English": "Suffice it to say that rhythm is as intrinsic to language as sense and that a too slavish attention to the order in which words fall, especially in that typical French sentence of many exquisitely dovetailed clauses, will result, in English, in a lurching sentence with a loose tail that seems to cover more ground than any self-respecting sentence should reasonably be expected to do."[48] Reviewing Alan Brown's retranslation of Roy's *Bonheur d'occasion* in 1991, she writes, "I wish I could say that Brown's version was as excellent as it should be, but regrettably there are too many awkward un-English phrases and a number of instances of the sort of mistake often made by people who live surrounded by another language."[49]

This sense of the importance of language is intimately linked to an appreciation of style. Marshall has remarked that translating a text gives a translator a unique perspective not only on the author's work, but also on the process of writing. On *The Road Past Altamont*, her first full-length translation, she observes: "I learned the craft from it, also much about writing and words and language—I have a knowledge of the structure and intricacy of the book that few ordinary readers could have, simply because my work took me, of necessity, right to the heart of it."[50] While not making it a condition *sine qua non* of a good translation, she has also observed that a translator who is her- or himself a writer is perhaps more likely to possess a sense of what style is (whether or not she or he can define her or his own style in so many words)[51] and of the ways it works to create textual unity. This does not mean that the act of translation is necessarily made easier. Once one has recognized another writer's style, it still remains to work out how to make the translated text hold together in the same way. When translating Roy's work, so "beautifully articulated, every bone, every muscle properly attached and in its place," admits Marshall, "my difficulty was always with the style. It is so simple, always so appropriate, so unobtrusive. Yet those lovely sentences go limp when turned into English. I never discovered why this is so. I simply fought and went on fighting.[52]

While it is useful, if one translates literature, to possess a well-developed sense of style, Marshall considers it to be "impertinent"[53] for the writer-translator to substitute her or his own style for that of the author, or to leave traces of the translator's own personality in the text: "I suppose if there were a writer whose thoughts and imaginative processes were identical, or almost identical, to my own," she admits, "I might slip into this rhythm without realizing that I was doing it." However, in the case of Roy, she states, such a practice would have been been "impossible," adding, "But when, as with Gabrielle Roy, not only the thoughts themselves but the structure of the thoughts, the use or withholding of detail, in fact the entire attitude, were idiosyncratic and unique, these thoughts, coloured as they were by the mind that inspired them, could not fit themselves into my particular way of forming sentences but had to find their own arrangement of words, vocabulary, and stress."[54] The need, as translator, to produce the same effects using the same means, or means as similar as possible, was made all the more challenging by the fact that she "didn't always find congenial, the way [Roy] obtained an effect—by which of course I mean her emotional, dramatic, or structural effect. But I was bound to use her way."[55]

However, if one envisions "translating someone else's words [as] a form of writing dialogue,"[56] as Marshall does, it is undoubtedly easier for a writer accustomed to the exercise of dialogue production, to let other voices speak. In her own fiction, as Marshall points out, "the characters don't all talk like me. And when I'm doing a translation it is not me who is talking. People have asked me about that: they seem to think that as a writer I would have my own way of putting things. But I just feel that this is somebody else. Of course I am also limited by the text. But as far as I am concerned, this is not me speaking."[57] Although she does not state it explicitly, Marshall seems to be suggesting here that the faculty or faculties—ability to distance oneself? ability to empathize? technical skill? all of the above?—that allow her to write effective dialogue also allow her to recognize and to convincingly mimic narrative voices (and by extension, authorial voices?) "belonging" to other writers—all elements that interact to produce textual unity and a distinctive style.

Writing Gabrielle Roy's Voice

Roy respected Marshall's understanding of her writing, and also her sense of what makes a narrative work, both in French and in English. On the several occasions when Marshall suggested changes to Roy's original or objected to those Roy proposed to make, the latter always agreed with her in the end.[58] By discussing their respective intentions and choices, and negotiating meaning, author and translator came to understand better how both texts—the source text and the translation—functioned. As Marshall says of Roy, "She went through every word not once but several times with her translator, pounding out each sentence as she unquestionably pounded out each sentence of the original....It was an exhausting and stimulating process, and the final English text was as close to the original version as two brains could get it."[59]

Roy, clearly, wanted the translation to be exact[60] and to sound like her, but she also wanted the reader to be able to forget that he or she was reading a translation. She would go through the text "ten times," then would say to Marshall, "We'll go through it again, and not even think of translation." This is also Marshall's conception of what a good translation should be: "Do I want my translations to stand as, and to have the status of, an original piece of writing? Yes, I do. There is one theory of translating which I've seen expressed, which is that translation should sound like the work of an educated foreigner. I don't think that's true. I think it should sound as if it were written in its new language."[61]

Accordingly, Marshall's respect for the original version did not extend to attempting to "inscribe the foreign" in the English text by anything other than conventional means (using the occasional French word, French proper nouns, and so forth). She appreciated the same approach in the work of other translators. Speaking of Philip Stratford and Wayne Grady's translations of Antonine Maillet, she remarks, "And when we come to [these translations] we come, I think, to real translation: they have found equivalents for Acadian idiom that are English, and have a charm and forcefulness of their own without sacrificing accuracy and precision."[62] Roy shared this preoccupation with correct usage and exactitude, even though she needed to be convinced that certain English words or constructions were indeed acceptable. As Marshall notes, "although she respected my knowledge of English, as she often told me and others, she felt obliged to make sure—not simply in general but every time a dispute arose—that I did indeed know what I was talking about."[63] Ultimately, however, while Roy was "the unquestioned authority on her own meaning and intention," Marshall, was "just as unquestionably the authority on English syntax and idiom."[64]

Conclusion(s)

In a brief text introducing Marshall's work as both writer and translator, the editors of an anthology including one of her short stories state that "Marshall's sensitivity in rendering French-Canadian literature into English is a product of her skill as a writer of fiction."[65] Similar comments implicitly or explicitly acknowledging this sensitivity have been made by writers and critics reviewing her translations of Roy's books.[66] Speaking of *Windflower*, Hugo Macpherson remarks that "Joyce Marshall preserves admirably the still simplicity of Gabrielle Roy,"[67] while Jean Remple notes that Marshall's "perceptive rendering of Gabrielle Roy's simple but vivid language is little short of superb."[68] Shirley Gibson, reviewing *Enchanted Summer*, is categorical: "Marshall is a writer herself and it's obvious that she 'hears' language. Thanks to her well-tuned ear we're left with the feeling that, aside from a few rough spots at the beginning, *Enchanted Summer* has come to us with the author's intention intact."[69]

Here I would like to come back to my earlier remarks about how I hear Joyce Marshall's translation voice, and connect them to her own observations about translation being an "extended exercise in dialogue-writing."[70] As Marshall suggests in the passage cited earlier, a writer, when writing dialogue, has to be able to sound like other people. This, to my mind, implies that one needs to be able to distance oneself from one's self in order to produce effective dialogue and—taking Marshall's claim to its logical conclusion—to produce effective translation. It is around this idea of distance that my questioning revolves. By "distance" I am referring to a form of (self-)awareness or consciousness that conditions or informs the authorial stance and that cannot be dissociated, I believe, from one's relationship to both one's language (or artistic idiolect) and one's mother tongue.

In my opinion, although their writerly voices and styles are completely different, and although they approach their material (characters, situations, and so forth) very differently, Gabrielle Roy and Joyce Marshall do share a similar type of linguistic and aesthetic awareness. Although I have no idea how I could go about "proving" this, I suspect that they have a similar feeling for how evocativeness works in their respective languages, on a stylistic level, a comparable sense of the ways it can be created through language, structure, setting, and narrative dynamic, although they do not necessarily use the same means to achieve it.

This is borne out by the remarks critics have made with respect to Joyce Marshall's own writing. Margaret Laurence, speaking of the stories collected in *A Private Place*, uses a lexicon that is familiar to anyone who has read criticism of Roy's works: "They contain a beautiful economy of style, the ability to convey a great deal in a few pages. There is as well something which I can only call wisdom, the somewhat distanced viewpoint which is nonetheless always vitally involved."[71] Russell Brown and Donna Bennett, editors of an anthology including "The Enemy," one of Marshall's stories from *A Private Place*, could almost be speaking of some of Roy's stories and novels: "The strengths of her narratives lie in her detailed and convincing studies of isolated characters, in her simple, direct style, and in her capacity for eliciting strong visual images."[72] Finally, the themes that Andrew Garrod and David Staines identify in Marshall's works are those that define much of Roy's: "The folly and fragility of love, the pain of the human predicament, the evocative power and deception of memory—such themes recur in her fiction with its careful focus on people and their interactions."[73]

What comes through in Joyce Marshall's translation voice—that sense of Gabrielle Roy's—seems to me to be the product of a sensitivity to Roy's voice and authorial distance that flows not only from Marshall's understanding and respect of Roy's thought processes and style, but also from certain shared "awarenesses." This results in translation choices—words, structures, rhythms, and tones—that in the aggregate express Roy's voice and distance by articulating them in analogous ways in English.[74] Marshall's understanding and affinities with Roy ultimately weigh more in the translation process than the fact that she did not always find "congenial" the way Roy produced certain effects.

This book is about some of the "pioneers" of English-language literary translation in Canada. Joyce Marshall qualifies as one, by virtue of her position within the literary institution as writer, editor, and translator, and by virtue of her involvement with the organizations working to protect and promote Canadian literature, literary translation, and their practitioners during the crucial decades when all the elements necessary for the professional recognition of literary translation fell into place or were prompted to do so—in part through the efforts of the writers and translators themselves. When Harry Binsse was translating Gabrielle Roy, he had no institutional support as such, and the literary translator was more or less invisible; by the time Alan Brown took over from Joyce Marshall in the mid-1970s, this support was in place and literary translators were beginning to see their work acknowledged. One of the people responsible for this transformation was Joyce Marshall, the "accidental translator."

NOTES

1 Joyce Marshall, interview with Jane Everett, December 28, 2000. See also Joyce Marshall, "The Writer as Translator: A Personal View," *Canadian Literature*, no. 117 (summer 1988): 25. Unless otherwise indicated, information concerning Marshall or quotations attributed to her are from the December 2000 interview or from telephone conversations with Jane Everett on September 11, 2002 and January 29, 2003.
2 Joyce Marshall, "An Interview with Joyce Marshall," interview by Linda Leith. *Matrix*, no. 29 (fall 1989): 38. Roy and Marshall met for the first time in 1959.
3 Marshall, "The Writer as Translator: A Personal View," p. 26.
4 Canon Chambers's father had been headmaster of a school in Pentridge, Derbyshire, before emigrating with his family to Stoneham, Québec, where he hoped to become a landowner, something that would have been impossible to do in England. Although he did buy several parcels of land and some livestock, the venture did not succeed, and he eventually moved to Montréal, where he

went back to his former profession of teaching. Canon Chambers was his second eldest son. The eldest, E.T.D. Chambers, was the author of a number of reports and guidebooks on the development of various regions of Québec, on raising foxes and game, on angling and on the *ouananiche* or land-locked salmon. A younger brother was a journalist; in later life, he was a Gentleman Usher of the Black Rod.
5 According to Marshall's father, a statue of Sir Walter Scott in Edinburgh is from the workshop of this sculptor; Marshall's great-grandfather is said to have sculpted the statue's hands.
6 A Greek and Latin scholar, he and his brothers had attended Heriot's Hospital in Edinburgh, a school for "the sons of poor burgesses." See Heriot-Watt University, "George Heriot," in *History of the University*, Archive, Records Management and Museum Service, Heriot-Watt University, <www.hw.ac.uk/archive/gheriot.htm>.
7 W.H. New, "Joyce Marshall," in *Dictionary of Literary Biography* [*DLB*], vol. 88, *Canadian Writers 1920–1959*, 2nd ser., ed. W.H. New (Detroit: Gale Research, 1989), p. 199.
8 New, "Joyce Marshall," *DLB*, p. 199.
9 New, "Joyce Marshall," *DLB*, pp. 199–200.
10 New, "Joyce Marshall," *DLB*, pp. 199–200.
11 The *Canadian Periodical Index, 1939–1947* lists thirty-nine poems published in *Saturday Night*, six in *Canadian Poetry* and one in the *Dalhousie Review*.
12 Published in *Queen's Quarterly, Saturday Night, Canadian Life, Canadian Home Journal, Seventeen, New Liberty, Montréaler, The Tamarack Review, Fiddlehead, Canadian Fiction Magazine, Matrix, Canadian Forum, Room of One's Own, Canadian Women's Studies*, and *Dandelion*.
13 New, "Joyce Marshall," *DLB*, p. 202.
14 For example, she was a judge for the SmithBooks/Books in Canada First Novel Award in 1995, an experience she later described in *Books in Canada*. See Joyce Marshall, "Book Review," *Books in Canada* 24, no. 3 (April 1995): 10–12.
15 As her unpublished correpondence with that publishing house and with Jack McClelland indicate. See McClelland and Stewart Fonds, William Ready Division of Archives and Research Collections, McMaster University Library, Hamilton, ON.
16 New, "Joyce Marshall," *DLB*, pp. 202–203.
17 Joyce Marshall, "Next Episodes," *Books in Canada* 21, no. 3 (April 1992): 27.
18 The entries for Bessette, Hébert, and Savard were co-authored by Norah Storey.
19 For more information about the founding of LTAC, see the portraits of Philip Stratford and Patricia Claxton in this volume.
20 Literary Translators' Association of Canada, "History," Literary Translators' Association of Canada, <www.attlc=ltac.org/history.htm>.
21 Patricia Claxton, "Discovering Friendship," in *Blood and Bone/En chair et en os* (Oakville, ON: Mosaic Press, 1995), p. ix.
22 Marshall, "An Interview with Joyce Marshall," p. 38.

23 Regarding the making of the CBC program and Marshall's role as intermediary with Jack McClelland, see Joyce Marshall, "Remembering Gabrielle Roy," *Brick*, no. 39 (summer 1990): 61–62.
24 Anne Denoon, "A Private Place," *Books in Canada* 23, no. 5 (summer 1994): 23.
25 The French original of *La rivière sans repos* included three short stories: "Les satellites," "Le téléphone," and "Le fauteuil roulant." Marshall translated these at the same time that she translated *Windflower*, but they were not published with the English version. Of the three translations done by Marshall—"The Wheelchair," "The Satellites," and "The Telephone"—only the second was eventually published (in 1978, in the *Tamarack Review*), although a condensed version of the third did appear in *Reader's Digest* in 1980. A second translation of "The Wheelchair," by Sherri Walsh, was published in *Arts Manitoba* in 1984; "The Telephone" was retranslated by Joyce Lubert and published in *Matrix* in 1988.
26 See Marshall, "The Writer as Translator," p. 26; Marshall, "Interview with Joyce Marshall," p. 23.
27 The letters have been grouped chronologically, the beginning and end dates corresponding to significant developments in the history of the colony of New France: 1632–41; 1642–50; 1651–62; and 1663–72 (Marie de l'Incarnation died in 1672).
28 Joyce Marshall, introduction to *Word from New France: The Selected Letters of Marie de l'Incarnation*, trans. and ed. Joyce Marshall (Toronto: Oxford University Press, 1967), p. 32–33. Anne Denoon remarks, "Marshall's introduction to this book not only reveals her own scholarship and intelligence, but demonstrates how a skilled fiction writer's sensitivity to character and detail can enrich the study of history" (Denoon, "A Private Place," p. 23). Two of the letters, "The Earthquake" and "Memories of Her Son," are included in the *Oxford Anthology of Canadian Literature*, 1973.
29 Carl F. Klinck, ed., *Literary History of Canada*, 2nd ed., vol. 3 (Toronto: University of Toronto Press, 1976), p. 75.
30 Joyce Marshall, translator's note, in *No Passport: A Discovery of Canada*, by Eugène Cloutier, trans. Joyce Marshall (Toronto: Oxford University Press, 1968), p. vii.
31 Marshall, translator's note, p. vii.
32 That is, prompted by the knowledge of how narrative is produced and how readers' interest can be engaged.
33 See Joyce Marshall, "Found in Translation," *Books in Canada* 20, no. 2 (March 1991): 30.
34 Joyce Marshall, "Gabrielle Roy 1909–1983," *Antigonish Review*, no. 55 (autumn 1983): 44. See also Marshall, "The Writer as Translator," pp. 25–26; Marshall, "Gabrielle Roy, 1909–1983: Some Reminiscences," *Canadian Literature*, no. 101 (summer 1984): 183–84; and Joyce Marshall, quoted in Sherry Simon and David Homel, "The Writer as Translator / The Translator as Writer," in *Mapping Literature: The Art and Politics of Translation* (Montréal: Véhicule Press, 1988), p. 19.

35 Marshall, "Remembering Gabrielle Roy," p. 58. See also Marshall, "Gabrielle Roy 1909–1983," p. 44.
36 See Marshall, "The Writer as Translator," p. 26.
37 "If there are tricks I never discovered them or problems with easy solutions I never found them, and when I did find a solution to a problem, any relief I might feel was quickly wiped out by the looming of some new equally formidable problem." (Marshall, "The Writer as Translator," p. 27).
38 Marshall, "Gabrielle Roy 1909–1983," p. 44.
39 Gabrielle Roy, "Les îles," in *Cet été qui chantait* (Montréal: Éditions françaises, 1972), p. 193.
40 Gabrielle Roy, "The Islands," in *Enchanted Summer*, trans. Joyce Marshall (Toronto: McClelland and Stewart, 1976), p. 119.
41 Marshall, "Gabrielle Roy, 1909–1983: Some Reminiscences," 184.
42 Gabrielle Roy, *La rivière sans repos* (Montréal: Beauchemin, 1970), p. 312.
43 Gabrielle Roy to Joyce Marshall, October or November 1969, Joyce Marshall fonds, P047/013/001.
44 Gabrielle Roy, *Windflower*, trans. Joyce Marshall (Toronto: McClelland and Stewart, 1970), p. 149.
45 Marshall, "Gabrielle Roy 1909–1983," p. 59.
46 Marshall, "Remembering Gabrielle Roy," p. 59.
47 Marshall, "The Writer as Translator," p. 27.
48 Joyce Marshall, "Françoise Mallet-Joris: A Young Writer on Her Way," *Tamarack Review*, no. 8 (summer 1958): 64.
49 Marshall, "Found in Translation," p. 30.
50 Joyce Marshall, afterword, in *The Road Past Altamont*, trans. Joyce Marshall (Toronto: McClelland and Stewart, 1989), pp. 149–50.
51 See Marshall's remarks to that effect in Simon and Homel, "The Translator as Writer," p. 18.
52 Marshall, "Remembering Gabrielle Roy," p. 59. See also Marshall, "Gabrielle Roy 1909–1983," p. 44.
53 Quoted in Simon and Homel, "The Translator as Writer," 19.
54 Marshall, "The Writer as Translator," p. 28.
55 Marshall, "The Translator as Writer," p. 27.
56 Quoted in Simon and Homel, "The Translator as Writer," pp. 18–19. See also Marshall, "The Writer as Translator," p. 28.
57 Quoted in Simon and Homel, "The Translator as Writer," pp. 24–25.
58 For example, Marshall read the manuscript of *La montagne secrète* and suggested changes to a scene, which Gabrielle Roy accepted. Roy also reversed a decision to insert a sentence—considered unnecessary by Marshall—into a crucial transition passage in *La rivière sans repos*.
59 Marshall, afterword, p. 150.
60 Roy was also a perfectionist about her own writing: Marshall had to throw out sixty pages of *Windflower* because of changes Roy had made to the French manuscript.
61 Quoted in Simon and Homel, "The Translator as Writer," p. 19.

62 Marshall, "Found in Translation," p. 31.
63 Marshall, "Remembering Gabrielle Roy," p. 61.
64 Marshall, "The Writer as Translator," pp. 25–26.
65 Russell Brown and Donna Bennett, "Joyce Marshall," in *An Anthology of Canadian Literature*, vol. 1, ed. R. Brown and D. Bennett (Toronto: Oxford University Press, 1982), p. 644.
66 For the most part, these are not reviews of the translations as such, but rather reviews of Roy's books with comments about the translation, when there are any, usually coming at the end.
67 Hugo Macpherson, "Blais, Godbout, Roy: Love, Art, Time," *Tamarack Review*, no. 57 (spring 1971): 88.
68 Jean Remple, "In Translation, Nothing Is Lost," *Montreal Star*, Nov. 28, 1970, p. 63.
69 Shirley Gibson, "She Ranges from the Infinite to a Commentary on Cows," *Globe and Mail*, Sept. 18, 1976, p. 39.
70 See Marshall, "The Writer as Translator," p. 28.
71 Margaret Laurence, "Stories with Wisdom: Marshall Book a Cause to Rejoice," *Montreal Gazette*, March 27, 1976, p. 51.
72 Brown and Bennett, "Joyce Marshall," p. 644.
73 Andrew Garrod and David Staines, "Joyce Marshall," In *Illuminations: The Days of Our Youth* (Toronto: Gage, 1984), pp. 109–10; quoted in McLean, "Joyce Marshall," p. 92.
74 My own affinities with both writers' voices are undoubtedly a part of the mix, as well.

BIBLIOGRAPHY

I. Primary Sources

Literary Translations

Guyart, Marie (Marie de l'Incarnation). *Word from New France: The Selected Letters of Marie de l'Incarnation*. Trans. and ed. Joyce Marshall. Toronto: Oxford University Press, 1967.

Roy, Gabrielle. "Grandmother and the Doll." Trans. Joyce Marshall. *Chatelaine*, Oct. 1960, 44–45, 82–86. Translation of "Grand-mère et la poupée." *Châtelaine* oct. 1960, 24–25, 44–46, 48–49.

———. *The Hidden Mountain*. Trans. Harry L. Binsse (1962), rev. Joyce Marshall. Toronto: McClelland and Stewart, 1974. Translation of *La montagne secrète*. Montréal: Beauchemin, 1961.

———. *The Road Past Altamont*. Trans. Joyce Marshall. Toronto: McClelland and Stewart, 1966. Translation of *La route d'Altamont*. Montréal: Éditions HMH, 1966.

———. "Le thème raconté par Gabrielle Roy" / "The Theme Unfolded by Gabrielle Roy." Trans. Joyce Marshall. In *Terre des hommes / Man and His World*, ed. Guy Robert. Ottawa: La Compagnie canadienne de l'Exposition universelle de 1967 / Canadian Corporation for the 1967 World Exhibition, 1967. 20–61.

———. *Windflower*. Toronto: McClelland and Stewart, 1970. Translation of *La rivière sans repos*. Montréal: Beauchemin, 1970.

———. *Enchanted Summer*. Trans. Joyce Marshall. Toronto: McClelland and Stewart, 1976. Translation of *Cet été qui chantait*. Montréal: Éditions françaises, 1972.

———. "The Satellites." Trans. Joyce Marshall. *Tamarack Review*, no. 74 (spring 1978): 5–28. Translation of "Les satellites." In *La rivière sans repos*. Montréal: Beauchemin, 1970.

———. "Barnaby's Telephone." Trans. Joyce Marshall. *Reader's Digest*, July 1980. Translation of "Le téléphone de Barnaby." In *Sélection du Reader's Digest*, juillet 1980: 36–40. Condensed version of "Le téléphone." In *La rivière sans repos*. Montréal: Beauchemin, 1970.

Other Translations

Casgrain, Thérèse F. *A Woman in a Man's World*. Trans. Joyce Marshall. Toronto: McClelland and Stewart, 1972. Translation of *Une femme chez les hommes*. Montréal: Éditions du jour, 1971.

Cloutier, Eugène. *No Passport: A Discovery of Canada*. Trans. Joyce Marshall. Toronto: Oxford University Press, 1968. Translation of *Le Canada sans passeport*. Montréal: HMH, 1967.

Kattan, Naïm. "Montreal Letter." Trans. Joyce Marshall. *Tamarack Review*, no. 30 (winter 1964): 48–52.

———. "Montréal and French-Canadian Authors: What They Mean to English-Canadian Novelists." *Tamarack Review*, no. 40 (summer 1966): 40–53.

———. "Montréal Letter. French-Canadian Plays." Trans. Joyce Marshall. *Tamarack Review*, no. 37 (autumn 1965): 60–64.

Pelletier, Gérard. *The October Crisis*. Trans. Joyce Marshall. Toronto: McClelland and Stewart, 1976. Translation of *La crise d'octobre*. Montréal: Éditions du jour, 1971.

Weilbrenner, Bernard. "New France under the Sun King." *Tamarack Review*, no. 35 (spring 1965): 90–95.

Works on Translation

Marshall, Joyce. Introduction. In *Word from New France: The Selected Letters of Marie de l'Incarnation*. Trans. and ed. Joyce Marshall. Toronto: Oxford University Press, 1967. 1–33.

———. Translator's Note. In *No Passport: A Discovery of Canada*, by Eugène Cloutier. Toronto: Oxford University Press, 1968. vii.

———. "Gabrielle Roy 1909–1983." *Antigonish Review*, no. 55 (autumn 1983): 35–46.

———. "Gabrielle Roy, 1909–1983: Some Reminiscences." *Canadian Literature*, no. 101 (summer 1984): 183–84.

———. "The Writer as Translator: A Personal View." *Canadian Literature*, no. 117 (summer 1988): 25–29.

———. Afterword. In *The Road Past Altamont* by Gabrielle Roy. Trans. Joyce Marshall. Toronto: McClelland and Stewart, 1989. 147–52.
———. "Remembering Gabrielle Roy." *Brick*, no. 39 (summer 1990): 58–62.
———. "Found in Translation." *Books in Canada* 20, no. 2 (March 1991): 30–32.

Literary Works
Marshall, Joyce. *Presently Tomorrow*. Boston: Little, Brown, 1946; Toronto: McClelland and Stewart, 1946.
———. *Lovers and Strangers*. Philadelphia: J.B. Lippincott, 1957.
———. *A Private Place*. Ottawa: Oberon, 1975.
———. *Any Time at All and Other Stories*. Toronto: McClelland and Stewart, 1993.
———. *Blood and Bone / En chair et en os*. Oakville: Mosaic Press, 1995.

Other Publications
Marshall, Joyce. "Françoise Mallet-Joris: A Young Writer on Her Way." *Tamarack Review*, no. 8 (summer 1958): 63–72.
———. "'…In the same country….'" *Tamarack Review*, no. 13 (fall 1959): 121–24.
———. "Some Recent Writing from French Canada." *Tamarack Review*, no. 23 (spring 1963): 96–101.
———. "Canadian Poets and Their Mythologies." *Montrealer* 39, no.10 (Oct. 1965): 40–43.
———. "Three from the Other Nation." *Tamarack Review*, no. 46 (winter 1968): 109–13.
———. "Aquin, Hubert," "Bessette, Gérard," "Blais, Marie-Claire," "Cloutier, Cécile," "Ducharme, Réjean," "Godin, Gérald," "Hébert, Anne," "Major, André," "Paradis, Suzanne," "Roy, Gabrielle," "Savard, Félix-Antoine," and "Vigneault, Gilles." In *Supplement (1967) to Oxford Companion to Canadian History and Literature*, ed. William Toye. Toronto: Oxford University Press. 1973. 5–6, 15–16, 18–19, 43–44, 69, 116, 127, 227, 241–42, 282–83, 286–87, 309.
———. "*La belle bête*," "Blais, Marie-Claire," "Godin, Gérald," "Major, André," "Marie de l'Incarnation," "Paradis, Suzanne," "Roy, Gabrielle," and "Vigneault, Gilles." In the *Oxford Companion to Canadian Literature*, ed. W. Toye. Toronto: Oxford University Press, 1983. 52, 72–74, 304, 502–503, 508, 635–36, 718–20, 813–14.
———. "An Interview with Joyce Marshall." By Linda Leith. *Matrix*, no. 29 (fall 1989): 38–39.
———. "Next Episodes." *Books in Canada* 21, no. 3 (April 1992): 27–29.
———. "Book Review." *Books in Canada* 24, no. 3 (April 1995): 10–12.
———. "*La belle bête*," "Blais, Marie-Claire," "Godin, Gérald," "Harvor, Elisabeth," "Major, André," "Marie de l'Incarnation," "Paradis, Suzanne," "Roy, Gabrielle," and "Vigneault, Gilles." In the *Oxford Companion to Canadian Literature*, 2nd ed., ed. E. Benson and W. Toye. Toronto: Oxford University Press, 1997. 93–94, 124–26, 471–72, 520, 721–22, 729–30, 903, 1023–24, 1155–56.

Unpublished Material

Marshall, Joyce. Joyce Marshall fonds. P047. Eastern Townships Research Centre, Bishop's University Archives, Lennoxville, QC.

Roy, Gabrielle. Fonds Gabrielle Roy. LMS-0082, 1982–11/1986–11: 17 (9–12). Literary Manuscript Collection. Library and Archives Canada, Ottawa, ON.

II. Secondary Sources

Benson, Eugene, and William E. Toye, ed. *The Oxford Companion to Canadian Literature*. Toronto: Oxford University Press, 1997.

Brown, Russell, and Donna Bennett. "Joyce Marshall." In *An Anthology of Canadian Literature*, vol. 1, ed. R. Brown and D. Bennett. Toronto: Oxford University Press, 1982. 644–51.

Claxton, Patricia. "Discovering Friendship." In *Blood and Bone / En chair et en os* by Joyce Marshall. Oakville: Mosaic Press, 1995. viii–x.

Denoon, Anne. "A Private Place." *Books in Canada* 23, no. 5 (summer 1994): 21–25.

Ellenwood, Ray. "Qui est Joyce Marshall?" Trans. Suzanne Saint-Jacques Mineau. In *Blood and Bone / En chair et en os* by Joyce Marshall. Oakville: Mosaic Press, 1995. xii–xvii.

Findley, Timothy. Afterword. In *Any Time At All and Other Stories* by Joyce Marshall. Toronto: McClelland and Stewart, 1993. 212–19.

Garrod, Andrew and David Staines. "Joyce Marshall." In *Illuminations: The Days of Our Youth*. Toronto: Gage, 1984. 109–10.

Gibson, Shirley. "She Ranges from the Infinite to a Commentary on Cows." *Globe and Mail*, Sept. 18, 1976, 39.

Heriot-Watt University. "George Heriot." In *History of the University*, Archive, Records Management, and Museum Service, Heriot-Watt University, <www.hw.ac.uk/archive/gheriot>.

Klinck, Carl F., ed. *Literary History of Canada*. 2nd ed. Vol. 3. Toronto: University of Toronto Press, 1976.

Laurence, Margaret. "Stories with Wisdom: Marshall Book a Cause to Rejoice." *Montreal Gazette*, March 27, 1976, 51.

Macpherson, Hugo. "Blais, Godbout, Roy: Love, Art, Time." *Tamarack Review*, no. 57 (spring 1971): 84–88.

McLean, Ken. "Joyce Marshall." In *Profiles in Canadian Literature*, vol. 7, ed. J.M. Heath. Toronto: Dundurn and Oxford University Press, 1991. 87–94.

New, W.H. "Joyce Marshall." In *Canadian Short Fiction: From Myth to Modern*, ed. W.H. New. Scarborough: Prentice-Hall Canada, 1986. 198–205.

———. "Joyce Marshall." In *Dictionary of Literary Biography*, vol. 88, *Canadian Writers 1920–1959*, 2nd ser., ed. W.H. New. Detroit: Gale Research, 1989. 197–205.

Remple, Jean. "In Translation, Nothing Is Lost." *Montreal Star*, Nov. 28, 1970, 63.

Roy, Gabrielle. "The Wheelchair." Trans. Sherri Walsh. *Arts Manitoba* 3, no. 4, (fall 1984): 47–53. Translation of "Le fauteuil roulant." In *La rivière sans repos*. 1970.

———. "The Telephone." Trans. Joyce Lubert. *Matrix*, no. 26 (spring 1988): 59–70. Translation of "Le téléphone." In *La rivière sans repos*. 1970.

Simon, Sherry, and David Homel, eds. "The Writer as Translator / The Translator as Writer." In *Mapping Literature: The Art and Politics of Translation*. Montréal: Véhicule Press, 1988. 15–27.

Toye, William E. "Marshall, Joyce." In Toye, *Supplement*, 229.

Toye, William E., ed. *Oxford Companion to Canadian Literature*. Toronto: Oxford University Press, 1983.

———. *Supplement (1967) to Oxford Companion to Canadian History and Literature*. Toronto: Oxford University Press, 1973.

Weaver, Robert. "Marshall, Joyce." In Toye, ed., *Oxford Companion to Canadian Literature*, 519–20.

———. "Marshall, Joyce." In Benson and Toye, eds., *Oxford Companion to Canadian Literature*, 744–45.

———, and William Toye, eds. *Oxford Anthology of Canadian Literature*. Toronto: Oxford University Press, 1973.

4

Philip Stratford
The Comparatist as Smuggler

GILLIAN LANE-MERCIER

 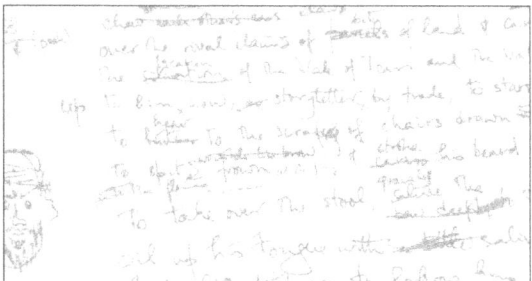

Poet, literary critic, translator, and professor, Philip Stratford (1927–99) was one of the most outspoken representatives of a generation of Canadian intellectuals who believed that translation could effectively bridge the cultural and political gap between English Canada and Québec. In a series of monographs, articles, prefaces, and translator's notes spanning almost thirty years, Stratford tirelessly pressed his point: whereas the United States has chosen the melting pot, Canada has opted for "collective differentiation and difference,"[1] an option that has not only placed the translation process at the very core of our cultural identity, but has also fostered a specifically Canadian approach to comparative literature in general and to translation in particular.

Stratford's career as a scholar and a translator offers significant insights into the ways in which translation, by "break[ing] down our cultural separatism,"[2] can serve as mediator between two communities that historically have shown little interest in one another. Together with other prominent translators such as Frank Scott and John Glassco, he was instrumental in formulating the conception of translation as "a bridge of sorts." The political and cultural duty of the anglophone translator, in his view, was both to create an awareness among English-Canadian readers of the nature of the crisis in Québec, and to acquaint them with Québec authors, thereby enabling a better understanding of the other and, by ricochet, of the self.

In the late 1970s, an alternative conception of translation also emerged in Stratford's work. Without relinquishing his defence of translation's communicative powers, Stratford brought to the fore aspects of the translation act that pragmatic approaches often neglect: translation as a paradoxical creative process in which author and translator enter into a "close yet critical discipleship"[3] based on faithfulness and betrayal, sameness and difference, servility and liberty. The richness of his reflections on literary translation stems from the manner in which they "bridge" two generations of translators and two conceptions of translation that Stratford the translator-poet deftly intertwined and between which Stratford the translator-scholar just as deftly distinguished.

As a practising translator whose renderings of Antonine Maillet's *Pélagie*, René Lévesque's *Memoirs*, and Robert Melançon's *Blind Painting* received national critical acclaim, Stratford was eloquent about the need for developing government policies to financially support and promote literary translation. He was at the forefront of a number of initiatives to establish an institutionally backed tradition of literary translation in Canada. As a teacher of English and comparative literature, Stratford spoke to the status of translated literature in the curriculum. His account of the emergence of Canadian comparative literary studies in the late 1960s reveals the degree to which translation practices in Canada during that period shared comparative literature's goal to bridge cultures, as well as certain aspects of comparative literature's methodological framework. Viewing the work of the translator as a creation "parallel and equal to the author's,"[4] Stratford was convinced that literary translation could play a crucial role in contributing to "the life and future of our country."[5]

The Making of a Smuggler[6]

The translator, wrote Stratford, is a "smuggler of literary products," a "literary contrabandier," a "useful mercenary" whose "vocation…is the arduous one of being alien in both countries. Paradoxically,…although he works in a sense to eliminate boundaries, he depends on them absolutely; he trades on the existence of frontiers and his own facility in crossing them.

He is by necessity a man of divided allegiances."[7] This definition could apply to Stratford's scholarly pursuits prior to becoming a literary translator: "Border countries," he once commented, "[are] a rather barren and forbidding terrain, the preserve of a few hard-bitten comparatists."[8] It might also explain his decision, upon his arrival in Montréal in 1964, to try his hand at translating a Québec novel into English: "It seemed a good way to infiltrate the new country while keeping lines of communication open with the old home."[9] Taking this trope of bridges and creative exchange to yet another level, this definition resonates with Stratford's conception of the poet, whose sole effort consists in an impossible attempt to perfectly capture—imitate, transcribe, translate—the unique inner voice of the poet-translator's "inevitable Other."[10] Indeed, as Antoine Sirois has suggested, "ce rôle de passeur de frontières, il l'a joué toute sa vie"[11] in his multiple capacities as teacher, translator, literary critic, poet, writer, and illustrator.

Philip Stratford was born on October 13, 1927 in Chatham, Ontario. He graduated with an Honours BA in English from the University of Western Ontario in 1950. After spending a year at the Université de Bordeaux (1950–51), he embarked on a doctoral program at the Sorbonne in Paris, which included a year of study at the University of London. In 1954 he defended his thesis, entitled "Le non-conformisme catholique dans le roman contemporain français et anglais, 1850–1940," for which he received "Mention très honorable."

Stratford's initial reasons for going to France were more a reflection of family influence and a personal interest in French culture than of academic objectives. Four of his uncles had been killed in the First World War, and two of them were buried in France. Stratford's father, who had not fought overseas but had written his chemistry thesis in Lyon, was himself a confirmed francophile. When Stratford enrolled at the Université de Bordeaux, it was with the intention of simply spending some time in France. The decision to prepare a doctoral thesis at the Sorbonne on a comparative study of Greene and Mauriac came later, upon the suggestion of a professor whom he met during his first year abroad. Further personal factors also come into play: in September 1952, Stratford married Jacqueline de Puteaux, a Parisian-born aristocrat with a background in the study of art, whom he had met in Paris in the winter of 1951.

Stratford's teaching career began in France. From 1950 to 1952, he taught English at lycées in Cognac (near Bordeaux) and Paris. Upon returning to Canada, he lectured for two years in English at Assumption University of Windsor, before moving to the English department of the University of Western Ontario in 1954. His first monograph, a revised version of his doctoral thesis entitled *Faith and Fiction: Creative Process in Greene and Mauriac*, appeared in 1964. The same year, Stratford successfully applied for a position in the Department of English at the Université de Montréal, seeking both to advance his career and to reimmerse himself and his family in a culturally richer, francophone environment. Department chair from 1969 to 1975, he was founding director of the university's comparative literature program (1967–69). He retired in 1992 and was appointed professor emeritus in 1993.

Stratford's commitment to academia rapidly took him far beyond the confines of the University. Responsible, as he himself put it, "for the back half"[12] of the first issue of *ellipse*, a bilingual poetry review co-founded by poet-translator Doug Jones in 1969, Stratford acted as consulting editor until 1981. He served on the editorial boards of *English Studies in Canada*, the *Journal of Canadian Studies* and *Literary History of Canada*, as president of the Association of Teachers of English in Québec (1968–69) and president of the Canadian Association of Comparative Literature (1973–75). In 1975, he co-founded the Literary Translators' Association of Canada and accepted a two-year mandate as its first secretary. A juror for the Grand Prix Littéraire of the City of Montréal and the Governor General's translation award, Stratford served on the board of directors of the Humanities Research Council of Canada (1974–76), and was a member of the Canadian Federation for the Humanities and Social Sciences' Translation Committee (1976–77), whose objective was to encourage translation in both official languages.

By training, Stratford was, first and foremost, a student of English and comparative literature, a Graham Greene scholar, and a specialist in the modern French and British novel. After moving to Québec, he quickly became an expert on Canada's two founding literatures and a pioneer of Canadian comparative literary studies. Besides *Marie-Claire Blais* (1971) and *All the Polarities: Comparative Studies in Contemporary Canadian Novels in French and English* (1986), which was awarded the Gabrielle Roy Prize by the Association for Québec and Canadian Writers, Stratford wrote a number of articles pertaining to Canada's national literatures for academic journals. In 1979, he spearheaded the first issue of the *Canadian Review of Comparative Literature* to be entirely devoted to comparative essays on Canadian topics.

The move to Québec was responsible for much more, however. Stratford began a "parallel" career as translator and scholar of literary translation, officially inaugurated in 1966 by the publication of *Convergence: Essays from Quebec*, a collection of articles by Montréal critic and journalist Jean Le Moyne. Over the next three decades, Stratford edited and/or translated eleven non-fictional, fictional, and poetic works, including *Second Chance*, by Diane Hébert, which won the 1988 Governor General's translation award. He also published several scholarly articles on translation, journalistic accounts of the situation of literary translation in Canada, and scores of reviews of translated Québec books for the *Globe and Mail*, *Quill and Quire* and the *Gazette*. His 1975 *Bibliography of Canadian Books in Translation: French to English and English to French* was described as "nearly comprehensive in its documentation of bilateral translation activity"[13] and hailed as an invaluable reference tool.

Stratford was also a poet and a writer. As much of his theoretical work suggests, this most certainly had a determining impact on his "parallel" conception of translation as creative exchange. Stratford composed and illustrated a children's book, *Olive: A Dog—Un chien*, published in 1976 as a bilingual edition. Three volumes of his poetry appeared in the 1990s: *The Rage of Space* (1992), *Seven Seasons* (1994) and *Verse Portraits* (1997), followed by a posthumous publication, *And Once More Saw the Stars* (2001), comprising a series of renga written in collaboration with the eminent Canadian poet P.K. Page. His memoir, *Hawthorn House* (1999), completed during the last year of his life, relates his childhood years and the influence of the surrounding natural world, so predominant in much of his poetry. Stratford died in Montréal on April 23, 1999. He is survived by his wife and their six children.

The Comparatist in Canada, or "News from the Front"

Stratford's particular itinerary as a literary translator can only be understood through an analysis of his work as a comparatist and the conceptual affinities that permeate his writing on both comparative literature and translation. Until the 1950s, comparative studies of English- and French-Canadian literature were virtually non-existent. In a 1979 article entitled "Canada's Two Literatures: A Search for Emblems," Stratford commented that although the situation had improved substantially, the results were still far from satisfactory. He attributed this rather surprising lag to the fact that, until the Second World War, both literatures "were heavily dependant on old-world models and designed for old-world tastes. Reputations were made abroad, not at home." Although distinctly Canadian literatures emerged in each language in the mid-forties, the two literatures developed along parallel lines. Not only "next-to-no sharing of experience on critical, cultural or creative levels" took place, but, barring a few notable exceptions, there was a display of "mutual ignorance and indifference" among writers.[14] Consequently, by the late 1970s English-Canadian and Québec authors had as yet exerted no visible influence on each other. This ignorance extended to the reading public which "remained largely ignorant of the literary accomplishments of their opposite numbers."[15] Further contributing factors were the greater prestige of worldwide comparative studies, and the "monoculturalism" of English and French departments in Canadian universities, traditionally reluctant to introduce topics in Canadian comparative literature.[16]

On a more positive note, Québec anglophone writers such as Frank Scott, John Glassco, G.V. Downes and A.J.M. Smith had already recognized the importance of translation in bridging the two solitudes, and making contemporary Québec literature accessible to an English-speaking readership. When Stratford took up his appointment at the Université de Montréal in 1964, he found himself "au coeur de cette effervescence pionnière d'ouverture vers l'Autre"[17] through translation. Given his self-avowed propensity for crossing borders and his allegiance to cultural nationalism, it is hardly surprising that he turned almost immediately to Québec literature and translation as a means to bring "news from the front"[18] to an anglophone public avid for a clearer understanding of the events unfolding in Québec. Nor is it surprising that he was quick to integrate translation into his university teaching. His research seminars provided the setting for innovative assignments that, in retrospect, were to be of prime importance to both the curriculum and the literary institution.

Stratford's first teaching experience at the Université de Montréal was "*FRAN 631: Littérature canadienne-anglaise*, an obligatory course for students in the French Department!" As he would later recall in *ellipse*, "the students and I shouldered our responsibilities: they read the authors in English, I lectured on them in French. *It was a happy comparative compromise*....Since the students seemed game for almost anything, as one assignment I set them the translation of some of the poems we were studying."[19] Rather than opting for a "passive" approach to the teaching of the literary other with everyone gathered on the same unilingual, unicultural shore, so to speak, he favoured a dynamic "compromise" that resulted in the constant criss-crossing of linguistic and literary boundaries.

In his very first article on translation, entitled "French-Canadian Literature in Translation" (1968), Stratford broadens this approach in an explicitly political statement, juxtaposing issues of cultural identity with questions of innovative course offerings:

English teachers [can] put some of the French-Canadian books already available in translation onto our Canadian literature reading lists..., and in this way begin to break down our cultural separatism.

More ambitiously, [they can] design courses and programs which truly reflect our cultural duality. We have a great deal to learn about one another in this country, and there is an interesting and totally unexplored field of comparative studies to be investigated here on many levels. Very often it is in learning more about others that we discover more about ourselves.[20]

In a 1979 special issue of the *Canadian Review of Comparative Literature*, Stratford re-examines the aim, place, and status of Canadian comparative studies within the academy. Once again he draws on his teaching experience to reach a more complex conclusion. A second set of classroom experiments, a comparison of twenty French and English novels from the 1960s, showed that despite some resemblances, "two quite distinct types of fiction were being practised."[21] As a consequence,

> comparative Canadian studies must be subtle enough to allow the apparent contradictions of a bifocal view....one must realize that there is no such thing as a Canadian literature and one should resist any political promptings to lump Canada's two literatures together in one sack, whether the sack bears a political label such as "Canadian Studies" or goes under a neutral scholarly tag like "Canadian Comparative Literature."[22]

Much can be gleaned from Stratford's teaching projects. His work in the classroom embodied the necessity of constructing bridges, together with concrete ways they could be built and crossed. Comparative literary studies was one way; translation, another; curriculum reform, yet another. These projects can be perceived as concrete responses to the political and cultural turmoil of the 1960s and 1970s; as such, they are at once context-specific and ideologically in keeping with the bilingual ideal of liberal federalism: "I would like to see," stated Stratford as early as 1968, "the word translation become as household and as vital a word for us as Trans-Canada."[23] More importantly, these projects enable us to gain insight into the reasons he chose to promote translation and to become a literary translator himself.

Choosing the Works to Be Smuggled

"I do not believe much in translation," noted Stratford, "where interest and even a sense of affinity are absent."[24] Indeed, despite their generic diversity and the various types of affinities—ideological, intellectual, thematic, stylistic—they embodied, Stratford's choice of works to translate remained consistent in political and aesthetic terms. On the one hand, Stratford selected works capable of relaying to English-speaking Canadians a view of contemporary Québec, together with its "deeply rooted," "vigorous and varied creative life."[25] "French-Canadian experience today is not so foreign after all," as he indicates in his translator's prefaces, "but is recognizably like our own while still remaining excitingly different....though outsiders ourselves, we hope to have represented *eux-autres* broadly, truly and sympathetically."[26] On the other hand, he preferred works that presented a creative challenge, allowing him to exercise his own stylistic inventiveness. These two basic liberties—of choice, of invention—formed the core of what he deemed to be the translator's freedom.

Stratford's idea of the translator's freedom of choice is symptomatic of the position occupied by translators within the literary institution throughout the 1960s, 1970s, and 1980s: "The Canadian translator is still in the privileged position of having a relatively free hand in a relatively clear field—that is, he can pick and choose what he wants to translate, but at a price. The price is that he must find and promote, himself, the book that he would like to see published in translation."[27] Stratford gives as an example of his own experiences with such (relative) freedom the circumstances surrounding his decision to translate Antonine Maillet's *Pélagie-la-Charrette* shortly after it appeared in 1979. His initial enthusiasm led him to publish a highly positive review of the book in the *Gazette*, "singling out its wonderful inventiveness and the uniqueness of its language and referring, *en passant*, to the 'possibly impossible' job of translating it."[28] He then approached, to no avail, several Canadian publishers, including McClelland and Stewart, encouraging them to consider a translation. Even Leméac, Maillet's Québec publisher, showed no interest. It was not until the book won the Prix Goncourt in November 1979 that Leméac entered into negotiations with New York-based Doubleday, and Stratford was asked to submit a ten-page sample. As he recalled a few years later, "Doubleday was negotiating for joint publication with the British publisher, John Calder. He read my sample and was enthusiastic. His support and Antonine's helped bypass their house translator and finally gave me the assignment."[29]

While this example is not paradigmatic of Stratford's experiences with publishers, it nevertheless provides a disclaimer for "the notion that the translator is an ivory-tower type. He really does get thickly covered in dust from the market place"[30] and his liberties are never absolute. It also reveals the principal motivating factors behind Stratford's decision to translate a particular work: an initial enthusiasm (affinity) for the "inventiveness and uniqueness" of the original, the "possibly impossible job of translating it" (creative challenge), and the desire to promote contemporary French-Canadian literature in English Canada (political agenda), supported by the willingness to initiate negotiations with a publisher. Each motivating factor can be seen as a derivative of the translator's right to choose and to invent: "As literary contrabandier the translator...stands for freedom, risk, excitement and adventure."[31]

For a better sense of Stratford's translation corpus, an ordering by genre rather than by chronology seems appropriate. *Convergence: Essays from Quebec* (1966), the collection of Le Moyne's essays, was followed by *André Laurendeau, Witness for Quebec: Essays* (1973) and two more anthologies that manifest Stratford's adherence to the conception of translation as cultural and political bridge. Consisting of a selection of one or more short stories by eighteen well-known contemporary Québec writers translated by seventeen English-Canadians,[32] *Stories from Quebec* (1974) sought to highlight various narrative techniques which Stratford, in his introduction, described as "typically Québecois." Made available to an anglophone public still shaken by the 1976 victory of the Parti Québecois, *Voices from Quebec: An Anthology of Translations* (1977), was much more eclectic and ambitious in scope. It contains eighty-six selections taken from fiction, poetry, drama, essays, popular songs, journalism, history, and film scripts written between the 1960s and the 1970s by French Canadians from Québec and the Maritimes.[33] What the editors wished to communicate was the palpable "strain of difference" at the root of Québec's refusal to conform to Anglo-American experiences and norms, and its "persistent drive for independence."[34]

Convergence: Essays from Quebec was praised for dispelling simplistic notions concerning ethnic solidarity and nationalism, and for introducing to an anglophone readership the "aggressive individualism" of Jean Le Moyne in a "lucid English version that omits almost nothing found in the original and adds only what is indispensable to our understanding."[35] *Voices from Quebec* was hailed as "an outstanding text in both conception and execution, a difficult but vital and undeniably successful mission," while its translators were lauded for their "sensitivity and fidelity to both style and content."[36]

Stratford's penchant for translating works of an autobiographical and/or political nature was given full rein several years later. In 1986, he was asked to produce an "instant translation" of René Lévesque's *Attendez que je me rappelle…*(1986), "which was translated as it was being written so that the two versions appeared simultaneously."³⁷ Not only does *Memoirs* stand out in Canadian translation as the first example of an instant translation—this was no doubt Stratford's main challenge—but it also stands out in Stratford's own translation corpus due to its pronounced "foreignness." The mediating powers of translation infiltrate the level of form as well as content, resulting in a translation that "makes it impossible for the reader to forget that s/he is reading about the former prime minister [sic] of Québec, a province not quite like the others."³⁸ *Memoirs* was followed in 1988 by the publication of *Second Chance*, Diane Hébert's account of her triple organ transplant.

In his landmark *Bibliography of Canadian Books in Translation: French to English and English to French* (1975; 1977), Stratford's goal was to found a tradition of literary translation in Canada. In his influential foreword, he summarized what had been accomplished over the past two decades and outlined a plan of action for improving the situation: more translations and retranslations of older works; revival of out-of-print translations; correction of significant omissions; cheaper editions.³⁹ He called for greater government support aimed at encouraging public interest in the other culture and inciting translators to translate literary texts. The *Bibliography* instantly became—and has remained—a model for the institutional analysis of literary translation in Canada.

Between 1968 and 1993, Philip Stratford translated six French-Canadian novels, if one includes Claire Martin's two autobiographical texts—united under the title *In an Iron Glove* (1968)—which initially qualified as fiction. *In an Iron Glove* was followed by *The Madman, the Kite and the Island*, by Félix Leclerc (1976); *Pélagie: The Return to a Homeland* (1982) and *The Devil Is Loose!* (1986) by Antonine Maillet and, in collaboration with David Lobdell, *Pierre*, by Marie-Claire Blais (1993).⁴⁰ With few exceptions, his renderings were praised by reviewers, notably for capturing the unique tone and stylistic quality of the original. His version of Martin's books was described as "a very good one": "it reads like English and it reads almost like Claire Martin, which is no mean feat for an author whose brio is so intimately bound to the syntax and idiom of her own language."⁴¹ His translation of Antonine Maillet's *Pélagie-la-Charrette* was considered "formidable and inspired."⁴² Similar praise was reserved for *The Devil Is Loose!* whose "salty, slightly archaic style…recall[s] the Atlantic provinces in the 1930's while avoiding the trap of a 'dialect' translation."⁴³

Not all readers were in agreement with Stratford's treatment of Maillet's prose, however. In her review of *The Devil Is Loose!* Barbara Godard calls into question Stratford's aim "to create the novel Maillet would have written were she writing in English, instead of foregrounding the text's difference."[44] Henri-Dominique Paratte chastises not only Stratford, but all Maillet's translators, for their lack of sufficient knowledge of Acadia and its idiom, together with their inadequate choice of an "equivalent" for the latter.[45]

In 1986, Stratford published *Blind Painting*, a collection of poems by Montréal poet Robert Melançon, whose *Peinture aveugle* had initially appeared in 1979. The volume was short-listed for the 1986 Governor General's Literary Award for Translation. *Air*, another much smaller collection of translated poems by Melançon followed in 1997. These two translations appear alongside the originals, in bilingual editions, a trend the review *ellipse* has done much to promote. *Blind Painting* further stands out due to the differences between this re-edition of *Peinture aveugle* and the 1979 original: some poems have been omitted, others have been revised, new poems have been added. Reviewers were quick to single out both the uniqueness of the authors' collaboration, which they likened to Anne Hébert and Frank Scott's *Dialogue sur la traduction* (1970), and the way in which *Blind Painting* illustrates the "catalytic action of translation"[46] by generating a "spiralling movement of re/writing," of "freewheeling creativity."[47]

Culture and Creativity: Stratford's Conception of Translation

While a brief translator's note, preface or introduction accompany most of Stratford's translations,[48] his conception of the translation act itself is more clearly exposed in his scholarly writings. Over half of the articles he published between 1968 and 1994 focus on the role of translation within the literary establishment. Their aim: to underline the fact that Canada "lack[ed] a vigorous and intelligently planned policy of translation."[49] This did not imply that translation in Canada was without a history or that it had never received institutional recognition. On the contrary, Stratford provides extremely accurate accounts of both, with a view to outlining "what had been left undone."[50] The underlying assumption, akin to the one at the root of the classroom projects, was that translation is not an art governed exclusively by aesthetic criteria or metaphysical ideals. It is an economically determined social practice whose future growth depends entirely on federal funding and "some heavy two-way traffic"[51] over the newly constructed institutional bridge. This is the only way to correct statistical imbalances, cultural disparities, and marketing difficulties: "translations remain marginal, economically uninteresting, technically difficult to handle, and hard to sell."[52]

Inseparable from the bilingual dream, Stratford's conception of translation was by no stretch of the imagination idealistic: bridges must be planned, budgeted for, engineered, maintained. Designed to link cultures, readerships, publishing companies, scholarly pursuits, university programs, and writers, the spanning process is perforce multifaceted, equally as imperative in the classroom as in the curriculum, the government, the literary institution, and the market place. In this sense, Stratford was a pragmatist, determined not to be content with images of bridges but to become a builder himself. At this level, his conception of translation could be interpreted as a context-oriented response to a historical situation that called for a political definition of literary translation and a plan of action.

On another level, however, Stratford's conception of literary translation could also be interpreted as deriving from more abstract factors grounded in intellectual and aesthetic assumptions. These assumptions form the basis for an alternative view of translation that emerged in his writing during the 1970s and that characterizes the other half of his scholarly texts. Here Stratford's idea of literary translation is informed not so much by a sense of urgency in the face of political ferment as by analogies he perceived between translation and comparative literature, which enabled him to pass with extraordinary ease from one to the other.

It was Stratford the comparatist who first referred to what Stratford the translator would subsequently associate with the more pragmatic metaphor of bridge-building, namely, the figure of the parallel. Early allusions to parallels are present in his monograph on Greene and Mauriac, where the traditional comparative model based on influence is replaced by a new method designed to identify, over and above the "common traits" already observed by critics, significant differences between the two authors' works. A much more refined description of the figure can be found in his articles published during the 1970s. In one of his classroom projects, students were asked to question Ronald Sutherland's "centralist" premise that French- and English-Canadian novels stem from a common historical denominator and Jean-Charles Falardeau's "separatist" contention that the two literatures run at right angles to each other, thereby diverging completely. Their conclusion opened up an innovative intermediate space: "neither the Sutherland nor the Falardeau theory is sufficient in itself."[53] The two literatures never converge, nor do they totally diverge. As "proximate but unlike phenomena," they must be apprehended in terms "not [of] sameness but [of] qualified similarity"[54] so as to avoid the traditional pitfall of giving precedence to similarities.[55]

By conceiving French- and English-Canadian literature as parallel lines that are at once independent (they never meet) and mutually dependant ("one parallel fixes and defines the other"[56]), Stratford laid out new methodological and theoretical foundations for the comparative study of Canada's two literatures. In *All the Polarities*, the notion of "polarity" was added to clarify the metaphor of parallel lines, which had been criticized by the influential Canadian comparatist E.D. Blodgett for its reductive binarism and insidiously imperialistic connotations of "anglophone hegemony."[57] Stratford defended his choice of metaphor, reaffirming its ability to "tolerat[e] difference as well as sameness" and recalling that "the movement of parallels admits of considerable diversity: they need not always run in straight lines; they can take an angle or a curve; moving into a third dimension they can spiral together into shapes as naturally convoluted as snail shells." He nonetheless admitted that the term "polarity" better captured the dynamic nature of the phenomena he was describing and the dialectical dimension of the "bifocal" method he had developed.[58] One must proceed "by successive *rapprochement* and distancing" of the two poles,[59] allowing for each similarity to be reconsidered in the light of the differences it concealed and for generalizations to be qualified by the uniqueness of the individual works. The plural—polarities—further implied multiple varieties of convergences/divergences as well as multiple sites from which to observe them.

The figure of the parallel also played a central role in Stratford's more abstract view of literary translation. In contrast to the contextual focus of his historical and institutional accounts of translation in Canada, where the latter was seen as a cultural *product*, this alternative vision construed translation as a creative *process* whose dynamism is a direct result of the polarities upon which it relies. The empirical considerations so prevalent in his non-theoretical writing are superseded by speculations pertaining to the translator's task, the function of translation, the nature of the translation process, and the sorts of polarities involved. Each polarity is described with a view to exposing paradoxical similarities and differences. While the original and the translation both propose something new, the translation, contrary to the original, belongs simultaneously to the author and the translator. The translator must "absolutely respect the integrity of his author's text" and, at the same time, "be perfectly true to [his] own idiom."[60]

Inhabited by an "imitative frenzy" and "the impulse to translate," the translator enters into an "act of empathy, or of sharing, or of possession"[61] of the original. Although literary training, and an astute understanding of foreign and domestic markets, languages, and cultures are prerequisites, this is not enough. The translator must "be able to write with flair and imagination";[62] he or she must go beyond critical textual analysis and the search for servile equivalencies to become a creator in his or her own right, delving into his or her own life experiences in order to discover or invent voices, tones, pitches, and ranges of vocabulary that at once "accommodate" those of the original and confirm the translator's presence in the translated text. "It is not a question of suppressing one's own individuality";[63] rather, the translator must strike a "paradoxical posture"[64] that allows him or her to become a creative imitator whose loyalty to the "spirit" of the original is constantly counterbalanced by the right to exercise stylistic freedom, to project him- or herself into the creative process. Therein resides the "true value" of the translated work: "Far from being a mere chameleon [the translator] has a character and style of his own, and translation, in the strictest sense, does not mean setting up an equation but setting up a *creative tension* between the translator's style and that of his subject."[65] In this way, the translation assumes its own "similar yet distinctive tone."[66]

The notion of stylistic innovation is embedded in Stratford's idea of creative liberty, itself a paradoxical phenomenon that "must be exercised if the translation is to have life" but must not "eclipse [the translator's] fidelity to the text."[67] What Stratford meant by creative liberty, or creative imitation, is best illustrated by the polarity he established between the translator and the writer. Just as translators walk the tightrope between servitude (loyalty) and creation (betrayal), writers, too, should refuse to adopt a posture based on servility (to reality, to literary conventions, to their inner voice).[68] As in the case of translators, writers must experiment, imitate creatively, and hence betray in order to sustain the "uneasy" tension between constraint and freedom. Moreover, by projecting themselves into the creative process, translators enjoy the same freedom of linguistic and stylistic choice as authors: "as every translator knows, any single word can usually be rendered in three or four ways."[69] And just as the author must keep the real world in abeyance, giving free rein to imagination, so the translator should avoid overly close contact with the author in order to remain free to translate "the life in the book":[70] "Taking his cue from the author, the translator must jealously keep his own possibilities of choice open."[71]

Stratford's evocation of the translator's creative freedom has at least two implications. First, the vigorous emphasis on the similarities between author and translator (they are both imitative creators) and, by extension, between original and translation ("translation is a second authoring")[72] threatens to momentarily suspend the dialectical tension so crucial to the concept of the parallel. Stratford, however, does not let this happen. The momentary *rapprochement* (which serves to reject conceptions of translation where "difference" is synonymous with "inferiority" and "derivation") gives way, in true dialectical fashion, to distancing, which in turn leads to the uncovering of a new difference between literary translators and writers. Because they have already read the book and know what's coming next, translators do not enjoy the same sense of excitement and discovery authors feel as their story unfolds. The freedom not to know is a one-sided freedom, specific to the act of writing. "The problem for the translator is how to reproduce this creative blindess"[73] and thereby exercise his or her creative liberty.

Creative blindness can be induced through various techniques, such as a cursory first reading of the original, purposeful forgetfulness, or a refusal to use a good dictionary. These techniques foster a parallel freedom that enables the translator "to nurture that vital element of surprise"[74] and, in this way, realign the act of translation with the act of creation without upsetting the indispensable polarity. The "illusion that you are not translating but putting the text back into its original language" is in fact a by-product of the translator's creative blindness, an indication that the fundamental creative tension between author and translator, far from having been dissolved, is operating at its highest possible level. In short, by defining the translator's work as "parallel and equal to the author's," Stratford dismantled conventional hierarchies in favour of the more complex notion of creative parity. And by showing the extent to which the reproduction of the author's creative blindness paradoxically fuels the translator's creative freedom, he reinforced the conceptual and methodological validity of the parallel in the area of literary translation.

The second implication of Stratford's definition of creative freedom concerns its relation to the literalism vs. fluency debate: is his conception of the translation act source-oriented or target-oriented?[75] Stratford made numerous passing allusions to the question of the translator's visibility as it relates to this debate. In 1971, he noted in *Canadian Studies*, "Personally, I prefer translations where the translator's own frame shows through the cloth....this contradicts the theory that the translator should be some kind of invisible, tasteless, odourless medium."[76] In other writings on translation, however, he seemed to favour a target-oriented approach: "The translation must be rooted in *la langue d'arrivée*—the 'target' language, just as deeply as the original was in *la langue de départ*, the 'source' language."[77] Notwithstanding his sense of creative freedom, this implied that "[the translator] must be ready to employ any ruse to get closer to his subject, and any device to bring his subject closer to his audience. He must work clandestinely to eliminate the distinctions between source-subject and target-audience....the translator must work to become the invisible and probably anonymous agent of a profoundly human exchange."[78] The primary assumption here is that translators, be they visible or invisible, must strive for fluency by bringing the source-text "closer to [their] audience" without falling into the trap of free adaptation.

In contrast, Stratford's strongest statements regarding his views on the debate engage quite different assumptions, exemplified by the neologism "to english": "In the age-old debate between those who swear by strict fidelity and those who demand poetic license in translation, between near-literalists and free-adaptors, I side with the former. I felt it was not my job to remodel *Pélagie*, but to render it. I like the verb 'to english a text'; I do not feel it is my duty to Anglicize the books I translate. For me, englishing a text even means allowing some foreign flavour to subsist, so that readers are occasionally reminded that they are reading a translation. Within these limits I had to exercise my own inventiveness, that was the challenge."[79]

In the face of these conflicting remarks, it is difficult to qualify Stratford's approach as purely target-culture oriented. The idea of the translator's visibility—or invisibility—together with the nature of the concept's founding criteria (subjective? stylistic? linguistic?) and underlying assumptions (fluency? foreignizing?), seems particularly unstable, undermined as it is by the desire to "deliver the man entire."[80] The temptation is strong to adopt one of two attitudes. One can either point to a cluster of contradictions within Stratford's conception of translation, which he was unable to resolve due, some might say, to the absence of a more systematic theoretical framework;[81] or, one can point to a manifestation of unproblematized tensions that Stratford implicitly assumed.[82] The contradictions can also be approached from another perspective, that of stylistic invention. The cues are provided by Stratford himself. On the one hand, he makes a clear distinction between liberty and license (or free adaptation). On the other hand, he refers to the translator as an (invisible) mediator of "a profoundly human exchange," thereby taking us back full circle to the pragmatic concept of translation as bridge and, by doing so, providing the essential link between what could otherwise appear as two disconnected conceptions of the act of translation.

Translation and Stylistic Invention

In his review of *The Devil Is Loose!* David Homel quotes Stratford: "Maillet didn't want a literal translation. She would tell me, 'Go ahead, be free.' That invitation to freedom let me be more inventive."[83] What Stratford did with that freedom is described in the three articles he devoted to his experience as translator of *Pélagie-la-Charrette*. His first task was to determine whether it was possible to find an English equivalent to Maillet's depiction of Acadian speech. Here "equivalent" is synonymous with "faithful" and opposed to "adaptation"; it is also associated with "authenticity" and "fluency," given that the equivalents identified by Stratford (Little Shemogue Irish, Nova Scotia Scotch, Newfoundland Outport English) entail real-world target idioms. His second task was to decide whether he was competent enough to translate Maillet's novel into one or the other of these equivalents, and if so, whether this was advisable from a readership perspective. The answers, both negative, are revealing: not only did he feel he was not competent due to a "lack of seaboard experience,"[84] but fluency at the local level meant quaintness at the international level. These considerations formed the basis for his choice of Low Standard North American English which, while more in keeping with reader expectations and Stratford's own rural background, nevertheless downplayed questions of strict equivalence in favour of enhanced fluency and a certain sense of translational latitude.

This choice was a mere starting point, however, for it coincided with only one dimension of Maillet's portrayal of Acadian speech. The other dimension consists of a variety of accents, images, rhythms, expressions taken from a large array of literary sources (Rabelais, Molière, folk tales) and combined with authentic acadianisms. What Maillet writes is not "pure" Acadian; rather it is "an imaginative equivalent of *acadien*,...a new language....That new language was what I would have to translate."[85] Once again, questions of equivalence are raised, but instead of involving the imitation of extratextual phenomena, this other dimension requires the imitation of creative invention—or, more precisely, the creative imitation of creative invention. The only literalism in play here is the constraint to invent: "if Antonine Maillet had created a language of her own, I was not only entitled but bound to create my own language as well....I was to translate her Mailletois into Stratfordese."[86] In order to do so, Stratford drew freely on his own literary background (Chaucer, Shakespeare, Twain) and his memories of Anglo-Irish-Scots-American-Southwestern-Ontario oral traditions, searching for the right voice that would enable him to establish a creative tension—similar yet different—between his tone and Maillet's.

The following excerpt from *Pélagie* is representative of this strategy. First the original text:

"Voyons, voyons asteur! Vous le prenez pour qui, l'ancêtre?"
"Je le prends pour ce qu'il était: un détraqué. Mais un détraqué qui fut peut-être le seul, en des temps aussi bout-ci, bout-là, à avoir trouvé une trac qui menait à quelque part."
"Une trac qui menait à sa charrette fantôme, halée par six chevals noirs."
"Où c'est que j'aboutirons tous un jour ou l'autre, tous tant que je sommes. Mais lui, au moins, il se tenait paré."[87]

And now Stratford's version:

"Hold on! Whoa, now! Just who do you take him for, this ancestor of ours?"
"I take him for what he was, a loony whose mind was off the track. But a loony who was perhaps the only one in those wishy-washy times to have a track that led somewhere."
"A track that led to his phantom cart hauled by six black horses."
"Where we'll all end up some day or other, sure as I'm alive. But he, at least, was ready for it."[88]

While Stratford's idea that the translator's freedom must be modeled on the author's means searching for plausible correspondences ("For her Rabelais, I had Chaucer"),[89] it has the important advantage of defining equivalence not as a given, but as a construction based on translational decisions conditioned by the translator's creative liberty. Just as Stratford the comparatist rejected Falardeau's and Sutherland's unilateral approaches to Canadian comparative literature, Stratford the translator opposed the non-dialectical extremes of radical literalism (read "word-for-word" translation) and radical fluency (read translational license). In their stead, he strove to achieve either an "uneven fluency," whereby the tone of his own voice could be heard alongside the author's, or a form of "mild literalism" designed to sporadically reproduce, over and above the original's tonal qualities, some of its stylistic and linguistic particularities. Both tendencies are aptly qualified by Stratford's verb "to english" insofar as they rely on notions of inventiveness (versus servility) and liberty (versus license).

Whereas Stratford's overall approach to literary translation could be described as "literal" in the sense of "creatively faithful" to the meaning and poetic qualities of the original, it cannot be classified as source-oriented. Despite the occasional Gallicism and recourse to the conventional technique of keeping place names, together with some of the less hermetic proper and common nouns (e.g., Acadie; Charles-à-Charles, the *curé* in French, his translations are predominantly fluent. One can find numerous deformations of the source-text designed to enhance the translation's readability. More complex proper nouns, for instance, or ones carrying an important semantic charge, are translated (e.g., Little Whirligig [la petite Girouette]; the Sea-Cow [*La Vache marine*]). When references risk being either too local or too culturally obscure, they are omitted, accompanied by explanations (e.g., the title of Lévesque's *Memoirs*) or simply replaced by more recognizable target-culture references (Maillet's allusion to Victor Hugo is "englished" into an allusion to Paul Bunyan).

On occasion, when passages are considered incompatible with current target-ideologies, they are eliminated (the final three paragraphs of *The Madman, the Kite and the Island* were deleted with Leclerc's consent). In the case of Martin's novels, clarification and rationalization lead to a diluting of the ironic dimension. In Maillet's book, while the renderings of Maillet's particular Acadian idiom eschew radical fluency, they are considerably more accessible to the average anglophone reader than the original is to the average francophone reader, due to the choice of a less localized and less culturally alienated target-dialect. As for the French-sounding "gargoyles and tirades" in *Convergence*, they are more a strategy for "deliver[ing] the man entire" to the target-audience than a sign of anti-annexationist literalism.

Scrupulous analysis of and respect for the letter, tone and style of the original, then, rarely results in foreignizing translations, as Stratford himself implicitly acknowledged when he described the translating of *Pélagie* as "the intellectual experience of struggling with Acadian words until they came up Canadian."[90] Although some English-speaking readers may be able to appreciate thematically based parallels, very few can capture, during the reading process, the full range of polarities Stratford sought to maintain: Stratfordese silences the alterity of Mailletois.

The only exception to the target-oriented tendency of Stratford's translations is *Memoirs*, where many colloquialisms are rendered literally, idiomatic phrases such as "n'est-ce pas" are not translated, and French words different from those in the original are introduced, as the following passage illustrates. First, René Lévesque's text:

> Point n'est besoin de dire que voilà ce que je fis sans perdre une minute. Pour me heurter à de grands airs étonnés et des phrases drôlement évasives. Je finis par harceler les Affaires extérieures où le chat sortit du sac. Ma très excellente interview, je le comprendrais sans peine, n'est-ce pas, avait le défaut d'être plutôt mauvaise pour l'honorable ministre....Alors, n'est-ce pas, on s'était permis de la mettre provisoirement sous embargo, mais rien ne m'empêcherait plus de la reprendre.[91]

Now, Stratford's translation:

> As you can guess, this is exactly what I immediately did, only to run into surprised expressions and excessively evasive explanations. I ended up hammering on the door of External Affairs, where the cat finally came out of the sack. My very excellent interview, as I would surely appreciate without too much difficulty, had just one flaw: it was rather hard on the Honourable Minister....So, as I would certainly understand, n'est-ce pas, they had taken the liberty to put a temporary embargo on it [Lévesque's dispatch from Moscow], though by now, of course, nothing stood in the way of my taking it up again.[92]

It is in this book that Stratford came the closest to producing a source-oriented translation in the current sense of the term,[93] together with a textual manifestation of his own notion of creative tension.

Stratford's theoretical articles on translation occupy a unique place in his scholarly production. Allusions to political missions, cultural bridges, and institutional matters have been replaced by aesthetic preoccupations centred on notions of creative blindness, paradox, and inventiveness. But does this mean they have been entirely abandoned? Indeed, one might well want to ask one final question: to what extent does this dual vision of translation as mediation and as creation constitute in itself a polarity that is inherent to his overall conception of translation? The answer should, by now, come easily, contained as it is in many of the excerpts quoted above. At the heart of Stratford's writing on translation lies not so much the idea of cultural *transfer* as the idea of cultural *exchange*—of bridges that, by spanning gaps, not only "serv[e] as a passage across two discreet cultural zones," but create an "intermediate space between them."[94] It is one thing to build bridges, Stratford once wrote, it is another to realize you are actually on one.[95] As a trope for intercultural transfer, bridges foster new possibilities for transit, "reminding us of the distances which made them necessary in the first place."[96] As a trope for intercultural exchange, bridges relativize binarisms, subvert cultural imperialism, and spark a dialogue between equals. They also provide a middle ground for sameness and otherness to interact freely in a space where hierarchical orderings and other such imbalances are neither operative nor legitimate, and where distances no longer seem to matter.

Of Contraband and Other Bridges

Philip Stratford never ceased to speak of bridges, be they of the ambassadorial, political sort, designed to join and inform, or of the aesthetic, imaginative sort, steeped in creative sympathy. Although the former emphasize transmission and the latter innovation, both facilitate two-way crossings for tourists, ambassadors, smugglers, and the like. Both imply divided allegiances, close critical discipleship, and renewed understanding. Over and above the opposition between political engagement and artistic disengagement it embodies, Stratford's dual conception of translation presents an ethical and epistemological unity based on a keen awareness of the artistic, cultural, historical, and institutional stakes involved in interlingual exchanges between English and French Canada in the second half of the twentieth century. It also concretizes his vision of Canadian comparative studies as predicated on "the difficult bifocal view," for which the figure of the parallel was the most appropriate metaphor.

Philip Stratford's conception of translation was inseparable from his definition of comparative literature. His teaching and writing helped rethink the implications of literary translation for Canadian comparative literature by giving them the broad theoretical, critical, and institutional attention they deserved. In turn, this led him to examine the role of literary translation in the construction and transmission of cultural identities. Not only must translation become a "household word," it must be recognized as part of "our perennial Canadian search for identity." Ostensibly a vehicle for acquiring a better understanding of the other, translation ultimately contributes to greater knowledge of the self.

Stratford's vision of translation was equally inseparable from the liberal ideals of cultural nationalism and institutionalized bilingualism. Upon moving to Québec, he became one of the leaders of a group of intellectuals whose self-imposed mandate was to promote a dialogue between the nation's founding communities. He relentlessly sought to provide translators with greater institutional support and to correct the imbalance caused by the precedence given to literary translation from French to English. "Passeur de frontières," amateur of "forbidding" borderline terrains, fully aware of the risks involved for those with enough resolve to venture forth, Stratford never hesitated about exactly which boundaries he was committed to crossing and what messages he wished to convey to his target public.

This commitment has been criticized by scholars such as E.D. Blodgett, who see it as assimilationist by virtue of the binary framework from which it derives and non-dialectical as a result of the over-emphasis accorded to difference. One must be careful, however, when dealing with potential anachronisms. In spite of his cultural ideals, Stratford was a pragmatist, and he picked his fights with care. His messages were geared to respond to a very real situation that he, as a bilingual anglophone Canadian newly arrived in Québec, felt compelled to confront head-on. The attention to difference was, for Stratford, a methodological and political necessity: methodological, in that it was designed to counteract a flaw in Canadian Studies, too often centred on similarities; political, in that as a staunch believer in Québec's cultural distinctiveness, he saw the urgency of dispelling the misconceptions ingrained in English-Canadian perceptions.

Whereas some might also criticize Stratford for having remained on the margins of the exciting theoretical debates of the last two decades or for the lack of systematization in his own theoretical articles, others have preferred to focus on the usefulness of accounts that combine personal anecdote with theoretical reflection. His writing offers an inspiring example of how translators can use "anecdotal theorizing [to] generat[e] new knowledge, new understanding."[97] For Stratford, this new understanding was multifaceted, generated as much by ideological preoccupations as by stylistic innovation. Above all, it was organically linked to the translator's freedom and to a realistic vision of bridge-building.

Stratford's legacy to literary translation as it stands today is substantial. One has only to point to the ongoing cultural, political, and aesthetic significance of his reflections on translation as creation and exchange, to the landmark importance of his institutional analyses, to the avant-garde nature of his simultaneous translation of Lévesque's *Memoirs*. As a professor, a translator, and a translation activist, Stratford has contributed significantly to forging the very tradition of literary translation he felt to be so cruelly lacking in 1977. As a comparatist, a literary critic, and a translation scholar, he helped lay the foundations for an institutional approach to the study of translation in Canada. As a poet and an author, he opposed discourses of subservience and re-placed the translator-poet at the heart of a paradoxical aesthetic process where, to return to his own metaphors, freedom and inventiveness produce creative exchanges and bridges over parallel lines.

NOTES

1 Philip Stratford, "Literary Translation: A Bridge between Two Solitudes," *Language and Society* 11 (1983): 8.
2 Philip Stratford, "French-Canadian Literature in Translation," *Méta* 22, no. 1 (1977): 184.
3 Philip Stratford, "The Poet as Translator," *Studies in Canada* 5 (1994): 1.

4 Philip Stratford, "The Anatomy of a Translation: *Pélagie-la-Charrette*," in *Translation in Canadian Literature*, ed. C. La Bossière (Ottawa: University of Ottawa Press, 1983), p. 128.
5 Stratford, "French-Canadian Literature in Translation," p. 183.
6 A great deal of the information included in this section was very kindly supplied by Jacqueline Stratford. I should like to thank her not only for her helpfulness, warmth, patience, and enthusiasm but also for the documents she took the time to photocopy for me.
7 Philip Stratford, "Translation as Creation," in *Figures in a Ground: Canadian Essays on Modern Literature; Collected in Honor of Sheila Watson*, ed. D. Bessai and D. Jackel (Saskatoon: Western Producer Prairie Books, 1978), p. 10.
8 Stratford, "Translation as Creation," p. 9.
9 Stratford, "The Anatomy of a Translation," p. 121.
10 Stratford, "The Poet as Translator," p. 1.
11 Antoine Sirois, "Avant-propos," *ellipse* 51 (1994): 4.
12 Stratford, "Translating Antonine Maillet's Fiction," in *Culture in Transit*, ed. S. Simon (Montréal: Véhicule Press, 1995), p. 97.
13 John O'Conner, "Translations," *University of Toronto Quarterly* 46, no. 4 (1976/77): 401.
14 Philip Stratford, "Canada's Two Literatures: A Search for Emblems," *Canadian Review of Comparative Literature / Revue canadienne de littérature comparée* 6, no. 2 (1979): 131, 132, 133.
15 Stratford, "Canada's Two Literatures," p. 132.
16 See Philip Stratford, introduction, *Canadian Review of Comparative Literature* 6, no. 2 (1979): 113.
17 Sirois, "Avant-propos," p. 5.
18 Quoted in Sherry Simon, *Culture in Transit: Translating the Literature of Quebec* (Montréal: Véhicule Press, 1995), p. 12.
19 Stratford, "Translating Antonine Maillet's Fiction," p. 97. My emphasis.
20 Stratford, "French-Canadian Literature in Translation," p. 184.
21 Stratford, "Canada's Two Literatures," p. 135.
22 Stratford, "Canada's Two Literatures," p. 136.
23 Stratford, "French-Canadian Literature in Translation," p. 183.
24 Stratford, "Translating Antonine Maillet's Fiction," p. 326.
25 Philip Stratford, introduction, to *The Madman, the Kite and the Island*, by F. Leclerc, p. 5.
26 Philip Stratford and Michael Thomas, eds. and trans., *Voices from Quebec: An Anthology of Translations* (Toronto: Van Nostrand Reinhold, 1977), p. iv.
27 Stratford, "The Anatomy of a Translation," p. 124.
28 Stratford, "Translating Antonine Maillet's Fiction," p. 326.
29 Stratford, "The Anatomy of a Translation," p. 124.
30 Stratford, "The Anatomy of a Translation," p. 125.
31 Stratford, "Translation as Creation," p. 10.
32 Stratford himself translated one story by Françoise Hertel and two by Claire Martin.

33 Stratford translated single-handedly close to one-third of the selections.
34 Stratford and Thomas, *Voices from Quebec*, p. iii.
35 David Hayne, "Aggressive Individualism," *Canadian Literature*, no. 32 (1976): 78.
36 John O'Connor, "Translations," *University of Toronto Quarterly* 47, no. 4 (1977): 384–85.
37 Barbara Godard, "Translations," *University of Toronto Quarterly* 57, no. 4 (1987): 92.
38 Godard, "Translations," p. 93.
39 Stratford, foreword to *Bibliography of Canadian Books in Translation*, pp. vi–vii. The impact of the plan was immediate, as Stratford's own reassessment of the situation in 1990 made clear: "On the basis of this survey various attempts were made in the late 1970s to rationalize translation activity: lists of untranslated works were circulated, grants were guaranteed for the translation of certain Canadian classics, an international wing was added to the Translation Programme, offering support for foreign translations of Canadian works in languages other than English and French." Stratford, "Translation," p. 101.
40 Original titles are as follows : *Dans un gant de fer* (1965) and *La joue droite* (1966); *Le Fou de l'île* (1962); *Pélagie-la-Charrette* (1979) and *Crache-à-Pic* (1984); *Pierre* (1986). In the case of Blais's novel, Stratford completed and revised the translation David Lobdell had begun prior to his death.
41 John Warwick, "Translating Brilliance," *Canadian Literature*, no. 42 (1969): 82.
42 Kathy Mezei, "Translations," *University of Toronto Quarterly* 52, no. 4 (1983): 386–87.
43 David Homel, "Antonine Maillet's Eternal Return of the Acadian Character," *Quill and Quire* 52, no. 6 (1986): 37.
44 Godard, "Translations," pp. 95–96.
45 See Henri-Dominique Paratte, "Deux littératures à mieux découvrir: notes sur la traduction des deux littératures du Nouveau Brunswick," in *Langues et littératures au Nouveau-Brunswick*, ed. R. Gair (Montréal: Éditions de l'Acadie, 1986), pp. 401–10.
46 Philip Lanthier, "Harnessing Energy," *Canadian Literature*, no. 115 (1987): 14.
47 Godard, "Translations," p. 77.
48 The only exceptions are the two novels by Maillet, *Pierre* by Marie-Claire Blais, and *Air* by Melançon. These introductory remarks usually provide information on the author, his or her social context, the thematic, structural, or sociopolitical importance of the original, and the translator's aim, although sometimes only one or two of these aspects are highlighted. The introduction to Lévesque's *Memoirs* is perhaps the most interesting as it combines aesthetic and pragmatic criteria.
49 Stratford, "French-Canadian Literature in Translation," p. 184.
50 Stratford, "Translation," p. 101. "Translations should be cheap, vigorously promoted and easy to get. They should appear simultaneously with the original books and be treated as major literary events. A serious effort should be made to catch up on the backlog of important untranslated books and at the same time

prevent a future backlog. Those who influence reading habits—teachers, critics and reviewers—should open for the public those doors to which translation is the key." Stratford, "Literary Translation," p. 12.
51 Stratford, "Literary Translation," p. 12.
52 Stratford, "Reconciling the Two Solitudes," p. 14.
53 Stratford, "Canada's Two Literatures," p. 136.
54 Philip Stratford, *All the Polarities: Comparative Studies in Contemporary Canadian Novels in French and English* (Toronto: ECW Press, 1986), pp. 3, 4.
55 "Too often the separateness of Canada's two cultures has been a challenge to well-meaning critics who wish to convince us of underlying similarities and unity of outlook and give short thrift to fundamental differences. The present examination…is an attempt to correct this imbalance." Philip Stratford, "*Kamouraska* and *The Diviners*," *Review of National Identities*, no. 7 (1976): 125.
56 Stratford, "Canada's Two Literatures," p. 137.
57 E.D. Blodgett, *Configuration: Essays in the Canadian Literatures* (Toronto: ECW Press, 1982), p. 9.
58 As for Blodgett's reference to cultural imperialism, Stratford simply states that he is "aware of putting more weight on [his] English foot than on [his] French one." Stratford, *All the Polarities*, pp. 8, 7, 9.
59 Stratford, *All the Polarities*, p. 7.
60 Stratford, "Translating Antonine Maillet's Fiction," p. 331.
61 Stratford, "The Anatomy of a Translation," p. 122.
62 Stratford, "Translation as Creation," p. 11.
63 Stratford, "Translating Antonine Maillet's Fiction," p. 331.
64 Philip Stratford, "Finding a New Language: Translating Antonine Maillet," Atti del 6e Convegno internationale di studi canadesi, *Cultural Straniera*, no. 12 (1986): 419.
65 Stratford, "Translation as Creation," p. 13. My emphasis.
66 Stratford, "Translation as Creation," p. 13.
67 Stratford, "Finding a New Language," pp. 416–17.
68 The poem is a translation of the poet's inner voice; the poet is a "loyal disloyal friend/validator and if need be/violator of his Word." Stratford, "The Poet as Translator," *Textual Studies in Canada*, no. 5 (1994): 1.
69 Stratford, "Translation as Creation," p. 12.
70 Stratford, "The Anatomy of a Translation," p. 129.
71 Stratford, "Translation as Creation," p. 12.
72 Stratford, "Finding a New Language," p. 416.
73 Stratford, "Finding a New Language," p. 417.
74 Stratford, "The Anatomy of a Translation," p. 128.
75 Caution must be exercised here. Stratford did not provide clear-cut definitions of terms such as "literal," "foreignizing," and "adaptation." It would be anachronistic to refer to the political and ethical overtones these terms have for A. Berman and L. Venuti, for instance, whose seminal texts were published, respectively, in 1984 and 1986. I see no indication of any direct influence of

these works on Stratford's scholarly writing. When he sides with the "near-literalist" approach, this should therefore not be confused with the neo-literalist approach that has gained currency over the past two decades under the ethical and political aegis of the foreign.

76 Philip Stratford, "Circle, Straight Line, Ellipse," *Canadian Studies*, no. 49 (1971): 89–90.
77 Stratford, "Translation as Creation," p. 13.
78 Stratford, "Translation as Creation," p. 17–18.
79 Stratford, "Translating Antonine Maillet's Fiction," p. 328. Here are similar statements: "I will frequently introduce a slightly French *tournure de phrase*, even risking a certain awkwardness, just to remind the reader, and myself, that this is a translation." Stratford, "Finding a New Language," p. 417). "My practice is to stay as close as possible, to take guidance, as it were, from the original French. In this I follow the example of Frank Scott and not that of John Glassco who liked to put the emphasis on the English poem that was to result." Philip Stratford, "A Bridge of Sorts," unpublished paper, p. 5.
80 "I have considered it my duty to English, not Anglicize, Le Moyne; so I have left in most of the gargoyles and tirades,...thinking this was the best way to deliver the man entire." Philip Stratford, translator's preface, in *Convergence; Essays from Quebec*, by J. Le Moyne (Toronto: Ryerson, 1966), p. x.
81 This seems to be the case in the following: "I personally favour reproducing every feature of the French as closely as possible....You will note that as [a writer] with English ears trained to English cadences, [I] use the standard English meter, iambic pentameter, rather than Nelligan's French hexameter." Stratford, translator's preface, *Convergence*, p. 3.
82 The second attitude is by far the more plausible (see Stratford, "Translation as Creation," pp. 16–17). In the following excerpt from *Faith and Fiction*, Stratford explains what he means by assuming a contradiction. Referring to "what Mauriac calls, in theology, 'the essential contradiction between man's liberty and divine prescience,'" Stratford adds, "This contradiction has special signification for the novelist who is at once a God over his creation and, through his characters, a creature in it. It is a contradiction which cannot be resolved, though it can be assumed in the novelist's paradoxically ambivalent attitude. One cannot expect from him either extreme of commitment or non-commitment." Philip Stratford, *Faith and Fiction: Creative Process in Greene and Mauriac* (Notre Dame, IN: University of Notre Dame Press, 1964), pp. 312–13.
83 Quoted in Homel, "Antonine Maillet's Eternal Return," p. 37.
84 Stratford, "Translating Antonine Maillet's Fiction," p. 327.
85 Stratford, "Translating Antonine Maillet's Fiction," p. 328.
86 Stratford, "Translating Antonine Maillet's Fiction," p. 328.
87 Antonine Maillet, *Pélagie-la-Charrette*, p. 192.
88 Antonine Maillet, *Pélagie: The Return to a Homeland*, trans. P. Stratford (Garden City, NY: Doubleday, 1982; Toronto: Doubleday Canada, 1982), p. 134.
89 Stratford, "The Anatomy of a Translation," p. 126.
90 Stratford, "Finding a New Language," p. 418.

91 René Lévesque, *Attendez que je me rappelle* (Montréal: Québec/Amérique, 1986), p. 180.
92 René Lévesque, *Memoirs*, trans. P. Stratford (Toronto: McClelland and Stewart, 1986), p. 10.
93 Once again, caution must be exercised. In his translator's note to *Memoirs*, Stratford informed his readers that he had abridged references that might seem too local and added a few explanatory notes—a practice more associated with adaptation (or fluency) than literalism.
94 Sherry Simon, "The Paris Arcades, the Ponte Vecchio and the Comma of Translation," *Méta* 45, no. 1 (2001): 78.
95 See Stratford, "Finding a New Language," p. 409.
96 Simon, "The Paris Arcades," pp. 76–77.
97 Douglas Robinson, "22 Theses on Translation," *Journal of Translation Studies*, no. 2 (June 1998): 92–117, rpt. on homepage, <http://members.tripod.com/douglas.robinson/id172.htm>.

BIBLIOGRAPHY

I. Primary Sources

Literary Translations

Blais, Marie-Claire. *Pierre*. Trans. D. Lobdell and P. Stratford. Toronto: Oberon Press, 1993. Translation of *Pierre*. Paris: Acropole, 1986.

Côte Melançon, Charlotte. "Fenêtre/Window" and "Poème dans l'esprit de Jean Follain/Poem in the Spirit of Jean Follan." Trans. P. Stratford. *Ellipse*, no. 40 (1988): 102–105.

Leclerc, Félix. *The Madman, the Kite and the Island*. Trans. and introd. P. Stratford. Toronto: Oberon Press, 1976. Translation of *Le fou de l'île*. Montréal and Paris: Fides, 1962.

———. "The Villon Legacy." Trans. P. Stratford. *Canadian Literature*, no. 121 (1989): 108–14.

Maillet, Antonine. *Pélagie: The Return to a Homeland*. Trans. P. Stratford. Garden City, NY: Doubleday, 1982; Toronto: Doubleday Canada, 1982. Rpt. *Pélagie The Return to Acadia*. Trans. Philip Stratford. Fredericton, NB: Goose Lane Editions, 2004. Translation of *Pélagie-la-charrette*. Montréal: Leméac, 1979.

———. "Two Saints." Trans. P. Stratford. In *The Oxford Book of French-Canadian Short Stories*, ed. R. Teleky. Oxford: Oxford University Press, 1983. 219–24.

———. *The Devil Is Loose!* Trans. P. Stratford. Toronto: Lester and Orpen Dennys, 1986. Translation of *Crache à pic*. Montréal: Leméac, 1984.

Martin, Claire. *In an Iron Glove*. Trans. P. Stratford. Toronto: Ryerson Press, 1968. Translation of *Dans un gant de fer*. Montréal: Cercle du Livre de France, 1965.

Melançon, Robert. *Blind Painting*. Trans. P. Stratford. Introd. P. Stratford and R. Melançon. Montréal: Signal Editions, 1986. Translation of *Peinture aveugle*. Montréal-Nord: VLB, 1979.

———. "Jean-Aubert Loranger" and "Air." Trans. P. Stratford. *Ellipse*, no. 40 (1988): 106-109.

———. *Air*. Trans. P. Stratford. Vancouver: Éditions L. Lambert, 1997. Translation of *Air*. Bilingual edition.

Nepveu, Pierre. "Mélodrame/Melodrama" and "Écrit dans la chambre/Written in my Room." Trans. P. Stratford. *ellipse*, no. 40 (1988): 98-101.

Non-Literary Translations

Hébert, Diane. *Second Chance*. Trans. P. Stratford. Toronto: Lester and Orpen Dennys, 1988.

Lévesque, René. *Memoirs*. Trans. and introd. P. Stratford. Toronto: McClelland and Stewart, 1986. Translation of *Attendez que je me rappelle*. Montréal: Québec/Amérique, 1986.

Anthologies

Le Moyne, Jean. *Convergence: Essays from Quebec*. Trans. P. Stratford. Toronto: Ryerson Press, 1966.

Laurendeau, André. *André Laurendeau: Witness for Québec; Essays*. Trans. P. Stratford. Introd. C. Ryan. Toronto: Macmillan, 1973.

Stratford, Philip, ed. *Stories from Québec*. Introd. P. Stratford. Toronto: Van Nostrand Reinhold, 1974.

Stratford, Philip, and Michael Thomas, eds. *Voices from Québec: An Anthology of Translations*. Trans. P. Stratford and M. Thomas. Toronto: Van Nostrand Reinhold, 1977.

Bibliographies

Stratford, Philip, and Maureen Newman. *Bibliography of Canadian Books in Translation: French to English and English to French / Bibliographie de livres canadiens traduits de l'anglais au français et du français à l'anglais*. Ottawa. HRCC/CCRH, 1975.

Stratford, Philip. *Bibliography of Canadian Books in Translation: French to English and English to French / Bibliographie de livres canadiens traduits de l'anglais au français et du français à l'anglais*, Ottawa. HRCC/CCRH, 1977.

Works on Translation

Stratford, Philip. "French-Canadian Literature in Translation." *Méta* 13, no. 4 (1968): 180-87.

———. "Literary Translation in Canada: A Survey," *Méta* 22, no. 1 (1977): 37-44.

———. "Translation as Creation." In *Figures in a Ground: Canadian Essays on Modern Literature; Collected in Honor of Sheila Watson*, ed. D. Bessai and D. Jackel. Saskatoon: Western Producer Prairie Books, 1978. 9-18.

———. "The Anatomy of a Translation: *Pélagie-la-Charrette*." in *Translation in Canadian Literature*, ed. C. La Bossière. Ottawa: University of Ottawa Press, 1983. 121-30.

———. "Literary Translation: A Bridge between Two Solitudes." *Language and Society*, no. 11 (1983): 8-13.

———. "Finding a New Language: Translating Antonine Maillet." Atti del 6e Convegno internazionale di studi canadesi, *Cultura Straniera* 12 (1986): 409–21.
———. "Translating Antonine Maillet's Fiction." *Quebec Studies* 4 (1986): 326–32. Rpt. in Simon, *Culture in Transit*, 93–100.
———. "Translation." In *Literary History of Canada*. Vol. 4, *Canadian Literature in English*, ed. W.H. New. Toronto: University of Toronto Press, 1990. 97–107.

Literary Works

Stratford, Philip. *Olive: A Dog, Un chien*. Montréal: Tundra, 1976.
———. *The Rage of Space*. Toronto: Oberon Press, 1992.
———. *Seven Seasons*. Toronto: Oberon Press, 1994.
———. *Verse Portraits*. Toronto: Oberon Press, 1997.
———. *Hawthorn House*. Ottawa: Buschek Books, 1999.
Stratford, Philip, and P.K. Page. *And Once More Saw the Stars: Four Poems for Two Voices*. Ottawa: Buschek Books, 2001.

Introductions, Notes, Prefaces, Reviews, and Other Works on Translation

Stratford, Philip. Translator's Preface. In *Convergence: Essays from Quebec* by J. Le Moyne. Toronto: Ryerson Press, 1966. ix–xii.
———. Translator's Preface. In *In an Iron Glove* by C. Martin. Toronto: Ryerson Press, 1968. v–vi.
———. "Circle, Straight Line, Ellipse." *Canadian Studies*, no. 49 (1971): 88–91.
———. Editor's Note. In *André Laurendeau: Witness for Quebec*, by A. Laurendeau. Toronto: Macmillon, 1973. xvii–xviii.
———. Introduction to *Tête Blanche* by M.-C. Blais. Trans. C. Fullman. Toronto: McClelland and Stewart, 1974. vii–xi.
———. Introduction to *The Madman, the Kite and the Island* by F. Leclerc. Toronto: Oberon Press, 1976. 5–9.
———. Foreward to *Bibliography of Canadian Books in Translation: French to English and English to French / Bibliographie de livres canadiens traduits de l'anglais au français et du français à l'anglais* by P. Stratford. Ottawa. HRCC/CCRH, 1977. i–vii.
———. "Anne Hébert's Romance of Evil." *Quill and Quire* 43, no. 5 (1977): 38.
———. "New Fiction Spans Cultural Gap." *Quill and Quire* 44, no. 17 (1978): 32.
———. "Quebec Writers and Translators Meet." *Quill and Quire* 45, no. 14 (1979): 14.
———. "Reconciling the Two Solitudes." *Quill and Quire* 45, no. 3 (1979): 12, 14.
———. "Existential Vertigo." *Essays in Canadian Writing* 16 (1979–1980): 213–18.
———. "Writer at Play." *Canadian Literature*, no. 85 (1980): 152–58.
———. "Marie-Claire Blais: Prowling the Periphery of Solitude." *Quill and Quire* 47, no. 6 (1981): 34.
———. "Fiction." *Quill and Quire* 48, no. 2 (1982): 38.
———. "Sparrows and Eagles." *Canadian Literature*, 102 (1984): 159–60.
———. Introduction to *Blind Painting* by R. Melançon. Trans. P. Stratford. Montréal: Signal Editions, 1986. 10.

———. Translator's Note. In *Memoirs* by R. Lévesque. Trans. P. Stratford. Toronto: McClelland and Stewart, 1986. 7.
———. "Completing the Elliptical Process." *ellipse*, no. 40 (1988): 97–109.
———. Afterword to *The Tin Flute* by G. Roy. Trans. Alan Brown. Toronto: McClelland and Stewart, 1989. 385–89.
———. "The Poet as Translator." *Studies in Canada*, no. 5 (1994): 1.
———. "A Bridge of Sorts." Unpublished conference paper.

Other Publications

Stratford, Philip. *Faith and Fiction: Creative Process in Greene and Mauriac*. Notre Dame, IN: University of Notre Dame Press, 1964.
———. *Marie-Claire Blais*. Toronto: Forum House, 1974.
———, ed. *The Portable Graham Greene*. Intro. P. Stratford. New York: Viking Press, 1973.
———. "*Kamouraska* and *The Diviners*." *Review of National Identities*, no. 7 (1976): 110–26.
———. Introduction. *Canadian Review of Comparative Literature/Revue canadienne de littérature comparée* 6, no. 2 (1979): 113–14.
———. "Canada's Two Literatures: A Search for Emblems." *Canadian Review of Comparative Literature/Revue canadienne de littérature comparée* 6, no. 2 (1979): 131–38.
———. *All the Polarities: Comparative Studies in Contemporary Canadian Novels in French and English*. Toronto: ECW Press, 1986.

II. Secondary Sources

Berman, Antoine. *L'épreuve de L'étranger*. Paris: Gallimard, 1984.
———. "La traduction comme épreuve de l'étranger." *Texte*, no. 4 (1985): 67–81.
Blodgett, E.D. *Configuration: Essays in the Canadian Literatures*. Toronto: ECW Press, 1982.
Cavell, Richard. "Transliterature." *Canadian Literature*, no. 106 (1985): 108–10.
Cook, Ramsay. "Acadian Odyssey." *Saturday Night* 97, no. 3 (1982): 54.
Dansereau, Estelle. "Robert Melançon, Philip Stratford." *Quarry* 36, no. 3 (1987): 82–86.
Elder, Jo-Anne. "The Non-Translation of Translation and the Tradition of Non-Translation." *ellipse*, no. 51 (1994): 23–37.
Everett, Jane. "Félix Leclerc, *The Madman, the Kite and the Island*, Trans. Philip Stratford." *Quarry* 26, no. 4 (Autumn 1977): 74–76.
Godard, Barbara. "Translations." *University of Toronto Quarterly* 57, no. 4 (1987): 77–98
Hayne, David. "Aggressive Individualism." *Canadian Literature*, no. 32 (1976): 77–78.
Homel, David. "Antonine Maillet's Eternal Return of the Acadian Character." *Quill and Quire* 52, no. 6 (1986): 37.
Issenhuth, Jean-Pierre. "Blind Painting." *Liberté*, no. 165 (1986): 138–41.

Jones, Doug. Foreword. *ellipse*, no. 51 (1994): 7–8.
Koustas, Jane. "Translations." *University of Toronto Quarterly* 66, no. 1 (1996/97): 291–301.
Lanthier, Philip. "Harnessing Energy." *Canadian Literature*, no. 115 (1987): 140–42.
Lennox, John. "Survivors from History." *Essays on Canadian Writing*, no. 28 (1984): 156–59.
Melançon, Robert. Introduction to *Blind Painting*. Montréal: Signal Editions, 1986. 11.
———. "Le poète est un traducteur." *Canadian Literature*, no. 117 (1988): 108–12
Mezei, Kathy. "Translations." *University of Toronto Quarterly* 52, no. 4 (1983): 385–97.
———. "A Bridge of Sorts: The Translation of Quebec Literature into English." *The Yearbook of English Studies* 15 (1985): 201–26.
———. "Speaking White. Literary Translation as a Vehicle of Assimilation in Quebec." *Canadian Literature*, no. 117 (1988): 11–24. Reprinted in *Culture in Transit: Translating the Literature of Quebec*, ed. S. Simon. Montréal: Véhicule Press, 1995. 133–48.
———. "Translation as Metonomy: Bridges and Bilingualism." *ellipse*, no. 51 (1994): 85–102.
O'Connor, John. "Translations." *University of Toronto Quarterly* 46, no. 4 (1976/77): 399–415.
———. "Translations." *University of Toronto Quarterly* 47, no. 4 (1977): 381–95.
Paratte, Henri-Dominique. "Deux littératures à mieux découvrir: notes sur la traduction des deux littératures du Nouveau-Brunswick." In *Langues et littératures au Nouveau-Brunswick*, ed. R. Gair. Moncton: Éditions de l'Acadie, 1986. 401–10.
Robinson, Douglas. *What Is Translation? Centrifugal Theories, Critical Interventions*. Kent, OH: Kent State University Press, 1997.
———. "22 Theses on Translation." *Journal of Translation Studies*, no. 2 (June 1998): 92–117. Rpt. on homepage, <http://members.tripod.com/douglas.robinson/id172.htm>.
Simon, Sherry. "Rites of Passage: Translation and Its Intents." *Massachusetts Review* 31, no. 1 (1990): 96–110.
———. *Culture in Transit: Translating the Literature of Quebec*. Montréal: Véhicule Press, 1995.
———. "The Paris Arcades, the Ponte Vecchio and the Comma of Translation." *Méta* 45, no. 1 (2001): 73–79.
Sirois, Antoine. "Avant-propos." *ellipse*, no. 51 (1994): 4–6.
Venuti, Lawrence. "The Translator's Invisibility." *Criticism* 28, no.2 (1986): 179–212.
Warwick, John. "Translating Brilliance." *Canadian Literature*, no. 42 (1969): 82–84.

On D.G. Jones
and Translating Outside

STEPHANIE NUTTING

D.G. Jones, to quote fellow writer George Bowering, "embodies the spirit of the Anglo-Saxon poet in a strange wintery land, the first morning outside [European] Eden";[1] Bowering's article is intriguingly entitled "Coming Home to the World." In his house in North Hatley, in the Eastern Townships of Québec, the award-winning poet and translator rests sideways to the fireplace, a white sweater hanging off his frame.[2] He has chosen to sit on a long pale couch in the living room, which contains the familiar professorial bric-a-brac of books and bookcases, wooden floors and framed prints. The room has the subdued ambiance of 1970s country decor, vaguely reminiscent of *Harrowsmith Magazine*. The wide windows on two sides of the living room show to great advantage an exquisite, evergreen-framed view overlooking Lake Massawippi. Although physically he appears fragile, Jones at 74 has lost none of his canniness. He has that unmistakable poised intensity that one commonly associates with poets. Indeed, D.G. Jones is a poet. Period. *Point à la ligne.*

Jones is also one of the most respected translators of poetry in Canada, but it would be shy of the mark to call him a professional translator per se. More correctly speaking, he is a Canadian anglophone poet who considers that writing poetry also includes regularly transforming francophone verse into English. This is perhaps a fine distinction, but it is a key one if Jones's pivotal role in literary translation in Canada is to be understood. His decision to translate Québécois poetry was a function of his choice, as a poet, to make more poetry accessible to English-Canadian readers. He is uncompromising in his devotion to his art and in his conviction that Canadian poetry in both languages would be better served if more readers were able to cross the linguistic divide that separates Canada's two solitudes. In 1969, with precisely this purpose in mind, Jones, along with his wife at the time, Sheila Fischman, and a small group of scholars, poets, and writers—Joseph Bonenfant and Richard Giguère, with consulting editors Roch Carrier, John Glassco, and Philip Stratford—founded *ellipse*, Canada's first magazine of poetry in both English and French in reciprocal translation.

An inside look at the North Hatley neighbourhood reveals the unusual microcosm that has both reflected and informed Jones's vision. In the 1970s and 1980s, a whole cluster of Anglo-Québécois poets lived next door to each other: D.G. Jones, Ronald Sutherland, and Ralph Gustafson. Other poets had summer residences nearby: A.J.M. Smith on Lake Memphremagog, F.R. Scott on Lake Massawippi, and Louis Dudek in Way's Mills. These poets exerted a centripetal force on other poets—anglophone and francophone—and by engaging in readings and various gatherings, turned this high-brow, English enclave into a bilingual, bohemian locus boasting an uncommonly high concentration of poetry. Ron Sutherland dubbed the sleepy village of 812 inhabitants the "Athens of the North."[3] Here is how Ralph Gustafson has described the physical, almost uncanny, proximity within which he and his fellow poets lived and worked: "I'll be at my typewriter and I'll need something to stimulate me, so I'll go to the kitchen, get a drink or make tea, and I look out my kitchen window at 2:00 in the morning, or 2:30, and lo and behold there's a bright light 50 or 20 yards up the hill, and it's Doug Jones in his eyrie, writing too."[4]

In the fall 2001 issue of *ellipse*, marking the end of an era (the editorship was being transferred from Sherbrooke to Fredericton), Jones writes with fondness of the heady times that had led to the creation of *ellipse* over thirty years before:

> Speaking personally, the excitement one felt in the nineteen-sixties with the exploration of the new English-Canadian poetry and then the discovery of the new Quebec poetry is hard for me to recover in

2001. It was a time when F.R. Scott made you feel that the poets, like himself, like P.K. Page and Margaret Avison and Phyllis Webb, like Birney, even like Souster and Dudek and Layton, even like Al Purdy, were recreating the collective culture of our society, and you too could join in. This was the time when F.R. Scott and John Glassco were translating Anne Hébert and Saint-Denys Garneau, and when by the end of the decade, with a lot of other poet-translators, Glassco put together the anthology French-Canadian Poetry in Translation. One began to discover Gaston Miron, Paul-Marie Lapointe, Roland Giguère, Fernand Ouellette, Michelle [sic] Lalonde and other poets who were writing their way out of solitude and *la grande noirceur*. A time when poets and singers and musicians were getting together for all night readings and performances—and touring the provinces like a grand national band.[5]

The stated goal in the inaugural issue of *ellipse* (1969) was "to generate a more intimate commerce between the two languages."[6] Declaring that translation, like charity, "begins at home," the founding editors were boasting the *grassroots* vitality—and virtue—of their scheme. And it was true. In one of those spectacular instances when the personal habitats of individual poets coincide with the literary institution within which they operate, the village, Jones's *home*, as it were, became both the reflection and nexus of the magazine.

Author of twelve books of poetry, translator of scores of contemporary Québec poets, retired professor of literature at the Université de Sherbrooke, D.G. Jones' achievements are lengthy and impressive. He has won the Governor General's Award twice: once in 1977 for his own collection of poetry, *Under the Thunder the Flowers Light up the Earth*, and again in 1993 for his translation of Normand de Bellefeuille's volume of poems, *Categorics: one, two and three*. The perfect symmetry of these awards, one for his own work and one for the translation of another poet's work, bespeaks an ongoing excellence and even-handed, indeed ambidextrous, commitment to both creation and translation. Yet his work has attracted recognition from many other sources: the President's Medal for Poetry at the University of Western Ontario for *The Lampman Poems* (1976), the A.J.M. Smith Award for Poetry at Michigan State University (1977), and the QSPELL A.M. Klein Prize for Poetry for both *Balthazar and Other Poems* (1989) and *The Floating Garden* (1995). In 1978, he was elected Fellow of the Royal Society of Canada. Four years later, in 1982, the University of Guelph conferred an honorary doctorate upon him for his literary achievements. However, a list of these distinctions, although impressive, does not allow a deep understanding of how and why Jones embraced the task of translating Québécois poetry.

Arriving in Québec

A review of his formative years sheds more light on the matter. Douglas Gordon Jones was born on January 1, 1929, in Bancroft, Ontario, a small community in the Canadian Shield in central Ontario, "where his father ran a lumber and pulpwood business."[7] After early schooling in Bancroft, Jones attended the Grove Preparatory College, a private school for boys in Lakefield, Ontario. In 1952, he earned a BA in English from McGill University, in Montréal, and, in 1954, a master's degree in English from Queen's University at Kingston. Subsequent teaching positions took Jones to the Royal Military College in Kingston (1954–55), and the Ontario Agricultural College (1955–61), later to become a part of the University of Guelph. In 1961, the Ontario years ended when he moved to the Québec Eastern Townships to take up a position at Bishop's University in Lennoxville (1961–63).

As E.D. Blodgett points out in a short biographical essay on Jones and his works, it was as an undergraduate at McGill that Jones "first gained recognition as a poet," winning a "number of prizes in creative writing."[8] Through the encouragement of one of his professors, Louis Dudek, he also started to publish his poetry in the small literary magazine *Contact*. Founded by Toronto-based poet Raymond Souster, *Contact* "served as an international crossroad for American, Canadian and European poetry," states Blodgett, but its "American dimensions were perhaps the most fruitful."[9] Dudek, who was "instrumental in shaping the editorial direction of the magazine"[10] had numerous American literary contacts from his years as a doctoral student at Columbia University and professor at City College, New York. Dudek's correspondence with American modernist poet Ezra Pound may well have influenced Jones more directly. At Queen's University, Jones completed a thesis on *The Cantos*, Pound's homage/translation of Homer's *Odyssey*, under the direction of George Whalley. This would prove to be a formative encounter for his future development as both poet and translator, reinforcing his sense of engagement with writing in Canada and stimulating his interest in translation, although the two activities were not yet to come together.

With colleagues from Queen's University and McGill, including Malcolm Ross, editor of the *Queen's Quarterly*, and poet/literary translator Frank Scott, Whalley co-organized an important Canadian Writers' Conference in Kingston in July 1955. Over eighty delegates from across the country were present, including many of the major figures in Canadian writing at the time, such as Adele Wiseman, Miriam Waddington, W.O. Mitchell, Morley Callaghan, Joyce Marshall, Dorothy Livesay, and Earle Birney, to name only a few. As Whalley writes, "when the delegates first arrived there was, of course, much 'knitting of severed friendships up.' But…a wholesome degree of mutual respect established itself."[11] The conference would adopt seven resolutions in aid of the, at the time, fledgling institution of English-Canadian literature. Two of these resolutions "urge all provinces to give an even more prominent place to Canadian literature in the school curricula,…and Canadian colleges and universities [to] include more of this literature in English courses, particularly in freshman survey courses." Other resolutions dealt with issues in publishing—"The Conference believes that to establish a continuing literary tradition in Canada signficant works by Canadians must be kept in print"—or government support for writing through awards to writers and "purchases of new Canadian writing for distribution among its Embassies and Consulates throughout the world."[12]

Jones, who appears in the delegates list as "Douglas Jones, Lake Paudash, Ontario,"[13] could not fail to be caught up in the momentum of the exchanges fostered by the conference through its formal papers, round tables and group discussions. A.J.M. Smith spoke engagingly of the role of poets as "tellers of unpleasant truths, as examiners of hidden guilt, as guardians and innovators of language" and, quoting verse by contemporary poets such as Irving Layton, observed that "modern poetry in Canada has become one of the lively arts."[14] Morley Callaghan evoked the difficulties of being published, and the grim, but nonetheless uplifting life of the writer. There were talks on the Canadian literary scene by representatives of publishers (John Gray of the Macmillan Company of Canada and S.P.S. Kite of Penguin Books, Canada), critics (Ralph Allen, editor of *Maclean's*), and broadcasting (Robert Weaver, program director at CBC). More importantly, at the instigation of Irving Layton, there were also lunchtime poetry readings, and Jones, like several of the other young poets present, read from his unpublished works. Poet Jay Macpherson recounts the "excitement that the readings generated in all of us, at any rate in those who read"; it was an experience that brought "home to us the sense of our community as a lively reacting organism, to be pleased or thwarted or argued with or transfigured," and gave "us something of which most of us stand in continuing need."[15]

As Scott points out, the Canadian Writers' Conference "was not attempting to discuss the problems that face the Canadian author who writes in French. Hence only very brief mention was made of the important question of translation in a bilingual country."[16] Subtly reinforced, perhaps nonetheless, by the conference, the more general notion of the interlinguistic communication of poetry was already a part of Jones's intellectual interests at the time. His choice of Pound's *The Cantos* as a dissertation subject had put him in intimate contact with one of the founding, and probably most controversial, figures in American translation theory.[17] Firmly anchored in his practice as a poet and his reflection on language, Pound's approach to translation evolved through his renderings of Anglo-Saxon and classical verse, and his experiments with reading Chinese characters. Situated "from the vantage point of modernist movements," Pound is seen by contemporary translation scholars, such as Lawrence Venuti, as "priz[ing] experiments with literary form as a way of revitalizing culture."[17] More specifically, observes Edwin Gentzler, "In *The Cantos* Pound's theory of translation is as visible as his theory of art. He thinks not in terms of separable languages, but of a mesh or interweaving of words that bind people regardless of nationalities. The threads of language run back in time, and as one traces them back, variable connections can be made. Peoples are joined by varying continuities of speech."[19]

Jones's thesis on Pound may have stimulated his reflections on the interconnective power of words in different languages, but the particular event that would weave together his own interests as poet, the excitement of writing in Canada at the time, the practice of translation, and his affection for Québécois poetry would come while Jones was still in Guelph, around 1958, in the form of an unexpected invitation. He was asked to attend the "Rencontre des poètes," an artists' retreat held at Morin Heights in the Québec Laurentians. Uncertain even why he was on the list for such an event (he assumed Frank Scott had suggested his name), he was immediately taken up by the energy of the conference atmosphere and the presence of so many well-known artists (he can still recall his pleasure in recognising the late Québec abstract painter, Guido Molinari, among the participants).

This conference ignited his interest in reading Québécois poets. Unilingual at the time, he had to rely on other writers, such as Jacques Godbout and Michèle Lalonde, to fill in the gaps for him in English. Despite his somewhat disconnected status, or perhaps due to it, Jones became keenly motivated to satisfy his curiosity about Québécois poems, which meant labouriously translating them for himself with the aid of dictionaries. A poem he later wrote, "Portrait of Anne Hébert"[20] was inspired by the reading of Hébert's poetry and by her brief appearance at the conference. Another poem, "Les masques de l'âme," he dedicated to Michèle Lalonde.[21]

The second and more decisive challenge came a few years later, in 1963, when he moved from anglophone Bishop's University to francophone Université de Sherbrooke.[22] Encouraged by Ronald Sutherland, who was then head of the English department, to take up the considerable task of building a master's program in Canadian-Québécois comparative literature, he lost no time in exploring the works of the major figures (past and emerging) in the field of French-Canadian poetry. To his dismay, he simultaneously discovered that most of the work of French-Canadian poets, or those who were being referred to more and more regularly as Québécois poets, had not been translated into English. Clearly, the opportunity for hands-on translation practice *sur le terrain* had begun.

Ironically, however, and at his own admission, Jones had done "badly" in French in high school. Motivated by a precocious interest in French verse, he managed to "get through the poetry"; but in his academic career, having been born and raised outside Québec was an impediment, especially in the fluid linguistic intermingling of the Québec Eastern Townships where the two official languages have co-existed for centuries and produced scores of bilingual residents. In this sense, one might say that Jones was and is something of an underdog, as his oral communication skills in his second language never did catch up with his deep affinity for and understanding of the written word.

The Founding of *ellipse*

The idea for *ellipse* had first come to Jones when his colleague, John Glassco, was preparing an anthology of French-Canadian poets for Oxford University Press. Although Jones did not work on the anthology himself, the synergy and enthusiasm generated by the project sparked the idea for the magazine and persuaded Jones that "this sort of work should be done continuously"; but it took a blunt challenge on the part of his wife at the time, Sheila Fischman, for him to act on the idea. Shortly thereafter, Jones elicited the help of his colleague and fellow poet at the Université de Sherbrooke, Joseph Bonenfant, who became the editor on the French side while Jones looked after the English texts. The first issue offered up a medley of writers: five poets from French Canada and five from English Canada. In subsequent issues, the format was altered to fit a binary approach that would pair together two writers, one from English Canada and one from French Canada, with original versions imprinted *vis-à-vis* the translations so that it was possible to see how the translator had recreated the new poem.

The choice of title can be traced back to a short piece by the French poet Eugène Guillevic (translated for *ellipse* by Teo Savory), which was placed in a prominent position immediately preceding the editorial pages. Thus, the founding editors chose, as an early emblem of the *ellipse* project, the reciprocal gaze of two separate centres simultaneously facing off and facing up to the tension that informs their distinctive curve. In this cultural geometry of poetry, it was the "poet-translators" (the designation is borrowed from Jones) who surveyed the pressure points from within *and without*, thereby managing the uneasy equilibrium that saves the structure from collapse: "With that pressure / From a crude exterior / On each of your points" / "Avec cette pression / En chacun de tes points / D'un extérieur informe."[23]

All the poet-translators of *ellipse* were convinced of the necessity of initiating a creative interface between poets and readers of Québec and English Canada; nevertheless, each poet espoused a slightly different approach. F.R. Scott was the impetus behind many of the introductions. Not only had he introduced Jones to the network of Quebec poets through the conference in Laurentians, but it was also thanks to him that Glassco had begun reading and translating the works of Saint-Denys Garneau. Scott was a dynamic and influential figure at the time, who favoured the strategy of *bonne entente*, a political and cultural *rapprochement* facilitated by mutual translation.

However, by the time *ellipse* was founded, in 1969, the odds in favour of a lasting and wide-scale *rapprochement* seem to have diminished. In its stead grew the patient but intense, one-on-one type of dialogue that the fledgling magazine was promoting. As Jones wrote in the foreword to one of the early issues of the magazine, "ironically, Canada has produced relatively few translators. But translation is now in the wind. One way or another, there will be a dialogue between Quebec and English-speaking North America."[24] The assertion *one way or another* hangs mysteriously between the phrases, certainly as an expression of the determination driving the editorial team, but also more generally as a type of caution. Dialogue, it would seem, is as subversive as spring water; it slips around obstacles and trickles along whatever route is open to it, and now translation was being called upon to open paths that politics would not or could not clear.

Teamwork

Given the collective beginnings of *ellipse* and Jones's role as a social stimulus for art and translation, it is impossible to sketch a portrait of Jones without including his fellow poet-translators. He gave form and future to a local groundswell. According to Philip Lanthier, *ellipse* grew out of a "legendary" poetry reading in August 1968, held at a pottery site owned and operated by Mildred Beaudin. The reading featured, among others, A.J.M Smith, F.R. Scott, D.G. Jones, and francophone poets Gérald Godin, Roland Giguère, and singer Pauline Julien.[25] That is not to say, however, that no tensions surfaced that night. The presentations were made in English only, a *faux pas* that offended Godin and Julien, and that organizers were careful to avoid in subsequent readings.

With the help of Joseph Bonefant and Sheila Fischman, a personal donation from J.G. McConnell (the owner of the *Montreal Star*), and grants from the Ministère des Affaires culturelles du Québec and the Arts Council of Ontario, *ellipse* survived the fragile nascent stage before the review was eligible to receive regular support from the Canada Council. Richard Giguère,[26] then a graduate student at the Université de Sherbrooke, brought with him his knowledge of Canadian poetry and his enthusiasm for contemporary Quebec poetry. Larry Shouldice, Diane Ally, and Patricia Godbout all did stints over the years as anglophone or francophone editors. At the same time, a large number of translators were recruited from across the country and across the ocean, from Yves Merzisen in Kamloops, BC, to C.R.P. May in Birmingham, England. With his fondness for anecdotes, Jones remembers "spending one memorable evening patching together pieces of *[e]llipse* proofs with scotch tape."[27]

Jones also participated in the Seventh Moon poetry readings along with his present wife, Monique Baril (known professionally as Monique Grandmangin); a colleague, Avrum Malus; and Malus's wife Monique Martin. The "earlier readings," Jones recalls, "represented mainly English-Canadian poets of the region and Montréal, but the late readings had a format more parallel to that of *ellipse*, one or two English-language poets, and one or two French-language poets." An educator and translator in her own right, Grandmangin translated some of Jones's poetry. Together with Ronald Sutherland, she also co-edited a collection of poetry by Gustafson, Jones, Roland Giguère, and Gaston Miron, which was published in the United States.[28] Grandmangin joined the *ellipse* team with the fourth issue. Many years later, in 1993 with the forty-ninth issue, she would become the review's francophone editor.

Grounds for Translation

"Why do we translate Quebec poetry?" asks Jones in his 1977 article "Grounds for Translation." At first, he advances a direct answer. It is "an immediate response" to French Canada's "cry to be heard." This quest for recognition, it should be noted, occurred in the context of the Quiet Revolution, a time of unprecedented literary activity and political change in Québec. Québec writers were producing innovative and provocative work that demanded an audience and caught the eye of some poets in English Canada. "And who is going to listen," Jones asks, " if English-Canadians do not, the people who have shared the same geography, the same history, who have been 'host' and 'hostis,' friend and enemy, for over two centuries?"[29] However, as Jones develops the strands of his argument, the answer to "why do we translate Quebec poetry" becomes more complex. As the focus shifts from the reciprocal shoring up of collective identities to the metaphysical metaphor of the sacrificial host, the translator's craft is recast in the light of sacred communion.

Quoting a hypothesis put forward by J. Hillis Miller,[30] whereby the critic is regarded as "host" in the double etymological sense of the term, as both "guest," or as "enemy," from the Latin *hostis*, Jones combines this concept with George Steiner's model of "hermeneutic motion." Defined by Steiner as the "act of elicitation and appropriative transfer of meaning,"[31] hermeneutic motion, as Jones applies the notion to the interplay between poet and translator, follows a sequence of "trust, invasion, incorporation, and restitution."[32] Although the process begins specifically with the betrayal of trust, successful translation radically transcends the well-worn axiom *traduttore traditore*. At the conclusion of the transfer of meaning, the separation of betrayal appears as a crucial, but temporary step, in a process based on mutual giving. Thus, in Jones' rereading and reworking of these two main theories, successful translation constitutes a literary form of fusion which bears a certain resemblance to the mystery of transubstantiation: "in such an act of translation, the original poet and his poem is the host, who is then eaten and digested, consumed and incorporated in the new body of the translation, of the translator, who now becomes the host within whom the original lives on, transformed." As Jones proclaimed earlier in the same article, citing Dennis Lee's fascination and identification in "Civil Elegies" with Saint-Denys Garneau,"Garneau lives on in Lee."[33]

Yet the exuberance for *le fusionnel* does not stop there. A secondary communion motif, this time one of sexual intercourse, is also woven into the fabric of this complex exposition: "Translation, we might say, is like sexual intercourse: it may be an expense of spirit in a waste of shame, or it may be a kind of death and resurrection into a new and larger life. In this more profound sense, neither a translation nor a poem aims at 'efficient communication' so much as at effective communion."[34] Although it is hard to know whether this declaration holds a hint of playful irony or not—if so, the irony was lost on R. Hoffpauir, who in his rebuttal to Jones's article dismissed the idea as "rather silly."[35] It is clear that such a treatment, in seeking to elevate the act of translation into a realm that is both sacred and intimate, constitutes a radical, even subversive, departure from the view of translation as an objective, mainly intellectual activity of looking for purely linguistic equivalents.

What this means in more concrete terms is that Jones, going back to Pound's modernist view, has always demonstrated his appreciation of translation as a means of connection, exchange, nourishment, and growth. It may be that translation affords a type of complicity and inspiration that many writers consciously or unconsciously crave. Certainly, Jones is a social translator; in his remembrance of past benchmarks, he often highlights the conferences and social gatherings he has attended as privileged moments that brought translators and poets together in an extraordinary celebration of the written and spoken word. When he talks of translation, he draws out of his memory anecdotes, producing them, one at a time, like semi-precious stones.

In a Strange and Wintery Land

One such story goes back to the early 1970s when Jones participated in a poetry reading in Pittsburgh, Pennsylvania, with Gaston Miron and Paul-Marie Lapointe. By that time, Jones was more or less the official translator of the two poets' work. At the event, they alternated between readings of translations by Jones and of the originals in French by Miron and Lapointe. How exactly it came to be that the three of them converged in Pittsburgh remains something of a mystery, but by all accounts, Naïm Kattan, then with the Canada Council, was instrumental in promoting the threesome within the United States.[36] This encounter ostensibly resulted in Samuel Hazo, director of the International Poetry Forum, overseeing the 1976 publication in the Pitt poetry series of *The Terror of the Snows*, a selection of Paul-Marie Lapointe's poems gathered in book form and translated by Jones. In his foreword, Hazo thanks Kattan, the Canada Council, and James Hosey of the United States Steel Foundation, which funded the publication.

Ten years later, *The March to Love*, a selection of poetry by Gaston Miron in translation, was also printed in Pennsylvania under the continued guidance of Hazo; however, this second book devoted to French-Canadian poetry was featured in the Byblos series. Whereas the translation of Lapointe's poetry was funded by the Steel Foundation, Miron's anthology in translation was made possible by funding from Michael D. Cheteyan II, in tribute to Alex Manoogian, the life president of the Armenian General Benevolent Union (AGBU).[37] One may wonder how Lapointe, via Jones, came to be promoted by the United States Steel Foundation; just as puzzling is how Miron, via Jones, came to be supported, albeit obliquely, by the Armenian General Benevolent Union. These examples of financial endorsement from outside are, from a contemporary perspective, a marvel in fundraising ingenuity, but in those years of political change and artistic *audace*, it seems that just about anything was possible and support could come from anywhere. These books also testify to the importance of personal contacts between Montréal and American intellectuals at the time. Like Louis Dudek, Ralph Gustafson, one of Jones's fellow Eastern Township poets, had extensive American connections, having spent the postwar years until 1963 in New York as a freelance writer and music critic. It is also worth noting that the initial impetus for the Canadian Writers' Conference in Kingston, for which Scott obtained a generous grant from the Rockefeller Foundation, came from an invitation F.R. Scott, A.J.M. Smith and A.M. Klein had received to attend the Poetry Conference at Harvard.[28]

Jones's appreciation of art's capacity to erase the boundaries between individuals and trigger a collective wave of identification and exhilaration is contagious. In "Grounds for Translation," he recounts the Lapointe/Miron/Jones literary reading in terms that are reminiscent of Nietszche's Dionysian æsthetic:

> I've seen an American reviewer, a Prof. of Humanities, dismiss Paul-Marie Lapointe's poetry, or my translations, with an irritated reference to the overly lush or fetid eroticism of two lines.
>
> On the other hand, as first the translator and then the poets read their work, I've seen an audience in Pittsburgh come alive to Paul-Marie Lapointe and Gaston Miron, so that for a few hours at least Lapointe and Miron and, indeed, Quebec existed on the banks of the Monangahela.[39]

What Jones does not write in *ellipse*, however, is how Miron stole the show; Jones recounts, "By the end, Gaston Miron took out his new harmonica and started playing French-Canadian folk songs." So thrilled by the reception of his work was Miron that he later asked Jones, "Do you think I could get a Guggenheim?" The clamour for a proper book of translation of Miron's poetry began that very evening, probably somewhere between the readings of translations and the folk music. It is a striking illustration of how quickly words that at one time existed outside one's frame of reference can strike up familiarity if the conditions are right, and a literary reading on the banks of the Monangahela acquire the atmosphere of a friendly get-together beside the Massawippi.

Translating the Whole Poem

The question of a translator's "most successful" translation is a vexed one. Although Jones is well known for his work on Miron, Lapointe, and de Bellefeuille, in terms of actual printings and reprintings, it is his translation of Michèle Lalonde's hugely popular poem "Speak White" that has been the most lucrative. Says Jones with a laugh, "it has made more bottles of scotch than any other poem." Of course, monetary reward, since translation is usually paid by the word, is not a major consideration when it comes to the translation of poetry: "It is nice to get some recognition, but you don't need public recognition to feel you are doing okay," states Jones. "There is satisfaction in having something to start with and trying to make it as good in your own language as it is in the original."

After forty years of writing poetry and translating other people's poems, Jones's approach to translation remains refreshingly straightforward. The principal task is to translate the whole poem: "I approach a translation as I would a poem. I work on both the same way. There are those who don't and it tends to be prosaic." For Jones, it is not necessary to be literally faithful to the original; indeed, he eschews "word for word" translation, although he admits he tries to stay fairly close to the tone of the original. If it is lyrical or rhetorical, the translation should have a lyrical or rhetorical punch, "so that it floats, it works, it doesn't sink."

Still, Jones is a cunning wordsmith, and he knows that in translation, as in poetry, there are no draftsman's charts for building a translation that "floats." Nor do his writings on the subject provide any. In fact, his 1988 article on translation, "Text and Context: Some Reflections on Translation," published in *Canadian Literature*, is unapologetically circular: to translate a poem one must first discover its meaning and then translate it into one's own language. However, in certain ways, this is an impossible task. Meaning is a tricky business given that it derives largely from the way culturally embedded semiotic codes are confirmed, nuanced, or subverted. It is particularly elusive if one stands outside the edge of cultural codes—which, to a lesser or greater degree, is almost always the position of the translator with respect to the original text—and it is always immediately altered by the choice of vocabulary in the translated text, however straightforward the translation process may appear to be.

Eventually and thankfully, Jones offers a way out of this conundrum by posing a challenge. He states that writing, be it creative writing or translating, is naturally and to a good extent intuitive and that not even the authors are fully conscious of the precise relationships that exist between their texts and the inherited code: "It is often assumed that when we are dealing with a poem or a translation we are dealing with packaged meanings. Rather we're dealing with meaningful packets of print or language, whose implications are always to some degree indeterminate. It is not a *truth* to be passed on truthfully. That may relieve some of the pressure on translators. It also may allow all kinds of approaches. Like the poem, it may be approached as a complex play, as political gesture, as relief from pain, even the pain of boredom."[40]

Outside the Ordinary

It is precisely this multiple, playful—critics might even say anarchic—vision of translation as interpretation that *ellipse* chose to illustrate in its remarkable fiftieth issue. The initial idea was to invite "fifty translators to translate two poems, twenty-five from French to English and twenty-five from English to French, and to comment on their translations."[41] The fact that the translators had to work with fairly difficult pieces—"Étrange capture" by Anne Hébert and "The Music" by Gwendolyn MacEwen—may account for the attrition; the actual number of printed variations dropped from fifty to forty-two. Yet the exact number of translators is of little consequence. The results are most important, and they are fascinating. They also echo Jones's personal approach, which has always embraced multiples of *other* approaches.

Although Jones rejects all formulaic and prescriptive approaches to translation, against the backdrop of other translators' work, certain of his strategic choices do inevitably stand out. For example Hébert writes,

> Du côté du pôle arctique
> On a remué le champ de neige
> À perte de vue désirant prendre au piège le soleil.

Jones's translation departs from the verb tense of the original by repeatedly choosing the present continuous form instead of the simple past or even the simple present:

> The North Pole, as far as the eye can see
> **they're shaking** up the snow
> **hoping** to catch the sun.[42]

Combined with the more direct choice of "shake" for "remuer" (compared to "plough" or "disrupt"), the effect captures the personal, active dimension of Hébert's present participle, "désirant," in contrast to the following rendition by Barbara Belyea:

> As far as the eye could see
> the polar snowfield **was ploughed** clear
> in order to trap the sun.

Philip Stratford offers yet another version:

> Up by the Arctic pole
> **they disrupted** the field of snow
> As far as the eye could reach trying to trap the sun.[43]

In the first line of the next stanza, it is the choice of the present perfect as verb tense used by Jones that stands in direct contrast to the passive or simple past used in other translations. The text reads as follows in the original: "On a tendu des filets de givre." Belyea opts for "Nets of frost **were laid down**" and Stratford for "**They spread out** nets of frost," while Jones writes, "**They've strung out** thin lines of frost."[44] The consistent choice of a vigorous present ("they're shaking") and present perfect ("they've strung"), along with the addition of the adjective "thin" for visual effect, create an immediacy that triggers a mood of subtle urgency. These are just two ways that Jones cleverly infuses his interpretation of "Strange Catch" with a hunterly sense of the imminent. In prose, it would probably be called suspense.

The Curve of Rhythms

To fully appreciate the temporal and lyrical tautness of Jones's work, however, one must explore a wider selection of his prodigious array of translations. The books of poetry by Paul-Marie Lapointe, Gaston Miron, and Normand de Bellefeuille in translation present an obvious corpus. Lapointe's *The Terror of the Snows* was Jones's first book of poetry in translation. It is a selection of Lapointe's poetry culled from four separate books: *The Virgin Burned* (*Le Vierge incendié*), *Choice of Poems* (*Choix de poèmes: Arbres*), *For All Souls* (*Pour les âmes*), and *The Canvas of Love and Other Poems* (*Tableaux de l'amoureuse*) in translation. In 1985, the selection was revised, enlarged, and published under the title *The Fifth Season*.

A comparison of Lapointe's "Fragile journée de Mica" with "Day Now Frail as Mica" reveals how Jones uses monosyllabic nouns at the end of lines for percussive effect. Under his pen, "fragile journée de mica où pourrissent les flaques / anémones d'un hiver soleil désirable" becomes "day now frail as mica when the puddles rot / a winter's anemones desirable sun."[45] Again, a tightening effect is achieved, although the hard monosyllabics in English contrast with the looser, more luxuriant syntax in the original. Nonetheless, Jones's claim to be more of a free translator is misleading. While he may tend to be less literal than, say, F.R. Scott,[46] there is without a doubt an unmistakable internal rigour to Jones's work. Throughout "Day Now Frail as Mica," he scrupulously adheres to what he calls, in describing Lepanto's aesthetic, the "curve" of rhythms.[47] Monosyllabic words—"rot," "sun," "chips," "fish," "heart," "rope," "dry," "out"—dot strategic parts of the poem like points within a curve. When the poem is viewed as a whole, it becomes clear that these words are strung together to create a tension strong enough to enable the poem to hold its own internal, and competing, syncopation, in keeping with the poetic intensity of the original.

Jones uses this strategy to similar effect in "Short Straws," his translation of Lapointe's poem "Courtes pailles." In French, the syntax mirrors the uneven tides of the poem's music, alternating between long tumbling lines and abrupt crashes of words. To preserve the curve of rhythms, Jones occasionally alters the sequence of the lines, as in segment 13 of "Short Straws":

> on ne soutient pas ce rythme
> cette immanence de la terreur
> où les poussins picorent[48]

In Jones's translation, this passage becomes

> the chicks peck about in the dirt
> this rhythm cannot be sustained
> imminent terror.[49]

Jones's translation of de Bellefeuille's poem "Désencombrer le monde entier," in *Catégoriques*, offers another illustration of his transformative strategies. In "Clearing Up the Entire World," the tightening effect characteristic of his translations is achieved, ironically, through a strategy of syntactic extension, in particular through the regular use of phrasal (two- and three-word) verbs. "Désencombrer" is simply rendered by "Clearing up." The final preposition snaps the meaning into place. But this is not all: by the time the poem is in full swing, the verb "désencombrer" ends up supplying so much semantic and syntactic capital that the phrase "chaque image **désencombre**"[50] yields a good half-dozen punchy words in English: "every image **does its bit to clear up**."[51]

This cheeky little riff should come as little surprise given Jones's assessment of de Bellefeuille as a type of modern musician—as de Bellefeuille has said himself, he "makes a racket with words."⁵² Jones adds to this assertion by observing that the poet makes "the racket consort with the song"; and so, we might add, does Jones. In his presentation of de Bellefeuille in *ellipse*, Jones makes it clear that the poet's attention to music is a central consideration in the double context of reading and interpreting (to be understood in the fullest, musical sense of the French word *interpréter*) his work: "His *Categorics, one, two, and three* is thematically organized around music—and dance, and painting. One is impressed by the rhythms of the sentences, by the repetitions of the sentences that, however strange in themselves or in the sequences, sweep the reader along as in a dance—as in music."⁵³ Alongside considerations of rhythm and tension, Jones's translations have deceptive semantic depth, as the translation of the title poem, "Categorics" ("Catégoriques") ably demonstrates. Here are the first two paragraphs of de Bellefeuille's text:

> Le prédicat. La famille. La viande parfois.
> Mais il y en a aussi de voix, de gestes, de rythmes dont on se dispute la qualité ou de signes alors, sans plus, dont le chiffre secret varie, indiscernable presque à leurs trois ombres emmêlées. Aristote. Kant. Nietzsche. Le concept. La boucherie. La phrase parfois; l'idéologie, mais sans la pesanteur.

Jones renders the same passage as follows:

> The predicate. The family. Sometimes the shambles.
> But there is also the question of voice, the gestures, the rhythms, whose precise implications we argue, or of signs, to put it simply, whose secret number is a matter of dispute, even—never mind the Gnostics—in the three mixed shades. Aristotle, Kant, Nietzsche. The concept. The shambles. Sometimes the whole sentence: ideology, but without much weight.⁵⁴

Jones has cleverly used his knowledge of language to move from meat ("la viande") to the less well-known English word "shambles," used here, as Jones says, in its meaning as "a place where they cut up meat," or slaughterhouse. The word is a technical gem because it captures and amplifies, on a deep level, the image of the "boucherie" that appears a few lines later in the poem. It is an elegant lesson about the layers of etymology in words, and Jones's ingenious manipulation of vocabulary.

Being Inside *and* Outside

The experience of reading de Bellefeuille through Jones's translations is best captured by Fred Wah: "What next, as we stand in the whoosh of sentence traffic, wait for the sign to change, the word-rumble to clear. *Categorics* is incisive in its displacement of syntax, in its cunning alterations of our anticipation for clarity and conclusion. Normand de Bellefeuille studies the ways in which language layers our world, our bodies, our desires. Sometimes we stand there with Doug Jones, the translator, looking both ways before crossing into the next world."[55] Standing on the outside is always disconcerting, but standing on the outside with a veteran poet like Jones guiding us makes the crossing to the inside of the other worth every second of bewilderment. There is a secret fearlessness in these translations as the original texts are very demanding, especially the ones in *Catégoriques*, but Jones is a seasoned craftsman, and the greater the challenge, the richer the experience. "'Impossible'; that was one of the adjectives I first noted in Quebec," he recalls. People would say that translations of poetry are *impossible* and that you should always read things in the original." Then he sums up his philosophy with grand simplicity by declaring, "It doesn't matter if people think it's impossible or not, you do it and it can be quite extraordinary."

Indeed, from the very beginning of his career Jones has sought out challenges and chosen to defy conventional opinions. Significantly, "The March to Love," his rendering of Gaston Miron's powerful lyrical poem "La marche à l'amour," appeared in the autumn 1970 issue of *ellipse*, the same month the author of *L'homme rapaillé* and fervent partisan of Québec's independence had been jailed for ten days under the War Measures Act. In a touching article included in the same issue, entitled "Gaston Miron: A Testimony," Jones writes with modesty, measure, and passion: "I don't know the whole of Gaston Miron's work. I don't even know his language very well. But I do know that what he has done as a poet and as an animator of poetry is one of the most important things a man can do, at any time but especially at this time. That is to recognize and express what he is, and also, what he may be. It is to free man from the prison of the unconscious, and from the possible prison of his own image of himself."[56]

As translator, Jones is conscious of the complexity of Miron's writing, with its "strange rhetoric, difficult enough to translate"; even the poems that affirm "the world of Eros, builder of cities, a celebration of the images of desire," contain solemn "declarations of love with the intentional force of declarations of war,"[57] as the following excerpt from *La Marche à l'amour* so aptly illustrates:

> dans les giboulées d'étoiles de mon ciel
> l'éclair s'épanouit dans ma chair
> je passe les poings durs au vent
> j'ai un coeur de mille chevaux-vapeur
> j'ai un coeur comme la flamme d'une chandelle
> toi tu as la tête d'abîme douce n'est-ce pas
> la nuit de saule dans tes cheveux
> un visage enneigé de hasards et de fruits
> un regard entretenu de sources cachées
> et mille chants d'insectes dans tes veines
> et mille pluies de pétales dans tes caresses[58]

Moving from outside to inside, Jones adjusts vocabulary and rhythm to recapture Miron's solemn sensuality:

> In sudden showers, stars bursting from my sky
> the lightning streams through my flesh
> and I go on fists clenched in the wind
> a thousand horsepower beating in my heart
> and in my heart a candle's flame
> and you, your head holds all the mystery of a sweet abyss
> is that not so
> your hair the night of willow trees
> your face is dusted with the snows
> and fruits of fortune, and your gaze
> is held still mistress to the hidden springs
> and in your veins a thousand insects sing
> and in your manifold caress a thousand petals rain[59]

The diction is for the most part sparce, although occasionally words, such as "Sudden showers" and the participle "bursting" for the forceful "giboulée," are added to preserve the clarity of the image. "Streams" is chosen to capture some of the ripening abundance of "s'épanouit." There is just a hint of rhetorical flair in the "mystery of a sweet abyss" and again in "still mistress to the hidden springs." Monosyllabic nouns dot the ends of lines in the English like incantatory beats, keeping the powerful intensity of the original poem's final two lines. As a fellow poet, Jones has set himself the task of translating the whole poem: putting his own poetic skills in the balance to assert with Miron "the dignity and the almost faceless vitality of the human being."[60]

As E.D. Blodgett observes, Jones's own poetry "cannot be 'placed,'" although "configurations of place seek each other everywhere in his work."[61] He has demonstrated an abiding interest in the mythopoeic dimensions of poetry, both in *Butterfly on Rock*, which explores an impressive range of verse by fellow Canadian poets, and in his own poetry. "Jones has tended to see his larger, more embracing forms in mythological terms," writes George Woodcock, "although he has been saved from the amorphous vagueness of much mythopoeic poetry...by an aesthetic precision, an economy of language, and a neo-imagist sharpness of outline."[62] Blodgett himself considers that the "distinctive quality of Jones' poetry...is what Phyllis Webb calls its peculiar 'syllabic grace.'"[63]

Certainly, Jones's sense of precision, economy, and rhythm has provided effective strategies in his translations. More tellingly, Jones has also acknowledged the importance, for his writing, of the visual world and painting, in a way that strangely recalls his approach to translation:

> One thing about paintings generally: they are other landscapes. One can go outside oneself and into another world in terms of painting, rather than in terms of real life...I in a sense inhabit landscapes in paintings as we all real ones [*sic*]. A painter like Ni Tsan, a Chinese painter, is very much a landscape poet—I mean, painter....As I was looking out my window in North Hatley in the middle of winter, I was looking at the real landscape, and also, in a sense, at Ni Tsan's landscape simultaneously. The two became one, in a measure. This was a way to reorganise my landscape, and as well, to make a rather heavy poem, I suppose, rather witty and light.[64]

This same ability to be both outside and inside, to reorganize his own landscape through an identification with the trees of the other, surfaces as well in Jones's remarks on his reading of Gaston Miron: "Gaston Miron has articulated a world, a land where the Québécois can settle in with his own language," Jones writes in his Testimony. He "has installed in his body not an iron cross but a green spruce." Using vocabulary reminiscent of the steps of trust, invasion, incorporation, and restitution of his vision of translation, Jones sees Miron's writing as at once an "act of demolition—spiritual, psychological, mythological," a "recognition of breakdown" that "makes possible a breakthrough, a new way of proceeding which is 'la marche à l'amour.'" Jones continues, "Naturally, as an Anglophone, born in a small town in Ontario with its own rocky hillsides, I hope that the horizons of this new development will not stop at the borders of Québec." Challenging the "all too rigid structures that imprison us within too narrow horizons, that twist us and set us against one another,"[65] the poet/translator concludes: "But even if language is one of the most dangerous gifts that has been given to man (and that's obvious, in several senses) making poems is one of the most innocent and most human of occupations. And Gaston Miron has been making poems for a long time. Because he is first and foremost a poet."[66] The same can be said of D.G. Jones himself, translator inside and outside, but *avant tout* poet.

NOTES

1 George Bowering, "Coming Home to the World," *Canadian Literature*, no. 65 (summer 1975): 7–8.
2 Interview with the author, North Hatley, Jan. 4, 2004. Unless otherwise indicated, all quotations of remarks by D.G. Jones refer to this interview.
3 Ron Sutherland, "The Athens of the North," in *Les Cantons de l'Est: Aspects géographiques, politiques, socio-économiques et culturels*, ed. Jean-Marie Dubois (Sherbrooke: Éditions de l'Université de Sherbrooke, 1989), p. 266. Quoted by Philip Lanthier in "English Poetry in the Eastern Townships," p. 17.
4 Quoted by David Homel, "Green, Wonderful Things," *Books in Canada*, Jan. 1984, p. 7. This cover article on the writers of North Hatley gives an excellent description of the milieu from the 1970s to the early 1980s. The author thanks Prof. Stephen Henighan of the University of Guleph for this research tip.
5 D.G. Jones, foreword, *ellipse*, no. 66 (fall 2001): 6–7.
6 D.G. Jones, editorial in *ellipse*, no. 1 (1969): 5.
7 E.D. Blodgett, *D.G. Jones and His Works* (Toronto: ECW Press, 1984), p. 1.
8 Blodgett, *D.G. Jones and His Works*, p. 2.
9 Blodgett, *D.G. Jones and His Works*, p. 3.
10 Frank Davey, "Dudek, Louis," p. 340.
11 George Whalley, preface to *Writing in Canada: Proceedings of the Canadian Writers' Conference Held at Queen's University July 1955*, ed. G. Whalley (Toronto: Macmillan, 1956), p. ix.
12 F.R. Scott, introduction to *Writing in Canada*, ed. George Whalley, pp. 8, 9.
13 Whalley, ed., *Writing in Canada*, p. 145.
14 A.J.M. Smith, "Poet," *Writing in Canada*, ed. G. Whalley, p. 22.
15 Jay Macpherson, "Report on Poetry Readings," *Writing in Canada*, ed. G. Whalley, p. 138.
16 Scott, introduction to *Writing in Canada*, p. 10.
17 As Susan Bassnett points out, Pound's *Homage to Sextus Propertius*, which the American poet conceived as a homage (as opposed to a translation), generated "savage attacks" from critics who expected a literal equivalence. Susan Bassnett, *Translation Studies* (London and New York: Routledge, 2002), p. 85; see also pp. 95–97, 98–101.
18 Lawrence Venuti "1900s-1930s," in *The Translation Studies Reader*, ed. L. Venuti (London and New York: Routledge, 2000), p. 11.
19 Edwin Gentzler, *Contemporary Translation Theories* (London and New York: Routledge, 1993), p. 23.
20 D.G. Jones, *The Sun Is Axeman* (Toronto: University of Toronto Press, 1961), p. 3.

21 D.G. Jones, "Tracing *Ellipse*," *ellipse*, no. 40 (1988): 19.
22 E.D. Blodgett tells an amusing anecdote about Jones running afoul of the local medical school brass: "His appointment at Bishop's was of rather short duration, and its termination may be attributed to another unhappy speech, this time to a group of nurses in neighbouring Sherbrooke, after which he was accused by doctors as being a hippy and a communist masquerading in a Sunday suit." Blodgett, *D.G. Jones and His Works*, p. 1.
23 Guillevic, "Ellipse," trans. Teo Savory, *ellipse*, no. 1 (fall/automne 1969): 3. The original poem first appeared in *Les Euclidiennes* (Paris: Gallimard, 1967). The translation originally appeared as "Ellipse," trans. Teo Savory, in *Guillevic* (Santa Barbara: Unicorn Press, 1968).
24 D.G.Jones, foreword, *ellipse*, no. 1 (fall/automne 1969): 5.
25 The author owes a debt of gratitude to Richard Giguère for his generous help with the research of this article. Unless otherwise indicated, all subsequent references to Richard Giguère are from an interview of Richard Giguère by the author, Sherbrooke, Dec. 4, 2003.
26 Philip Lanthier, "English Poetry in the Eastern Townships," in *Anthologie de la poésie des Cantons de l'Est au vingtième siècle / Anthology of Twentieth-Century Poetry of the Eastern Townships*, ed. R. Giguère, P. Lanthier, and André Marquist (Montréal: Les Éditions Triptyque and Véhicule Press, 1999), pp. 18–19.
27 D.G. Jones, "Tracing *Ellipse*," p. 20.
28 Monique Grandmangin and Ronald Sutherland, eds., *Dentelle/Indented: Ralph Gustafson, Roland Giguère, Gaston Miron, D.G. Jones*, trans. M. Grandmangin and R. Sutherland (Colorado Springs: Press at Colorado College, 1982). See also *ellipse*, no. 13, for a variety of single poems by Jones translated by Grandmangin, as well as *ellipse*, no. 43 for her translation of Jones's essay on Robyn Sarah. D.G. Jones, "D'entretien domestique et de musique: La poésie de Robyn Sarah," trans. M. Grandmangin, *ellipse*, no. 43 (1990): 53–63.
29 D.G. Jones, "Grounds for Translation," *ellipse*, no. 21 (1977): 78.
30 J. Hillis Miller, "The Critic as Host," *Critical Inquiry* 3, no. 3 (spring 1977): 447; quoted by Jones, "Grounds for Translation," p. 70.
31 George Steiner, *After Babel: Aspects of Language and Translation* (New York: Oxford, 1975), p. 296. See also chapter 5 "The Hermeneutic Motion."
32 Jones, "Grounds for Translation," p. 82.
33 Jones, "Grounds for Translation," pp. 84, 82.
34 Jones, "Grounds for Translation," p. 84.
35 Richard Hoffpauir, "A Response to D.G. Jones's 'Grounds for Translation,'" *ellipse*, no. 22 (1978): 112.
36 Over thirty years later, Pittsburgh is still an epicentre of Québec culture in the United States. As the site of Festival Québec, presented by the Pittsburgh Cultural Trust, the city planned a wide array of events featuring Québécois arts, music, theatre, cinema, and poetry for the spring of 2004.
37 Cf. the dedication in Gaston Miron, *The March to Love*, ed. D.G. Jones. Trans. D.G. Jones, Marc Plourde, Louis Simpson, Brenda Fleet, John Glassco, and Dennis Egan. N.p.: International Poetry Forum, Byblos Editions, 1986.

38 Whalley, ed., *Writing in Canada*, p. vii.
39 Jones, "Grounds for Translation," p. 78.
40 Jones, "Text and Context: Some Reflections on Translation," *Canadian Literature*, no. 117 (summer 1988): 10.
41 D.G. Jones, foreword to *ellipse*, no. 50 (1993): 6.
42 Anne Hébert, "Étrange capture," *ellipse*, no. 50 (1993): 10; Anne Hébert, "Strange Catch," trans. D. G. Jones, *ellipse*, no. 50 (1993): 34. Emphasis mine.
43 Anne Hébert, "Strange Arrest," trans. Barbara Belyea, *ellipse*, no. 50 (1993): 12; Anne Hébert, "Strange Capture," trans. Philip Stratford, *ellipse*, no. 50 (1993): 56. Emphasis mine.
44 Anne Hébert, "Étrange capture," p. 10; Anne Hébert, "Strange Arrest," trans. Barbara Belyea, p. 12; Anne Hébert, "Strange Capture," trans. Philip Stratford, p. 56; Anne Hébert, "Strange Catch," trans. D. G. Jones, p. 34. Emphasis mine.
45 Paul-Marie Lapointe, *Pour les âmes* (Montréal: L'Hexagone, 1964), p. 26; Paul-Marie Lapointe, *The Terror of the Snows: Selected Poems by Paul-Marie Lapointe*, trans. D.G. Jones, (n.p.: University of Pittsburgh Press, 1976), p. 46.
46 As Richard Giguère states, "Scott tenait à une fidélité au texte de départ." (Scott was concerned with being faithful to the original text). Jones also exposes this trait in his written portrait of Scott as translator: "Certainly Scott's translations, besides being accurate and English, by which I mean free of the peculiar wow in idiom and in sense that betrays the influence of another language, retain the sharpness, the syntactic directness, and the concrete eloquence of the originals." D.G. Jones, "F.R. Scott as Translator," in *On F.R. Scott: Essays on His Contributions to Law, Literature and Politics*, ed. S. Djwa and R. St. J. Macdonald (Montréal and Kingston: McGill-Queen's University Press, 1983), p.162.
47 D.G. Jones, foreword to *The Terror of the Snows*, by Paul-Marie Lapointe, p. xv.
48 Paul-Marie Lapointe, "Courtes pailles," in *Pour les âmes*, pp. 32–49;
49 Paul-Marie Lapointe, "Short Straws," trans. D.G. Jones, in *The Terror of the Snows*, pp. 49–54.
50 Normand de Bellefeuille, *Catégoriques un, deux et trois* (Trois-Rivières: Écrits des Forges, 1986), p. 57. Emphasis mine.
51 Normand de Bellefeuille, *Categorics One, Two and Three*, trans. D.G. Jones (Toronto: Coach House Press, 1992), p. 55. Emphasis mine.
52 "C'est comme *composer*/du bruit" writes de Bellefeuille in "La fille qui était liège (Douleur: dansée)." Normand de Bellefeuille, *La Marche de l'aveugle sans son chien* (Montréal: Éditions Québec Amérique, 1999), p.73. The full quotation for Jones's remark is as follows: "The danger in his [Normand de Bellefeuille's] case may be that the reader thinks of his writing as merely music. He says himself in *The Way of the Blind Man without His Seeing-eye Dog* that he makes a racket with words, disheveled and tireless words, he makes, disheveled, a racket, but he works, a bit like a modern musician, to make the racket consort with the song." D.G. Jones, foreword in *ellipse*, no 65 (spring 2001): 8.
53 D.G. Jones, foreword in *ellipse*, no. 65 (spring 2001): 8.

54 de Bellefeuille, *Catégoriques*, p. 9; de Bellefeuille, *Categorics*, trans. D.G. Jones, p. 7.
55 Fred Wah, back cover of Normand de Bellefeuille, *Categorics one, two and three*, trans. D.G. Jones.
56 D.G. Jones, "Gaston Miron: A Testimony," *ellipse*, no. 5 (autumn 1970): 55.
57 D.G. Jones, "Editorial," *ellipse*, no. 5 (autumn 1970): 7.
58 Gaston Miron, "La marche à l'amour," *ellipse*, no. 5 (1970): 14.
59 Gaston Miron, "The March to Love," trans. D. G. Jones, *ellipse*, no. 5 (1970): 15.
60 Jones, "Editorial," p. 7.
61 Blodgett, *D. G. Jones and His Works*, p. 3.
62 George Woodcock, "Jones, D.G.," in the *Oxford Companion to Canadian Literature*, ed. Eugene Benson and William Toye (Toronto: Oxford University Press, 1997), p. 585.
63 Blodgett, *D. G. Jones and His Works*, pp. 3–4.
64 D.G. Jones in interview with Mary Hamilton, quoted by Blodgett, *D.G. Jones and His Works*, p. 5
65 Jones, "Gaston Miron: A Testimony," pp. 56, 57.
66 Jones, "Gaston Miron: A Testimony," p. 57.

BIBLIOGRAPHY

I. Primary Sources

Literary Translations (Books)

Blouin, Louise, D.G. Jones, and P. Bernard, eds. *Esprit de Corps: Québec Poetry of the Late Twentieth Century in Translation*. Trans. D.G. Jones. Trois-Rivières: Écrits des Forges; Winnipeg: The Muses' Company, 1997.

de Bellefeuille, Normand. *Categorics: One, Two and Three*. Trans. D.G. Jones. Toronto: Coach House Press, 1992. Translation of *Catégoriques un deux et trois*. Trois-Rivières: Écrits des Forges, 1986.

Lapointe, Paul-Marie. *The Terror of the Snows: Selected Poems by Paul-Marie Lapointe*. Trans. D.G. Jones. n.p.: University of Pittsburgh Press, 1976.

———. *The Fifth Season: Poems by Paul-Marie Lapointe*. Trans. D.G. Jones. Toronto: Exile Editions, 1985. Rev. ed. of *The Terror of the Snows*.

Martel, Émile. *For Orchestra and Solo Poet*. Trans. D. G. Jones. n.p.: Muses' Company, 1996. Translation of *Pour orchestre et poète seul*. Trois-Rivières: Écrits des Forges, 1995.

Miron, Gaston. *The March to Love: Selected Poems*. Ed. D.G. Jones. Trans. D.G. Jones, Marc Plourde, Louis Simpson, Brenda Fleet, John Glassco, and Dennis Egan. n.p.:International Poetry Forum, Byblos Editions, 1986. Translation of *La Marche à L'Amour*.

Literary Translations (Poems)

Alonzo, Anne-Marie. "[Excerpt from *Seul le désir*]." Trans. D.G. Jones. *ellipse*, no. 39 (1988): 21.

———. "[Two excerpts from *Seul le désir*]." Trans. D.G. Jones. *ellipse*, no. 39 (1988): 23.
Beaulieu, Michel. "garlands of fame (an entertainment)." Trans. D.G. Jones. *ellipse*, no. 36 (1986): 103–105. Translation of "fleurons glorieux (divertissement)."
Beausoleil, Claude. "Excerpt from Du texte et du doute (essai fictionnel)." Trans. D.G. Jones. *ellipse*, no. 23/24 (1979): 69–73. Translation of "Extrait: Du texte et du doute (essai fictionnel)."
———. "Endless Montreal." Trans. D.G. Jones. *ellipse*, no. 56 (1996): 57–59. Translation of "Sans fin Montréal."
de Bellefeuille, Normand. "[Untitled from *Heureusement, ici il y a la guerre*]." Trans. D.G. Jones. *ellipse*, no. 44 (1990): 61–63.
———. "Clearing Up the Entire World." Trans. D.G. Jones. *ellipse*, no. 65 (spring 2001): 47. Translation of "Désencombrer le monde entier."
———. "The Severed Head of Iokanaan." Trans. D.G. Jones. *ellipse*, no. 65 (spring 2001): 49 Translation of "La tête tranchée de Iokanaan."
Brault, Jacques. "Short Song." Trans. D.G. Jones. *ellipse*, no. 7 (spring 1971): 9. Translation of "Chanson brève."
———. "From d'Amour et de mort." Trans. D.G. Jones. *ellipse*, no. 7 (spring 1971): 9 Translation of "from d'Amour et de mort."
———. "Louange XIII (extract)." Trans. D.G. Jones. *ellipse*, no. 7 (spring 1971): 27 Translation of "Louange XIII (extract)."
———. "The Birth of Clouds." Trans. D.G. Jones. *Poems by Jacques Brault* (1984). Etchings by Lucie Lambert. *ellipse*, no. 48 (1992): pp. 93–111. Translation of "La naissances des nuages."
Brossard, Nicole. "Text: Metamorphoses and Butchered Language." Trans. D.G. Jones. *ellipse*, no. 6 (winter 1971): p. 25. Translation of "Texte: Métamorphose et langage tronqué."
———. "Tabernak." Trans. D.G. Jones. *ellipse*, no. 6 (winter 1971): 27–31. Translation of "Tabernak."
———. [Untitled]. Trans. D.G. Jones. *ellipse*, no. 12 (1973): 28.
———. "[Untitled from 'Aube à la saison']." Trans. D.G. Jones. *ellipse*, no. 53 (1995): 23.
———. "She Was Then without Narrator." Trans. D.G. Jones. *ellipse*, no. 53 (1995): 35. Translation of "Elle était lors sans narrateur."
Caccia, Fulvio. "[Untitled from 'Scirocco']." Trans. D.G. Jones. *ellipse*, no. 54 (1995): 39.
———. "Blind Travel." *ellipse*, no. 54, 1995, p. 41 (translation of "Le voyage blanc").
———. "Scirocco." Trans. D.G. Jones. *ellipse*, no 54 (1995): 43–45. Translation of "Scirocco."
Chamberland, Paul. "The Unspeakable (excerpts)." Trans. D.G. Jones. *ellipse*, no. 8/9 (1971): 43–61. Translation of "L'Inavouable (extraits)."
Chiasson, Herménégilde. "Blue," "White," "Red." Trans. D.G. Jones. *ellipse*, no. 63 (spring 2000): 29–31. Translation of "Bleu," "Blanc," "Rouge."

Des Roches, Roger. "[excerpt from *L'imagination laïque*]." Trans. D.G. Jones. *ellipse*, no. 42 (1989): 25–27.

Desrochers, Alfred. "Hymn to the North Wind (excerpt)." Trans. D.G. Jones. *ellipse*, no. 25/26 (1980): 17–19. Translation of "Hymne au vent du nord (extrait)."

Dostie, Gaétan. "The Frenzy of Fear." Trans. D.G. Jones. *ellipse*, no. 6 (winter 1971): 17–23. Translation of "La Peur délire."

Escomel, Gloria. "[Untitled]." Trans. D.G. Jones. *ellipse*, no. 58 (fall 1997): 37.

Gagnon, Madeleine. "From *Pensées du poème*." Trans. D.G. Jones. *ellipse*, no. 33/34 (1985): p. 21. Translation of "extraits de *Pensées du poème*."

Garneau, Michel. [Untitled]. Trans. D.G. Jones. *ellipse*, no. 27/28 (1981): 11.

———. [Untitled]. Trans. D.G. Jones. *ellipse*, no. 27/28 (1981): 35.

Garneau, Saint-Denys. "[Leave this impossible mound]." Trans. D.G. Jones. *ellipse*, no. 37 (1987): 39–41. Originally "[Quitte le monticule]."

Garneau, Sylvain. "The Deal-Maker, or 'La bonne entente.'" Trans. D.G. Jones. *ellipse*, no. 55 (1996): 49–51. Translation of "La bonne entente."

———. "The Just." Trans. D.G. Jones. *ellipse*, no. 55 (1996): 53. Originally "Les justes."

Giguère, Roland. "The Hand of the Hangman Finally Rots." Trans. D.G. Jones. *ellipse*, no. 2 (winter 1970): 19. Translation of "La main du bourreau finit toujours par pourrir."

———. "Mémoire d'ombre." Trans. D.G. Jones. *ellipse*, no. 2 (winter 1970): 23–25. Translation of "Mémoire d'ombre."

———. "Saisons mortes." Trans. D.G. Jones. *ellipse*, no. 2 (winter 1970): 25. Translation of "Saisons mortes."

———. "Our Houses Put to the Torch." Trans. D.G. Jones. *ellipse*, no. 2 (winter 1970): 29. Translation of "Nos châteaux livrés au feu."

———. "The Age of the Word." Trans. D.G. Jones. *ellipse*, no. 2 (winter 1970): 29. Translation of "L'âge de la parole."

Godin, Gérald. "[from 'Cantouque de l'écoeuré']." Trans. D.G. Jones. *ellipse*, no. 45 (1991): 103. Translation of an excerpt from "Cantouque de l'écoeuré."

———. "The Secret Passage." Trans. D.G. Jones. *ellipse*, no. 45 (1991): 113–115. Translation of "Porte dérobée."

Grandbois, Alain. "Let Us Close the Cupboard." Trans. D.G. Jones. *ellipse*, no. 14/15 (1974): 25–27. Translation of "Fermons l'armoire."

———. [Untitled]. Trans. D.G. Jones. *ellipse*, no. 14/15 (1974): 81.

Hébert, Anne. "Strange Catch." Trans. D.G. Jones. *ellipse*, no. 50 (1993): 34–35. Translation of "Étrange capture," *ellipse*, no. 50 (1993): 10.

Hébert, François. "Exercices de l'amitié." Trans. D.G. Jones. *ellipse*, no. 60 (fall 1998): 33. Translation of "Exercices de l'amitié."

Hénault, Gilles. "Bestiary." Trans. D.G. Jones. *ellipse*, no. 18 (1976): 37–39. Translation of "Bestiaire."

Jacob, Suzanne. "[Untitled from *Le deuil de la rancune*]." Trans. D.G. Jones. *ellipse*, no. 61 (1998): 39.

Lalonde, Michèle. "The Spent Silence." Trans. D.G. Jones. *ellipse*, no. 3 (spring 1970): 9. Translation of "Le silence effrité."

———. "The Delirium of Noon." Trans. D.G. Jones. *ellipse*, no. 3 (spring 1970): 11. Translation of "Le jour halluciné."

———. "The Polar Night Comes Down." Trans. D.G. Jones. *ellipse*, no. 3 (spring 1970): 23. Translation of "Il fait nuit lente."

———. "Speak White." Trans. D.G. Jones. *ellipse*, no. 3 (spring 1970): 25–31. Translation of "Speak White."

Langvin, Gilbert. [Untitled]. Trans. D.G. Jones. *ellipse*, no. 13 (1973): 29.

———. "Catacombs" Trans. D.G. Jones. *ellipse*, no. 13 (1973): 31. Translation of "Catacombes."

Lapointe, Paul-Marie. "Trees." Trans. D.G. Jones. *ellipse*, no. 11 (1972): 17–27. Translation of "Arbres."

Lasnier, Rina. "Belling Sea." Trans. D.G. Jones. *ellipse*, no. 22 (1978): 21. Translation of "Cloche de mer."

———. "The Palm Tree." Trans. D.G. Jones. *ellipse*, no. 49 (1993): 25. Translation of "Le palmier."

———. "The Tortoise, Bishop of the Desert." Trans. D.G. Jones. *ellipse*, no. 49 (1993): 25. Translation of "La tortue, évêque du désert."

———. "Malemer." Trans. D.G. Jones. *ellipse*, no. 49 (1993): 31–47. Translation of "La malemer."

Leblanc, Raymond. "Time for Saying." Trans. D.G. Jones. *ellipse*, no. 16 (1974): 9. Translation of "Le temps de dire."

———. "Land of Acadia." Trans. D.G. Jones. *ellipse*, no. 16 (1974): 11. Translation of "Pays d'Acadie."

Leclerc, Michel. "Ode For a Civil Morning—1." Trans. D.G. Jones. *ellipse*, no. 12 (1973): 49–57. Translation of "Ode pour un matin public—1."

Lefrançois, Alexis. "A Long Silence: Un ange passe." Trans. D.G. Jones. *ellipse*, no. 46 (1991): 33. Translation of "Un ange passe [la tête]."

———. "Vaugelas." Trans. D.G. Jones. *ellipse*, no. 46 (1991): 35. Translation of "Vaugelas."

Loranger, Jean-Aubert. "I Look through the Window at the Outside." Trans. D.G. Jones. *ellipse*, no. 20 (1977): 13–15. Translation of "Je regarde dehors par la fenêtre."

Lozeau, Albert. "The Dust of the Day." Trans. D.G. Jones. *ellipse*, no. 38 (1987): 27. Translation of "La poussière du jour."

Miron, Gaston. "My Sad One and Serene." Trans. D.G. Jones. *ellipse*, no. 5 (autumn 1970): 11. Translation of "Ma désolée sereine."

———. "La marche à l'amour." Trans. D.G. Jones. *ellipse*, no. 5 (autumn 1970): 13–23. Translation of "La Marche à l'amour."

Nelligan, Émile. "Winter Evening." Trans. D.G. Jones. *ellipse*, no. 40 (1988): 113. Translation of "Soir d'hiver."

Nepveu, Pierre. [Untitled]. Trans. D.G. Jones. *ellipse*, no. 32 (1984): 15.

———. [Untitled]. Trans. D.G. Jones. *ellipse*, no. 32 (1984): 27.

Ouellette, Fernand. "And We Loved." Trans. D.G. Jones. *ellipse*, no. 1 (fall 1969): 29–31. Translation of "Et nous aimions."

———. "Agony of Wings." Trans. D.G. Jones. *ellipse*, no. 10 (1972): 13 Translation of "Sanglot d'aile."

———. "Geology." Trans. D.G. Jones. *ellipse*, no. 10 (1972): 29. Translation of "Géologie."

———. "Periplum." Trans. D.G. Jones. *ellipse*, no. 10 (1972): 39–43. Translation of "Le Périple."

———. "The Sun." Trans. D.G. Jones. *ellipse*, no. 10 (1972): 45. Translation of "Le Soleil."

———. "The Vertical Stream." Trans. D.G. Jones. *ellipse*, no. 10 (1972): 25–26. Translation of "Le Fleuve vertical."

Perrault, Pierre. "The Oak and the Reed (A Fable)." Trans. D.G. Jones. *ellipse*, no. 62 (1999): 25. Translation of "Le chêne et le roseau."

———. "The Song of Marie." Trans. D.G. Jones. *ellipse*, no. 62 (1999): 25. Translation of "La chanson de Marie."

Piché, Alphonse. "Departure." Trans. D.G. Jones. *ellipse*, no. 47 (1992): 45. Translation of "Départ."

———. "[Two untitled poems: one from *Dernier profil*, the other from *Sursis*]." Trans. D.G. Jones. *ellipse*, no. 47 (1992): 57–61.

Préfontaine, Yves. "Exode." Trans. D.G. Jones. *ellipse*, no. 52 (1994): 31. Translation of "Exode."

———. "Night Sentences." Trans. D.G. Jones. *ellipse*, no. 52 (1994): 55. Translation of "Phrases de nuit."

Rilke, Rainer Maria. "The Roses." Trans. D.G. Jones. *ellipse*, no. 66 (fall 2001): 87–89. Translation of "Les Roses."

Tanguay, Bernard. "[Untitled]." Trans. D.G. Jones. *ellipse*, no. 17 (1975): 48–68.

Thibodeau, Serge Patrice. "Chipoudie, 1679–1755." Trans. D.G. Jones. *ellipse*, no. 57 (spring 1997): 39. Translation of "Chipoudie, 1697–1755."

———. "Crossing the Valley." Trans. D.G. Jones. *ellipse*, no. 57 (spring 1997): 45. Translation of "Le passage dans la vallée."

———. "Farewells." Trans. D.G. Jones. *ellipse*, no. 57 (spring 1997): 43. Translation of "Les Adieux."

———. "Madawaska, 1789." Trans. D.G. Jones. *ellipse*, no. 57 (spring 1997): 41. Translation of "Madawaska, 1789."

———. "Nomades." Trans. D.G. Jones. *ellipse*, no. 57 (spring 1997): 53. Translation of "nomades."

———. "The Poet's Mausoleum." Trans. D.G. Jones. *ellipse*, no. 57 (spring 1997): 47. Translation of "Le mausolée du poète."

———. "The Return." Trans. D.G. Jones. *ellipse*, no. 57 (spring 1997): 49. Translation of "Le retour."

Uguay, Marie. "[Seven untitled poems]." Trans. D.G. Jones. *ellipse*, no. 31 (1983): 11–13.

Literary Works (Poetry)

Jones, D. G. *Frost on the Sun*. Toronto: Contact Press, 1957.

———. *The Sun Is Axeman*. Toronto: University of Toronto Press, 1961.

———. *Phrases from Orpheus*. Toronto: Oxford University Press, 1967.
———. *Under the Thunder the Flowers Light Up the Earth*. Toronto: Coach House Press, 1977.
———. *A Throw of Particles: New and Selected Poems*. Toronto: General Publishing, 1983.
———. *Doucet-Saito: Concepts in Clay*. Illus. Doucet-Saito. North York, ON: Koffler Gallery, c.1985.
———. *Balthazar and Other Poems*. Toronto: Coach House Press, 1988.
———. *A Thousand Hooded Eyes*. Ltd. ed. Wood engravings by Lucie Lambert. Vancouver: Éditions Lucie Lambert, 1991.
———. *Le Soleil Cogne*. Trans. Camille Fournier. Montréal: Éditions du Noroît; Beuvry (France): Maison de la Poésie Nord-Pas-de-Calais, 1995. Originally published as *The Sun Is Axeman*. Toronto: University of Toronto Press, 1961.
———. *The Floating Garden*. Toronto: Coach House Press, 1995.
———. *Wild Asterisks in Cloud*. Montréal: Empyreal Press, 1997.
———. *Grounding Sight*. Montréal: Empyreal Press, 1999.

Works on Translation

Jones, D. G. "D.G Jones / Fred Cogswell." Discussion: Eva Kushner and Yves Merzisen. *ellipse*, no. 21 (1977): 98–101.
———. "Grounds for Translation." *ellipse*, no. 21 (1977): 58–91. Trans. Joseph Bonenfant as "Raisons d'être de la traduction," *ellipse* no. 21 (1977). Rpt. in *The Insecurity of* Art, ed. Ken Norris and Peter Van Toorn. Montréal: Véhicule Press, 1982. 67–80.
———. "F.R. Scott as Translator." *On F.R. Scott: Essays on His Contributions to Law, Literature and Politics*, ed. Sandra Djwa and R. St. J. Macdonald. Kingston and Montréal: McGill-Queen's University Press, 1983. 160–64.
———. "Text and Context: Some Reflections on Translation." *Canadian Literature*, no. 117 (summer 1988): pp. 6–10.

Other Publications (Literary Criticism)

Jones, D. G. *Butterfly on Rock: A Study of Themes and Images in Canadian Literature*. Toronto: University of Toronto Press, 1970.
———. "Gaston Miron: A Testimony." *ellipse*, no. 5 (autumn 1970): 55–57.
———. "An Interview with Michèle Lalonde." *ellipse*, no. 3 (spring 1970): 33–41.
———. "La vraie révolution est celle de l'imagination." *ellipse*, no. 6 (winter 1971): 91–97.
———. "Adam's Inventory: Aspects of Contemporary Canadian Literature." In *Readings in Commonwealth Literature*, ed. William Walsh. Oxford: Clarendon Press, 1973. Previously published in *Social Education* [Washington] 35, no. 6 (October 1971).
———. "Myth, Frye, and Some Canadian Writers." *Canadian Literature*, no. 55 (winter 1973): 7–22.
———. "Paysage intérieur et paysage." Trans. Brigitte Franchomme. *ellipse*, no. 12 (1973): 118–31.

———. "Cold Eye and Optic Heart: Marshall McLuhan and Some Canadian Poets. *Modern Poetry Studies* 5, no. 2 (autumn 1974): 170–87.

———. "David Helwig's New Timber." *Queen's Quarterly* 81, no. 2 (summer 1974): 202–14.

———. "George Johnston." *Canadian Literature*, no. 59 (1974): 81–87.

———. "In Search of America." *Boundary*, no. 2 (fall 1974): 227–46.

———. "A Postcard from Chicoutimi." *Studies in Canadian Literature* 1, no. 2 (summer 1976): 170–82.

———. "Art, Technology, and Silence: The Poet in Canada in the 1980s." *The Written Word/Prestige de l'écrit*, ed. A.G. McKay. Ottawa: Royal Society of Canada, 1980.

———. "Un bricoleur parmi les technologues: La vision pastorale de Purdy." Trans. Yvette Gonzalo-Francoli. *ellipse*, no. 27/28 (1980): 94–105.

———, ed. and introd. *The Lines of the Poet: 13 Poems*. Illus. Morton Rosengarten. Toronto: Monk Bretton Books, 1981.

———. "Al Purdy's Contemporary Pastoral." *Canadian Poetry* no. 10 (spring/summer 1982): 32–43.

———. "Preface to *Mainstream*: An Unpublished Anthology (1973)." In *The Insecurity of Art: Essays on Poetics*, ed. Ken Norris and Peter Van Toorn. Montréal: Véhicule Press, 1982. 62–66.

———. "Private Space and Public Space." In *On F.R. Scott: Essays on His Contributions to Law, Literature and Politics*, ed. Sandra Djwa and R. St. J. Macdonald. Kingston and Montréal: McGill-Queen's University Press, 1983. 44–54.

———. "Canadian Poetry: Roots and New Directions." *Credences: A Journal of Twentieth-Century Poetry and Prose*, n.s., 2, no.2/3 (fall/winter 1984): 229–36.

———. "The Mythology of Identity: A Canadian Case." In *Driving Home: A Dialogue between Writers and Readers*, ed. Barbara Belyea and Estelle Dansereau. Waterloo, ON: Published for the Calgary Institute for the Humanities by Wilfrid Laurier University Press, 1984, pp. 39–56.

———. "Le mérite d'Archibald Lampman." Trans. Patricia Godbout. *ellipse*, no. 38 (1987): 89–95.

———. "Steel Syntax: The Railroad as Symbol in Canadian Poetry." In *Symbols in Life and Art*, ed. James Leith. Kingston and Montréal: Published for the Royal Society of Canada by McGill-Queen's University Press, 1987.

———. "Émile Nelligan." *ellipse* no. 40 (1988): 111.

———. "Tracing *Ellipse*." *ellipse*, no. 40 (1988): 18–21.

———. "Notes on a Poetics of the Sacred." In *Silence, the Word and the Sacred*, ed. E.D. Blodgett and H.G. Coward. Waterloo, ON: Pub. for the Calgary Institute of the Humanities by Wilfrid Laurier Press, 1989: 67–82.

———. "Carman: Animula vagula blandula." In *Bliss Carman: A Reappraisal*, ed. Gerald Lynch. Ottawa: University of Ottawa Press, 1990: 33–41.

———. "Criticism and Creativity, or *les éperons de la muse*." *Métonymies: Essais de littérature canadienne comparée / Essays in Comparative Canadian Literature*. Cahiers de littérature canadienne comparée no. 2. Sherbrooke: Université de Sherbrooke, 1990.

———. "D'entretien domestique et de musique: la poésie de Robyn Sarah." Trans. Monique Grandmangin. *ellipse*, no. 43 (1990): 53–63.
———. "The Hexagon Poets and the Continuing Revolution in Quebec Poetry." In *Studies on Canadian Literature*, ed. Arnold E. Davidson. New York: Modern Language Association of America, 1990. 226–47.
———. "Blodgett's Poetry." *Canadian Literature*, no. 129 (summer 1991): 238–41.
———. "Earle Birney: La tournée en vers du monde." Trans. Patricia Godbout. *ellipse*, no. 45 (1991): 9–21.
———. "Identité et différence: remarques comparatives sur la poésie de Margaret Avison et Rina Lasnier." Trans. Patricia Godbout. *ellipse*, no. 49 (1993): 104–15.
———. Foreword to *ellipse*, no. 50 (1993): 4–6.
———. Foreword to *ellipse*, no. 65 (spring 2001): 6–9
———. Foreword to *ellipse*, no. 66 (fall 2001): 6–7.

II Secondary Sources

Bassnett, Susan. *Translation Studies*. 3rd ed. London and New York: Routledge, 2002.
Blodgett, E.D. " The Masks of D.G. Jones." *Canadian Literature*, no. 60 (spring 1974): 64–82. Rpt. in *Poets and Critics: Essais from* Canadian Literature *1966–1974*, ed. George Woodcock. Toronto: Oxford University Press, 1974. 159–78.
———. *D.G. Jones and His Works*. Toronto: ECW Press, 1984.
Bowering, George."Être chez soi dans le monde." Trans. Rodolphe Lacasse. *ellipse*, no.13 (1973): 82–103. Rpt. in "Coming Home to the World. " *Canadian Literature*, no. 65 (summer 1975): 7–27.
Davey, Frank. "Dudek, Louis." in the *Oxford Companion to Canadian Literature*, 2nd ed., ed. Eugene Benson and William Toye (Don Mills, ON: Oxford University Press, 1997).
de Bellefeuille, Normand. *La Marche de l'aveugle sans son chien*. Montréal: Éditions Québec Amérique, 1999.
———. *Catégoriques un deux et trois*. Trois-Rivières: Écrits des Forges, 1986. Editorial in *ellipse*, no. 5 (1970): 6–7.
Gentzler, Edwin. *Contemporary Translation Theories*. London and New York: Routledge, 1993.
Giguère, Richard, Philip Lanthier, and André Marquis, eds. *Anthologie de la poésie des Cantons de l'Est au vingtième siècle/Anthology of Twentieth Century Poetry of the Eastern Townships*. Montréal: Éditions Triptyque and Véhicule Press, 1999.
Gonzalo-Shepherd, Danielle. "D.G. Jones, poète du devenir: étude et traduction du recueil *Sous le feu du tonnerre, les fleurs illuminent la terre*." PhD. diss. Universitéde Sherbrooke, 1991.
Grandmangin, Monique, and Ronald Sutherland, eds. *Dentelle/Indented: Ralph Gustafson, Roland Giguère, Gaston Miron, D.G. Jones*. Trans. Monique Grandmangin and Ronald Sutherland. Colorado Springs: Press at Colorado College, 1982.

Guillevic, Eugène. "Ellipse." Trans. Teo Savory. *ellipse*, no. 1 (fall 1969): 3. Originally published in *Les Euclidiennes*. Paris: Gallimard, 1967. Translation originally appeared as "Ellipse." Trans. Teo Savory. *Gaillevic*. Santa Barbara: Unicorn Press, 1968.

Hébert, Anne. "Strange Arrest." Trans. Barbara Belyea. *ellipse*, no. 50 (1993): 12

———. "Strange Capture." Trans. Philip Stratford. *ellipse*, no. 50 (1993): 55.

Hoffpauir, Richard. "A Response to D.G. Jones's 'Grounds for Translation.'" *ellipse*, no. 22 (1978): 107–15.

Homel, David. "Green, Wonderful Things." *Books in Canada*, January 1984, p. 7.

Lanthier, Philip. "An Interview with Doug Jones." *Matrix*, no. 22 (spring, 1986): 63–70.

———. "English Poetry in the Eastern Townships." In *Anthologie de la poésie des Cantons de l'Est au vingtième siècle / Anthology of Twentieth Century Poetry of the Eastern Townships*, ed. Richard Giguère, Philip Lanthier, and André Marquis. Montréal: Les Éditions Triptyque and Véhicule Press, 1999. 16–25.

Lapointe, Paul-Marie. *Pour les âmes*. Montréal: L'Hexagone, 1964.

Macpherson, Jay. "Report on Poetry Readings." In Whalley, ed., *Writing in Canada*. 136–39.

Scott, F.R. Introduction to *Writing in Canada*, ed. G. Whalley. 1–10.

Smith, A.J.M. "Poet." In Whalley, ed., *Writing in Canada*. 13–24.

Steiner, George. *After Babel: Aspects of Language and Translation*. New York: Oxford, 1975.

Sutherland, Ron. "The Athens of the North." In *Les Cantons de l'Est. Aspects géographiques, politiques, socio-économiques et culturels*, ed. Jean-Marie Dubois. Sherbrooke: Éditions de l'Université de Sherbrooke, 1989.

Venuti, Lawrence, ed. *The Translation Studies Reader*. London and New York: Routledge, 2000.

Whalley, George, ed. *Writing in Canada: Proceedings of the Canadian Writers' Conference Held at Queen's University July 1955*. Toronto: Macmillan Company of Canada, 1956.

Woodcock, George. "Jones, D.G." In the *Oxford Companion to Canadian Literature*, ed. Eugene Benson and William Toye. Toronto: Oxford University Press, 1997. 585.

6

Patricia Claxton
A Civil Translator

AGNES WHITFIELD

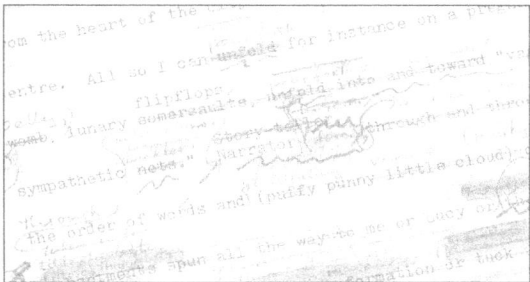

Patricia Claxton embodies the role of the translator as a civil agent, with rights and responsibilities within a civic society, and more specifically, like the civil engineer, called upon to ensure the constructive and logistical functions that facilitate the safe circulation of people and ideas. The term "civil" has a wide variety of meanings and associations: relating to a community or citizens, touching the normal rights of individuals, conforming to the normal standards of politeness, designating what is legally recognized (civil year) or legally determined (civil liabilities). Civil rights are the traditional rights of citizens with respect to state control. Strands of all these meanings come together in the motivations that have led Claxton to become a translator. A deeply held conception of citizenship and civic duty underlies her vision of translation's vital contribution to furthering a healthy intellectual debate within bilingual Canadian society, her sense of responsibility towards the authors and texts she translates, her dedication to "getting it right,"[1] and her commitment to the legal structures that ensure translation's place within a civic society in a context of respectful cultural exchange.

Since 1968, when she published her first translation, an article by Pierre Elliott Trudeau from *Cité Libre*, Claxton has translated some twenty books and countless articles, short stories, and poems on a wide variety of topics, including pressing Canadian political issues, feminist fiction, and a Canadian journalist's view of human tragedy in the Rwandan genocide of 1994. She has penned into English texts by distinguished Québec historians Marcel Trudel and Fernand Ouellet, such well-known contemporary Québécois writers as Nicole Brossard, France Théoret, Jacques Godbout, Jean-Paul Daoust, and Gil Courtemanche, and popular children's author Cécile Gagnon. For the Canadian public, however, Claxton's name is perhaps most often linked with that of Gabrielle Roy, the grande dame of Canadian and Québec letters. Claxton received the Governor General's Award for her translation of Roy's posthumous autobiography, *Enchantment and Sorrow*, in 1987, and again in 1999 for *Gabrielle Roy, a Life*, by François Ricard, with whom she also shared the same year, as translator, the Drainie-Taylor Biography Prize.

Throughout her career, Claxton has been a strong advocate of the translation profession. As a member of the executive of the Société des traducteurs du Québec, precursor of the Ordre des traducteurs, terminologues et interprètes agréés du Québec (OTTIAQ), she was responsible for the development of accreditation examination procedures and standards. Founding president of the Literary Translator's Association of Canada (LTAC), she was successful in lobbying the Canadian government for codification of copyright protection for Canadian translators. The recognition of translators as authors in their own right remains a fundamental issue for her, and she continues to monitor on behalf of LTAC any proposed federal legislation with implications for translators. Through her teaching, articles, and numerous speaking engagements across the country, she has contributed generously to a better public awareness of the complexities of the translator's craft and the importance of intercultural exchange within Canada.

Early Crossings

Difference and displacement have always been present in Claxton's life. The exotic appeal of otherness as well as its dangerous potential for violence and division, the excitement of vast distances and boundaries to cross, and a deep sense of the vulnerability of human life against the political tides of war and illness resurfaced in varied forms throughout her life, shaping her experience, framing her approach to translation, and above all, giving her intimate knowledge of the vital importance of establishing civil communication networks for the safe transit of people and ideas.

Claxton's exposure to two very different worlds, and more importantly her sense of moving from one to the other, is inscribed in the very process of her birth. Born in Kingston, Ontario, in 1929, she was conceived in British India, as it was called before Partition. A sign perhaps of things to come, the translator's task being to give texts from other cultures new life in her own, Claxton undertook her first crossing, the long passage back home from India over land and sea, as a child in her mother's womb. Dorothy Carson had almost died giving birth to her first children, male twins, and for her next two deliveries, undeterred by the uncertainties of the voyage, she preferred to return to the comfortable town on Lake Ontario where both she and her husband, Frederick, had been born. Before she was a year old, Claxton, the youngest of the family, was once more on the high seas, on her way back to Lahore. She was to live there, part of a small English-speaking enclave, until she was almost eleven.

Claxton's parents were second- and third-generation Canadians of British stock, her father of Irish and her mother of Scottish parentage. Their families were part of Kingston's town-and-gown society: her mother had attended private school in Toronto, and her father was a graduate of Royal Military College. After a tour in the First World War, he joined the Royal Engineers of the British Army, as a means to an end, Claxton recalls, a way to "do exciting things in exotic places." Until his retirement in 1940, he was stationed in Lahore, where he worked as an engineer on the construction of the North Western Railway across Pakistan and India. By Canadian standards, Claxton's childhood in Lahore was an unusual one. She did not attend school as such, but shared her lessons with a half-dozen other young English-speaking children under the supervision of their governesses. Although Claxton had an English nanny and not an Indian *ayah*, she nonetheless enjoyed her interaction with Indian culture, including sharing riding lessons with a young Indian prince and his tutor. Summers were spent in Kashmir, which she loved. As Canadians, her parents were somewhat more interculturally open-minded than other members of the predominantly English enclave. Her mother, contrary to most of her English neighbours, was a great admirer of Gandhi.

While Claxton's father's retirement in 1940 was opportune in the Indian context, as the political tensions and violence between Hindu and Muslims escalated before Partition, the family's return to Canada was set against other pressing international tensions, where the political would have an even greater effect on the personal. They were to come back via the Pacific, but as Claxton recounts, "My father was going to join us in Hong Kong when my mother got a telegram. Dunkirk had occurred and he had decided to volunteer." Her father spent part of the Second World War in London cleaning up from the Blitz, before being sent to Iraq to oversee the construction of a railway supply line linking the Persian Gulf to the Soviet Union. As a young adolescent, Claxton was certainly able to appreciate the risks of war and the concerns her mother must have felt for their own ocean crossing, but she seems most of all to have admired her father for his sense of duty. Perhaps something of the vulnerability, uncertainty, and deep sense of displacement she must have felt nonetheless surfaces in her short but telling statement: "I hated coming back."

The movies and ice cream cones of quiet wartime Kingston could not compete with the horses and camels, the snake charmers, and the rich and varied colours of India. Claxton remembers her early years abroad with great intensity. Returning to Canada was a departure from paradise. Coming back also meant, for the first time, attending a regular school with classrooms and peers, first at Sydenham Public School and then at Kingston Collegiate and Vocational Institute. Claxton had fought hard against being sent away as a boarder to Havergal, her mother's alma mater in Toronto. Perhaps she knew instinctively that these were precious years. Dorothy Carson died in 1945, and at fifteen years of age, Fred Carson having been appointed vice-president of the Montreal Locomotive Works, Claxton found herself once more on the move, this time to Montréal. Her arrival in Québec was a renewal with difference. Claxton's experience of French was limited. Although her classmates at the Study, a private school in Westmount, had learned the language since kindergarten, Claxton had to make do with one year of Ontario High School French. Looking back now from the distance of her accomplishments as a translator, Claxton is critical of the way French was taught then, "as a dead language like Latin or Greek, not as a living language, a means of communicating." When she arrived at McGill, she was drawn to philosophy, economics, and comparative religion, dropping French as soon as she could. She graduated with a General BA in Arts, got her first real job as an investment analyst for Sun Life, and shortly after married a young Montréal lawyer, John Claxton, with whom she had two sons.

On the surface, little in Claxton's formal education and what she herself refers to "as a relatively undistinguished record" as a university student could foretell her accomplished future as a Canadian literary translator; yet a personal sense of the essential importance of intercultural crossings, or more precisely, a realization of their troubling contentiousness, was already forming in her mind. Claxton remembers vividly having difficulty understanding the geographic borders of francophone and anglophone Montréal when she arrived in the city: "There was a wall," Claxton recalls, "you didn't go any further east than [the department store] Morgans; any French Canadian who came west spoke English." English and French Montréalers lived in separate worlds. Sports provided one of the few opportunities to cross the boundaries. Her father had wonderful hockey tickets just behind the Canadiens' bench. More significant for Claxton was the excitement she felt on those rare occasions when she "crossed the line" with her fencing teammates into parts of Montreal that, as an anglophone, she would never have otherwise visited.

As a child, Hindustani, omnipresent in the streets and shops around her, was first and foremost a language to be deciphered. However, the ensuing steps of language acquisition required for bringing the language of the other home, literally and metaphorically, were impeded by the colonial context in which she lived. If Claxton has a regret about her childhood in India, it is that she learned to speak only a little Hindustani, the lingua franca of India before Partition.

Years later, in social functions in Montreal in the mid-fifties, as the wife of a young professional, she was once again confronted with a linguistic barrier: "If we were in a group with francophones," she recalls, "I couldn't participate. This wasn't right." This time, she was determined to complete the learning process. With two small children at home, time was limited, but Claxton resourcefully kept a French dictionary by the kitchen sink for easy consultation whenever she had a free moment. When the boys were at school, she was able to devote herself more seriously to her task, picking up provincial night-school courses, then courses at McGill University where she became friends with one of her professors, Nicole Deschamps, who introduced her to Laurent Duval, a journalist at Radio Canada. She began to read *Cité libre*.

The early 1960s were heady, many would say turbulent, times in Québec. After the *grande noirceur* of the narrow clericalism of the Duplessis years, an irreversible tide of change was transforming Quebec society. Caught up in the excitement of the broad exchange of new ideas surrounding her, many of which she was hearing or reading about in French, Claxton was also ready for intellectual challenge. Translating a French text into English, she decided, just for her own purposes, would be both an exercise in self-discipline and a concrete way to hone her new linguistic skills. She found an article by a writer with a compelling style, of a length she thought she could handle, and set painstakingly about her first translation. After much editing and re-editing, she showed her work to Duval, whose reaction was categoric: "You have worked very hard, and I commend you for it," he told her, as she relates, "But if you're going to translate what this fellow wrote, you have to write what he said, and not what you think he ought to have said."

Undaunted, Claxton took the tough advice to heart (it still resonates in her ears) and once again plunged into revising her translation. She showed the new version to the author, who liked what he read, told her she had a flair for this kind of thing, and encouraged her to pursue her work. The title of the text was "La nouvelle trahison des clercs," and its author, Pierre Elliott Trudeau. Although she did not realize it at the time, Claxton had embarked upon what would become her life's work.

Engineering the Crossing

The meeting with the young Montréal lawyer and parliamentarian who would become prime minister of Canada in 1967 was decisive in another, more concrete way. Through a mutual friend, Trudeau introduced her to Jean-Paul Vinay, a professor of comparative stylistics in the Department of Linguistics at the Université de Montréal and, along with his colleague Jean Darbelnet, one of Canada's pioneers in translation theory. Claxton enrolled in Vinay's course, and before she knew it, she was on the way to completing the master's degree in translation she earned in 1971. She describes Vinay as a marvellous pedagogue. The program was structured around what she refers to as "guided doing," practical translation exercises in a variety of fields, into both French and English. Well suited to her own self-directed, hands-on learning style, her studies at the Université de Montréal were to give her the tools she needed to set out the course, to engineer the crossing, so to speak, both for herself as translator and for others as readers.

"From the beginning, from the time of *Cité libre*," she recalls, "I knew translation was a way of communicating something important to people who did not speak French. Big changes were happening in Quebec and English-speaking Canadians needed to understand what they were about." Her passionate sense of the broader social function of translation within Canada is pungently evident in her first article on literary translation, a short text entitled "Culture Vulture," published in 1967 in the Université de Montréal review *Méta: Journal des traducteurs / Translators Journal*.

Excerpts from Québec nationalist writer Hubert Aquin's seminal novel *Prochain épisode* had just appeared in the popular *Maclean's* magazine, and Claxton was appalled by the abysmal quality of the translation: "French syntax is followed throughout, with French punctuation, and where the straight literality or *calque* yields something that is just too, too garbled for words, the translator cooks up something else which is pure invention in varying degrees of inaccuracy (or leaves it out altogether—O happy solution!)."[2]

At stake are two issues of fundamental importance for Claxton: the incomprehensibility of the translation for an English readership, and its lack of historical and artistic integrity. The translator, she points out, referring to another passage, "has missed an obvious allusion" to the Québec patriots of the 1837 rebellion, while "certain sustained images of quite lyrical beauty, and allusions to other parts of the book...are completely lost."[3] Both shortcomings, and this is why Claxton takes the translator to task so bluntly, prevent the translated text from carrying out what she sees as its primary function: to provide Canadian anglophone readers with accurate and informed access to Aquin's text and ideas.

From the particular case of *Prochain épisode*, Claxton moves on to a scathing attack on the dismal state of literary translation in Canada in general: "I have seen enough that is bad and read and heard enough exasperated comment to be convinced that we could and should do better." With a surprising breadth of vision and commitment for one so early in her translation career, she then proceeds to outline why and how the situation can be improved: "A glance over the fence on the part of either of our two cultures," she affirms forthrightly, "is not likely to be habit-forming unless it pleases."[4] The Canada Council program of subsidies will only be successful, she warns, if both the council and the publishers who receive its grants make a serious commitment to verifying translation quality. Nor is she content to wait for good translators to simply "appear."[5] With considerable foresight, she calls for "the institution of a program of advanced formal study intended specifically to prepare literary translators," offers an outline of the types of courses such a program might include, and recommends the establishment of a "Governor-General's Prize, or an equivalent," and "a vigilant committee set up by the profession [with] as its principal function to award stars in ascending multiples for good translations and some other appropriate symbol for bad ones; skulls and cross-bones, I suggest."[6]

Six years and many advocacy efforts later, in 1973, the Canada Council would add translation to the categories for its prestigious literary prizes, renamed the Governor General's Awards in 1986. Eight years later, in

1975, Claxton would be one of the fourteen founding members and first president of the Literary Translators' Association of Canada (LTAC). While it has yet to assign star and lemon ratings to published translations, LTAC has contributed significantly to improving the professionalism of literary translation in Canada.

When acknowledging the central role Claxton has played within the literary translation community in Canada, it is difficult not to call to mind both the extensive organizational abilities of her mother and the indomitable engineering eye of her father scanning the vast horizon of northwestern India or the formidable deserts of Iraq, mapping out the position of the rails to be laid. Dorothy Carson was a very strong woman with a highly developed sense of public service, an active organizer, in Second World War Kingston, of the IODE,[7] the blood clinic, and parcels to soldiers on the front. Fred Carson was knighted in 1942 for his railway work in India. Claxton remembers her mother's impatience to get things done, and her father's sheer Irish bull-headedness. Endowed with both parents' sense of public commitment, Claxton would need to call on both their strengths in her advocacy for literary translation in Canada.

One of the thorniest issues for Canadian literary translators was, and remains, professional recognition. Concretely, this includes having their name on the book cover, mention of their work in book reviews, protection of their rights in the publishing contract, and participation in royalties. "An early LTAC initiative," writes Claxton, "was the adoption of a watchdog role for the Association, scrutinising reviews of translations and notifying editors of newspapers and magazines when translators were not properly acknowledged."[8] Claxton was at the forefront of the association's initiative to develop a standard publishing contract for translators, and beginning in 1977, she spearheaded its determined efforts to have translators' rights included in the changes being made to the Canadian Copyright Act. As draft after draft of amendments to the legislation were reviewed, no funds being available to hire professional counsel, Claxton found herself, as LTAC president and later copyright chair, researching British and Canadian case law, making presentations before various federal Parliamentary committees, and filing legal briefs. She still remembers the derisory attitude of many of the officials she met for whom translation was an inferior form of activity, and "translators did not count." To give one a flavour of the debates, according to one draft amendment to the act, tabled in Parliament on May 27, 1987, "tables, compilations and computer programs"[9] were considered literary works, but not, hard as this is to believe now, translations.

One catches a glimpse of the determination and intelligence with which Claxton tackled the legal dimensions of these lobbying efforts, and the time and energy she devoted to the cause, in a six-page "Brief on Copyright" she filed on June 10, 1985, before the Sub-Committee of the Standing Committee on Communications and Culture on the Revision of Copyright, this time with advice from expert legal counsel.[10] Claxton outlines succinctly LTAC's position that "case law precedent clearly identifies translations as original literary works in the meaning of the Copyright Act,"[11] and that translations should accordingly be added to the list of specific inclusions (maps, charts, plans, tables and compilations) described in the act as literary works.

She also examines in considerable depth a proposal put forward to include translations as "derivative works," noting that the term "is pejorative, meaning just short of plagiaristic and therefore contemptible." To avoid the impact of these negative connotations on the perception of translation, she suggests the wording "derived works" as a more positive term, "totally neutral, meaning simply 'works which have been derived,' and which, besides, finds a totally natural and accurate equivalence with the French *oeuvres dérivées*."[12] Furthermore, she points out, "derivative works" is American terminology, and she argues against its use "on the grounds that there should be no encouragement to introduce American case law into our courts, since it would lead to confusion between the two regimes."[13] She then proceeds to analyze the substantive aspects of including translation among the derived works in the new legislation, and offers precise recommendations based on an analysis of the Copyright Act and case law in both the United Kingdom and the United States. She ends the brief by outlining numerous "examples of abuses and confusion"[14] affecting translators, which could and should be remedied in the new legislation.

Nor were Claxton's efforts limited to the preparation and submission of briefs. In 1987 she wrote to Flora Macdonald, minister of Communications, protesting the inclusion in draft legislation of computer programs as literary works, but not translations. The letter was copied to the Standing Committee on Communication and Culture as well as to Harvey André, minister of Consumer and Corporate Affairs, for both departments were concerned, complicating Claxton's task. The letter was also sent to a variety of anglophone and francophone arts groups, including the Canadian Conference of the Arts, the Conférence des associations de créateurs et créatrices du Québec, the Council of Translators and Interpreters of Canada, the League of Canadian Poets, the Société des traducteurs du Québec, the Writers' Union of Canada, and the Union des écrivains québécois, all of whom Claxton had regularly consulted and mobilised over the ten years of networking and advocacy required to finally have translation included in the Canadian Copyright Act.

During this same period, she also generously shared the results of her research on the question with other translators, through a series of articles she published in English and French in professional reviews, such as *L'Antenne* and *Circuit*. Unfailingly modest about her part in ensuring the recognition of translators' rights in the revised Copyright Act passed by Parliament on December 11, 1987, Claxton states simply, "These efforts were successful, translations are now mentioned as literary works in the law." Ever vigilant, the determined civic agent adds, "this had to be fought for." Until 1994, she continued to represent LTAC at the Conférence des associations de créateurs et créatrices du Québec, a working group of arts creators formed for the joint study of copyright and the submission of consensus positions on the continuing revision of the Canadian Copyright Act.

Claxton's fight for professional recognition for translators has gone hand in hand with a similar commitment to setting up the structures that ensure professional responsibility. In keeping with her bold recommendations in "Culture Vulture" and her concern for translation quality, Claxton devoted considerable energy throughout the 1970s and early 1980s to the issue of translator accreditation. Within Québec and Canadian translators' associations, these were key years for issues related to professional development. From 1972 to 1974, as executive member of the Société des traducteurs du Québec, Claxton chaired the Admissions Examination Committee, with responsibility for devising and implementing examination procedures. From 1978 to 1982, she represented her provincial association on the Conseil des traducteurs et interprètes du Canada (CTIC), the pan-Canadian accreditation board. In 1981–82, as chair of the CTIC Standard Examination Board, she oversaw a major reorganization of the national accreditation procedures and prepared a procedural guide to be used by member associations from six provinces. That same year, she was also responsible for the administration of the Canada-wide certification examinations in English-French, French-English, along with a variety of other language combinations. Her professional contributions have also extended to the international arena. She has represented LTAC at the Fédération internationale des traducteurs that groups together professional translation associations from over sixty different countries. As a member of PEN International, she has taken up the cause of translators imprisoned for their work.

The Spirit of Passage

Claxton's commitment to the civic role of translators informs her own style and work. Her concern for establishing a respectful social framework for the practice of translation as intercultural exchange, for engineering the crossing, so to speak, is reflected in many different ways within the spirit of her own translation passages. Certainly, a consistent interest in Canadian social issues links the wide range of books, articles, and other works Claxton has translated since her maiden voyage with *Cité libre*. Her early commercial translations include sections of the federal Commission of Inquiry into the Non-Medical Use of Drugs (Ledain Commission), articles on labour policy and income security, and a chapter of the Royal Commission on Bilingualism and Biculturalism (Laurendeau-Dunton Commission). Her first major translations placed her squarely in the intercultural debate on the history of Québec, with books by eminent Québec historians Marcel Trudel (*The Beginnings of New France, Atlas of New France, Canadian History Textbooks: A Comparative Study*) and Fernand Ouellet (*Lower Canada, 1791–1840: Structural Change and Nationalism*). She took on articles about Québec's Quiet Revolution, including texts by Gérard Pelletier, Jacques Hébert, and Fernand Ouellet for Thomas Axworthy and Pierre Trudeau's edited volume *Towards a Just Society*, and she continued to translate articles by the great man himself. However, increasingly uncomfortable with Trudeau's constitutional positions, and particularly with his fierce opposition to the Meech Lake and Charlottetown Agreements, Claxton discreetly passed on the opportunity to translate the former prime minister's memoirs. "I had become very disillusioned with his ideas," Claxton recalls, "I felt I had contributed, through my translations, to what he was doing, and I did not want to contribute any longer."

Trudel's book *The Beginnings of New France* gave Claxton her first nomination for the Canada Council (now the Governor General's) Award in translation (she was to be shortlisted five more times and would win the award on two occasions). New translation challenges soon arose. Remaining true to her fundamental interest in important social issues, Claxton undertook three books (*Turn of a Pang, French Kiss or a Pang's Progress,* and *Baroque at Dawn*) by well-known Québec feminist Nicole Brossard, as well as several short works by Suzanne Jacob and France Théoret. Short stories by Iraqi-Canadian writer Naïm Kattan explore themes from immigration, Ronald Lavallée's historical novel about the Métis, *Tchipayuk, or the Way of the Wolf*, and Gabrielle Roy's autobiography, *Enchantment and Sorrow*, address respectively the sombre side of Métis and minority francophone life in the Canadian West. Claxton's most recent translation, *A Sunday at the Pool in Kigali*, by Québec journalist Gil Courtemanche, is set in Rwanda during the April 1994 Hutu-led, government-orchestrated genocide against the Tutsi people.

Claxton's sense of the translator as a civic agent also underlies her approach to the process of translation. As her critique of the initial translation of *Prochain épisode* so cogently demonstrated, she is intensely aware of the profound differences between languages and cultures. Not unlike her early crossings from India to Canada as a young child, intercultural passages can be arduous, slow zigzags over hostile waters, and their ultimate destination can be uncertain. Although there may be some consolation in not being alone for the passage, the presence of others increases the complexity of the crossing. Much depends on the languages themselves, the authors involved, the attitudes of the publishers, and the perceived expectations of the final readers. Claxton's need to engineer the crossing and her resulting attention to the contractual framework of the translation process reflect both her recognition of the inevitably dialogic nature of this process and her own search for respectful and secure balance within the troubled waters of negotiated passage. It is in this sense that her dedication to "getting it right" is to be understood, not merely as a question of finding the right grammatical or terminological structure, but one of finding the exact point on the compass where a variety of forms of respect can intersect: respect for the ideas and artistic integrity of the original text, respect for the author's underlying project, respect for the forms and values of the target language that ensure the comprehensibility of the translated text, and respect for the translator herself and her work.

How complex these multiple layers of negotiation can be, and how limited the rules of passage given one can be, were made painfully clear to Claxton very early in her career when she was translating Trudel and Ouellet's historical studies. Both books were part of the McClelland and Stewart Canadian Centenary Series directed by Desmond Morton. As such, they had to conform to certain restrictions in length and format, and Claxton was asked to condense both original texts. Needless to say, this further complicated the arduous translation process. Ouellet was so incensed that "a mere translator should be cutting down his text" that Claxton had to ask both Morton, as series editor, and David Farr, the president of the Canadian Historical Association, to intervene. "In the end, Ouellet decided that I really was on his side, recalls Claxton, and both he and Morton thanked me in their prefaces to the book.[15] In a review published in the *Globe and Mail*, historian Ramsay Cook also paid homage to the translator's efforts, noting that "the book has been beautifully translated and adapted by Patricia Claxton."[16]

In Trudel's case, the French text was already a condensed version of three volumes, the last of which had never been published (the manuscript had been destroyed in a fire). This meant that Claxton had no original reference point for her own process of paring down the text: "Integrating contemporary quotations into the text was another headache," she adds. In their presentation of Trudel's book, Desmond Morton and Donald Creighton are clearly pleased to welcome the "best French scholarship" to the series, noting that "such a contribution, moreover, greatly aids the growing integration of the Series: enfin les fleurs-de-lys!"[17] They discuss the "difficulties of organising and executing such a series," but make no mention of the translation, nor of the choices Claxton was forced to make to have the lengthy French text fit the series format.

In fact, these choices reflect several strategies generally associated with the more intrusive process of adaptation, as opposed to translation. Claxton chose to eliminate certain chapters entirely, and in other cases to cut introductory remarks and secondary themes. As a result, the transitions between chapters and paragraphs had to be reworked in order to keep the flow of the amputated text coherent. Considerable judgement and attention to detail were required to ensure that the leaner text remained true to the spirit of the original, and that both the logical and chronological organization was maintained.

"Tooling" the Vessel

Through this meticulous process, Claxton developed an attentiveness to the external referent that was to stay with her throughout her practice as a translator. Checking the accuracy of references to time and place and making subsequent modifications are for her clearly part of the civil contract the translator undertakes with his or her reader. "Even in fiction," she states categorically, "references to real people and places should be right."[18] While such details might be considered merely technical in nature, for Claxton they are part of the essential underpinnings of the text. If the vessel is to be seaworthy in the target language, if the new readers are to find it credible, adjusting the tooling is fundamental to safe passage.

In her translator's note in Gabrielle Roy's *Enchantment and Sorrow*, published in 1986, Claxton mentions several small referential details that needed to be revised. Some, such as having a character speak of the First World War in 1938 before there was a Second World War, were simply "potentially distracting anomalies"[19] to be corrected. The autobiography was published posthumously and did not benefit from Gabrielle Roy's usual careful editing. Others touch on specific local knowledge of bus routes or the length of time it takes to walk from one point to another, details that, when inaccurate, the informed reader could find troubling: "Since Charing Cross is at one side of Trafalgar Square," notes Claxton, "a bus leaving Trafalgar Square and heading north towards Epping Forest [one of Gabrielle Roy's destinations], will not pass Charing Cross ten minutes or so later [as indicated in the original], though it will almost certainly pass King's Cross." She continues, "A morning's walk from just outside Nice to St-Tropez is clearly intended to telescope a distance of some hundred kilometres. Still, such a walk rather severely taxes the imagination for one who may know the region."[20] In yet other cases, the translation activates different historical classifications: "To Gabrielle Roy, 'Saxon' appears to mean 'old English' in a broad sense," writes Claxton, "but 'Saxon cottages,' thatched and half-timbered, are more accurately Tudor, and Boedicea lived before the coming of the Saxons and was therefore not a Saxon but a British queen." She adds, "Still, designating Boadicea as 'British' might allow an impression that she was a rather recent queen, whereas if she is identified with the ancient Britons her antiquity is no longer in doubt."[21]

Besides the practical clarification they provide, such details enable Claxton to establish an unintrusive, yet communicatively effective, dialogue with her readers about the translation process. By focussing on issues of external reference, as opposed to elements of a more interpretive nature, Claxton subtly sets the framework for the reception of the translated text within a dialogical space where difference can be discussed in a civil fashion, unhindered by precipitous judgements. Her friendly and unassuming tone contributes to the opening of a common space where author, text, source language, translator, target language and reader can meet for pleasant exchange. By offering to "share at least a few gleanings" from her research and reflection as translator, she communicates her own curiosity about the other to her reader: "I was puzzled by the way in which Gabrielle Roy speaks of 'Pembina Mountain,'" she writes conversationally, "I learned that this, in the early days of Manitoba was the name used collectively for a group of small settlements on the slopes of the Pembina Escarpment." Demystifying linguistic categorisation, she adds that she "also learned that in the Canadian Prairies the berries called 'pembinas,' from which pembina jelly is made, are also known as 'mooseberries,' and are elsewhere more prosaically called 'highbush cranberries.'"[22] By citing such concrete examples where they will be the least contested, Claxton discreetly validates the right to difference more generally and places the reading of the translation firmly within a framework of civil dialogue.

Ronald Lavallée's historical novel *Tchipayuk, or the Way of the Wolf* takes Claxton into the core of intercultural collision in nineteenth-century Manitoba. In her translator's note, she first draws attention to Lavallée's extensive research, "ensuring the authenticity of countless details," and then carefully draws a link, through terminology, between colonial past and present: "The early French penetration of the continent has left a surprising number of familiar terms and place names in English, some adapted first from Indian tongues....I wonder how many English speakers realise that the sled driver's command, 'Mush!' was originally (and more sensibly) 'Marche!'"[23] In *A Sunday at the Pool in Kigali*, anticipating "that readers might appreciate knowing more about the background of Rwandan politics," she has discreetly "provided a few additional footnotes and now and then added a clarifying word or two to the body of the book, hoping to give a maximum of information with a minimum of disruption to the story."[24]

Nor is dialogue confined to the readers' space. As the latter comment implies, loyalty to the text and its author are equally essential for Claxton. In her translator's notes—she significantly refuses the more authoritarian appellation of preface—she is careful to refrain from offering interpretations of the book she has translated. She respectfully lets the text stand for itself and leaves the reader to judge on his or her own. In this respect, her minute presentation of terms and details also reveals how scrupulous she is about even the smallest change she feels required to introduce in the translation. As an "interpretive translator," one who gives priority to the readability of the text in the target language, "intervening is part of my duty," she states in a recent, as yet unpublished, article entitled "Translating the Implied."[25]

She clearly finds such interventions troubling, however, and she notes conscientiously that "all the interventions discussed...were approved by the respective authors before publication of the books in translation." Even more revealing, after more than thirty years of professional practice, she remains "intrigued" at "how often [she has] found it necessary or desirable to add something not strictly called for at first sight, either to avoid ambiguity or downright inaccuracy, or to heighten the accuracy, sharpen the perception, bolden or soften the atmosphere...In other words, to fill in, in the target language, something implied in the source language."[26] Less frequently, she finds herself "ellipsing expressions in the target language because they seemed redundant, essential though their equivalents may have been in the source language." Her preoccupation with such changes is such that in the drafts of her translations, she now "inserts a symbol enabling her to locate interventions of both kinds, primarily to enable [her] to come back and reconsider them and eventually clear certain of them with [her] author."[27]

Her translation of Gabrielle Roy's *Ma chère petite soeur: Lettres à Bernadette 1943–1970* offers a looking-glass view into how her desire for readability and her equally intense loyalty to the text and its author play themselves out in the process of translating. In her translator's note, she carefully sets out the frame of the letters, and at the same time presents her own translation strategy. As she explains, "Bernadette's religious name was Soeur Léon de la Croix.…When Gabrielle addressed her as *ma chère petite soeur* she was using the word *soeur* in the double sense of 'sister,' and avoiding the formal name, which she found forbidding.…Being aware of this at the outset may be helpful to English readers."[28] The need to "keep the double meaning," or "special significance of this phrase," she adds, "was the principal reason for leaving the letter openings in French." On the other hand, "Since the French closings are often foreign to English, I have adapted those, lest they bewilder the reader and intrude on the substance and tone of the letters."[29]

She also draws the reader's attention both to the form of the letters, their "freshness and spontaneity," and to what they reveal about the relationship between the two sisters: "after Bernadette falls seriously ill, the spontaneity does not really disappear; what is new is a depth and intensity of emotion that are glimpsed but not sustained in the family chit-chat and ups and downs of events and preoccupations in the previous letters." Claxton admits that she has "been very conscious of these things in her translation, as well as of the fact that spontaneity and polish, while not mutually exclusive, are found in different proportions in personal letters as compared to writing intended for publication."[30]

Both challenges are present in the following passage from a letter Roy wrote to her sister from Paris, on June 22, 1948:

> Ma chère petite soeur,
>
> Il fait bon venir t'écrire quelques moments. Ta dernière lettre nous a donné à tous deux beaucoup de joie. Je crois d'ailleurs y avoir répondu, mais qu'importe, je suis contente de répéter que tes lettres nous apportent un gentil souvenir des heures heureuses de Kenora.
>
> J'ai écrit à Lucille et je vais l'aider dans ses études. Plus tard, elle pourra aider sa petite soeur à son tour, et un peu de bien fera ainsi, je l'espère, beaucoup de bonheur en fin de compte.[31]

To accommodate her own literary context, Claxton has gently moved the syntax and vocabulary to a slightly more formal note in English:

> Ma chère petite soeur,
>
> It's good to sit down and write to you for a few minutes. Your last letter brought much delight to both of us. I think I've already answered it, but never mind, I enjoy saying again that your letters bring us sweet memories of happy times at Kenora.
>
> I have written to Lucille and will help her with her studies. Later on it will be her turn to help her younger sister, and this way, I hope, a little good will end up bringing much happiness.[32]

At the same time, the colloquial expression, "never mind," helps maintain the balance, and Claxton has very carefully translated the emotional vocabulary, paying special attention to the fine distinctions between such common, yet often elusive, expressions as "il fait bon," "beaucoup de joie," "contente," "gentil," "heureuses," "beaucoup de bonheur." She also makes a small expansion, or "insertion," in the initial sentence to capture more concretely the familiar gesture of putting pen to paper, or sitting down to write.

In the following passage, taken from a letter near the end of the volume, written just a month before Bernadette's death, Roy's prose is much more intense:

> La beauté du monde m'est encore plus visible qu'avant grâce à toi. Tu m'enseignes aussi la générosité, l'oubli de soi et de penser aux autres. Et ce qui compte, c'est que tu m'enseignes tout cela, non par les mots qui ne laissent pas grande trace, mais par l'exemple qui, lui, est indélibile. Aujourd'hui le temps hésite entre le sombre et l'ensoleillé, entre le gris et le radieux, un peu à la manière de nos vies suspendues entre le sourire et les larmes, entre la peur et la confiance.[33]

Once again, Claxton has restructured the first sentence and deftly intermingled spoken and written syntactical forms:

> Thanks to you, I can see the beauty of the world even more clearly than before. You also teach me generosity, unselfishness, and thoughtfulness of others. And what really counts is that you teach me these things not with words, which fade without much trace, but through example, which cannot be erased. Today the weather is wavering between dull and sunny, between dismal and radiant—rather the ways our lives are, somewhere between tears and laughter, between fear and confidence.[34]

This time, to render the depth of Roy's emotion, Claxton has chosen her equivalents for their concision and lyrical qualities. Her own judicious use of sound and rhythm echoes Roy's writerly expressivity, particularly in the touching allusion to the ephemeral nature of the written word. There is no doubt that Claxton has engaged her own sensibilities on the side of Roy, as she literally feels her way through the process of re-expression into English for her readers.

Passage Home

Claxton's first ocean crossing, coming home to Canada for her own birth, is a striking image of the translative passage. In such a context, the essential moment of the voyage, the final destination to which it aspires, would seem to be the arrival itself, the new beginning. When speaking of her conception of the translation process, Claxton does indeed declare herself to be an interpretive translator, or *cibliste*. Within translation studies, Claxton's attention to the readerliness of the text and her insistence on conformity to target language norms are associated with what is called a fluent or transparent translation strategy, one that gives the reader the impression, or illusion, that he or she is reading an original text.

Contemporary theorists such as Lawrence Venuti have been quick to point out that such a strategy is not value-neutral. On the contrary, it "performs a labour of acculturation which domesticates the foreign text, making it intelligible and even familiar to the target-language reader [...], enacting an imperialism that extends the dominion of transparency with other ideological discourses over a different culture."[35] Yet an examination of Claxton's translation process, as we have seen, offers important nuances to Venuti's dichotomy, which, in the tradition of Walter Benjamin, equates interpretive or readerly translation strategies necessarily with a domesticating approach and literalist strategies with a foreignizing orientation.

In her own life, Claxton has made the reverse crossing, back towards the other, and her interpretive orientation is tempered by an equal respect for opening up home to the foreign. More specifically, within the Canadian/Québec context in which she has chosen to live, home is both self and other, identity and difference. Claxton's translation practice is thus more accurately situated in the framework of postcolonial theories of translation, where, as Susan Bassnett points out, "linguistic exchange [is seen] as essentially dialogic, as a process that happens in a space that belongs to neither source nor target absolutely."[36] Indeed, postcolonial theorist Homi Bhabha uses the term translation "not to describe a transaction between texts and languages but in the etymological sense of being carried across from one place to another."[37] From this perspective, "translation is now rightly seen as a process of negotiation between texts and cultures during which all kinds of translations take place mediated by the figure of the translator."[38] Claxton's personal contribution to an understanding of how this negotiated carrying across takes place lies in her sense of the civil structures necessary for a secure framework for intercultural respect.

Some of her most gratifying moments are her encounters with her fellow-travellers, the exchanges prompted by each text, the letters from enchanted readers, the meetings with new and touching fictional people: "I particularly enjoyed some of the characters," she recalls of her experience translating Gabrielle Roy's autobiography. "I also wept at times, because I felt her emotions so deeply. I was less anxious when doing the second part, the pressure was not as great when I was finished with her exceptionally painful childhood."[39] Working with the authors whom she conveys through the space in between difference has led to many privileged moments. In a break from historical texts, Claxton translated Nicole Brossard's transgressive, postmodern, feminist text, *Turn of a Pang*. She remembers with pleasure Brossard's endless curiosity about language, and their numerous discussions first to clarify the meaning of the French, and then to check that the English corresponded to Brossard's feeling about her own text. Undoubtedly, Gil Courtemanche speaks for many of Claxton's authors when he thanks Patricia Claxton "for the skill and great care she has brought to the task. As a result of our discussions, we made a few useful modifications and I took her counsel and the opportunity she offered to clarify some additional points. A good translation improves a text, and I feel this is certainly true in this case."[40] For Claxton, learning she has contributed through her translation to the success of Courtemanche's book in the English-speaking world, and even in other languages (as the rights sold at the Frankfurt book fair often depended on a reading of the English translation), is profoundly rewarding.

"I couldn't imagine translating without contact with the author," she recalls thinking, when invited to translate *Enchantment and Sorrow*. She consequently asked the publisher if Joyce Marshall, who had herself translated a number of books by Roy, and had known her well, could be her editor. Claxton speaks both fondly and respectfully of Marshall's editing: "Joyce is very low-key," she recalls, and "so my more colourful terms often needed to be toned down."[41] Marshall, along with her friend and mentor Philip Stratford, were Claxton's major influences, and she generously acknowledges their invaluable contribution to helping her learn her craft.

She is also grateful to her fellow literary translators within LTAC for "so much enrichment and friendship."[42]

Nor is the passage home devoid of family strife. Claxton's frustrations inevitably pinpoint relations with her publishers. Negotiating with inexperienced copy editors can be particularly trying. During her translation of *Enchantment and Sorrow*, for instance, she had decided, and Joyce Marshall had agreed, to use contractions throughout the book: "the publisher's copy editor, an untried beginner at creative work, arbitrarily took them all out and introduced all kinds of further problems. The result was disastrous and demanded weeks of rewriting."[43] When mistakes occur during the preparation of the printed copy, she is simply shattered. Coach House speeded up the publication of *French Kiss, or A Pang's Progress* in order for the book to be available for an important colloquium Nicole Brossard was attending in Australia. Claxton was not given an opportunity to check the page proofs containing graphics. As a result, three important words, the punch line, in fact, of a comic strip in the book, were left out. Seventeen years later, Claxton's reaction is poignant. Opening up the page, she says, her voice filled with emotion, "It breaks my heart." In an unexpected turn of events, Claxton was contacted early in 2003 by the new Coach House Books, interested in republishing *Turn of a Pang, French Kiss*, and *A Book*, translated by the late Larry Shouldice, in one volume, under the title *The Blue Books*. The publisher was "anxious to put all the old errors right" and Claxton was, as she says, "overjoyed."

Claxton lives in Montréal, with her husband, Jim McLeod, a retired dentist, with whom she enjoys playing a tough game of tennis and skiing down the slopes in the Green Mountains, especially when the snow is soft powder, or as Jim says, "une belle poudreuse." Her friends come from both anglophone and francophone milieux, and several, like Jori Smith, from the Québec artistic community. She is firmly rooted in her bilingual home where francophones and anglophones no longer live separate lives and the borders are more permeable. Over her thirty-year career, the spirit of her own translation passages has evolved: "I used to try to 'get into the author's skin,'" Claxton confides, "but couldn't always do so and felt guilty. Now I try to hear what the writer has to say, and choose an appropriate way of relating it, but without suppressing my own voice."[44]

Paradoxically, translation has enabled her, through penning the lines of others, to discover her own voice, the words and rhythms, the colours and emotions, the sounds and riggings of the passage itself.

NOTES

1 Patricia Claxton, Interview with the author, Montreal, Oct. 30 and 31, 2002. Unless otherwise indicated, all quotations of remarks by Patricia Claxton refer to this interview.
2 Patricia Claxton, "Culture Vulture," *Méta* 12, no. 1 (March 1967): 9.
3 Claxton, "Culture Vulture," p. 9.
4 Claxton, "Culture Vulture," pp. 9, 12.
5 Harry Lorin Binsse, "An Intellectual Iron Curtain?" *Montreal Star*, Sept. 22, 1962, Entertainment Section, p. 2.
6 Claxton, "Culture Vulture," p. 13.
7 Imperial Order Daughters of the Empire.
8 Patricia Claxton, "Introduction: Looking Back," in "La Traduction littéraire au Canada / Literary Translation in Canada," *Méta* 45, no. 1 (Apr. 2000): 9. During this same period, professional recognition, including visibility on book jackets, was also an important issue for American translators. See Marilyn Gaddis-Rose, "Like the Paths Around Combray, Humanistic Translation Theories Diverge and Converge," in *Translation Horizons: Beyond the Boundaries of Translation Spectrum*, ed. M. Gaddis-Rose, Translation Perspectives 9 (Binghampton: Center for Research in Translation, State University of New York, 1996), pp. 62, 66.
9 Claxton, "Introduction: Looking Back," p. 9.
10 Patricia Claxton, translator's note, in Gabrielle Roy, *Enchantment and Sorrow: The Autobiography of Gabrielle Roy* (Toronto: Lester and Orpen Dennys, 1987), pp. viii, ix.
11 The lawyer was Marian Hebb. She had some input with the brief, in particular, as Claxton recalls, as to how to best structure it, and was beside Claxton when the latter made the presentation: "She was in Ottawa for other clients, which meant that her fee to LTAC was modest."
12 Patricia Claxton, Brief on Copyright Introductory Remarks presented before the Sub-Committee of the Standing Committee on Communications and Culture on the revision of Copyright on behalf of the Literary Translators' Association of Canada, June 10, 1985, p. 1. For an indication of translation and copyright issues in Europe and the United States, see Cay Dollerup, "Copyright and Translation," in *Beyond the Western Tradition*, ed. M. Gaddis-Rose, Translation Perspectives 11 (Binghampton: Center for Research in Translation, State University of New York, 2000), pp. 347–49; and Marilyn Gaddis-Rose, "The Indispensable Details of Copyright and Permissions," in *Beyond the Western Tradition*, ed. M. Gaddis-Rose, Translation Perspectives 11 (Binghampton: Center for Research in Translation, State University of New York, 2000), pp. 351–53.
13 Claxton, Brief on Copyright Introductory Remarks, p. 2.
14 Claxton, Brief on Copyright Introductory Remarks. This latter argument was Hebb's.
15 Claxton, Brief on Copyright Introductory Remarks, p. 5

16 "I must finally thank Patricia Claxton who has assumed the difficult task of translating and adapting *Le Bas-Canada* for the Canadian Centenary Series," writes Ouellet. Fernand Ouellet, *Lower Canada, 1791–1840: Structural Change and Nationalism*, trans. P. Claxton (Toronto: McClelland and Stewart, 1990), p. xiv. The book, writes Morton in his preface, "has been skillfully and painstakingly adapted for the Series by the translator, Patricia Claxton." In Ouellet, *Lower Canada, 1791–1840*, p. x.
17 Cook, "Lower Canada 1791–1840."
18 W.L. Morton and D.G. Creighton, "The Canadian Centenary Series," in *The Beginnings of New France 1524–1663*, by Marcel Trudel, trans. P. Claxton (Toronto: McClelland and Stewart, 1973), p. x.
19 Patricia Claxton, "Enchantment and Sorrow in the Life of a Literary Translator," Interview with Mary Plaice, *Circuit*, no. 21 (June 1988): 21.
20 Claxton, translator's note in Roy, *Enchantment and Sorrow*, p. viii.
21 Claxton, translator's note in Roy, *Enchantment and Sorrow*, p. viii.
22 Claxton, translator's note in Roy, *Enchantment and Sorrow*, pp. viii.
23 Ronald Lavallée, *Tchipayuk, or the Way of the Wolf* (Vancouver: Talon Books, 1994), p. ix.
24 Patricia Claxton, translator's note, in Gil Courtemanche, *A Sunday at the Pool in Kigali*, trans. Patricia Claxton (Toronto, Alfred A. Knopf Canada, 2003), n.p.
25 Patricia Claxton, "Translating the Implied," unpublished manuscript, p. 2.
26 Claxton, "Translating the Implied," pp. 2, 3–4.
27 Claxton, "Translating the Implied," p. 4.
28 Patricia Claxton, translator's note, in Gabrielle Roy, *Ma chère petite soeur: Lettres à Bernadette 1943–1970* (Montréal: Boréal, 1988), p. vii.
29 Claxton, translator's note in Roy, *Ma chère petite soeur*, pp. vii, viii.
30 Claxton, translator's note in Roy, *Ma chère petite soeur*, p. vii.
31 Gabrielle Roy, *Ma chère petite soeur: Lettres à Bernadette 1943–1970*, p. 27.
32 Gabrielle Roy, *Letters to Bernadette*, trans. P. Claxton, ed. François Ricard (Toronto: Lester and Orpen Dennys, 1990), p. 12.
33 Roy, *Ma chère petite soeur*, p. 207.
34 Roy, *Letters to Bernadette*, p. 167.
35 Lawrence Venuti, *Rethinking Translation: Discourse, Subjectivity, Ideology* (London and New York: Routledge, 1992), p. 5.
36 Susan Bassnett, *Translation Studies*, 3rd ed. (London and New York: Routledge, 1998), p. 6.
37 The synthesis of Bhabha's position is given by Bassnett, *Translation Studies*, p. 6.
38 Bassnett, *Translation Studies*, p. 6.
39 Claxton, "Enchantment and Sorrow in the Life of a Literary Translator," p. 20.
40 Gil Courtemanche, *A Sunday at the Pool in Kigali*, trans. P. Claxton (Toronto: Alfred A. Knopf Canada, 2003), n.p.
41 Patricia Claxton, telephone interview, November 1, 2002.
42 Claxton, "Introduction: Looking Back," p. 11–12.
43 Claxton, "Enchantment and Sorrow in the Life of a Literary Translator," p. 21.
44 Claxton, "Enchantment and Sorrow in the Life of a Literary Translator," p. 20.

BIBLIOGRAPHY

I. Primary Sources

Translations

Brossard, Nicole. *Turn of a Pang*. Trans. P. Claxton. Toronto: Coach House: 1976. Translation of *Sold Out: Étreinte-illustration*. Montréal: Éditions du Jour, 1973. Rpt. in *The Blue Books*. Toronto: Coach House Books, 2003. 117–225.

———. *French Kiss, or A Pang's Progress*. Trans. P. Claxton. Toronto: Coach House, 1986. Rpt. in *The Blue Books*. Toronto: Coach House Books, 2003. 227–341. Excerpted in *Erotica: An Anthology of Women's Writing*. London: Pandora Press, 1990, and in *The Girl Wants To*, ed. Lynn Crosbie. Toronto: Coach House, 1993. Translation of *Kiss: Étreinte-exploration*. Montréal: Éditions du Jour, 1974; Quinze, 1980.

———. "Matter and Our Shoulders." Trans. P. Claxton. *ellipse*, no. 53 (1995): 51–53. Translation of "La matière et nos épaules."

———. *Baroque at Dawn*. Trans. P. Claxton. Toronto: McClelland and Stewart, 1997. Translation of *Baroque d'aube*. Montréal: Hexagone, 1995.

———. "The Giant Nature of Words and Silence Around Identity." Trans. P. Claxton. Second Shirley Greenberg Lecture. Ottawa: Presses de l'Université d'Ottawa, 2001. Translation of "La nature géante des mots et du silence autour de l'identité."

Courtemanche, Gil. *A Sunday at the Pool in Kigali*. Trans. P. Claxton. Toronto: Alfred A. Knopf Canada, 2003. Translation of *Un dimanche à la piscine à Kigali*. Montréal: Boréal, 2000.

Daoust, Jean-Paul, "It's Snowing." Trans. P. Claxton. *ellipse*, no. 66 (fall 2001): 34–35. Translation of "Il neige." *Les Saisons de l'ange*, 1997.

———. "Self-Portrait." Trans. P. Claxton. *ellipse*, no. 66 (fall 2001): 48. Translation of "Auto-portrait." *Les saisons de l'ange*, 1999.

Gagnon, Cecile. *Hello, Tree*. Trans. P. Claxton. Illus. Darcia Labrosse. Toronto: McClelland and Stewart, 1988. Translation of *Bonjour l'arbre*. Montréal: Éditions du Raton Laveur, 1985.

———. *I'm Hot*. Trans. P. Claxton. Illus. Darcia Labrosse. Toronto: McClelland and Stewart, 1988. Translation of *J'ai chaud*. Montréal: Éditions du Raton Laveur, 1986.

———. *I'm Hungry*. Trans. P. Claxton. Illus. Darcia Labrosse. Toronto: McClelland and Stewart, 1988. Translation of *J'ai faim*. Montréal: Éditions du Raton Laveur, 1986.

———. *A New House*. Trans. P. Claxton. Illus. Darcia Labrosse. Toronto: McClelland and Stewart, 1988. Translation of *Un nouveau logis*. Montréal: Éditions du Raton Laveur, 1988.

Godbout, Jacques. *The Golden Galarneaus*. Trans. P. Claxton. Toronto: Coach House, 1995. Translation of *Le temps des Galarneau*. Paris: Seuil, 1993.

Guillet, Jean-Pierre. *The Cliff Case*. Trans. P. Claxton. Illus. Huguette Marquis. Waterloo, QC: Quintin Publishers, 1994. Translation of *Enquête sur la falaise*. Waterloo, QC: Éditions Quintin.

———. *The Magdalen Islands Mystery*. Trans. P. Claxton. Illus. Huguette Marquis. Waterloo, QC: Quintin Publishers, 1994. Translation of *Mystère aux îles-de-la-Madeleine*. Waterloo,QC: Éditions Quintin.

Hébert, Jacques. "Legislating for Freedom." Trans. P. Claxton. In *Towards a Just Society*, ed. Thomas S. Axworthy and Pierre Elliott Trudeau. Toronto: Viking (Penguin Canada), 1990. 131–147. Translation of "Le législateur au service de la liberté."

Jacob, Suzanne. Five untitled poems from *La part du feu*. Trans. P. Claxton. *ellipse*, no. 61 (spring 1999): 41–47.

Kattan, Naïm. "Abu Nuas Street." Trans. P. Claxton. In *The Neighbour and Other Stories*. Toronto: McClelland and Stewart, 1982. 61–77; Also published in *Journal of Canadian Fiction* 17/18 (1976): 50–56; and in *Ottawa: A Literary Portrait*, ed. John Bell. Lawrencetown Beach, NS: Pottersfield Press, 1992. 176–87. Translation of "Rue Abou Nouas." In *Dans le désert*. Montréal: Leméac, 1974. 21–35.

———. "The Picture." Trans. P. Claxton. In *The Neighbour and Other Stories*. Toronto: McClelland and Stewart, 1982. 49–60. Translation of "Le tableau." In *Dans le désert*. Montréal: Leméac, 1974. 9–19.

Lavallée, Ronald. *Tchipayuk, or the Way of the Wolf*. Trans. P. Claxton. Vancouver: Talonbooks, 1994. Translation of *Tchipayuk, ou le chemin du loup*. Paris: Albin Michel, 1987.

Maillet, Andrée. "A Little Parlour Game." Trans. P. Claxton. *Contemporary Literature in Translation* 21 (summer 1975): 20–21. Translation of "Un petit jeu de société." In *Le lendemain n'est pas sans amour*. Montréal: Beauchemin, 1963. 83–90.

Major, André. "The Thief of Bonsecours Market." Trans. P. Claxton. In *Stories from Quebec*, ed. Philip Stratford. Toronto: Van Nostrand Rheinhold, 1974. 153–60. Translation of "Le voleur du marché Bonsecours." In *La Chair de poule*. Montréal: Éditions Parti Pris, 1965.

Ouellet, Fernand. *Lower Canada, 1791–1840: Structural Change and Nationalism*. Trans. P. Claxton. Toronto: McClelland and Stewart, 1980. Translation and adaptation of *Le Bas-Canada 1791–1840: Changements structuraux et crise*. Ottawa: Université d'Ottawa, 1976.

———. "The Quiet Revolution: A Turning Point." Trans. P. Claxton. In *Towards a Just Society*, ed. Thomas S. Axworthy and Pierre Elliott Trudeau. Toronto: Viking (Penguin Canada), 1990. 313–41. Translation of "La révolution tranquille, tournant révolutionnaire."

Pelletier, Gérard. "1968: The Mood in Quebec and the Language Policy." Trans. P. Claxton. In *Towards a Just Society*, ed. Thomas S. Axworthy and Pierre Elliott Trudeau. Toronto: Viking (Penguin Canada), 1990. 207–25. Translation of "1968: L'humeur du Québec et la politique des langues."

Ricard, François. *Gabrielle Roy: A Life*. Trans. P. Claxton. Toronto: McClelland and Stewart, 1999. Translation of *Gabrielle Roy: Une vie*. Montréal: Boréal, 1996.

Roy, André. "Flagrant Poems." Trans. P. Claxton. In *Les stratégies du réel / The Story So Far 6*, ed. Nicole Brossard. Toronto: Coach House, 1979. 101–11. Translation of "Flagrants poèmes."

Roy, Gabrielle. *Enchantment and Sorrow: The Autobiography of Gabrielle Roy*. Trans. P. Claxton. Toronto: Lester and Orpen Dennys, 1987. Translation of *La Détresse et l'enchantement*. Montréal: Boréal, 1984.

———. *Letters to Bernadette*. Trans. P. Claxton. Ed. François Ricard. Toronto: Lester and Orpen Dennys, 1990. Translation of *Ma chère petite soeur: Lettres à Bernadette*. Montréal: Boréal, 1988.

———. *The Tortoiseshell and the Pekinese*. Trans. P. Claxton. Toronto: Doubleday Canada, 1989. Translation of *L'Espagnole et la Pékinoise*. Montréal: Boréal, 1986.

Théoret, France. "Tongues Afire." Trans. P. Claxton. In *Les strategies du réel / The Story So Far 6*, ed. Nicole Brossard. Toronto: Coach House, 1979. 195–217. Translation of "Feu de langues."

Tougas, Daniel. "A Frisbee in the Park." Trans. P. Claxton. *Prairie Fire* 11, no. 1 (spring 1990): 148–50. Translation of "Dans le parc d'à côté, des jeunes jouaient au frisbee." 144–47.

Trudeau, Pierre Elliott. "New Treason of the Intellectuals." Trans. P. Claxton. In *Federalism and the French Canadians*. Toronto: Macmillan, 1968. 151–81. Abridged version in *Quebec States Her Case*, eds. Frank Scott and Michael Oliver. Toronto: Macmillan. 57–69. Rpt. in *Who Speaks for Canada?* ed. Desmond Morton. Toronto: McClelland and Stewart, 1999. Translation of "La nouvelle trahison des clercs." *Cité Libre*, April 1962.

———. "The Values of a Just Society." Trans. P. Claxton. In *Towards a Just Society*, ed. Thomas S. Axworthy and Pierre Elliott Trudeau. Toronto: Viking (Penguin Canada), 1990. 357–85. Translation of "Des valeurs d'une société juste."

———. "The Poverty of Nationalist Thinking in Quebec." Trans. P. Claxton. In *Towards a Just Society*, ed. Thomas S. Axworthy and Pierre Elliott Trudeau. Eds. Toronto: Viking (Penguin Canada), 1990.

———. "Postscript." In *Towards a Just Society*, trans. P. Claxton, ed. Thomas S. Axworthy and Pierre Elliott Trudeau. 2nd ed. Toronto: Viking (Penguin Canada), 1992. 430–41. Also appeared as "Trudeau Speaks Out." *Maclean's*, Sept. 28, 1992. 22–26.

Trudel, Marcel. *The Beginnings of New France*. Trans. P. Claxton. Toronto: McClelland and Stewart, 1973. Translation/condensation of *Les vaines tentatives 1524–1601*. Montréal: Fides, 1963; *Le Comptoir 1664–1622*. Montréal: Fides, 1966; and *La seigneurie des Cent-Associés. 1627–1663*. Montréal: Fides, 1979.

———. *Atlas of New France / Atlas de la Nouvelle-France*. Trans. P. Claxton. Québec: Presses de l'Université Laval, 1968.

———. *Canadian History Textbooks: A Comparative Study*. Trans. P. Claxton. Studies of the Royal Commission on Bilingualism and Biculturalism 5. Ottawa: Queen's Printer, 1970. Translation of *Manuels d'histoire canadienne : étude comparative*. Ottawa: Queen's Printer, 1970.

Vien, Rossel. "Coming Back to Saskatoon." Trans. P. Claxton. *Prairie Fire* 11, no. 1 (spring 1990): 137–42. Translation of "Retour à Saskatoon." 130–36.

Unpublished Translations

Arcand, Denys. "The Last Shot II." Screenplay. Trans. P. Claxton. Translation of "La femme idéale," 1991.

Brossard, Nicole. "Women Writers in Quebec Literature." Trans. P. Claxton. Conference paper given by Nicole Brossard in New York, 1979.

Daoust, Jean-Paul. "Butterflies." Trans. P. Claxton. Translation of "Les Papillons." In *Les saisons de l'ange I*. 1997. 91–92.

———. "Landscape." Trans. P. Claxton. Translation of "Paysage." In *Les saisons de l'ange I*. 1997. 12.

———. "The Window." Trans. P. Claxton. Translation of "Remugles." In *Les saisons de l'ange II*. 1999. 38.

Langevin, André. Trans. P. Claxton. Translation of *L'Élan d'Amérique*. Montreal: Cercle du Livre de France, 1972.

Non-Literary Translations

Boisseau, Natalie-Pascale. "Circus of the Sun: The Circus Isn't Just for Children any More." Trans. P. Claxton. *Shambala Sun*, July 1994, 48–52. Translation of "Le Cirque du Soleil: Une discipline du regard et de la présence."

Brunet, Michel. "Quebec and the French Presence in North America." Trans. P. Claxton. *Forces* 43, no. 2 (1978): 102–104. Translation of "Le Québec et la présence française en Amérique."

Commission of Inquiry into the Non-medical Use of Drugs (Ledain Commission). "Additional Conclusions and Recommendations of Marie-Andrée Bertrand." Trans. P. Claxton. In *Final Report*. Ottawa: Information Canada, 1973. 241–53.

———. "Appendix M: Innovative Services." Trans. P. Claxton. In *Final Report*. Ottawa: Information Canada, 1973.1079–102.

Dubuc, Robert. "Termium: System Description." Trans. P. Claxton. *Méta* 17, no. 4 (Dec. 1972): 203–19.

Dussault, Ginette. "Labour Policy and the Labour Market." Trans. P. Claxton. In *Canada under Mulroney: An End-of-Term Report*, ed. A.B. Gollner and Daniel Sale. Montréal: Véhicule Press, 1988.

Lachapelle, Guy. "Between Income Security and Family Equalization." Trans. P. Claxton. In *Canada under Mulroney: An End-of-Term Report*, ed. A.B. Gollner and Daniel Sale. Montréal: Véhicule Press, 1988.

Martin, Fernand. *Montreal: An Economic Perspective*. Trans. P. Claxton. Montréal: Accent Quebec Programme, C.D. Howe Research Institute, 1979. Translation of *Montréal: Les forces économiques en jeu*.

Royal Commission on Bilingualism and Biculturalism (Laurendeau-Dunton Commission). Foreword in *Book IV*. Trans. P. Claxton. Ottawa: Queen's Printer, 1970. xxv–xxvi.

———. Introduction in *Book IV*. Trans. P. Claxton. Ottawa: Queen's Printer, 1970. 3–14.

———. "Some Examples of Linguistic Policies in Business." Trans. P. Claxton. In *The Work World*. Ottawa: Queen's Printer, 1970. 491–518.

Published and Unpublished Texts on Translation
Claxton, Patricia. "Culture Vulture." *Méta* 12, no. 1 (March 1967): 9–13.
———. "Best Friend or Worst Enemy?" *New Book News from Quebec* 1, no. 2 (April 1972).
———. "A Model Contract for Translators." In *La traduction: Une profession / Translating: A Profession, Proceedings of the Eighth World Congress of the International Federation of Translators*, ed. Paul A. Horguelin. Montréal: Conseil des Traducteurs et Interprètes du Canada, 1977. 225–29.
———. "Copyright for Translators." *L'Antenne* 10, no. 6 (April 1979): 3.
———. "Problems of Literary Translation." Address to a training division of the Translation Bureau, Secretary of State Department, Hull, QC, April 18, 1979. Unpublished.
———. "Le droit d'auteur et vous." *L'Antenne* 14, no. 4 (March 1983): 3.
———. "Droit d'auteur: Où en sont les traducteurs?" *L'Antenne* 15, no. 4 (August 1984): 3.
———. "Translation and Creation." In *Traduction et qualité de langue*. Québec: Éditeur officiel du Quebec, 1984. 74–78.
———. Brief on Copyright Introductory Remarks presented before the Sub-Committee on Communications and Culture on the Revision of Copyright on behalf of the Literary Translators' Association of Canada, June 10, 1985.
———. "Enchantment and Sorrow in the Life of a Literary Translator." Interview by Mary Plaice. *Circuit*, no. 21 (June 1988): 20–21.
———. Mémoire présenté à la Commission parlementaire de la culture, Quebec, sur le Projet de Loi 78 (Loi sur le statut des artistes des arts visuels, des métiers d'art et de la littérature et sur leurs contrats avec les diffuseurs), November 29, 1988.
———. "Translation Contracts in Canada," Paper presented at the Third International Feminist Book Fair, June 14, 1988. Unpublished.
———. "Translating Gabrielle Roy." Guest lecture at the University of Alberta, Edmonton, and at the University of Calgary, Calgary, September 14 and 15, 1989. Unpublished.
———. "Translation, Business, and the Ivory Tower." Address to the Alberta Translators' and Interpreters' Association, Calgary, Alberta, September 16, 1989. Unpublished.
———. "The Translator's World as Stage." Address to the Society of Translators of Quebec, January 18, 1989. Unpublished.
———. "Remarks on the Occasion of the Launching of a Special Edition of *Prairie Fire*" (issue on "Franco-Manitoban Writing," Prairie Fire 11, no.1 [spring 1990]), March 29, 1990. Unpublished.
———. "Ruminations on Translation." Guest lecture followed by workshop at Collège universitaire de Saint-Boniface, Saint-Boniface, Manitoba, March 30, 1990. Unpublished.

———. "The Translator as Voyeur." In *Les acquis et les défis / Achievements and Challenges: Proceedings of the 2nd Conference of the Canadian Translators and Interpreters Council*. Montreal, 1990. 261–67.

———. "Interpretive License in Translation." Guest lecture at McGill University, Montréal, April 2, 1991. Unpublished.

———. "Concept in Translation." Address to the Alumni Circle of the School of Translators and Interpreters. University of Ottawa, Ottawa, October 24, 1992. Unpublished.

———. "Cultural and Language Policies and Their Repercussions for Literary Translation." In *Translating in North America: A Community of Interests; Proceedings of the Third North American Congress of the International Federation of Translators*. Montreal, May 27–29, 1992. 247–54

———. "Discovering Friendship." In *Blood and Bone / En chair et en os*, by Joyce Marshall. Oakville: Mosaic Press, 1995. viii–x.

———. "Traduire pour le cinéma." *Perspectives d'avenir en traduction / Future Trends in Translation*, ed. Marie-Christine Aubin. Saint-Boniface, MB: Presses universitaires de Saint-Boniface, 1995. 75–89.

———. "Sur les traces de Gabrielle Roy: Recherches et errances liées à la traduction de *La detresse et L'enchantement*." In *Actes du Colloque internationale Gabrielle Roy*, ed. André Fauchon. Saint-Boniface: Presses universitaires de Saint-Boniface, 1996. 703–16.

———. "Introduction: Looking Back." *Méta*, 45, no. 1 (2000): 7–12.

———. "Translating the Implied." Unpublished manuscript.

II. Secondary Sources

Aquin, Hubert. *Prochain épisode*. Montréal: Cercle du livre français, 1965.

———. *Prochain Episode*. Trans. Penny Williams. Toronto: McClelland and Stewart, 1967.

Bassnett, Susan. *Translation Studies*. 3rd ed. London and New York: Routledge, 1998.

Binsse, Harry Lorin. "An Intellectual Iron Curtain?" *Montreal Star*, Sept. 22, 1962, Entertainment Section, p. 2.

Cook, Ramsay, "Lower Canada 1791–1840." *Globe and Mail*, August 16, 1980.

Dollerup, Cay. "Copyright and Translation" In *Beyond the Western Tradition*, ed. M.Gaddis-Rose, Translation Perspectives 9. Binghamton: Centre for Research in Translation, State University of New York, 2000. 347–49.

Gaddis-Rose, Marilyn. "Like the Paths around Combray, Humanistic Translation Theories Diverge and Converge." In *Translation Horizons: Beyond the Boundaries of* Translation Spectrum, ed. Marilyn Gaddis-Rose, Translation Perspectives 9. Binghamton: Center for Research in Translation, State University of New York, 1996. 59–67.

———. "The Indispensable Details of Copyright and Permissions." In *Beyond the Western Tradition*, ed. Marilyn Gaddis-Rose, Translation Perspectives 11. Bing-

hamton: Center for Research in Translation, State University of New York, 2000. 351–53.
Morton, W.L. and D.G. Creighton, "The Canadian Centenary Series," in *The Beginnings of New France 1524–1663*, by Marcel Trudel, trans. P. Claxton. Toronto: McClelland and Stewart, 1973.
Venuti, Lawrence, ed. *Rethinking Translation: Discourses Subjectivity Ideology*. London and New York: Routledge, 1992.

7

Sheila Fischman
The Consummate Professional

PAMELA GRANT

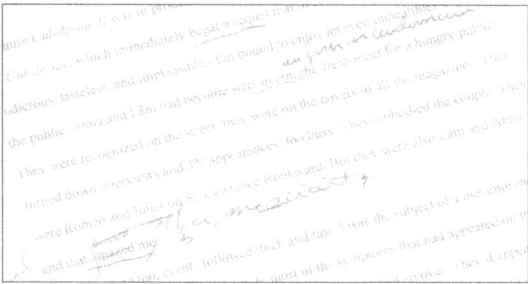

Sheila Fischman is doubtlessly one of the best-known and most prolific literary translators working in Canada today.[1] An enthusiastic promoter of contemporary Québec literature with close to one hundred book-length translations to her name, she has been a major force in creating an English-speaking audience for the authors of Québec. Over the last thirty years, she has given Canadian anglophones access to many of Québec's leading writers, including Anne Hébert, Michel Tremblay, Marie-Claire Blais, Roch Carrier, Yves Beauchemin, and Jacques Poulin, and, more recently, Gaétan Soucy, Élise Turcotte, and Christiane Frenette. Her accomplishments have won her numerous national and international honours, including Columbia University's Félix-Antoine Savard Prize (1989, 1990) and the Canada Council Translation Prize (1974, 1984). In 1998, she was awarded the IBBY[2] Certificate of Honour for translation, as well as the Governor General's Literary Award for Translation, for which she has also been frequently shortlisted. She holds honorary doctorates from the University of Ottawa (1999) and the University of Waterloo (2001); in 2000, she was made a Member of the Order of Canada. One of the few full-time literary translators in Canada, Fischman has earned this recognition through her masterful command of written English, her affinities with the authors and the literature that she translates, and her rigorous application of her talents to the profession of literary translation.

The Formative Years

Sheila Leah Fischman was born in Moose Jaw, Saskatchewan, on December 1, 1937, the daughter of Anna (née Adelkind) and Samson Fischman. Her maternal grandfather was born in Russia, and her paternal grandfather in Poland. When she was two years old, her parents moved to Elgin, Ontario, a village of three hundred inhabitants located north east of Kingston. Here her parents ran a general store—they were equal partners—and she and two younger sisters attended the local public school. A precocious reader, she found refuge in books, relishing that time in August when boxes of schoolbooks filled the store. They were the only Jewish family in the village, and this gave her an early awareness of cultural difference.[3] When Fischman was ready to enter high school, her parents decided to move to Toronto so that she and her sisters would have access to broader educational opportunities. Her parents valued education highly, and took it for granted that their daughters would go on to university for undergraduate and possibly graduate studies.

It was in grade nine at Forest Hill Collegiate in Toronto that Fischman started to learn French. It was a compulsory subject, and she continued to study it throughout high school, initially with English-speaking teachers. In grades twelve and thirteen, however, she had the good fortune to have as a teacher a Franco-Ontarian, T.J. Casaubon, who brought the language to life for her: "He made me realize at a certain level that French was not just a subject like chemistry . . . but a language, a living language that was used for communicating, for talking to your kids, for going to the bank, for living in."[4] She also recalls being introduced to French literature and enjoying in particular stories from Alphonse Daudet's *Lettres de mon moulin*. So great was Casaubon's influence on her that, years later, she would dedicate her first book-length translation to him.[5]

At the University of Toronto, she majored in chemistry but also enjoyed her anthropology and French courses. Although "neither chemistry nor anthropology presented itself as a serious career choice,"[6] her studies in anthropology (she completed an MA in the discipline) fueled her understanding of cultural identities and difference. In 1959, after graduation, she found office work at the CBC. In her words, "I was searching." She wrote book reviews for the *Globe and Mail* and worked in the promotion department of the University of Toronto Press for five years, writing jacket and catalogue blurbs. As the publisher's representative at an annual conference of the Learned Societies,[7] she attended a paper given by D.G. Jones, a professor of comparative literature at the Université de Sherbrooke and an eminent Canadian poet; they were married in 1968.

Finding Her Vocation

Settled with Jones in North Hatley, a scenic village of nine hundred located one hundred miles from Montréal on the shores of Lake Massawippi in the Eastern Townships, Fischman found herself in an ideal setting to foster her interest in literature and improve her command of French. North Hatley was home to two thriving but separate communities of English-speaking and French-speaking writers, artists, and artisans. Shortly after her arrival, she brought together both English- and French-language local poets for a high-spirited, alcohol-fueled, and at times confrontational evening of French and English poetry-reading and literary exchange. In her words, "That evening was the beginning of the rest of my professional life....I determined I would devote the energy and skill I could muster to attempting, only attempting, to break down some of the barriers between French- and English-speakers."[8]

At the time, Fischman's command of French was still limited: high-school and university courses had taught her the basics of the language and introduced her to the classics, but she had difficulty carrying on a conversation. She was determined to learn French as it was spoken and written in contemporary Québec. Jones (who is also profiled in this volume) had started translating Québec poetry (he would go on to win two Governor General's Literary Awards, one of which would be for translation),[9] and Fischman decided to try translating a Québec writer as a linguistic exercise.

The story of how she began her career as a translator has been told frequently.[10] Defying the conventional wisdom that one needs to be fluently bilingual in order to translate, she first tackled *Le Torrent* by Anne Hébert but found it too difficult. When her neighbour, Roch Carrier, gave her a collection of his short stories, she decided to translate one of them, "L'Oiseau," from *Jolis Deuils*, with the help of a dictionary. When that endeavour proved successful, she undertook to translate Carrier's new novel *La Guerre, Yes Sir!* Carrier's wife Diane assured her that it was a simple book with simple language.[11] Fischman soon realized that understanding the book was far from easy, but what she lacked in fluency, she made up for in resourcefulness. She consulted friends and acquaintances, and used dictionaries extensively. And, most importantly, she found that she was connecting with the story: "It was an amazing experience....It was as if I knew why he was writing it and what the subtext was and all the rest. And at the same time, I don't know, the definitions of the unfamiliar words just seemed to pop into my head."

Roch Carrier was a supportive and willing collaborator. It was Fischman's first exposure to Québécois *jurons*, so Carrier gave her "a course on swearing,"[12] explaining that the curses in *La Guerre, Yes Sir!* were based on liturgical articles used in the Catholic Church. Faced with the challenge of conveying this language to an English readership, she decided to retain the original French wording in such passages as "*Calice de ciboire d'hostie! Christ en bicyclette sur son Calvaire!* So you think we enjoy ourselves in the war?"[13] She sent her completed translation to several publishers, including the Bodley Head in London, and others in Canada. In 1970, it was finally accepted by a new small press that had just started up in Toronto: the House of Anansi.

During this same period, Fischman worked closely with Jones on *ellipse*, a review that presents selected work of French and English writers—primarily poets—in the original and in translation. In collaboration with Joseph Bonenfant, Richard Giguère, John Glassco, and Philip Stratford, they published the first issue in 1969. In 1971, Fischman was responsible for proposing an issue on the traumatic events of the 1970 Crise d'octobre, with texts by Nicole Brossard and Paul Chamberland, along with expressions of solidarity with Québec writers "imprisoned under the *War Measures Act*, such as Gaston Miron and Gérald Godin."[14] Fischman was a member of the editorial board of *ellipse* from 1969 to 1972, and consulting editor from 1973 to 1979. Although she did not translate the poetry the review specialized in, she did translate prose passages for the publication.[15] Moreover, she took care of many of the day-to-day tasks: "I remember writing to poets and publishers and advertisers, hauling copy to the printer, correcting proofs...addressing and stamping by hand the envelopes."[16]

A Distinguished Career in the Making

The success of *La Guerre, Yes Sir!* launched Fischman's career as a literary translator. She continued to translate, first in North Hatley and then in Montréal, where she would move in 1972 after her marriage to Jones ended. Her first literary translations were of Carrier's books: after publishing *La Guerre, Yes Sir!* in 1970, she went on to complete the trilogy with

Floralie, Where Are You? (1971) and *Is It the Sun, Philibert?* (1972), followed by *They Won't Demolish Me!* (1974). She also worked on some nonfiction, including a series of pamphlets on Québec arts and crafts for les Éditions Format.

The remarkable surge of translation of Québec literature into English was fuelled in part by political interest,[17] but there was more to it than that. "The reason that it started to blossom, at least from French to English," Fischman comments, "was because there was this explosion of new writing talent in Québec and a few of us who were there wanted to make this known." Moreover, this was a time when literary translation was beginning to gain support and recognition through the Canada Council Translation Grants Program, the Canada Council translation prizes, and the Association des traducteurs littéraires du Canada / Literary Translators' Association of Canada, of which Fischman was a founding member.[18]

As her reputation grew, she began to be solicited by various publishers and authors. In 1973, she agreed to translate Marie-Claire Blais's *Le Loup*. Despite some mixed reviews, her translations of *The Wolf* (1974) and of Carrier's *They Won't Demolish Me!* won her the first Canada Council Translation Prize in 1974. The same year, Harvest House published her translation of Jacques Benoît's *Jos Carbone*. By 1975, she wrote in a letter to Dave Godfrey at Porcépic Press: "A number of translations or projects are in the air and I find myself in the delightful position of having to be selective."[19] A few years later, she undertook her second translation of Marie-Claire Blais: *Une liaison parisienne*, which she titled *A Literary Affair* (1979).

She was keen to translate *Neige noire*, a disjointed, disturbing story by Hubert Aquin, the noted Québec nationalist writer whose work had won numerous awards, including the Governor General's award for fiction in 1969 (which he had refused). Two of his first three novels had been translated by Alan Brown, and Fischman was hesitant to infringe on Brown's interests. She took the initiative of sending a letter to Anna Porter, editor-in-chief of McClelland and Stewart, in which she wrote, "I've read [*Neige Noire*] and am knocked out by it. It would be fantastic to translate, but I'd want to be sure that both Hubert and Alan Brown agreed. In fact I've mentioned it to Alan, who sees no problems as far as he's concerned, but he's so closely associated with Aquin that I'm reluctant to intrude. On the other hand, I'm pretty sure that I could do a good translation."[20] Aquin agreed, and was supportive throughout her translation, consulting with her, answering her queries, and reading and approving the final version and its title, *Hamlet's Twin*. Aquin was to commit suicide at forty-seven in

1977, before publication of the translation of his final book, and Fischman was concerned that it be known that he had approved the translation before his death. *Hamlet's Twin* was well received;[21] even reviewers who had reservations about the original lauded the translation.[22] There were, however, some questions about her translation of the title, and, despite the fact that Aquin himself had given his blessing to her version, she was later to be accused of "culturally anglicizing Aquin."[23]

The translation of Aquin's dark story of violence, incest, and death left an enduring impression on Fischman. In 1986, she told Nicole Beaulieu in an interview, "I was haunted...by the ideas, the characters, the language,"[24] and she voiced the same sentiments thirteen years later in an address she gave upon receiving an honorary doctorate from the University of Ottawa: "Translating takes you deep inside the text, the language, the culture, the mind of the writer. It's a thrilling place to be, but it can sometimes be dangerous also. I still recall the troubled sleep, the nightmares even, that I suffered during and after the translation of *Neige Noire*."[25] Some twenty-five years later, Fischman would be asked by David Staines, the general editor of the New Canadian Library, to produce a new translation of Aquin's first novel, *Prochain épisode*. Published under the title *Prochain Episode* in 1967, Penny Williams's translation of this acclaimed, complex work had been strongly criticized for its numerous mistranslations and omissions,[26] and had been called "a disaster"[27] by Joyce Marshall (who is also profiled in this volume). Fischman's translation, *Next Episode*, would appear in 2001 and be chosen as the CBC's prestigious 2003 "Canada Reads" selection.

From the beginning of her career, Sheila Fischman had worked to promote those Québec authors whose work she loved. In the early 1970s, Roch Carrier arranged for her to meet a friend, Jacques Poulin. She read his first novel, *Mon cheval pour un royaume* (1967), liked it very much, and read the next two, *Jimmy* (1969) and *Le coeur de la baleine bleue* (1971). Determined to get these books translated and read by an English audience, she approached English-language publishers with the suggestion of combining the three novels, published separately in French, into a single volume. It took five years before House of Anansi finally published *The Jimmy Trilogy* (1979).

In 1976, she was also to add Naïm Kattan to her ever-growing list of authors: *Farewell Babylon*, her translation of Kattan's *Adieu Babylone*, was published to rave reviews.[28] Several years later, she translated Kattan's sequel, *Les Fruits arrachés*, as *Paris Interlude* (1979). At the same time, Coach House Press was looking for "innovative" and "experimental" work for its new translation program co-edited by Frank Davey and Barbara Godard. Fischman was asked to translate Victor-Lévy Beaulieu's *Jack Kérouac: Essai poulet*, a book about Kérouac's French-Canadian roots and influence; she would also translate Beaulieu's *Don Quichotte de la démanche* several years later under the title *Don Quixote in Nighttown* (1978).

By now, she was living her life more and more in French. When she worked on André Major's *L'Épouvantail*, the first completed draft of the translation contained numerous gallicisms that she was literally not aware of. The publisher, McClelland and Stewart, arranged to have Joyce Marshall read the translation critically and consult with Fischman to improve the text. Fischman appreciated the opportunity to work with Marshall, for whom she has great respect and affection. *The Scarecrows of Saint-Emmanuel* was published in 1977.

A characteristic of Fischman's career that was fast becoming apparent was her loyalty to "her" authors. Her first translations of Roch Carrier's work had marked the beginning of both an enduring friendship and one of the most successful relationships in Canadian letters. She would go on to translate all of Roch Carrier's work. Through her translations, Carrier has been embraced by a large English-speaking audience. His story *The Hockey Sweater* has become a children's classic: it was published in picture book form and also made into an animated film, which won more than fifteen international awards and an Oscar nomination. A quotation from this story, in both the original French and her English translation, appears on the Canadian five dollar bill today. Indeed, Carrier has achieved the odd distinction of being more popular in English-speaking Canada than in his native Québec.[29]

Throughout the following years she would also continue to promote Jacques Poulin's work enthusiastically, and, as with several other of her authors, the two have established a continuing working relationship and friendship: "What I love about Jacques Poulin's work," she observes, "is his ability to create and establish a mood in very few words...I like his minimalist style and his *intimiste* way of writing." This is also her translation challenge: "I know how he sweats and bleeds over every fragment of a sentence, how he strips away and strips away and strips away....And it's partly my awareness of how much creative effort has gone into the making of these perfectly limpid sentences that encourages me to strive and strive again to come up with something that reflects what he has done."[30]

As the 1980s approached, she also added to her regular authors two of Québec's most illustrious and best-loved writers, Anne Hébert and Michel Tremblay. Hébert, poet and novelist, was one of the most translated writers that Québec had known;[31] Fischman would translate her last seven novels into English, beginning with *Héloïse* (1982). In her tribute to Hébert in *Traduction d'Anne Hébert*, she describes how she went to Paris to research the setting. There she also met Hébert at her home, "tenant fébrilement le premier jet de ma traduction d'une main et quelques fleurs de l'autre."[32] It was the beginning of an illustrious working relationship. Her second translation of Hébert was the poetic, elliptical novel *In the Shadow of the Wind* (1984); the original, *Les Fous de Bassan*, had won France's Prix Femina for 1982. Of all her translations, this is the work that Fischman has most enjoyed translating.[33] The critical reception of her translation in the *New York Times Book Review* was excellent: "The power in this haunting book—a power that seems in no way diminished in translation—comes from the language, the rich, inventive images, the heated, melodious prose."[34]

Fischman continued to translate Hébert's work, including *The First Garden* (1990), originally *Le Premier jardin*, which won her the Félix-Antoine Savard Prize from the Translation Center at Columbia University in 1990, and *Est-ce que je te dérange?* published as *Am I disturbing you?* (1999) and nominated for the Giller Prize in 1999.[35] She had already begun to translate *Un habit de lumière*, Hébert's last novel, when the author died. In her translator's afterword to Hébert's *A Suit of Light*, Fischman wrote the following tribute:

> A translator is above all a reader, a close and careful reader: she reads a work—in this case a novel—again and again, probing its deepest secrets, attempting to comprehend and reinterpret the author's chosen images and words. I have performed this labour of love on six novels by Anne Hébert, and now on this, her final one. While a translator's interpretation of a text will necessarily determine its form in the new language, the author's way of looking at and interpreting the world of her fiction will mark the translator, too. Anne Hébert has changed forever the way in which I view and interpret aspects of certain landscapes, landscapes both natural and emotional. Above all, she has left me, she has left all her readers, with a vision of a world in which, despite prevailing darkness, the ultimate victor is light.[36]

In its tribute to Anne Hébert upon her passing, the *Globe and Mail* (January 24, 2000) asked Sheila Fischman, "a senior figure in her own right," to comment on Hébert's contribution to Québec and Canadian literature.[37]

At about the time she began to translate Anne Hébert, Fischman also undertook her first work by Michel Tremblay, the multiple-award-winning Québec playwright and novelist. John Van Burek and Linda Gaboriau, also profiled in this book, have translated many of his plays, but Fischman has translated all six of the novels in his semi-autobiographical Chronicles of the Plateau Mont-Royal series.[38]

The 1980s and 1990s saw her career reach new heights: she continued to receive national and international awards and to translate the works of Poulin, Tremblay, Hébert, and Carrier. She also translated a further work by André Major—*Une vie provisoire*, translated as *A Provisional Life* (1997)—and two more novels by Marie-Claire Blais: *Visions d'Anna ou Le vertige* as *Anna's World* (1985); and *Soifs*, which had won the 1996 Governor General's Literary Award for fiction in French, as *These Festive Nights* (1997). "The bounteous and terrible world of Marie-Claire Blais's great novel *Soifs*," she recalls, "was both disturbing and enriching."[39]

Her close acquaintance with the Québec literary scene allowed her to add a number of new authors to her list of "golden oldies."[40] She translated two books by Yves Beauchemin: *Le Matou* (in English, *The Alley Cat*, published in 1986), and *Juliette Pomerleau* (in English, *Juliette*, published in 1993).[41] The first, *Le Matou*, a runaway bestseller in both Québec and France, provoked some controversy centred on speculation that the novel's supernatural villain—Ratablavasky—was a Jewish stereotype. Fischman denied this: "The villain is not Jewish.…Beauchemin doesn't have an anti-Semitic bone in his body.…But he was so upset by the incident that he asked me not to use the word Jew or Jewish in the English translation."[42] She also took on other new authors, including Tony Cartano,[43] Jacques Savoie, Jean Lemieux, Hélène Le Beau, François Gravel[44] and Lise Bissonnette. By the mid-1990s, she could say, "Quite literally not a week goes by that I do not receive a call from a writer asking me to consider translating their work."[45]

In more recent years, Sheila Fischman has discovered a particular affinity for the new generation of Québec authors. She came upon Christiane Frenette's work when both she and Frenette won a Governor General's award in the same year. As Fischman recalls, "when one of the speeches around the time of the award gave a brief description of the novel in question, which was called in French *La Terre Ferme*…I said to myself, 'That is my kind of book.' And I bought it right then and there and I just loved it." She discovered a similar affinity with Élise Turcotte, whose French publisher had described her to Fischman as being "la petite soeur de Jacques Poulin." Gaétan Soucy's work also impressed and fascinated her: "He makes the French language do some things you wouldn't think the French language was capable of doing. And so I have the huge challenge but the great pleasure of trying to put that into English. And it's been very very gratifying." *The Little Girl Who Was Too Fond of Matches*, her rendering of *La petite fille qui aimait trop les allumettes*, is rightly described as "a superb translation."[46] Her creation of unusual turns of phrase to parallel the unconventional use of French is masterful; in this dense, dark story of a young girl and her brother who grow up on an isolated estate, cut off from the outside world and speaking a language of their own making, Fischman comes up with such inventive terms such as "stoppit" for "figette" (an attack or seizure), "secretarious" for "secrétarien" (a writer), and "inflations" for "enflures" (breasts).

These new affinities and friendships are evident in her current and upcoming projects: Gaétan Soucy's *Music-Hall!* (which she has translated as *Vaudeville!*) has just appeared, and she will be working on new works by Frenette, Turcotte, Gravel, and Poulin. Although her primary focus has been Québec novels, she has made some exceptions through the years. She translated two long prose poems by friend Roland Giguère, and she has translated a number of works for film and television, as well as the occasional play. As a professional translator, she has also undertaken some works of non-fiction.

A Full-Time Professional

Fischman has shaped her career by choosing to translate authors with whom she has an affinity. She observes, "I believe that to make a successful translation, you must choose books that 'speak' to you, for which you feel an affinity, emotional as well as stylistic. Indeed, without the emotional affinity, it's impossible, for me anyway, to render the style."[47] But this affinity with her authors and her evident skill with the written word are only part of the equation. In the end, her success rests on the fact that writers and publishers trust her with their works, and this trust is earned through hard work, high professional standards, and careful research: "I think [authors and publishers] trusted me too because I'm—if I may say so—a very meticulous translator. I spend a lot of time in dictionaries; I spend a lot of time rewriting and revising. I will research the smallest problem that I encounter in the French, research it with the author or with other people or reference books until I'm satisfied that I understand not just what the words or the phrase means, but also why the author wrote it in that way."

A full-time literary translator, Fischman approaches her work rigorously and methodically. She may work seven days a week, six hours a day, without a break. She works on only one translation at a time: "Translating a book means, for me at any rate, becoming totally absorbed, not only in it, but by it. It takes over my life. It certainly takes over my inner life. I seem to be constantly translating in my head. I usually have a notebook with me so that if I'm taking a walk or what have you and something snaps into my mind, I can make a note of it. It's a very intense and intensive experience and for me, it wouldn't be intellectually possible, it wouldn't be emotionally possible to divide myself between two or more translations." She produces the first draft as quickly as possible, "in one fell swoop...it's sort of like plunging into the cold lake water and then catching your breath for a bit before starting to swim with elegance and style."[48] Then, "the artistic work takes over. I work on it the way the writer works. The ideas are someone else's, but the writing is mine."[49] She emphasizes the importance of a translator's reading voraciously and becoming familiar with the flow of language, with the sound of dialogue, with idiomatic expressions, and with different shades of meaning: "A literary translator ideally should be able to write well in his or her own language...should be receptive to not just the sense but also the music of the other language and be able to transpose it into another key or for another instrument."[50]

Fischman does not like to let anyone see her first drafts. Years ago, she had an unpleasant experience when she reluctantly complied with a request for a printout of an early draft of the first few chapters of a translation. The draft ended up being passed about to a number of people, including to a US publisher—who assumed it was a finished work—without her knowledge or authorization. When she used to work with a typewriter, she would type each of her three or four drafts in full, revising and rewriting each one, researching expressions, querying the author, and wrestling with stubborn passages until the translation read to her satisfaction. Since she started to use a computer in 1983, she makes many of her revisions on screen, and then on paper, continually polishing the text and doing even more rewriting because it is technologically easier to do so. In her words, "I'm a furious re-writer and would probably rewrite my translations if I could afford to." She is her own harshest taskmaster, a perfectionist who must first be satisfied with her work herself. In one instance, she abandoned a translation project, reimbursing her advance, because she was not satisfied with the English version she was producing.[51]

Throughout the process, Fischman consults with the author, inquiring about difficult passages and meanings that are unclear to her. She sends a copy of the finished manuscript to the author before it goes to the publisher; she considers this a courtesy. It can also be useful: the author may catch some errors. But she refuses to use the word "collaboration" or "partnership" to describe her working relationship with the authors of the books she translates: these terms fail to acknowledge that, with the exception of a few hours of consultation, the translator works alone for the many weeks or months a translation requires. Other than her experience working with Joyce Marshall, she has rarely collaborated with another translator—not even with her partner, Donald Winkler, himself a literary translator (and, like Fischman, a winner of the Governor General's Literary Award for Translation)[52] as well as a filmmaker. Years ago, they tried collaborating on the translation of a children's book by Gilles Vigneault that was never published. They haven't collaborated closely on a translation since: "We are too alike and too stubborn."

To help handle the business side of her work, she has an agent. She hired John Goodwin to represent her in 1978 when she was commissioned to translate a play by Roland Lepage, *Le temps d'une vie*, for Tarragon Theatre in Toronto, since there were royalties and box office receipts involved. Goodwin continued as her agent in ensuing years, and since his death, his daughters have continued to represent her.

She has used her literary and publishing contacts and know-how to promote literary translation in a variety of ways. In her numerous contacts with publishing houses, she has urged, pushed, prodded, and nagged publishers to present Québec works to English-speaking readers. She has initiated the translation into French of a number of English novels, putting writers into contact with translators and publishers. She has often been called upon to speak for Canadian literary translators and has appeared on numerous panels, sat on juries, and given countless interviews. She has lobbied for recognition of the translator, even writing letters of protest to journalists and reviewers who have failed to acknowledge that certain books are translations. Fischman believes that translators should get equal billing and has worked, from her early days in translation, for the recognition of the translator: "We don't want to be anonymous. Translation is a work of creation that should be judged as such."[53]

Ironically, in the spring of 2003, when her translation of Hubert Aquin's *Prochain épisode* was being acclaimed by the CBC "Canada Reads" selection committee and she was participating in a discussion of translator recognition at the Blue Metropolis International Literary Festival in Montréal,[54] the House of Anansi,[55] who had been the first publisher of her translations of Québec literature, announced that it had stopped crediting translators on book covers. The new policy was to start with the publication of Fischman's translation of Lise Bissonette's *An Appropriate Place*. Anansi editor Martha Sharpe justified the decision by claiming that many readers "dismiss translations out of hand...it's hard to get a readership to embrace a book that's translated. The more we talked to readers and booksellers the more we realized that [translation] is a strike against the book in the marketplace."[56] Needless to say, Fischman disagreed with Anansi's decision, as well as the rationale behind it: she condemns the practice of disguising a translation as an original and argues, "Booksellers tell me that having my name on a translation brings more sales. The translator is a known quantity, while the author may not be."[57] Sharpe has now reversed that decision and Fischman's name is front and centre on her translation of Gaétan Soucy's *Music-Hall!* under the English title *Vaudeville!*

Fischman has also been a writer, reviewer, and editor. In addition to her early contracts as a broadcaster for the CBC, she has worked as a columnist for Toronto's *Globe and Mail*; she was literary editor of the *Montreal Star* in the 1970s and was a book columnist for the Montréal *Gazette*. She directed a collection of English-Canadian literature in translation for Éditions du Roseau from 1987 to 1991: as editor of the Calliope collection, she selected English novels to be translated into French, reading numerous books, reviewing documentation, and meeting with publishers, writers, and translators. These activities have provided her with additional avenues through which to act as a cultural advocate for Canada's two literatures.

Researchers and translators interested in studying the translations and related work of Sheila Fischman have a wealth of material available to them: she has donated her papers to Library and Archives Canada, and materials covering her career from 1968 to 1998 are housed in the Archives' Special Collections.[58] Her manuscripts provide insight into the translation process: for each work translated, the archives provide full annotated typescripts of each draft, complete with her handwritten corrections, marginal notes, and queries, as well as annotated page proofs and printed page excerpts from the original French works. Also included are publicity materials, reviews, and works never finished or published. Students and scholars of translation can trace the translating, decision-making, and writing processes as the translation evolves from the first draft to the final version. Her painstaking recording and documentation of each step of the translation process is further evidence of her meticulous work methods. Of particular interest is her extensive correspondence with publishers and authors. The friendly, informal, and at times affectionate tone of letters she has both sent and received from the many literary figures she has worked with underscores the personal nature of her professional relationships and affinities.

Style and Strategy

In her translations, Sheila Fischman strives to capture and reflect the style of the original author. She says that, ideally, a translator should "climb right into the skin of the author, even try to assume his or her personality" to convey the same mood and meaning as the original: "It's a process of re-creation."[59] As she puts it, "I have no style as a translator...I hope. I hope that no-one picks up a translation of mine and says, 'Oh yes, this sounds like Fischman.' If it did, I would hang up my dictionaries. I hope that when I translate Carrier, it reads like Carrier in English and so forth...with the other writers. A translator should be invisible."[60]

This chameleon-like ability to capture the voice of the original author is astounding in light of the variety and number of authors she has translated. She has managed to retain in translation the original flavour of Hébert's elegant prose, Tremblay's vivid, rich descriptions, Carrier's whimsical irony, Marie-Claire Blais's dark torment, and Bissonnette's detached voice, to name but a few.

She frequently stays deliberately close to an author's syntax and wording, refusing to adapt the prose to a more idiomatic English. For example, Marie-Claire Blais's *Soifs* is heavy with run-on sentences, the text containing almost no sentence, paragraph, or chapter breaks, and Fischman's translation, *These Festive Nights*, carefully reproduces Blais's unconventional and dense style. On the other hand, *Am I disturbing you?*, her translation of Hébert's *Est-ce que je te dérange?*, in many passages reflects Hébert's elliptical style through a close translation:

> Trop de lueurs, trop de tâches de soleil persistent pourtant dans mes yeux.[61]

Fischman translates directly:

> Too many glimmers, too many spots of sunlight still persist in my eyes.[62]

In another example, Hébert uses sentence fragments to convey emotion:

> Trop fraîche son image. Sans passé ni patine. D'hier seulement. Maigre. Sans profondeur.[63]

Fischman keeps the same syntax for similar effect:

> Her image is too fresh. Without past or patina. Only from yesterday. Thin. Without depth.[64]

Similarly, she captures the feeling of Poulin's deceptively simple prose, as this passage from *Volkswagen Blues* illustrates:

> Jack Waterman n'était pas très content de lui-même en tant qu'écrivain. D'une manière générale, il ne s'aimait pas beaucoup (il se trouvait trop maigre et trop vieux et trop renfermé), mais ce qu'il détestait par-dessus tout, dans sa propre personne, c'était sa façon de travailler.[65]

Fischman's translation is economical, yet evocative:

> Jack Waterman was not very pleased with himself as a writer. He didn't like himself very much in general (he thought he was too thin and too old and too withdrawn), but what he hated about himself more than anything was his way of working.[66]

Fischman's respect for the style of the original is apparent not only in her syntax, but also in her handling of verb tenses. Deciding how to render, in English, the French historic and dramatic present is always an issue for a translator, and in a number of her translations Fischman has chosen to reflect the tense used in the original, rather than to use the more standard past tenses that an English reader would expect.[67] For example, much of Hébert's *L'Enfant chargé de songes* is written in the present tense, and the narrative frequently switches between the past and the present, sometimes even within one paragraph:

> Aline, après le depart de Julien, s'est étirée, toute nue devant la fenêtre, oubliant que la veille encore elle n'avait jamais assez de vêtements pour se cacher aux yeux du monde. Du haut de sa fenêtre elle regarde les maisons, les rues, les voitures, les petits personnages circulant sur les trottoirs, la ligne des montagnes.[68]

Fischman's translation, *Burden of Dreams*, faithfully reflects this use of tense:

> After Julien had gone, Aline stretched, naked, at the window, forgetting that only the night before she never had enough clothes to hide her from the eyes of the world. From her window, she looks down on the houses, the streets, cars, small individuals walking along the sidewalks, the line of mountains in the distance.[69]

She is careful to respect the cultural and linguistic origins of the original,[70] and her sense of "invisibility" leads her to defer to the original author and retain traces of that author's style. The slightly foreign flavour that sometimes results is deliberate: "It's important that the reader feel as if he or she is reading or is listening to a real person but at the same time that person must always—so to speak—be speaking French, even though the words are English."[71] As a result, "Reading her work is somewhat like conversing with a fluent non-native speaker whose accent, while it does not interfere with the message, reminds one of the 'other' language....The novel may be in English, but, for those familiar with the original, it still "sounds" like Anne Hébert, Roch Carrier, or Michel Tremblay."[72]

Yet Fischman does not adhere slavishly to the original; she will artfully rework the wording when a close translation will not do. For example, she recounts how she toiled over the opening lines of Hébert's *In the Shadow of the Wind* (*Les fous de Bassan*), which initially seemed untranslatable:[73]

> La barre étale de la mer, blanche, à perte de vue, sur le ciel gris, la masse noire des arbres, en ligne parallèle derrière nous.[74]

Starting with a literal translation ("The slack bar of the sea . . ."), she worked and reworked the sentence, eventually coming up with a striking final version:

> A strand of sea poised between tides, white, as far as the eye can see, and against the gray sky, in a parallel line behind us, the black bulk of trees.[75]

She also has not hesitated to translate freely when a book title does not lend itself to a close translation. In addition to the controversial *Hamlet's Twin*, she has "tin-fluted"[76] a number of titles, including *Les fous de bassan / In the Shadow of the Wind*, *Les vues animées / Bambi and Me*, *Soifs / These Festive Nights*, and *L'Île de la Merci / The Body's Place*.

Perhaps one of the most difficult challenges that Fischman has had to face in her translation of Québec novels has been the rendering of the distinctive flavour of Québec French. She has faced this challenge from the outset: *La Guerre, Yes Sir!* contained numerous Québec swear words. She took a stand at that point, deciding to retain the original French wording in the translation and justifying her choice in a translator's note at the beginning of the book: "The swearing has been left in French....the relationship of the villagers to the Church is perhaps the novel's single most important theme...rebellion is achieved in a figurative way by the use of a most amazing collection of oaths and curses, which call on virtually every object of religious significance to Roman Catholics....To translate them [by Anglo-Saxon expletives] would have been to distort the values of the people who use them; on the other hand, literal translations would have been at best perplexing, more often simply absurd."[77]

However, her strategy towards ecclesiastical swearing in French texts appears to have changed from her early translations of Carrier's work, in which she made a point of retaining *jurons*.[78] In Tremblay's *Bambi and Me*, as in other more recent translations, characters use more conventional

English swear words. In *Les vues animées*, for example, "Quel gros mot? J'ai-tu dit un gros mot, moé? J'ai-tu dit crisse? J'ai-tu dit tabarnac?" becomes "What dirty words? Did I say something dirty? Did I say shit? Did I say fuck?"[79]

There is no real equivalent of *joual* in English, and this is particularly problematic for the translator of Michel Tremblay, for whom the use of *joual* is so characteristic. While the English slang that Fischman uses is inevitably more standard than the French, her ear is finely tuned to the nuances of dialogue. As can be illustrated by this quick exchange from *Les vues animées*, the oral quality of "Ben c'est là, épais. Pis arrêtez de me faire pardre mon temps! Riez-vous de moé, coudonc?" is faithfully conveyed by the colloquial "That's it then, dummy! Now quit wasting my time! Are you laughing at me or what?"[80]

However, particularly when the dialogue reflects phonetic features of the oral French, a certain amount of loss is inevitable. A sentence such as "I don't spy on you when I'm on stage" does not really capture the flavour of Tremblay's "J't'espionne pas, moé, quand chus en scène."[81] Fischman readily admits the problems of translating Tremblay's dialogues: "There's tension between the French and English language. His urban characters speak in a style that's faintly English...the words and also some of the syntax. I decided a long time ago it's impossible to translate that without having it contorted. We both regret it, but we both accept that we have to live with it."[82]

The related issue of how to, or whether to, indicate the use of English in the French source text poses an ongoing dilemma for translators and translation scholars. As Kathy Mezei observes, "When translators choose to ignore, or omit to indicate, English-language usage in the French source text, they contribute to a de-politicization of the French text and a flattening of the levels of linguistic irony and play."[83] Yet there is rarely a subtle, fluent way to indicate code switches and English borrowings. In response to criticism that she does not mark switches into English in some of Tremblay's original dialogue—for example, by using italics—Fischman explains that such typographical solutions interfere with her esthetic concerns: "In the case of such specific uses of English,...I have to acknowledge that part is 'lost in translation.' If [Tremblay's] novels rested only on that, they'd be pretty thin works....But they're not. They are extremely rich; for one thing their character studies are astonishing. And that, fortunately, is translatable."[84]

Fischman places a priority on aesthetic concerns in the literature she translates. Hubert Aquin's *Prochain épisode* is a complex, multi-layered work that invites readings on a number of levels. Despite criticism that her retranslation, *Next Episode*, focussed on the spy narrative and depoliticized the original,[85] Fischman successfully captured what Penny Williams's earlier translation, *Prochain episode* (1967), had, in Joyce Marshall's words, failed to reflect: "the speed and lightness that gave the original its wonderful sense of improvisation, its air of being written before our eyes."[86]

A Passion for Literature

Sheila Fischman and Donald Winkler have lived in their home near Saint-Laurent Boulevard in Montréal's Plateau Mont-Royal for over sixteen years and are at home in the neighbourhood and in the city. They enjoy "the general cultural things": going to the theatre, to concerts, to the opera. They like to travel; a favourite destination is France, although they do not get there often enough for her liking. She loves to cook and to garden; one of the benefits of her small perennial flower garden is that it gives her the excuse to go more often to the Jean Talon market. She is a remarkably modest, unpretentious person who relishes quiet, everyday activities. Above all, she loves to read, especially contemporary Québec literature, whether it is something she plans to translate or not.

At the beginning of her career, she admits, political concerns were part of her motivation, but explains, "I've changed some of my opinions...now it's language that thrills me more than my potential for effecting political change,"[87] and elsewhere, "I confess that in my earlier days there was a naive political component to what I thought I was doing. I thought that creative writers are better placed to give a sense of a culture, of a society, of a political movement, than are the various analysts or 'logues.' Their take on society is more immediately accessible perhaps to people than is the work of specialists. There was a time, long ago, when I thought that being instrumental in bringing contemporary writers to the attention of non-French speaking readers might perform a kind of political function. I don't think I'd be so naive as to use that kind of language now."[88] Although translation is her profession and her livelihood, Fischman maintains that literary passion is the real driving force behind her work:

> My role is to share my enthusiasm, my passion for particular writers' work. To share that with as many people as I can. I am one of those rather obnoxious people who will sit and talk about a book that I have liked and will say, "Here, take it, you have to read it." And so I am doing that I suppose on a larger scale, by making these books accessible, available, to people who aren't able to read them in the orig-

inal. It is really at that rather intimate level that I see my role. Now people, when they are writing about translation, bring out all those metaphors—the *passeur*, the bridge, the ambassador, all of that. These are all true, of course, but it's not in those terms that I see my work, that I see what I do. It's a matter of sharing with others something that I am enthusiastic about.

She considers literary translation to be not just what she does: it's who she is; it defines her. In fact, her career is a model of artistic professionalism: through her approach to her work, she has integrated the idealistic artist who works for the sheer pleasure of the experience and the hard-working, knowledgeable professional who skilfully manages her time and shapes her career.

NOTES

1 In Sherry Simon's words, "If anyone in Canada knows anything at all about translation, they will know the name of Sheila Fischman." See Sheila Fischman, "Esthetic Affinities: An Interview with Sheila Fischman," interviewer S. Simon, in *Culture in Transit: Translating the Literature of Quebec*, ed. Sherry Simon (Montréal: Véhicule Press, 1995), p. 185.
2 The International Board on Books for Young People.
3 Nicole Beaulieu, "La voix discrète d'une traductrice de fond," *Actualité*, Dec. 1986, p. 159.
4 Claire Helman, dir., *Talking Translation: Sheila Fischman and Roch Carrier*, National Film Board of Canada, 1993.
5 The dedication reads, "The translation is for my teacher, T.J. Casaubon." Roch Carrier, *La Guerre, Yes Sir!* trans. S. Fischman (Toronto: Anansi, 1970).
6 Sheila Fischman, Interview with Pamela Grant, Montréal, August 7, 2003. Except where otherwise indicated, all quotations from Sheila Fischman are taken from this interview.
7 This conference is now called the Congress of the Humanities and Social Sciences.
8 Sheila Fischman, "A Night in August," *Matrix*, no. 20 (spring 1986): 26.
9 D.G. Jones has won the Governor General's Literary Award twice: once in 1977, for poetry, with *Under the Thunder the Flowers Light Up the Earth*, and again in 1992, for translation from French into English, with *Categorics One, Two and Three*, by Normand de Bellefeuille.
10 Beaulieu, "La voix discrète," pp. 157–59; Albert Manguel, "Le mot juste," *Saturday Night*, July 1983, pp. 53–54; Marion McCormick, "Life in Translation," *Books in Canada*, Oct. 1977, pp. 21–22; Joel Yanofsky, "Learning French Blossomed into a Thriving Career," *Canadian Jewish News*, Feb. 4, 1988, p. 17.
11 McCormick, "Life in Translation," p. 21.
12 Helman, *Talking Translation: Sheila Fischman and Roch Carrier*.

13 Carrier, *La Guerre, Yes Sir!* trans. S. Fischman, p. 69.
14 "Le premier numéro de 1971 est également digne de mention, puisqu'à l'initiative de Sheila Fischman, *ellipse* serre alors de très près la bouleversante actualité des événements d'octobre 1970, en publiant des texes de Paul Chamberland, Nicole Brossard et d'autres, auxquels font écho ceux d'Eli Mandel ou d'Al Purdy. En plus d'exprimer sa solidarité envers ses amis écrivains emprisonnés en vertu de la *Loi des mesures de guerre*, comme Gaston Miron et Gérald Godin, *ellipse* voulait ainsi montrer aux Québécois qu'il y avait aussi de la sympathie au Canada anglais. 'Bien entendu,' dit Sheila Fischman, 'ce sont de bien grands mots pour une si petite revue, mais on travaille avec les moyens qu'on a, et c'est un document qui reste.'" Quoted in Patricia Godbout, "Bientôt trente ans de traduction poétique à la revue *ellipse*," *Circuit* (fall 1998): 11.
15 See issues 1, 4, 6, 13, 14–15, 19, and 21 of *ellipse*.
16 Sheila Fischman, "Leafing through the First Issue of *ellipse*," *ellipse*, no. 40 (1988): 13–14.
17 "On a eu l'impression que le Canada anglais s'était gratté la tête en disant: Mais d'où ça vient tout ça? Et beaucoup de gens croyaient qu'ils pourraient trouver dans la littérature des réponses à certaines questions." Quoted in Patricia Godbout, "Bientôt trente ans de traduction poétique à la revue *ellipse*," p. 11.
18 She was one of the Stanley House Group, a gathering of fourteen literary translators (including Joyce Marshall, Pierre Nepveu, Alan Brown, and Patricia Claxton) who met in the Gaspé in 1975 at a seminar organized by Philip Stratford and created the LTAC/ATTLC. The association has worked to improve the image and recognition of literary translators in Canada, for example, by ensuring that publishers acknowledge the translator on the cover of a book and by persuading the Canada Council to establish a program to provide publishers with funds to pay translators. See Patricia Claxton,"Introduction Looking Back," *Méta* 45, no. 1 (2000): 7–12.
19 Sheila Fischman, letter to Dave Godfrey, Sheila Fischman Fonds, Library and Archives Canada, Ottawa. Porcépic Press, July 31, 1975.
20 Sheila Fischman, letter to Anna Porter, editor-in-chief of McClelland and Stewart, July 31, 1975.
21 See Peter McBride, "*Hamlet's Twin* a First-Class Novel," *Hamilton Spectator*, May 19, 1979; Sherry Simon, "Final Episode: H.A.'s Novel Retains Brilliance in Translation," *Gazette*, Jun. 2, 1979; Geoffrey Inverarity, "Confusion as Style: A Bizarre Exploration of Chaos," *Whig-Standard*, Aug. 24, 1979; John J. O'Connor, "Translations," *University of Toronto Quarterly* 51, no. 4 (summer 1982): pp. 391–403; and Linda Leith, "Rights of Memory," *Canadian Forum*, Sept. 1979, p. 28.
22 See David W. Atkinson, "Hamlet's Twin," *Lethbridge Herald*, July 28, 1979.
23 "Une volonté d'angliciser culturellement Aquin" is the expression used by Chantal de Grandpré in "La canadianisation de la littérature québécoise: le cas Aquin," *Liberté* 27, no. 3 (June 1985): 58.
24 "J'étais hantée…par les idées, les personnages, le langage." Quoted in Nicole Beaulieu, "La voix discrète," p. 157.

25 Sheila Fischman, "Translation Matters / En guise de traduction," Address given at the University of Ottawa on the occasion of the awarding of an honorary doctorate, June 6, 1999.
26 See Patricia Claxton, "Culture Vulture," *Méta* 12, no. 1 (1967): 9–13; Joyce Marshall, "Three from the Other Nation," *Tamarack Review*, no. 46 (winter 1968): 109–11.
27 Joyce Marshall, "Three from the Other Nation," p. 110.
28 Tom Saunders, "Sensitive Portrayal of the Journey into Manhood," *Winnipeg Tribune*, Oct. 2, 1976.
29 See Pierre Hébert, "Roch Carrier au Canada anglais," *Oeuvres et critiques: Le roman québécois contemporain (1960–1986) devant la critique*, 14, no. 1 (1989): 101–13.
30 Fischman, "Esthetic Affinities," p. 187.
31 Anne Hébert's earlier novels were translated by Gwendolyn Moore (*The Torrent*), Kathy Mezei (*The Silent Rooms*), Norman Shapiro (*Kamouraska*), and Carol Dunlop-Hébert (*Children of the Black Sabbath*).
32 Sheila Fischman, "Témoignage: Hommage d'une traductrice à Anne Hébert," trad. Patricia Godbout, in *Traductions d'Anne Hébert* (Ville Saint-Laurent: Fides, 2001), p. 16. The text was originally read in English at an evening of tribute to Anne Hébert at the Blue Metropolis festival in Montreal, April 2000.
33 Fischman, "Témoignage: Hommage d'une traductrice à Anne Hébert," p. 17.
34 Bryan, C.D.B., "Six Narrators in Search of an Explanation," *New York Times Book Review*, July 22, 1984, p. 7.
35 This was the subject of controversy (as was Nancy Huston's winning of the Governor General's award the same year) because such nominations "blur the distinction between the original and the translation." Jane Koustas, "Translations," *University of Toronto Quarterly* 70, no. 1 (winter 2000/01): 271.
36 Sheila Fischman, translator's afterword in Anne Hébert, *A Suit of Light*, (Toronto: Anansi, 2000), p. 105.
37 Jane Koustas commented, "There is no questioning the observations of one of Canada's most influential and successful translators. Having translated seven of Hébert's novels, Fischman was indeed well placed to reflect on her impact. However, that the *Globe and Mail* turned to a translator illustrates yet again the importance of translation and English Canada's dependence on this process." Koustas, "Translations," *University of Toronto Quarterly* 70, no.1 (winter 2000/01): 271
38 John J. O'Connor praised her translation of *The Fat Woman Next Door Is Pregnant* for "containing much excellent work, especially in the translation of dialogue." O'Connor, "Translations," *University of Toronto Quarterly* 51, no. 4 (summer 1982): 395.
39 Fischman, "Translation Matters / En guise de traduction."
40 She uses this term in a CBC ArtsCanada interview to refer to, for example, Poulin, Hébert, Tremblay, and Carrier. Interview with Sheila Fischman, "In Translation," *CBC Arts Canada*, 2003.

41 *Juliette*, along with *Volkswagen Blues* and *In the Shadow of the Wind*, are singled out as "distinguished works" of translation by John O'Connor. In John O'Connor, "Translations: French to English," *Oxford Companion to Canadian Literature*, ed. Eugene Benson and William Toye (Toronto: Oxford University Press, 1997), pp. 1127–32.
42 Joel Yanofsky, "Learning French Blossomed into a Thriving Career," p. 17.
43 Tony Cartano is the only non-Quebec author she has translated.
44 François Gravel, well known as a children's author, won the Governor General's Award for children's literature in 1991 for *Deux heures et demie avant Jasmine*.
45 Sheila Fischman, "Esthetic Affinities," p. 186.
46 Koustas, "Translations," *University of Toronto Quarterly* 70, no. 1 (winter 2000/01): 126.
47 Fischman, "Translation Matters / En guise de traduction."
48 Sheila Fischman, letter to Ellen Godfrey of Press Porcépic, March 15, 1977. Sheila Fischman Fonds, Library and Archives Canada, Ottawa.
49 Tom Spears, "Translating Bare Words in Artistry," *Toronto Star*, Books, n.d.
50 Helman, *Talking Translation: Sheila Fischman and Roch Carrier*.
51 She had undertaken to translate Victor-Lévy Beaulieu's *Blanche forcée* in 1977, but was not able to "click" with the text. Sheila Fischman, letter to Frank Davey, Coach House Press, Feb. 21, 1980.
52 Donald Winkler won the Governor General's Literary Award for Translation (French to English) in 1994, for *The Lyric Generation: The Life and Times of the Baby Boomers*, by François Ricard.
53 Quoted in Tom Spears, "Translation Is Creation," [Calgary] *Albertan*, May 15, 1978.
54 This workshop was called "L'affaire du 5 piastres / The $5 Bill Event," a reference to the fact that her name, unlike author Carrier's, does not appear on the currency in question along with her English translation of the French quotation from *The Hockey Sweater*.
55 The House of Anansi was sold to Stoddart Publishing in 1989. See James Polk, "Anansi, House of," in the *Oxford Companion to Canadian Literature*, 2nd ed., ed. Eugene Benson and William Toye (Toronto: Oxford University Press, 1997), p. 33.
56 Ray Conlogue, "Translators Drop Off Book Fronts," *Globe and Mail*, May 28, 2003, p. R4.
57 Conlogue, "Translators Drop Off Book Fronts," p. R4.
58 Sheila Fischman Fonds, First Accession 1992-22 (covers 1968–91), prepared by Chris Berry and Pierre Beaudreau, March 1997; and Sheila Fischman Fonds, Second Accession, 1999-01 (covers 1977–98), prepared by Catherine Hobbs, July/August 1999. Library and Archives Canada, Ottawa, ON.
59 Barbara Black, "Introducing the Translators," *Gazette*, Aug. 4, 1984, p. C1.
60 Helman, *Talking Translation: Sheila Fischman and Roch Carrier*.
61 Anne Hébert, *Est-ce que je te dérange?* (Paris: Seuil, 1998), p. 34.
62 Anne Hébert, *Am I Disturbing You?* trans. S. Fischmann (Toronto: Anansi, 1999), p. 21.

63 Hébert, *Est-ce que je te dérange?* p. 34.
64 Hébert, *Am I Disturbing You?* p. 21.
65 Jacques Poulin, *Volkswagen Blues* (Montréal: Québec/Amérique, 1984), p. 47.
66 Jacques Poulin, *Volkswagen Blues*, trans. S. Fischman (Toronto: McClelland and Stewart, 1988), p. 35.
67 In her articles in the *University of Toronto Quarterly*, Jane Koustas points to several translations in which Fischman has chosen to reflect the French use of verb tense: Hébert's *Burden of Dreams*; Carrier's *Lament of Charlie Longsong* and *The End*; Gravel's *Miss September;* Savoie's *The Blue Circus;* Major's *A Provisional Life*. Jane Koustas, "Translations," *University of Toronto Quarterly* 65, no. 1 (winter 1995/96): 128–42; Jane Koustas, "Translations," *University of Toronto Quarterly* 69, no. 1 (winter 1999/2000): 104–14; Koustas, "Translations," *University of Toronto Quarterly* 70, no. 1 (winter 2000–2001).
68 Anne Hébert, *L'enfant chargé de songes* (Paris: Seuil, 1992), p. 122.
69 Anne Hébert, *Burden of Dreams*, trans. S. Fischman (Toronto: Anansi, 1994), p. 122.
70 Koustas, "Translations," *University of Toronto Quarterly* 70, no. 1.
71 Helman, *Talking Translation: Sheila Fischman and Roch Carrier*.
72 Koustas, "Translations," *University of Toronto Quarterly* 65, no. 1 (winter 1995/96): 130–31.
73 Fischman, "Témoignage: Hommage d'une traductrice à Anne Hébert," p. 17.
74 Anne Hébert, *Les fous de Bassan* (Paris: Seuil, 1982), p. 13.
75 Anne Hébert, *In the Shadow of the Wind*, trans. S. Fischman (Toronto: Stoddart; New York: Beaufort, 1984), p. 9.
76 For more on this term, which refers to the title of the English translation of Gabrielle Roy's *Bonheur d'occasion*, see David Homel, "Tin-Fluting It: On Translating Dany Laferrière," in *Culture in Transit: Translating the Literature of Quebec*, ed. S. Simon (Montréal: Véhicule, 1995).
77 Fischman, foreword, in Roch Carrier, *La Guerre, Yes Sir!* pp. 1–2.
78 Barbara Godard points this out: "In [*The Alley Cat*], contrary to her practice in translating Carrier, Fischman opts for translating swearing into English: 'Il a dû vous parler des ses mérites pour le ciel et de tout le saint bataclan...n'en croyez pas un maudit mot' becomes 'He must have praised himself to the skies and what have you, but don't believe a bloody word he says.'" Barbara Godard, "Translations," *University of Toronto Quarterly* 57, no. 1 (fall 1987): 97. Two years later, in the same journal, Godard writes, "Fischman's strategies have shifted from her early translations of Roch Carrier's work, where she so scrupulously retained the French 'sacre' to mark cultural difference. Now her Québécois have abandoned terms like 'sacre ton camp' for the ordinary English 'screw off.'" Barbara Godard, "Translations," *University of Toronto Quarterly* 59, no. 4 (summer 1990): 102.
79 Michel Tremblay, *Les vues animées* (Montréal: Leméac, 1990), p. 60; Michel Tremblay, *Bambi and Me*, trans. S. Fischman (Burnaby, BC: Talonbooks, 1997), p. 48.

80 Tremblay, *Les vues animées*, p. 31; Tremblay, *Bambi and Me*, trans. S. Fischman, p. 26.
81 Michel Tremblay, *News from Édouard*, trans. S. Fischman (Burnaby, BC: Talonbooks, 2000), p. 12; Michel Tremblay, *Des nouvelles d'Édouard* (Montréal: Leméac, 1994), p. 15.
82 Quoted in Tom Spears, "Translating Bare Words in Artistry."
83 Kathy Mezei, "Translation as Metonomy: Bridges and Bilingualism," *eilipse*, no. 51 (1994): 92. Also see Barbara Godard, "Translations," 1986, p. 77–98 and "Translations," 1988, 84–111.
84 Fischman, "Esthetic Affinities: An Interview with Sheila Fischman." p. 190.
85 Agnès Whitfield, "Translations/Traductions," *University of Toronto Quarterly*, 1 (winter 2002/2003): 304.
86 Marshall, "Three from the Other Nation," p. 110.
87 Fischman, "A Night in August," p. 27.
88 Fischman, "Esthetic Affinities: An Interview with Sheila Fischman," p. 189.

BIBLIOGRAPHY

I. Primary Sources

Literary Translations

Aquin, Hubert. *Hamlet's Twin*. Trans. S. Fischman. Toronto: McClelland and Stewart, 1974. Translation of *Neige noire*. Montréal: Éditions La Presse, 1974.
———. *Next Episode*. Trans. S. Fischman. New Canadian Library. Toronto: McClelland and Stewart, 2001. Translation of *Prochain épisode*. Paris: Cercle du Livre de France, 1965.
Beauchemin, Yves. *The Alley Cat*. Trans. S. Fischman. Toronto: McClelland and Stewart, 1986. Translation of *Le matou*, Montréal: Québec/Amérique, 1981.
———. *Juliette*. Trans. S. Fischman. Toronto: McClelland and Stewart, 1993. Translation of *Juliette Pomerleau*. Montréal: Québec/Amérique, 1989.
Beaulieu, Victor-Lévy. *Jack Kerouac: A Chicken Essay*. Trans. S. Fischman. Toronto: Coach House Press, 1975. Translation of *Jack Kérouac: Essai poulet*. Montreal: Éditions du Jour, 1972.
———. *Don Quixote in Nighttown*. Trans. S. Fischman. Erin, ON: Porcépic, 1978. Translation of *Don Quichotte de la démanche*. Montréal: Éditions de l'Aurore, 1974.
Benoit, Jacques. *Jos Carbone*. Trans. S. Fischman. Montréal: Harvest House, 1974. Translation of *Jos Carbone*. Montréal: Éditions du Jour, 1967.
Billon, Pierre. *The Children's Wing*. Trans. S. Fischman. Montréal: Robert Davies Publishing, 1996. Translation of *L'Enfant du cinquième Nord*. Montréal: Québec/Amérique, 1982; Paris: Seuil, 1982.
Bissonnette, Lise. *Following the Summer*. Trans. S. Fischman. Toronto: Anansi, 1993. Translation of *Marie suivait l'été*. Montréal: Boréal, 1992.
———. *Affairs of Art*. Trans. S. Fischman. Toronto: Anansi, 1996. Translation of *Choses crues*. Montréal: Boréal, 1995.

---. *Cruelties*. Trans. S. Fischman. Toronto: Anansi, 1998. Translation of *Quittes et doubles*. Montréal: Boréal, 1997.

---. *An Appropriate Place*. Trans. S. Fischman. Anansi, 2002. Translation of *Un lieu approprié*. Montréal: Boréal, 2001.

Blais, Marie-Claire. *The Wolf*. Trans. S. Fischman. Toronto: McClelland and Stewart, 1974. Translation of *Le Loup*. Montréal: Éditions du Jour, 1972.

---. *A Literary Affair*. Trans. S. Fischman. Toronto: McClelland and Stewart, 1979. Translation of *Une liaison parisienne*. Montréal: Stanké/Quinze, 1975.

---. *Anna's World*. Trans. S. Fischman. Toronto: Lester and Orpen Dennys, 1985. Translation of *Visions d'Anna, ou Le vertige*. Montréal: Stanké, 1982.

---. *These Festive Nights*. Trans. S. Fischman. Toronto: Anansi, 1997. Translation of *Soifs*. Montréal: Boréal 1995.

Carrier, Roch. *La Guerre, Yes Sir!* Trans. S. Fischman. Toronto: Anansi, 1970. Translation of *La Guerre, Yes Sir!* Montréal: Éditions du Jour, 1968; 1998.

---. "The Bird." Trans. S. Fischman. *ellipse*, no. 4 (summer 1970): 8. Rpt. in *Invisible Fictions: Contemporary Stories from Quebec*, ed. Geoff Hancock. Toronto: Anansi, 1987. 149–50.

---. "Bread." Trans. S. Fischman. *ellipse*, no. 4 (summer 1970): 30–31.

---. "Fate." Trans. S. Fischman. *ellipse*, no. 4 (summer 1970): 10–11.

---. "The Ink." Trans. S. Fischman. *ellipse*, no. 4 (summer 1970): 19–20. Rpt. in *Invisible Fictions: Contemporary Stories from Quebec*, ed. Geoff Hancock. Toronto: Anansi, 1987. 157–58.

---. "The Invention." Trans. S. Fischman. *ellipse*, no. 4 (summer 1970): 17–19.

---. "The Precious Stone." Trans. S. Fischman. *ellipse*, no. 4 (summer 1970): 21–24.

---. "The Room." Trans. S. Fischman. *ellipse*, no. 4 (summer 1970): 25–29. Rpt. in *Invisible Fictions: Contemporary Stories from Quebec*, ed. Geoff Hancock. Toronto: Anansi, 1987. 159–64.

---. "Steps." Trans. S. Fischman. *ellipse*, no. 4 (summer 1970): 11–12. Rpt. in *Invisible Fictions: Contemporary Stories from Quebec*. Toronto: Anansi, 1987. 151–52.

---. "The Telephone." Trans. S. Fischman. *ellipse*, no. 4 (summer 1970): 15–17.

---. "The Wedding." Trans. S. Fischman. *ellipse*, no. 4 (summer 1970): 13–15. Rpt. in *Invisible Fictions: Contemporary Stories from Quebec*, ed. Geoff Hancock. Toronto: Anansi, 1987. 153–56.

---. *Floralie, Where Are You?* Trans. S. Fischman. Toronto: Anansi, 1971. Translation of *Floralie, où es-tu?* Montréal: Éditions du Jour, 1969.

---. *Is It the Sun, Philibert?* Trans. S. Fischman. Toronto: Anansi, 1972. Translation of *Il est par là, le soleil*. Montréal: Éditions du Jour, 1970.

---. *They Won't Demolish Me!* Trans. S. Fischman. Toronto: Anansi, 1974. Translation of *Le Deuxmillième étage*. Montréal: Éditions du Jour, 1973.

---. *The Garden of Delights*. Trans. S. Fischman. Toronto: Anansi, 1978. Translation of *Le Jardin des délices*. Montréal: La Presse, 1975.

---. *The Hockey Sweater and Other Stories*. Trans. S. Fischman. Toronto: Anansi, 1979. Translation of *Les enfants du bonhomme dans la lune*. Montréal: Stanké, 1979.

———. *No Country without Grandfathers*. Trans. S. Fischman. Toronto: Anansi, 1981. Translation of *Il n'y a pas de pays sans grands-pères*. Montréal: Stanké 1979.

———. *Lady with Chains*. Trans. S. Fischman. Toronto: Anansi, 1984. Translation of *La Dame qui avait des chaînes aux chevilles*. Montréal: Stanké, 1981.

———. *The Hockey Sweater*. Trans. S. Fischman. Montréal/Plattsburgh: Tundra Books, 1984. Translation of *Le chandail de hockey*. Montréal/Plattsburgh: Les Livres Toundra, 1984.

———. *Heartbreaks along the Road*. Trans. S. Fischman. Toronto: Anansi, 1987. Translation of *De l'amour dans la ferraille*. Montréal: Stanké, 1984.

———. "What Languages Do Bears Speak? Canadian Feature Issue: English Literature and Littérature du Québec." Special issue, ed. Clark Blais and Sheila Fischman, *Translation: The Journal of Literary Translation*, no. 20 (Spring 1988): 175–81.

———. *The Boxing Champion*. Trans. S. Fischman. Montréal: Tundra Books, 1991. Translation of *Un champion*. Montréal: Les Livres Toundra, 1991.

———. *Prayers of a Very Wise Child*. Trans. S. Fischman. Toronto: Viking, 1991. Translation of *Les prières d'un enfant très, très sage*. Montréal: Stanké, 1988.

———. *The Man in the Closet*. Trans. S. Fischman. Toronto: Viking, 1993. Translation of *L'homme dans le placard*. Montréal: Stanké, 1991.

———. *The Longest Home Run*. Trans. and adapted by Sheila Fischman. Montréal: Tundra Books, 1993. Translation of *Le plus long circuit*. Montréal: Les livres Toundra, 1993.

———. *The End*. Trans. S. Fischman. Toronto: Viking, 1994. Translation of *Fin*. Montréal: Stanké, 1994.

———. *The Basketball Player*. Trans. S. Fischman. Toronto: Tundra Books, 1996. Translation of *Le joueur de basket-ball*. Montréal: Les livres Toundra, 1996.

———. *The Lament of Charlie Longsong*. Trans. S. Fischman. Toronto: Viking, 1998; Toronto: Penguin, 1999. Translation of *Petit homme tornade*. Montréal: Stanké, 1996.

———. *Prayers of a Young Man*. Trans. S. Fischman. Toronto: Viking, 1999; Penguin, 2000. Translation of *Prières d'un adolescent très, très sage*. Montréal: Stanké, 1998.

Cartano, Tony. *Blackbird*. Trans. S. Fischman. New York: Macmillan, 1986. Translation of *Blackbird*. Paris: Éditions Buchet/Chastel, 1980.

Frenette, Christiane. *Terra Firma*. Trans. S. Fischman. Dunvegan, ON: Cormorant, 1999. Translation of *La terre ferme*. Montréal: Boréal, 1997.

Giguère, Roland. *Miror and Letters to an Escapee*. Trans. S. Fischman. Erin, ON: Press Porcépic, 1976. Translation of *Miror et Lettre à l'évadé*. Extraits de *La Main au feu*. Montréal: L'Hexagone, 1973.

Gravel, François. *Benito*. Trans. S. Fischman. Toronto: Lester and Orpen Dennys, 1990. Translation of *Benito*. Montréal: Boréal, 1987.

———. *Felicity's Fool*. Trans. S. Fischman. Dunvegan, ON: Cormorant, 1992. Translation of *Bonheur fou*. Montréal: Boréal, 1990.

———. *My Life as a Crow*. Trans. S. Fischman. Toronto: Lorimer, 1993. Translation of *Corneilles*. Montréal: Boréal, 1989.

———. *Waiting for Jasmine*. Trans. S. Fischman. Toronto: Groundwood, 1993. Translation of *Deux heures et demie avant Jasmine*. Montréal: Boréal, 1991.
———. *Ostend*. Trans. S. Fischman. Dunvegan, ON: Cormorant, 1996. Translation of *Ostende*. Montréal: Éditions Québec/Amérique, 1994.
———. *Miss September*. Trans. S. Fischman. Dunvegan, ON: Cormorant, 1998. Translation of *Miss Septembre*. Montréal: Éditions Québec/Amérique, 1996.
———. *A Good Life*. Trans. S. Fischman. Dunvegan, ON: Cormorant, 2001. Translation of *Fillon et frères*. Montréal: Québec/Amérique, 2000.
Hébert, Anne. *Héloïse*. Trans. S. Fischman. Toronto: Stoddart, 1982. Translation of *Héloïse*. Paris: Seuil, 1980.
———. *In the Shadow of the Wind*. Trans. S. Fischman. Toronto/New York: Stoddart / Beaufort Books, 1984. Translation of *Les fous de Bassan*. Paris: Seuil, 1982.
———. *The First Garden*. Trans. S. Fischman. Toronto: Anansi, 1990. Translation of *Le premier jardin*. Paris: Seuil, 1988.
———. *Burden of Dreams*. Trans. S. Fischman. Toronto: Anansi, 1994. Translation of *L'Enfant chargé de songes*. Paris: Seuil, 1992.
———. *Aurélien, Clara, Mademoiselle, and the English Lieutenant*. Trans. S. Fischman. Toronto: Anansi, 1996. Translation of *Aurélien, Clara, Mademoiselle et le lieutenant anglais*. Paris: Seuil, 1995.
———. *Am I Disturbing You?* Trans. S. Fischman. Toronto: Anansi, 1999. Translation of *Est-ce que je te dérange?* Paris: Seuil, 1998.
———. *A Suit of Light*. Trans. S. Fischman. Toronto: Anansi, 2000. Translation of *Un habit de lumière*. Paris: Seuil, 1999.
———. *Collected Later Novels*. Trans. S. Fischman. Introd. Mavis Gallant. Toronto: Anansi, 2003.
Kattan, Naïm. *Farewell, Babylon*. Trans. S. Fischman. Toronto: McClelland and Stewart, 1976. Translation of *Adieu Babylone*. Montréal: Éditions La Presse, 1975.
———. *Paris Interlude*. Trans. S. Fischman. Toronto: McClelland and Stewart, 1979.Translation of *Les fruits arrachés*. Montréal: Hurtubise HMH, 1977.
Le Beau, Hélène. *No Song, But Silence*. Trans. S. Fischman. Toronto: Coach House, 1995. Translation of *La Chute du corps*. Paris: Gallimard; Montréal: Boréal, 1992.
Lemieux, Jean. *Red Moon*. Trans. S. Fischman. Dunvegan, ON: Cormorant, 1994. Translation of *Lune rouge*. Montréal: Québec/Amérique, 1991.
Major, André. *The Scarecrows of Saint-Emmanuel*. Trans. S. Fischman. Toronto: McClelland and Stewart, 1977. Translation of *L'Épouvantail*. Montréal: Éditions du Jour, 1974.
———. *A Provisional Life*. Trans. S. Fischman. Ottawa: Oberon, 1997. Translation of *Une vie provisoire*. Montréal: Boréal, 1995.
Poulin, Jacques. *The Jimmy Trilogy*. Trans. S. Fischman. Toronto: Anansi, 1979. Translation of *Mon cheval pour un royaume*. Montréal: Éditions du Jour, 1967; Montréal: Éditions du Jour, 1969; *Le coeur de la baleine bleue*. Montréal: Éditions du Jour, 1971.

———. *Spring Tides.* Trans. S. Fischman. Toronto: Anansi, 1986. Translation of *Les grandes marées.* Montréal: Leméac, 1977.
———. *Volkswagen Blues.* Trans. S. Fischman. Toronto: McClelland and Stewart, 1988. Translation of *Volkswagen Blues.* Montréal: Québec/Amérique, 1984.
———. *Mr. Blue.* Trans. S. Fischman. Montréal: Vehicule, 1993. Translation of *Le Vieux Chagrin.* Montréal: Leméac, 1989.
———. *Autumn Rounds.* Trans. S. Fischman. Toronto, ON: Cormorant, 2002. Translation of *La tournée d'automne.* Montréal: Leméac, 1993.
———. *Wild Cat.* Trans. S. Fischman. Toronto, ON: Cormorant, 2003. Translation of *Chat sauvage.* Montréal: Leméac, 1998.
Savoie, Jacques. *The Revolving Doors.* Trans. S. Fischman. Toronto: Lester and Orpen Dennys, 1989. Translation of *Les Portes tournantes.* Montréal: Boréal Express, 1984.
———. *Blue Circus.* Trans. S. Fischman. Dunvegan, ON: Cormorant, 1997. Translation of *Le cirque bleu.* Montréal: La Courte échelle, 1995.
Soucy, Gaétan. *Atonement.* Trans. S. Fischman. Toronto: Anansi, 1999. Translation of *Acquittement.* Montréal: Boréal, 1997.
———. *The Little Girl Who Was Too Fond of Matches.* Trans. S. Fischman. Toronto: Anansi. 2000. Translation of *La petite fille qui aimait trop les allumettes.* Montréal: Boréal, 1998.
———. *Vaudeville!* Trans. S. Fischman. Toronto: Anansi, 2003. Translation of *Music-Hall!* Montréal: Boréal, 2002.
Tremblay, Michel. *The Fat Woman Next Door Is Pregnant.* Trans. S. Fischman. Vancouver: Talonbooks, 1981. Translation of *La grosse femme d'à côté est enceinte.* Montréal: Leméac, 1978.
———. *Thérèse and Pierrette and the Little Hanging Angel.* Trans. S. Fischman. Toronto: McClelland and Stewart, 1984; Burnaby, BC: Talonbooks, 1996. Translation of *Thérèse et Pierrette à l'école des Saints-Anges.* Montréal: Leméac, 1980.
———. *The Heart Laid Bare.* Trans. S. Fischman. Toronto: McClelland and Stewart, 1989. Toronto: Talonbooks, 2002. Also published as *Making Room.* London: Serpent's Tail, 1990. Translation of *Le Cœur découvert.* Montréal: Leméac, 1986.
———. *The First Quarter of the Moon.* Trans. S. Fischman. Vancouver: Talonbooks, 1994. Translation of *Le premier quartier de la lune.* Montréal: Leméac, 1989.
———. *Bambi and Me.* Trans. S. Fischman. Burnaby, BC: Talonbooks, 1997. Translation of *Les vues animées.* Montréal: Leméac, 1990.
———. *A Thing of Beauty.* Trans. S. Fischman. Burnaby, BC: Talonbooks, 1998. Translation of *Un objet de beauté.* Montréal: Leméac, 1997.
———. *The Duchess and the Commoner.* Trans. S. Fischman. Burnaby, BC: Talonbooks, 1999. Translation of *La duchesse et le roturier.* Montréal: Leméac 1982.
———. *News from Édouard.* Trans. S. Fischman. Burnaby, B.C: Talonbooks, 2000. Translation of *Des nouvelles d'Édouard.* Montréal: Leméac, 1994.
———. *Twelve Opening Acts.* Trans. S. Fischman. Vancouver: Talonbooks, 2002. Translation of *Douze coups de théâtre.* Montréal: Leméac, 1992.

———. *Birth of a Bookworm.* Trans. S. Fischman. Vancouver: Talonbooks, 2003. Translation of *Un ange cornu avec des ailes de tôle.* Montréal: Leméac, 1994.

Turcotte, Élise. *The Sound of Living Things.* Trans. S. Fischman. Toronto: Coach House, 1993. Translation of *Le bruit des choses vivantes.* Montréal: Leméac, 1991.

———. "Vintage Clothes." Trans. S. Fischman. *Matrix*, no. 46 (Aug. 1995): 37–39.

———. *The Body's Place.* Trans. S. Fischman. Toronto, ON: Cormorant, 2003. Translation of *L'île de la Merci.* Montréal: Leméac, 1997.

Yaugud, Louar (Raoul Duguay). "Lettre damour à Toulmonde. " Trans. S. Fischman. *ellipse*, no. 6 (winter 1971): 32–47.

Non-Literary Translations

Barcelo, François. Introduction to *Montreal.* Trans. S. Fischman. Photographs by Mia and Klaus. Montréal: Leméac, 1983.

Brault, Jacques. "Some Notes on the Translation of Poetry." Trans. S. Fischman. *ellipse*, no. 21 (1977): 11–35.

Carrier, Roch. *Canada.* Trans. S. Fischman. Montréal: Éditions Libre Expression / Art Global, 1986. Translation of *Canada.* Montréal: Éditions Libre Expression / Art Global, 1986.

———. *Our Life with the Rocket: The Rocket Richard Story.* Trans. S. Fischman. Toronto: Viking, 2001. Translation of *Le Rocket.* Montréal: Stanké, 2000.

Dumont, Fernand. *The Vigil of Quebec.* Trans. Sheila Fischman and Richard Howard. Toronto: University of Toronto, 1974. Translation of *La Vigile du Québec.* Montréal: Hurtubise, 1971.

Dupont, Pierre. *How Lévesque Won.* Trans. S. Fischman. Toronto: Lorimer, 1977. Translation of *15 novembre 76.* Montréal: Les Quinze, 1976.

Fournier, Pierre. *A Meech Lake Post-Mortem: Is Quebec Sovereignty Inevitable?* Trans. S. Fischman. Montreal: McGill-Queen's University Press, 1991. Translation of *Autopsie du Lac Meech: La souveraineté, est-elle inévitable?* Montréal: VLB Éditeur, 1990.

Gros-Louis, Max. *First among the Hurons.* Trans. S. Fischman. Montréal: Harvest House, 1974. Translation of *Le Premier des Hurons.* Montréal: Éditions du Jour, 1973.

Hébert, Jacques. *The World Is Round: A Long and Winding Letter on Canada, the World and Youth.* Trans. S. Fischman. Toronto: McClelland and Stewart, 1976. Translation of *La terre est ronde: Longue, interminable lettre, où il est question de la jeunesse, du Canada et du monde.* Montréal: Fides, 1976.

———. *Have Them Build a Tower Together: About Katimavik, a Meeting Place, about Youth, about Hope.* Trans. S. Fischman. Toronto: McClelland and Stewart 1979. Translation of *Faites-leur bâtir une tour ensemble, òu il est question de Katimavik, lieu de rencontre, et de la jeunesse, et de l'espérance.* Montréal: Éditions Héritage, 1979.

Moisan, Clement. "The Contemporary Poetry of Quebec." Trans. S. Fischman. *ellipse*, no. 1 (1969): 6–15.

Potvin, Gilles. *MSO: The First Fifty Years*. Trans. S. Fischman. Montréal: Stanké, 1984. Translation of *OSM: Les Cinquante premières années*. Montréal: Stanké, 1984.
Sioui, Georges. *For an Amerindian Autohistory*. Trans. S. Fischman. Montreal: McGill-Queen's, 1992. Translation of *Pour une autohistoire amérindienne*. Québec: Les Presses de l'Université Laval, 1991.
Tardivel, Jules-Paul. *For My Country*. Trans. S. Fischman. Toronto and Buffalo: University of Toronto Press, 1975. Translation of *Pour la patrie: Roman du vingtième siècle*. Montréal: Cadieux et Derome; Hurtubise HMH, 1974.

Selected Translations for the Stage, Screen, and Radio

Carrier, Roch. *The Celestial Bicycle*. Trans. S. Fischman. Play. 1982. Traduction de *La Celeste bicyclette*.
———. *The Hockey Sweater and Other Stories*. Sound Recording. Dramatized by Alexander Hausvater. Fredericton, NB: BTC Audiobooks, 2001.
Godbout, Jacques. *A Hunting Lesson.* (animated film) Directed by Jacques Drouin, produced by Thérèse Descary, Jean-Jacques Leduc. Adapted by Sheila Fischman.
Hébert, Anne. *L'île de la Demoiselle*. Unpublished play.
Lepage, Roland. *Le temps d'une vie*. Play. Commissioned by Bill Glassco for Tarragon Theatre, Toronto, 1978.
Tardif-Delorme, Paule. *Beyond the Sound Barrier*. Children's play. Translated for Theatre Beyond Words, 1983.
———. *Tale of a Bird*. Translation of *Le conte de l'oiseau*. Monologue set to music performed by André Prevost. Sound recording. Montréal: Société nouvelle de l'enregistrement 1982.
Tremblay, Larry. *Talking Bodies*. 4 plays: *A Trick of Fate; Anatomy Lesson; The Dragonfly of Chicoutimi; Ogre*. Vancouver: Talonbooks, 2001. Translation of *Le déclin du destin*. Montréal: Leméac, 1989; *Leçon d'anatomie*. Montréal: Éditions Laterna Magica, 1992; *The Dragonfly of Chicoutimi*. Montréal: Les Herbes Rouges, 1995; *Ogre*. Carnières-Morlanwelz, Belgium: Éditions Lansman, 1997). *Anatomy Lesson* also published separately: New York: Ubu Repertory Theatre, 1995.

Works on Translation

Blaise, Clark, and Sheila Fischman, eds. "Canadian Feature Issue: English Literature and Littérature du Québec." Special issue, *Translation: The Journal of Literary Translation* 20 (spring 1988).
CBC. Arts Canada: Writing Quebec. "In Translation," interview with Sheila Fischman. http://artscanada.cbc.ca/artscanada.jsp.startingPieceLabelwriting quebec. 2003-06-10
Fischman, Sheila. "French and English Texts in Tandem: The Editing of *ellipse*." In *Editing Canadian Texts*, ed. F.G. Halpenny. Toronto: Hakkert, 1975. 81–94.
———. "The Literature of French Quebec." In *Quebec Literature in Translation: A Resource Guide for the Teaching of Canadian Literature*, ed. Quebec Work

Group (Sheila Fischman, co-ord.). Toronto: Writers' Development Trust, 1977. 49–55.

———. "The Watchdog Writers of Quebec." *Book Forum: An International Transdisciplinary Quarterly*, no. 4 (1978): 113–18.

———. "A Night in August." *Matrix*, no. 22 (spring 1986): 23–27.

———. "Leafing through the First Issue of *ellipse*." "*ellipse* a vingt ans/*ellipse*: Twenty Years." Special issue, *ellipse*, no. 40 (1988): 13–14.

———. "Esthetic Affinities: An Interview with Sheila Fischman." In *Culture in Transit: Translating the Literature of Quebec*, ed. Sherry Simon. Montréal: Véhicule Press, 1995. 185–93.

———. "Translation Matters / En guise de traduction." Address given at the University of Ottawa on the occasion of the awarding of an honourary doctorate, June 6, 1999. Unpublished.

———. "Témoignage: Hommage d'une traductrice à Anne Hébert." Trad. Patricia Godbout. In *Traductions d'Anne Hébert, Les Cahiers Anne Hébert 3*, ed. Patricia Godbout and Christiane Lahaie. Ville Saint-Laurent: Fides, 2001. 15–20. (Originally read in English at an evening of tribute to Anne Hébert at the Blue Metropolis festival in Montreal, April 2000).

Helman, Claire, dir. *Talking Translation: Sheila Fischman and Roch Carrier*. Prod. Tamira Lynch. National Film Board of Canada, 1993.

Homel, David. "Solving the Difficulties: A Panel Discussion with Alberto Manguel, Julia O'Faolain, Paul Wilson, Leila Vennewitz, and Sheila Fischman." *Translation Review*, no. 20 (1986): 9–13.

II. Secondary Sources

Aquin, Hubert. *Prochain Episode*. Trans. Penny Williams. Introd. Ronald Sutherland. New Canadian Library 84. Toronto: McClelland and Stewart, 1967.

Atkinson, David W. "Hamlet's Twin." *Lethbridge Herald*, July 28, 1979.

Black, Barbara. "Introducing the Translators." *Gazette*, Aug. 4, 1984: C1.

Bryan, C.D.B. "Six Narrators in Search of an Explanation." *New York Times Book Review*, July 22, 1984, 7.

Beaulieu, Nicole. "La voix discrète d'une traductrice de fond." *L'Actualité*, Dec. 1986, 157–59.

Claxton, Patricia. "Culture Vulture." *Méta* 12, no. 1 (1967): 9–13.

———. "Introduction: Looking Back." *Méta* 45, no 1 (2000): 7–12.

Conlogue, Ray. "Translators Drop Off Book Fronts." *Globe and Mail*, May 28, 2003, R4.

De Grandpré, Chantal. "La canadianisation de la littérature québécoise: Le cas Aquin." *Liberté* 27, no. 3 (June 1985): 50–59.

Godard, Barbara. "Translations." *University of Toronto Quarterly* 57, no. 1 (fall 1987): 77–98.

———. "Translations." *University of Toronto Quarterly* 59, no. 4 (summer 1990): 84–111.

Godbout, Patricia. "Bientôt trente ans de traduction poétique à la revue *ellipse.*" *Circuit* (fall 1998): 10–11.
Hébert, Pierre. "Roch Carrier au Canada anglais. " *Oeuvres et critiques. Le roman québécois contemporain (1960–1986) devant la critique* 14, no. 1 (1989): 101–13.
Homel, David. "Tin-Fluting It: On Translating Dany Laferrière." In *Culture in Transit: Translating the Literature of Quebec,* ed. Sherry Simon. Montréal: Véhicule, 1995.
Inverarity, Geoffrey. "Confusion as Style: A Bizarre Exploration of Chaos." *Whig-Standard* [Kingston], Aug. 24, 1979.
Koustas, Jane. "Translations." *University of Toronto Quarterly* 65, no. 1 (winter 1995/96): 128–42.
———. "Translations." *University of Toronto Quarterly* 69, no. 1 (winter 1999/ 2000): 104–14.
———. "Translations."*University of Toronto Quarterly* 70, no. 1 (winter 2000/01): 271–87.
———. "Translations." *University of Toronto Quarterly* 71, no. 1 (winter 2001/02): 115–31.
Larue-Langlois, Jacques. "Sheila Fischman: Une schizophrénie très confortable." *Devoir,* July 24, 1982, 11, 12.
Leith, Linda. "Rights of Memory." *Canadian Forum,* Sept. 1979, 28.
Manguel, Albert. "Le mot juste." *Saturday Night,* July 1983, 53–54.
Marshall, Joyce. "Three from the Other Nation." *Tamarack Review,* no. 46 (winter 1968): 109–11.
McBride, Peter. "*Hamlet's Twin* a First-Class Novel." *Hamilton Spectator,* May 19, 1979.
McCormick, Marion. "Life in Translation." *Books in Canada,* Oct. 1977, 21–22.
Mezei, Kathy. "*Hamlet's Twin.*" Review. *Queen's Quarterly,* 1987, 161–63.
———. "Translation as Metonymy: Bridges and Bilingualism." "De la traduction / On Translation: En hommage à / In Honour of Philip Stratford." Special issue, *ellipse,* no. 51 (1994): 85–102.
O'Connor, John J. "Translations." *University of Toronto Quarterly* 49, no. 4 (summer 1980): 383–98.
———. "Translations." *University of Toronto Quarterly* 51, no. 4 (summer 1982): 391–403.
———. "Translations: French to English." In *Oxford Companion to Canadian Literature,* 2nd ed., ed. Eugene Benson and William Toye. Toronto: Oxford University Press, 1997. 1127–32.
Polk, James. "Anansi, House of." In *Oxford Companion to Canadian Literature,* 2nd ed., ed. Eugene Benson and William Toye. Toronto: Oxford University Press, 1997. 33.
Saunders, Tom. "Sensitive Portrayal of the Journey into Manhood." *Winnipeg Tribune,* Oct. 2, 1976.
———. "Quebecer's Last Novel an Erotic Masterpiece." *Winnipeg Free Press,* June 9, 1979.

Simon, Sherry. "Final Episode: H.A.'s Novel Retains Brilliance in Translation." *Gazette*, June 2, 1979.
Spears, Tom. "Translating Bare Words in Artistry." *Toronto Star* Books, n.d.
———. "Translation Is Creation." [Calgary] *Albertan*, May 15, 1978.
Viets, Deborah. "Sheila Fischman Translating a Love for Language." *Quill and Quire*, Apr. 1988, 27.
Whitfield, Agnès. "Translations/Traductions." *University of Toronto Quarterly 72*, no. 1 (winter 2002/2003): 291–307.
"Words Are Like Gemstones: 'Sharp, Clear, Fine," *Globe and Mail*, January 24, 2000, R1.
Yanofsky, Joel. "Learning French Blossomed into a Thriving Career." *Canadian Jewish News*, Feb. 4, 1988, 17.

8

Transformations of
Barbara Godard

KATHY MEZEI

In 1974, the newly formed Association for Canadian and Québec Literatures (ACQL) held an inaugural conference at the Learned Societies Congress in Toronto.[1] It was a heady moment in scholarly exchange and the institutional legitimization of our two "national" literatures.[2] As the on-site program organizer, Barbara Godard helped Sandra Djwa plan the session on literary theory and suggested names of scholars from Québec. Bilingual, energetic, steeped in both Québec and English-Canadian literary traditions, ready to push beyond boundaries of canon, gender, and nation, Godard had already embarked upon her quest to understand and explain connections and differences, and to facilitate dialogue between the French and English communities.

Concealed behind other scholarly fields and the more visible arts, translation has all too often played a shadowy role in our two cultures. Through comparative literary studies, the practice of literary translation, and the editing of journals and collections featuring both literatures, Godard has helped reveal translation as an original art form and valid field of study. With her inventive translations and her conversations with experimental Québec feminists Nicole Brossard (*These Our Mothers, Lovhers, Picture Theory, Intimate Journal*) and France Théoret (*The Tangible Word*), she has contributed to forging a distinct Canadian feminist translation practice and theory.

From Space Science to Québec Feminism...

Born in 1941 to William and Margaret Thompson, Godard grew up in Toronto, where she attended elementary and secondary school. Although she remembers enjoying the translation parts of Latin and German examinations, it was in English and History that she received her Honours BA from the University of Toronto in 1964. At the Université de Montréal, where she completed her MA in 1967 with a thesis on the city of Montréal in the two literatures, she worked hard at improving her French writing skills. She audited courses on comparative stylistics by Jean-Paul Vinay and became involved with a reading group of Québec literature students that led to the establishment of the literary journal, *Lettres et écritures* (1964–66), forerunner to *Voix et images du pays*.

During her doctoral studies in France (1967–71), Godard attended seminars by Lucien Goldmann and Roland Barthes at the École des Hautes Études Pratiques, "reading Balzac through Lukacs with one and Flaubert and the failed revolution of 1848 with the other."[3] During those exhilarating years in Paris, recalls Godard, "feminism was still around the corner, although Hélène Cixous was teaching in a related UER [Unité d'enseignement et de recherche], and Cixous and Christine Brooke-Rose were writing their innovative fiction." In 1976, Godard became a full-time professor at York University, where she teaches English, French, Social and Political Thought, and Women's Studies.

To date, Godard has published five book translations, along with translations of dozens of poems, essays, and fictional excerpts in journals and books. She has written over twenty significant, often provocative, articles on translation in Canada, translation theory, the history of Canadian literary translation, and gender and translation. She edited the Coach House Press Translation Series with Frank Davey (1974–85), and contributed the annual *Letters in Canada* review on "Translations" in the *University of Toronto Quarterly* (1986–88). Through scrupulous editing, membership on juries for prizes and grants, organization of and participation in conferences, panels, workshops and associations, and public promotion of writers in translation in newspaper, radio, and television interviews, she has steadfastly served the translation community.

Godard has significantly contributed to the recognition of translation as a vital literary activity and theoretical site, bringing the experimental and theoretical work of Québec, particularly women, writers to the attention of the rest of Canada and the global literary community. Through her prefaces, translator's journal, and theoretical articles on translation as well as her self-reflective and densely theorized translations, one can track the evolution of her theories on translation from the early 1970s, when she first began to translate literary texts, to an increasingly refined and sophisticated articulation of the contested position of translators and translations.[4]

When asked the inevitable question of how she became involved in translation, Godard replied that she first started translating to earn money as a graduate student at the Université de Montréal. While studying Québec literature with Albert LeGrand, she supported herself by taping drills for English as a Second Language (ESL) courses and teaching English conversation in the summer-school language program in the linguistics department. She was subsequently approached by Marie-Andrée Bertrand and Denis Szabo in the newly formed criminology program to translate their papers for presentation at a conference. While studying in France, she translated essays on space science for members of her husband's research team in geophysics and space science. Although there were specific terminological dictionaries published by Dunod for all the sciences, she was confronted with the challenge of discipline-related vocabulary. The prepositions and conjunctions that clarified the nature of the team's experiments with rockets launched into the ionosphere during auroras were also problematic.

In 1973, while on temporary contract at York University and worried about finances, she was offered, but refused, the position of co-ordinator of the new Translation Grant Program at the Canada Council. She decided nonetheless that since there would be money around for translation, she would become a translator if she could not get permanent work teaching. Translation interested her because of her place at a crossroads between French and English: "Translating seemed to be a way to formally create a barrier between the languages again by making me pay attention to the crossover."

Crossing Over...

Godard first turned her hand to literary translation in Canada in the early 1970s, stimulated by contemporary Québec writing and the interest in translation among the writers associated with Coach House Press. *Open Letter* was also publishing an animated discussion about translation within the Toronto Research Group (bp nichol, Steve McCaffery, and Barbara Caruso). Intrigued by Godard's comments on the Québec literary scene, Frank Davey, with whom she was team-teaching a course, suggested she translate some of these experimental writers for the magazine.

This was the beginning of a period of significant translation activity. From 1972 to 1978, Godard published a series of political/poetical manifestos by key Québec nationalist poets, including Michèle Lalonde, Jacques Brault, Paul Chamberland, and Raoul Duguay, in *Open Letter*. In papers delivered during the peak of the Québec independence movement at a momentous gathering—the Québec Writers Conference, Sainte-Adèle, May 27–30, 1971, and in other works, these four Québec poets vigorously challenged the colonized condition of Québec. Their impassioned inventory and invention of a *pays* resonated with an emerging English-Canadian nationalism and literature. By means of these early translations, Godard engaged with avant-garde writers who were disrupting the codes and conventions of language, syntax, and genre, and sought to ensure that their voices would be heard in English Canada. For her, as for several translators in the 1970s, translation signified a political as well as a creative act.

In 1973 or 1974, according to Godard, Davey approached her about the feasibility of organizing a translation series for Coach House Press. Godard's role was to seek out avant-garde Québec writers, communicate with publishers and translators—an often thankless task—, and edit the translations. Davey presented the proposed texts to the press's board, negotiated contracts, and guided the translations through the publication process. Initially, their focus was the vibrant experimental fiction emerging from Québec under the influence of the French nouveau roman, which contrasted with the predominantly realist fiction being published in English Canada.[5] In 1979, Godard was influential in arranging the publication of two feminist texts: *The Story So Far*, a bilingual collection of new writing from Québec compiled by Brossard, and *A Clash of Symbols*, Linda Gaboriau's translation of the feminist collaborative drama, *La nef des sorcières*. In total, seven books by Brossard would appear in the series.

Godard and Davey experienced numerous hurdles, in particular the lack of experienced translators at this stage in our translation history and Québec publishers' indifference to potential English-Canadian audiences. In 1985, Davey resigned as editor, citing Coach House's editorial collective's disapproval of the number of Brossard translations in the series and their reluctance to allow Davey and Godard to retain their editorial independence.

Whatever problems existed within the press, the series was, in retrospect, highly influential. It introduced experimental writers like Brossard, Jacques Ferron, and Victor-Lévy Beaulieu to language-centred poets and novelists in the rest of Canada, including Fred Wah, George Bowering, and Daphne Marlatt, and it stimulated lasting exchanges and conversations between Québécois and English-Canadian writers. As Davey remembers "the translation series initially set out—at least as I saw it—to make francophone and anglophone writers in Canada more aware of each other's writing and writing theories."[6]

In 1978, Godard herself embarked upon a book translation project with Antonine Maillet's Governor General's Award-winning *Don l'Orignal* (1972). Undertaken initially for Coach House Press, *The Tale of Don l'Orignal* appeared under the imprint of Clarke Irwin. After the latter collapsed, the translation was republished in paperback under the New Press heading from Stoddard, a fact Godard discovered quite by chance. With its Acadian dialect, neologisms, and playful exuberance, Maillet's works posed dilemmas for her translators. As Godard herself points out, "translators' strategies have ranged from Douglas Mantz's phonetic transcription to create the shock and novelty of acadian as literary language, to Godard...and Stratford's creation of a synthetic language to stand for writer's idiolect—'Mailletois' into 'Stratfordese' with *Pélagie* (1982)...In contrast, Ben Shek's translation of *Mariaagelas*...retains many Acadianisms."[7]

While she may falter in tackling Maillet's dialect, particularly in the idiosyncratic speech of her earthy heroine/narrator, "La Sagouine," Godard's own rendering captures many features of the tall tale in a fluid, lively style. There is just a whiff of foreignness to convey Maillet's evocative recounting of wondrous places and events. The result is a mix of archaic English, American rural South, and slang diction and syntax. Here is la Sagouine in the original:

> Djeu le Père, qu'elle disait pieusement, c'est à toi que je parle. Essaie pas de faire mine que tu'entends pas. Tu sais que Citrouille est parti pour la guerre. Ç'a rien de drôle, une guerre. Il pourrait se faire casser quelque chose, mon fi. C'est à toi d'y voir."

Godard's translation renders la Sagouine's prayer in colloquial slang:

> "God the Father," she said piously, "its ya I'm talkin to. Mind ya don't pretend ya don't hear me. Ya know Citrouille's gone off to war. Ain't nothing funny about them wars. My son just might break somthin, lemme tell ya. And it's up to you to keep an eye on him.[8]

In translating Maillet, as in translating the poetic manifestos for *Open Letter*, Godard was developing tactics for difficult texts replete with neologisms, dialect, and semantic and syntactic disruption. She was paying close attention to the sound, rhythm, and orality of the text, a habit that would characterize all her later translations. As well, she retained the names of characters in the original French—Don l'Orignal, Citrouille, Noume—a practice she continues to maintain, and one that emphasizes the strangeness and playfulness of both target and source text.

The Translator as Ventriloquist

In the 1980s, influenced by the new French feminists such as Luce Irigaray, for whom she acted as translator during the Toronto International Summer Institute on Semiotics in June 1987, and by Québec feminist writers like Nicole Brossard, Louky Bersianik, and France Théoret, Godard began her project of "charting the sexual differences operating in language."[9] This turn to feminist theory and her articulation of the conjunction of feminism and translation denotes another crossing over. In a series of articles, prefaces, and translations of Brossard and Théoret, she incorporates their experiments in gender and language into her own practice.

In 1981 she translated a suite of poems by Nicole Brossard, "Tentation" ("The Temptation"), for a conference/reading in Toronto called Writers in Dialogue. The performance of a translation, especially the location and occasion, forms part of the extra-linguistic context that shapes the translation, a crucial aspect of Godard's translation position. She is careful to contextualize the act of translation.[10] Encountering Brossard's elliptical, oral, sensual style, a style characterized by doubles, repetitions, polysemic words, puns, ellipses, intertextual references, neologisms, white blank spaces, and typographic designs, Godard deliberated on how to render Brossard's meaning and sound. Casting herself as translator as ventriloquist, she stated: "Consciously, I sacrificed sense to sound" a declaration and practice that roused some controversy and misunderstanding about the translator's dilemma.[11]

In clarifying her translation strategy, which she has pointedly adjusted to the textual innovations of Brossard but which she also aligns with her own theoretical positions, Godard writes, "Complicity…is the nature of the relationship between translator and writer in such translations, when translation becomes creation but also subversion.…My signaling to an anglophone audience the orality of Brossard's text has made clear themes within the text as well as placing it at the crossroads of two relevant discourses, that of contemporary feminism and avant-garde concrete verse...the only two francophones...in the audience, affirmed that the poems indeed sounded just like Brossard. The translator becomes ventriloquist."[12]

Characteristic of her translation practice, Godard's collaboration with original authors (Brossard, Théoret) and dialogue with editors (Ray Ellenwood) and writers (Daphne Marlatt, Lola Lemire Tostevin) contributes to her sense of herself as an active and visible participant in the rewriting of a text. Consultation with Ellenwood, for example, resolved the problem of the title, *Amantes*—often the translator's *bête noire*. She credits him with suggesting the letter "h" in *Lovhers*, which made the grammatical element, always central to Brossard, much clearer.[13]

In 1983, Coach House Press published *These Our Mothers; Or, The Disintegrating Chapter*, Godard's translation of *L'amèr*, the first volume of Nicole Brossard's lesbian triptych. Here Godard begins a practice, followed in all subsequent translated books, of offering the anglophone reader a preface. As she would write later in the preface to *Lovhers*, "one could write a history of theories of translation, a history of the relationships between author and translator, indeed between author and reader, by writing a history of the preface as genre."[14]

With such gestures, Godard signals her visibility as translator and her refusal to concede to the concept of translator and translation as transparent. She also initiates a pattern of explication that recurs in all her prefaces. By outlining the source author's ideas, theoretical framework and stylistics, and the place of this text within this author's oeuvre, she situates the text she is translating. At the same time, she delineates her specific translation strategies and decisions, the difficulties the source text presents, and her solutions, along with the sometimes complex and disingenuous process by which she arrived at these solutions. For the *Tessera* issue on translation (no. 6), the editors each translated a poem from Lola Lemire-Tostevin's "sophie," accompanied by a brief commentary, in effect constructing a serial and conversational "translation." Godard remarked that her own "Water-Music: Theme and Vers-if-ications" was the first "preface" composed during the translation process rather than after; as self-reflective commentary, it muses and meanders; by turns associative, spiraling, like her translations, it engages in a combinatory practice.

In the preface to *These Our Mothers*, Godard draws our attention to the influence of Jacques Derrida and Gilles Deleuze on Nicole Brossard in references to difference, erasure, and repetition. She also underlines the prevalence of doubleness in Brossard's language and meaning, and her reworking of the relation between gender and grammar. For Godard, there is a serendipitous but consciously developed interaction between Deleuzian deconstruction, the act of translating Brossard, and the articulation of her own particular position on translation. In the midst of pondering how to translate certain terms in *L'amèr*, she attended a talk at York University by Constantin Boundas on Deleuze. This enabled her to "recogniz[e]...the serial system of Brossard's fiction and its exploration of 'surfaces of sense,' of making the textual body a virtual surface for the inscription of desire,...which unfolds as a mapping of new configurations of sense in an unsettling movement of 'deterritorialization.'" When she later asked Brossard about Deleuze, Brossard replied she had one of his books, *Logique du sens*, open on her desk.[15]

Coincidence, serendipity or the translator's intuition? With this input, Godard began to understand how Brossard had reworked Deleuze's ideas on difference and repetition (which is "never the return of the same as it is within representation ever subordinate to the exigencies of identity") into a theory of sexual differences that opens up a space for lesbian sexuality. At the same time, through her intricate reading of Deleuze, Godard expresses and refines her own translation practice, and her opposition to the dominance in English-language translations of "a naturalizing target-language strategy valuing transparency...as though [they] had been written in English."[16]

Confronted with the polysemic and gender neutral title and central trope, *l'amèr*—bitter, sea, and mother (*mère*), in which the absent "e" signifies the absent mother, the silenced feminine—Godard proposes as her title and subject "These our mothers": The Se / The Sour / The Smothers. With its graphic setup and multiple meanings, this rendering is an example of Godard's preference for transformation, an attempt to recreate rather than to repeat Brossard's many-layered signifier.[17]

While some of Godard's innovative, imaginative solutions may seem contrived or self-conscious, this self-consciousness is deliberate and a flaunting of the translator's signature, as can be seen in her translation of the following lines from the unsettling opening of *l'amèr*:

> J'ai tué le ventre. Moi ma vie été la lune. Moi ma mort. Trente ans me séparent de la vie, trente de la mort. Ma mère, ma fille. Mamelle, une seule vie, la mienne. Réseau clandestin de reproduction. Matrice et matière anonymes.

Godard responds to the repetitiveness of "moi" and "ma" by italicizing "*my*." The playful polysemy of "mamelle" is re-created in "Mamma, Mam*elle*, Mamilla":

I killed the womb. *My* life in summer the moon. *My* death. Thirty years separate me from life, thirty from death. My mother, my daughter. Mamma, Mam*elle*, Mamilla, a single life. Clandestine's system of reproduction. Anonymous matrix and matter.[18]

Godard's translations of Brossard are a veritable *tour de force*, offering anglophone and bilingual readers the pleasure of entering into Brossard's brilliantly (de)constructed, elliptical "reality." Indeed, Brossard affirms the collaboration—in both senses of the word[19]—and the reciprocal relation between author and translator: "what we choose to hide in the text must now be unveiled....I must face what I had consciously and scrupulously hidden. To be translated is to be the subject of an inquiry not only into what one believes oneself to be, but also into the way of thinking in a language and the way we are thought by a language."[20]

The Translator as She

Godard's earlier investigations into discourse, feminist theory, and translation were influenced by formalism and structuralist semiotics, which attempted to uncover deep structures and codify the communication act."[21] During the late 1970s and 1980s, while translating Brossard and other major experimental Québec feminist poets and novelists, including Louky Bersianik, Yolande Villemaire, Marie Uguay, and Louise Cotnoir, Godard was also pursuing her reflections on translation. Working her way through French feminist theorists Luce Irigaray and Hélène Cixous, Godard sought to differentiate male/female translation practices in relation to the body, desire, sexuality, and voice. In the 1989 *Tessera* issue devoted to "La traduction au féminin/Translating Women," she makes the connection that women "translate" when they enter the public realm, that women like translators are silenced, invisible, the other, the servant, and that woman herself is translated through discourse and patriarchal institutions and hierarchies. As she would note later, translation foregrounds "the work of gender in a feminization of diction and retention of sound images as connectives to disrupt syntax"[22]

With the publication of "Theorizing Feminist Discourse/Translation" in this issue of *Tessera*, Godard moves from a relatively essentialist explication of discourses towards a more deconstructive, pluralist model. "Feminist discourse," she writes, "is translation in two ways: as notation of 'gestural' and other codes from what has been hitherto 'unheard of,' a muted discourse, and as repetition and consequent displacement of the dominant discourse."[23] In advocating for and making visible what has been concealed, Godard's stance becomes ideological and political in that she hopes that feminist discourse and translation will be emancipatory, subversive, and affirmative. As creative transformation, translation opens up to include imitation, adaptation, quotation, pastiche, parody, and repetition. Difference(s) rather than sameness or equivalence are traced through the translation act. "Translation theory joins feminist textual theory," she observes, "in emphasizing the polyphony of the translated text in that it foregrounds the self-reflexive elements of the translator's/rewriter's discourse and flaunts its work, its textuality."[24]

This transformative process of translation is particularly evident in her rendition of *Lovhers* (1986), the third book in Brossard's lesbian triptych, which Godard started working on in 1981. Brossard negotiated the translation with Antonio d'Alfonso at Guernica. Godard met with Brossard on several occasions, and also attended a session of Brossard's graduate class at Queen's University in Kingston on *Picture Theory*. As with *These Our Mothers*, Brossard read the final draft.

In her preface to *Lovhers*, Godard compares the two translations; *Lovhers*, she notes, has developed a more lyric line and resorts less to grammatical play than *These Our Mothers*. She explains that puns like "delire" (reading and unreading, delirious) are paraphrased rather than translated, while neologisms intended to disrupt conventions of gender in grammar are, in contrast, paradoxically translated rather than paraphrased. The translation effect, therefore, is one of a relatively literal rendering of Brossard's fragmented, elliptical syntax, traces, and repetitions, one that reproduces her deconstruction of conventional patterns.[25] In contrast, the "translation" of Brossard's puns and wordplay is relatively free. For example, the repeated polyphonic phrase "JE N'ARR TE PAS DE LIRE" becomes "I DON'T STOP READING/ DELIRING." This is paraphrase; moreover, "deliring" imposes a foreignizing effect on the translation by means of a neologism in English that elicits the memory of the French "lire." The translator is overtly self-conscious. In translations such as "glaze and phrase" for "verre et du verbe," Godard as ventriloquist strives to capture the sound rather the meaning, although, in these cases, she seems adroitly to achieve both.

Here is Brossard's version of the first "Tentation":

j'ai succombé à toutes les visions
séduite, surface, série et sérieuse
en toute mobilité et paysages
concentrée sur chaque épisode

territoire et joue, masquée/ démasquée:
out of space ou pleine d'intonations
dans le climat, délirante autour
de toutes les figures, aérienne
dans l'emploi du verre et du verbe[26]

Godard skilfully recreates Brossard's rupture and resistance of syntax and play with language:

The Temptation
i succumbed to all the visions
seduced, surface, series and serious
in all mobility and landscapes
concentrated on each episode
territory and cheek. masked/unmasked:
hors l'espace or full of intonations
in the climate delirious around
all the figures, aerial
in the use of glaze and phrase[27]

Nicole Brossard's *Picture Theory* continues her exploration of the lesbian subject and text through images of light, the hologram, and Ludwig Wittgenstein's picture theory. Working on the translation, published in 1990, sent Godard back to Wittgenstein's *Tractatus*, Djuna Barnes, Gertrude Stein, and Julia Kristeva to spin a convoluted web of texts, intertexts, associations, and conversations. Godard creates what she calls her own "network of signifiers." In her preface to this book, which mixes philosophy, poetry, fictional narrative, and typographic play in a search for a new discourse, a new pictorial representation of woman, Godard warns us that the English version differs greatly from the French version, and yet it remains a translation, a playful, transformative translation, and not an adaptation or a Poundian homage.[28]

She alerts us that phrases in English in the original will be in boldface, and French phrases, unlike those in other languages—German, Italian, etc.—will not be italicized. The opening section of Book 3, "Thought," offers examples of Godard's use of boldface, along with her responsiveness to Brossard's elliptical syntax and word play:

Les cités de verre s'étaient éteintes. Dernier jour dans l'île, j'étais déjà "dans les eaux de Curaçao" en ville prise par cette tension qui m'incite au présent. Michèle Vallée, livre trois, rue Laurier (MOTHER SICK—STAYING IN NEW YORK—WILL WRITE—LOVE—CLAIRE).[29]

Godard's translation preserves the eruption of English into Brossard's narrative:

> The glass cities were extinct. Last day on the island, I was already "in the waters of Curaçao" in the city, caught by this tension which urges me into the present. Michèle Vallée, book three, rue Laurier **(MOTHER SICK—STAYING IN NEW YORK—WILL WRITE—LOVE—CLAIRE)**.[30]

By retaining the original English sentence in bold, Godard recreates the element of multiplicity in the source text; by maintaining the original address "rue Laurier" instead of translating it into "Laurier St.," she firmly locates the text in Montréal. In a literal flaunting of the translator's signature, Godard mischievously inserts herself into the last section of the book, the book within the book, "Hologram," by inscribing "translated from the French by Barbara Godard" on the cover and title pages. In this kind of translation/transformation, the anglophone reader experiences a different text and participates in the self-reflexive dynamic of a translator negotiating a new linguistic and discursive network of signifiers.

Translating by Lapses and Bounds[31]

In "A Translator's Journal" (1995), which she was tempted to call "Essays/ons traduction/translation," and of which excerpts have been published as "Re/configurations" (an expression perhaps worth investigating as a term for translation?), Godard concocts "a sort of log book of a translation."[32] She peregrinates through the mechanics of translation—tenses, rhythm, definition, how to translate the numerous quotations—and through the false starts and felicitous solutions.[33]

Bakhtin, always an important figure for Godard as her ideas on translation germinate, resurfaces in the journal through her reflections on dialogism: "I've been interested in exploring a metonymic or contingent theory of translation...in which languages, texts, social texts, touch each other interanimating. In this contamination, the translator-function works like the author-function to fix momentarily the circulation of meaning within a contingent network of texts and social discourses, difference that produces a transformation between linguistic versions. Translation here is not a carrying across, but a reworking of meaning."[34] The process of translating Brossard and interrogating representation, language, gender and grammar, subjectivity, and the "author" as construct has been (re)configured into a theory of translation. For Godard, praxis and theory have merged in the signifier, "translation," to suggest a layered reading, interpretation, and rewriting of other acts of writing.

Although Godard has not yet translated or adapted theatrical pieces, she has written two complex and important studies on the translation, adaptation, performance, and performativity of plays. In a 1990 article, "(Re)Appropriation as Translation," she examines the concepts of transformation and adaptation through a detailed perusal of Sally Clark's *Jehanne of the Witches* and the *Trial of Judith K*. She observes how, in adapting novels for the stage and rewriting them with female protagonists, Clark creates a "textual web of variations, adaptations, ramifies,"[35] and carefully and sympathetically scrutinizes Clark's own position as a female playwright and the destabilization of gender in both plays and performances. In "Between Performative and Performance: Translation and Theatre in the Canadian/Quebec Context," she tries to "disentangle the problematic of theatre as translation / translation as theatre from translation in theatre...to distinguish the performativity of translation from translation in performance." She observes "the tendency in English to confound the act of translating a play-text across different "national" languages with the act of transposing a written text onto the stage....[In contrast] francophone critics...have examined the social effects of translated theatre texts in [the context of] the political relations of Québec and the rest of Canada from the perspective of the margin constituted by the national and global hegemony of English."[36]

In 1991, Godard published *The Tangible Word*, a translation of four early texts by France Théoret: *Bloody Mary, Une voix pour Odile, Vertiges*, and *Nécessairement putain*. As the French titles indicate, Théoret undoes different constructions of woman—as subject, as icon, as Québécoise, harshly exposing woman's silenced voice, her invaded body, her stereotyped maternal role, her necessary whoredom. Like Brossard, Théoret has been at the forefront of the interrogation of gender, subjectivity, and language; her prose is similarly elliptical, subversive, and disruptive. As Godard writes in her preface, "although Théoret elaborates a theory of textuality as translation,...her textual praxis challenges the translator [and the reader, one might add (K.M.)]. Godard met with Théoret on one or two occasions to discuss translation issues. Because Théoret had "a stylistic feature of making grammatical parallelisms in unusual places and ways," she needed to "clarify that these were not typographical errors." Théoret had a vast vocabulary drawing on different linguistic registers, many from the old *parler français du Canada* about which Godard would also raise questions. Théoret wanted Godard to use her revised version (1991), which was more readable and less elliptical; this Godard did when it resolved a translation impasse.

In *Bloody Mary*, a short, syncopated, angry text, Théoret presents the literal and textual disfigurement of the Virgin Mary. The virginal and maternal figure of a "holy" Virgin Mary, who is also every woman, is brutally gutted and murdered along with Catholic traditions, teachings, and practices. Violence, blood, death, rape, and scatology are presented in a series of monstrous images meant to shock and disturb. The opening line, "Le regard du dedans furieusement tue," is strikingly memorable. Godard retains the knifelike incisiveness that cuts sharply through language and convention with "The gaze from inside furiously throttles."[37] Other barbed and multi-levelled phrases like "Avant toujours j'écris le couteau," and the bloody refrain or slogan, "Du sang l'en mange / Du sang l'on chie" are tautly rendered as: "Before always I write knife" and "Blood to eat / Blood to shit," which retain the rhythm and precision of the original text (in the latter case, even improving its conciseness). Neologisms, such as "l'encensfantsilonlaire" and "l'enfantfansilaire," are cleverly transformed into "incensefantisilonary" (which, like the original, en (cens)fant, plays with "infant") and "infantfansilary."[38] Godard's decision to keep the phrase "Où's qu'y a que ça s'pogne que ça s'plotte que ça s'mette" (20) in French maintains Théoret's visual symmetry and ensures that the violent and staccato sounds of the original disturb the anglophone reader with their foreignness.[39]

Contextualizing Canadian Literary Translation

Preparing the "Translations" review for the *University of Toronto Quarterly's* annual *Letters in Canada* issue from 1987 to 1989 provided Godard with a diversity of translations and studies of translations from which she could discern patterns and trends. Writing in 1988 about the previous year's crop of translation, she observed, "With the appearance of such sophisticated translations, which recognize the complexity of writing in the source text and exhibit a matching creative energy in rewriting it, the situation of translation in Canada seems flourishing...however, the theory of translation in anglophone Canada is ambiguous, divided between those who conceptualize meaning as unitary and recoverable, hence transferrable [*sic*] between transparent languages, and those who understand texts to be always already written and meaning to be elusive."[40]

In her writings on translation, including "Translation as Culture: A Canadian School of Translation" (1997), Godard has, herself, contributed significantly to the visibility and dissemination of Canadian literary translation as practice and as a challenging field of scholarly inquiry. In recognition of the importance of both her translation practice and her critical writing, not only in Canada, but also internationally, she was asked to contribute two articles to the *Encyclopedia of Literary Translation in English* (2000). In "Gender and Gender Politics in Literary Translation," she explores the history of gender in translation, its effacement yet perseverance throughout history, and its resurgence particularly in Canada in combination with feminist theory and feminist writers and translators. In "French-Canadian Writers in English Translation," she packs not only a wealth of historical detail, but also locates the theoretical and institutional shifts and turns in our translation history. In 2000, she was awarded the Canadian Association for Translation Studies' Vinay-Darbelnet prize for her article "Une littérature en devenir: La reécriture textuelle et dynamisme du champ littéraire; Les écrivaines québécoises au Canada anglais."

"This rewriting is and is not translation"—Godard's closing comment on the process of translating *The Tangible Word* reflects the paradox of translating and her own parodic, playful, and transformative sense of translation.[41] Quite fittingly, her most recent creative dialogue is *Intimate Journal* (2004), a translation of Brossard's *Journal intime ou voilà donc un manuscrit*.

NOTES

1 Sessions were held jointly with the Canadian Comparative Literature Association and the Association of Canadian University Teachers of French.
2 The list of conference participants included Jack Warwick, Gilbert Drolet, Pierre Nepveu, Näim Kattan, Clara Thomas, Desmond Pacey, Paul-André Bourque, Clément Moisan, Philip Stratford, Northrop Frye, Hubert Aquin, Gérard Bessette, Louis Dudek, David Hayne, Jean-Charles Falardeau, Sheila Fischman, Kathy Mezei, and Alan Brown.
3 Email interview with Barbara Godard, October 6 and 13, 2001; all subsequent quotations are from this interview unless otherwise indicated. I wish to thank Barbara Godard for her gracious co-operation with this portrait.
4 As Sherry Simon notes, "Godard's search for innovative modes through which the translator's position can be spoken make her work central to any formulation of feminist translation" Sherry Simon, *Gender in Translation: Cultural Identity and the Politics of Transmission* (London: Routledge, 1996), p. 22.
5 See also Frank Davey's essay "A History of the Coach House Press Québec Translations," delivered at the Learned Societies, ACQL, Montréal, June 1995, p. 5. Godard and Davey each attribute the origin of the idea to the other. Davey writes that Godard suggested that the press "undertake a series of translations of new Québec writing…that reflected political and artistic concerns similar to those of writers whom Coach House was already publishing."
6 Davey, "A History of the Coach House Press Québec Translations," p. 15.

7 Barbara Godard, "French-Canadian Writers in English Translation," in *Encyclopedia of Literary Translation into English, vol.1*, ed. Olive Classe (London: Fitzroy Dearborn, 2000), 480–81.
8 Antonine Maillet, *Don l'Orignal* (Montréal: Leméac, 1972), pp. 47–48; Antonine Maillet, *The Tale of Don l'Orignal*, trans. B. Godard (Toronto: New Press, 1978), p. 35.
9 Barbara Godard, "Language and Sexual Difference," *Atkinson Review of Canadian Studies* 2, no. 1 (1984): 14.
10 "More than just a transference of 'meaning' from one set of language signs to another though competent use of the dictionary and grammar, the process of translation involves a whole set of extra-linguistic criteria." See Barbara Godard, "The Translator as She," in *In the Feminine: Women and Words / Les femmes et les mots*, ed. Ann Dybikowski, Victoria Freeman, Daphne Marlatt, Barbara Pulling, and Betsy Warland (Edmonton: Longspoon, 1985), p. 193. Godard has also observed, "The second 'transformational' modality, translation establishes relations to an outside and creates a new semiotics." Barbara Godard, "Deleuze and Translation," *Parallax* 6, no. 1 (2000): 63.
11 Barbara Godard, "The Translator as Ventriloquist," Prism International 20, no. 3 (1982), p. 35. For reactions to the performance see Robyn Gillam 'The Mauve File Folder: Notes on the Translation of Nicole Brossard," *Paragraph* 17, no. 2 (fall 1995), pp. 8–12, and Godard's considered reply in a letter to the Editors, *Paragraph*, 17, no. 3 (winter/spring 1995/96): 39–40.
12 Godard, "The Translator as Ventriloquist," *Prism International* 20, no. 3: 36.
13 Godard, "Language and Sexual Difference," p. 19.
14 Preface to *Lovhers*, by Nicole Brossard, trans. Barbara Godard (Montréal: Guernica, 1986), p. 7.
15 Barbara Godard, "Deleuze and Translation," *Parallax* 6, no. 1 (2000): 58.
16 Godard, "Deleuze and Translation," p. 59.
17 Godard explains that exchanging puns with Daphne Marlatt over the telephone helped her with this title. She also states that the intended title could not be reproduced on the cover, only on the inside, and that the meanings had to be spelled out more clearly for the readers as "the translation from *These Our Mothers* to the graphic sign was gradually worked out." Godard, "Language and Sexual Difference," p. 19.
18 Nicole Brossard, *L'amèr, ou le chapitre effrité* (Montréal: Quinze, 1977), p. 11; Nicole Brossard, *TheSe our Mothers; or, The Disintegrating Chapter*, trans. Barbara Godard (Toronto: Coach House Press, 1983), p. 13.
19 Colloboration, defined in French and English as co-operation especially in artistic and scientific endeavours, can also imply capitulation, deceit, and duplicity as in the case of French "collaboration" with the Nazis during the Second World War.
20 Nicole Brosssard, quoted by Godard, "The Translator as She," p. 197.
21 See Godard, "The Translator as She," p. 194.
22 Godard, "French-Canadian Writers in English Translation," p. 481.
23 Barbara Godard, "Theorizing Feminist Discourse/Translation," *Tessera*, no. 6 (1989): 46.

24 Godard, "Theorizing Feminist Discourse/Translation," in *Translation, History and Culture*, ed. Susan Bassnett and André Lefevere (London: Pinter, 1990), p. 92.
25 Barbara Godard, preface to *Lovhers*, by Nicole Brossard, trans. Barbara Godard, p. 9.
26 Nicole Brossard, "Tentation," in *Amantes* (Montréal: Quinze, 1980), p. 75.
27 Nicole Brossard, "Temptation," in *Lovhers*, trans. Barbara Godard (Montréal: Guernica, 1986), p. 76.
28 The translation of *Picture Theory*, according to Godard, was initiated by Roof Books in New York, with a co-edition by Guernica. The Roof edition, she says, came out without a preface and with many errors. This time, Godard sent her questions to Brossard by mail: "Generally the answers came back as I expected; by then I knew her system and that the ambiguity was indeed intentional. We talked as much about the ideas and the form of the books as about specific passages."
29 Nicole Brossard, *Picture Theory* (Montréal: Nouvelle Optique, 1982), p. 105.
30 Nicole Brossard, *Picture Theory*, trans. Barbara Godard (Montréal: Guernica, 1991), p. 91.
31 See Barbara Godard, "Gender and Gender Politics in Literary Translation," in *Encyclopedia of Literary Translation into English, vol. 1*, ed. Olive Classe (London: Fitzroy Dearborn Publishers, 2000), pp. 501–12.
32 Barbara Godard, "A Translator's Journal," in *Culture in Transit: Translating the Literature of Québec*, ed. Sherry Simon (Montréal: Véhicule Press, 1995, p. 69.
33 Describing Godard's technique in this journal, Sherry Simon remarks: "Godard's tracking of her own intellectual footsteps, her attentiveness to the workings of her own mind restores the reality of translation as a truly associative process, an ongoing appeal to memory and to a private thesaurus, a ping pong of potentially infinite rebounds." (Simon, *Gender in Translation*, p. 23.)
34 Godard, "A Translator's Journal," p. 77.
35 Barbara Godard, "(Re)Appropriation as Translation," *Canadian Theatre Review*, no. 64 (1990): 35.
36 Barbara Godard, "Between Performativity and Performance: Translation and Theatre in the Canadian/Quebec Context," *Modern Drama*, 43, no. 3 (fall 2000): 332–34, 340–41.
37 France Théoret, *The Tangible Word*, trans. Barbara Godard (Montréal: Guernica, 1991), p. 19.
38 Théoret, *The Tangible Word*, trans. Barbara Godard, p. 21.
39 Théoret, *The Tangible Word*, trans. Barbara Godard, p. 20.
40 Barbara Godard, "Translations," *University of Toronto Quarterly* 59, no. 1 (1989): 98.
41 Barbara Godard, "Translating Translating Translation," introduction to *The Tangible Word*, by France Théoret, trans. Barbara Godard (Montréal: Guernica, 1991), p. 14.

BIBLIOGRAPHY

I. Primary Sources

Literary Translations (Books)

Brossard, Nicole. *These Our Mothers; Or, The Disintegrating Chapter.* Trans. Barbara Godard. Toronto: Coach House Press, 1983. Translation of *L'amèr ou le chapitre effrité.* Montréal: Quinze, 1977.

———. *Lovhers.* Trans. Barbara Godard. Montréal: Guernica, 1986. Translation of *Amantes.* Montréal: Quinze, 1980.

———. *Picture Theory.* Trans. Barbara Godard. Montréal: Guernica, 1991. Translation of *Picture Theory.* Montréal: Nouvelle Optique, 1982.

———. *Intimate Journal, or Here's a Manuscript.* With an introduction, "The Moving Intimacy of Language," by Barbara Godard. Trans. Barbara Godard. Toronto: Mercury Press, 2004. Translation of *Journal intime ou voilà donc un manuscrit.* Montréal: Les Herbes Rouges, 1984. 5–23.

Maillet, Antonine. *The Tale of Don l'Original.* Trans. Barbara Godard. Toronto: Clarke-Irwin, 1978; Toronto: New Press, 1989. Translation of *Don l'Original.* Montréal: Leméac, 1972.

Théoret, France. *The Tangible Word (1977–1983).* Trans. Barbara Godard. Montréal: Guernica, 1991. Translation of *Bloody Mary.* Montréal: Les Herbes Rouges, 1977; *Une voix pour Odile.* Montréal: Les Herbes Rouges, 1978; *Vertiges.* Montréal: Les Herbes Rouges, 1979; and *Nécessairement putain.* Montréal: Les Herbes Rouges, 1980.

Translations in Journals or Edited Volumes

Amyot, Geneviève. "These Two Are Real Birds." Trans. Barbara Godard. *The Story So Far*, no. 6 (1979): 131–46.

Bersianik, Louky. "Moli mi tangere." Trans. Barbara Godard. *Room of One's Own* 4, no. 1 (Sept. 1978): 98–110.

Brault, Jacques. "The Writer and Power." Trans. Barbara Godard. *Open Letter* 2nd ser., no. 3 (fall 1972): 22–25.

Brossard, Nicole. "from *L'amèr ou le chapitre effrité.*" Trans. Barbara Godard. *Essays on Canadian Writing*, no. 7/8 (fall 1977): 7–16.

———. "My Continent." Trans. Barbara Godard. *Fireweed*, no. 13 (1982): 105–107; Rpt. in *Spelles: Poetry by Canadian Women*, ed. Judith Fitzgerald. Windsor: Black Moss, 1986. 31–33. Rpt. in *Fireworks: The Best of Fireweed*, ed. Makeda Silvera. Toronto: Women's Press, 1986. 111–13.

———. "The Temptation." Trans. Barbara Godard. In *Amantes* introduction, 67–75. *Prism International* 20, no. 3 (spring 1982): 30–34; rpt. in *Prism International* 23, no. 2 (winter 1984): 160–61.

———. "The Act of the Eye on Purple," from *These Our Mothers.* Trans. Barbara Godard. In *Lords of Winter and of Love*, ed. Barry Callaghan. Toronto: Exile, 1983. 93.

———. "My Memory of (Love)" and "The Barbizon Hotel for Women." In *Lovhers*, pp. 53–64; pp. 68–75. Trans. Barbara Godard. *Exile* 9, no. 2/3/4 (1984): 240–50.

———. Selection from *The/Se/our/Mothers*. Trans. Barbara Godard. *Radical Reviewer*, no.10 (June 1984): 13.

———. Section of *Journal Intime* for *Canadian Women Writer's Engagement Calendar*. Trans. Barbara Godard. Ed. Adele Wiseman. 1986.

———. Section of "Perspective." Trans. Barbara Godard. In *Picture Theory*, pp. 129–44. Rpt in *Raddle Moon*, no. 10 (spring 1991): 86–98.

———. "Certain Words." Trans. Barbara Godard. In *Collaboration in the Feminine: Writing on Women and Culture from Tessera*. Toronto: Second Story Press, 1994. 47–52.

———. "Skin Screen Too." Trans. Barbara Godard. In *Picture Theory*, pp. 129–44. *Public*, no. 12 (1995): 66–71.

———. "The Textured Angel of Desire." Trans. Barbara Godard. *Yale French Studies*, no. 87 (1995): 105–14.

———. "Igneous Woman, Integral Woman." In *Lovhers*, pp. 45–52. Rpt in *Out of Everywhere: Linguistically Innovative Poetry by Women in North America and the UK*, ed. Maggie O'Sullivan. London: Reality Street Editions, 1996. 112–14.

———. "The Barbizon Hotel for Women" and "The Temptation." Trans. Barbara Godard. In *Lovhers*, pp. 68–75; pp. 76–84. Rpt in *Poems for the Millenium*, vol. 2, ed. Pierre Joris and Jerome Rothenberg. Berkeley: University of California Press, 1997. 712–17.

———. "Act of the Eye." Trans. Barbara Godard. In *Moving Borders: Three Decades of Writing by Women*, ed. Mary Margaret Sloan. Jersey City: Talisman House, 1998. 100–104, 107–12.

———. "Geometrical." Trans. Barbara Godard. In *These Our Mothers*, p. 64. [illus. broadside]. Burlington, VT: Association of College and Research Libraries, 1999.

———. Section 2 of *Journal Intime*. Trans. Barbara Godard. In *Verdure* [Buffalo], no. 56 (2002): 82–90.

Chamberland, Paul. "The Revolution of the Writer." Trans. Barbara Godard. *Open Letter* 2nd ser., no. 3 (fall 1972): 26–28.

———. *I Have No*. Trans. Barbara Godard. *Open Letter* 2nd ser., no. 7 (summer 1974): 5–17.

Cloutier, Cécile. Ten poems from *Chaleuils*. In Evelyn Voldeng, "La Production Poétique comme duplication on derivation textuelle d'une langue à une autre?" in *La Traduction: l'Universitaire et le practicien*, ed. A. Thomas and J. Flamand. Ottawa: Presses de l'Université d'Ottawa, 1984. 150–59.

———. Selections from *Chaleuils* and *Ostraka*. Trans. Barbara Godard. *Fireweed*, no. 56 (winter 1996): 56–58; rpt. in *Trans Lit*, no. 4 (1999): 27–32.

Cotnoir, Louise. "Writing Ourselves with, in and against Language." Trans. Barbara Godard. *Room of One's Own* 8, no. 4 (fall 1983): 50–52.

———. "The Marked Gender." Trans. Barbara Godard. *In the Feminine: Women and Words / Les femmes et les mots*. Edmonton: Longspoon, 1985. 99–104.

Duguay, Raoul. "The Future of the Writer / The Writer of the Present / The Power of the Writer." Trans. Barbara Godard. *Open Letter* 2nd ser., no. 3 (fall 1972): 29–31.

Gauvin, Lise. "What? You Too?" Trans. Barbara Godard. In *Collaborations in the Feminine: Writing on Women and Culture from Tessera*. Toronto: Second Story Press, 1994. 214–20.
Hébert, Anne. "Strange Capture." Trans. Barbara Godard. *ellipse*, no. 50 (1993): 26–28.
Lalonde, Michèle. "Writers and the Revolution." Trans. Barbara Godard. *Open Letter* 2nd ser., no. 4 (spring 1973): 29–37.
Lamoureux, Joanne. "The Museum Flat." Trans. Barbara Godard. *Public*, no. 1 (1989): 71–84.
Lanctôt, Mireille. "The Claybaker." Trans. Barbara Godard. *Room of One's Own* 14, no. 1 (September 1978): 87–91.
La Rue, Monique. "Power or 'Unpower' of the Fictional Subject: A Letter to Lise Gauvin in Reply to 'What? You Too?'" Trans. Barbara Godard. *Collaboration in the Feminine: Writing on Women and Culture from* Tessera. Toronto: Second Story Press, 1994. 221–27.
Massé, Carole. "The Subject at Stake." Trans. Barbara Godard. *Collaboration in the Feminine: Writing on Women and Culture from* Tessera. Toronto: Second Story Press, 1994. 218–20.
Perrault, Marie. *Roberto Pellegrinuizzi*. Trans. Barbara Godard. Lethbridge: Southern Alberta Art Gallery, 1988.
Uguay, Marie. Untitled Poem. Trans. Barbara Godard. *ellipse*, no. 31 (1983): 15.
Vezina, Medje. "My Sorrow Knows No Bounds." Trans. Barbara Godard. *ellipse*, no. 35 (1986): 28–31.
Villemaire, Yolande. "My Heart Beats Like a Bolo." Trans. Barbara Godard. *Room of One's Own* 4, no. 1 (sept. 1978): 111–28.
Wittig, Monique. "*The Constant Journey:* An Introduction and a Prefatory Note." Trans. Barbara Godard. *Modern Drama* 39, no. 1 (1996): 156–59.

Works on Translation

Godard, Barbara. "The Translator as Ventriloquist." *Prism International* 20, no. 3 (1982): 35–36.
———. "Language and Sexual Difference: The Case of Translation." *Atkinson Review of Canadian Studies* 2, no. 1 (1984): 13–20.
———. "Translating and Sexual Difference." *Resources for Feminist Research* 13, no. 3 (1984): 13–16.
———. "Translation Poetics, from Modernity to Post-Modernity." Rpt. in *Translation, Translation*, ed. Susan Petrilli. Amsterdam: Rodopi, 2003. 87–99.
———. "The Translator as Ventriloquist." *Prism International* 22, no. 2 (1984): 60–61.
———. "The Translator as She: The Relationship between Writer and Translator." In *In the feminine: Women and words/les femmes et les mots*, ed. Ann Dybikowski, Victoria Freeman, Daphne Marlatt, Barbara Pulling, and Betsy Warland. Edmonton: Longspoon, 1985. 193–98.
———. "Preface to *Lovhers*," by Nicole Brossard. Trans. Barbara Godard. Montréal: Guernica, 1986. 7–12.

———. "Translations." *University of Toronto Quarterly* 57, no. 1 (1987): 77–98.
———. "Translations." *University of Toronto Quarterly* 58, no. 1 (1989): 76–98.
———. "Theorizing Feminist Discourse/Translation." *Tessera*, no. 6 (1989): 42–53.
———, et al. "Translation: The Relationship between Writer and Translator," *Méta* 34, no. 2 (1989): 209–24.
———. "Translations." *University of Toronto Quarterly* 59, no. 1 (1989): 81–107.
———. "(Re)Appropriation as Translation." *Canadian Theatre Review*, no. 64, 1990): 22–31.
———. "Theorizing Feminist Discourse/Translation." In *Translation: History and Culture*, ed. Susan Bassnett and André Lefevere. London: Pinter, 1990. 87–96; London: Pinter, 1995; Italian ed. *La Traduzione tra Storia e Cultura*. Milan: Crocetti, 1995.
———. "*from* Re/configurations." *Raddle Moon*, no. 10 (spring 1991): 76–85.
———. "Preface to *Picture Theory*," by Nicole Brossard. Trans. Barbara Godard. Montréal: Guernica, 1991. 7–11.
———. "Translating Translating Translation." Introduction to *The Tangible Word* by France Théoret. Montréal: Guernica, 1991. 7–15.
———. "Translating (*with*) the Speculum." *TTR: Traduction, terminologie, rédaction* 4, no. 2 (1991): 85–121.
———. "Traduzione: soggetto / il in transito." In *Questioni di teoria femminista*, ed. Paola Bono. Milan: La tartaruga edizioni, 1993. 163–83.
———. "A Translator's Journal." In *Culture in Transit: Translating the Literature of Quebec*, ed. Sherry Simon. Montréal: Véhicule Press, 1995. 69–82.
———. Letter to the Editors. *Paragraph*, 17, no. 3 (winter/spring 1995/96): 39–40.
———. "Translation as Culture: A Canadian School of Translation Theory?" In *Translation and Multilingualism in Post-Colonial Context: Indian and Canadian Experiences*, ed. Shanta Ramakrishna. Delhi: Pencraft, 1997. 157–82.
———. "Une littérature en devenir: La réécriture textuelle et le dynamisme du champ littéraire; Les écrivaines québécoises au Canada anglais." *Voix et images* 24, no. 3 (spring 1999): 495–527.
———. "Millennial Musings on Translation." *Athanor* [Italy] 10, no. 2 (1999–2000): 46–56.
———. "Between Performativity and Performance: Translation and Theatre in the Canadian/Quebec Context." *Modern Drama* 43, no. 3 (fall 2000): 327–58.
———. "Deleuze and Translation." *Parallax* 6, no. 1 (2000): 56–81.
———. "French-Canadian Writers in English Translation." In *Encyclopedia of Literary Translation into English. Vol. 1*, ed. Olive Classe. London: Fitzroy Dearborn, 2000.
———. "Gender and Gender Politics in Literary Translation." In *Encyclopedia of Literary Translation into English. Vol. 1*, ed. Olive Classe. London: Fitzroy Dearborn, 2000. 501–12.
———. "Translation." *Public*, no. 20 (2000): 89–94.
———. "Dialogue sur la traduction entre féminists canadiennes et québécoises." *Athanor* 12, no 4 (2001): 116–27.

———. "L'Ethique du traduire: Antoine Berman et le 'virage éthique' en traduction." *TTR: Traduction, terminologie, rédaction* 14, no. 2 (2001): 49–82.

———. "La Traduction comme reception." *TTR: Traduction, terminologie, rédaction* 15, no. 1 (2002): 65–101.

II. Secondary Sources

Bassnett, Susan, and André Lefevere, ed. *Translation, History and Culture.* London: Pinter, 1990.

Davey, Frank, "A History of the Coach House Press Québec Translations." Paper delivered at the Learned Societies, ACQL, Montréal, June 1995. Unpublished.

Gillam, Robyn. "The Mauve File Folder: Notes on the Translation of Nicole Brossard." *Paragraph* 17, no. 2 (fall 1995): 8–12.

Simon, Sherry. *Gender in Translation: Cultural Identity and the Politics of Transmission.* London: Routledge, 1996.

9

Ray Ellenwood
The Translator as Activist

BARBARA KERSLAKE

An eloquent and impassioned advocate of the importance of translation to Canadian culture, Ray Ellenwood has been an outspoken champion for those who choose the difficult path of literary translation for the love of it. One of the first presidents of the LTAC (the Literary Translators' Association of Canada) and a long-time member of the executive, Ellenwood has persistently drawn public attention to the government policies and publishing practices that have served to marginalize literary translation in Canada.[1]

His own interests have drawn him to works that in some way challenge the social, political, or artistic status quo. He counts among his numerous translations, Marie-Claire Blais's first openly lesbian novel, *Nights in the Underground* (1979), Jacques Ferron's political and social satire, *The Penniless Redeemer* (1984), and *Signals for Seers*, a selection of poems by social militant Gilles Hénault (1988). Perhaps his deepest passion has been for the Automatist movement led by painter Paul-Émile Borduas. He translated the group's famous radical artistic manifesto, *Refus global*, in 1985, and has also tackled two works by a close collaborator of Borduas, surrealist poet and playwright Claude Gauvreau: *Entrails*, for which he won the Canada Council's Translation Prize in 1981, and *The Charge of the Expormidable Moose*, published in 1996.

A professor of English at Atkinson College, York University, Ellenwood shares a house with his wife, Brenda, a potter and amateur botanist, in the Beaches, an area of Toronto known as an artistic community. Around the pine table in their kitchen/family room, there are children's toys and equipment for the grandchildren, and pottery and memory-objects on the shelves, with enough space around everything to give a sense of roominess and tidiness. The brightly coloured, non-figurative art on the walls speaks of the Ellenwoods' shared appreciation for modern art. This is inhabited art. It includes some pieces that they have worked on together. A certain sense of this artistic creativity and playfulness, even daring, can be found as well in Ellenwood's practice as translator. As energetic advocate of the authors he has translated and steadfast defender of translators' rights, Ellenwood has had his share, too, of colourful moments.

From Geordie Accents to French Surrealism

William Ray Ellenwood was born in Edmonton in August 1939, into a middle-class family from a farming background. His antecedents were mostly English, and his mother, Anne Spensley, was born in England. His father, Harry Ellenwood, was a native of Red Deer, Alberta. Of the two families, the Ellenwoods were the more intellectual. Ellenwood's paternal grandfather, William Rogers Ellenwood, a native of Nova Scotia, had a BA in Divinity from McGill. After several stressful years of teaching in remote areas from Québec to British Columbia, William bought a farm near Red Deer. He knew Latin and owned an excellent library; Ellenwood describes him as "a real Victorian."[2] His son Harry, a very practical man, was a professional engineer.

Ellenwood's maternal grandparents, Will and Mary Spensley, had come to Canada from the north of England and had strong Geordie accents. Hearing this distinctive way of speaking, very different from his own, made him more sensitive to speech patterns and the sound of languages. Ellenwood attributes his later ability as a translator to this childhood experience. Nan, as his mother was called, may not have had an intellectual upbringing, but she was nevertheless very interested in art and culture. One of her great pleasures was listening to the opera broadcasts on Saturday afternoons. This was greeted with howls of derision from her children—"a bunch of savages," as Ellenwood describes himself and his two brothers. It was from his mother that he inherited his lifelong passion for visual art. From her, and from his own wide experience, he has learned to see through and into paintings.

In elementary and secondary school in the working-class and lower-middle-class district of South Edmonton where he grew up, Ellenwood appears to have been very much like his peers—resolutely shunning culture and drawn to sports. However, he showed a certain talent for writing and took a creative writing course in high school. He entered university with the feeling that English was the subject that he did best. It was not until his second year at the University of Alberta, ironically after failing first-year French, that his love for that language and its culture began to develop seriously. Knowing another language then became, in his words, a mixture of "romantic fantasy, necessity and will," French being a required subject at the time.

After graduating in 1961, he decided to continue at the University of Alberta, and he pursued a master's degree in English. His thesis examined the role of the fictitious editor in the periodicals of Steele and Addison in eighteenth-century England. From a French professor who was on an exchange program at the University of Alberta, he found out about the French government's Assistantship Programme, whereby English-speaking graduates could live and work in France, teaching English to French high-school students. With this goal in mind, Ellenwood worked hard at improving his French by taking combined literature and conversation courses. He obtained a key to the language lab and went through the entire series of *Voix et images* tapes about French life and culture.

In 1963, having received his master's degree, he married Brenda Brown, whom he had known since high school. Their initial project was to create a life together and apart, spending holidays together and working in different countries. They applied for teaching posts abroad, she in England and he in France. A few months later, however, Brenda joined Ellenwood in Narbonne, the southern French city where he was teaching at the Lycée Victor Hugo. It was here that he really became proficient in French, and here also that his interest in art history blossomed. Ellenwood was keen to acquire as much of this new culture as he could, by reading eclectically and looking at as many paintings as possible. The next year was spent together in Essex, England, where Ellenwood was an assistant English master at Palmer's Grammar School for Boys, and Brenda learned pottery and also taught. In 1965 they returned to Alberta, where Ellenwood became a full-time sessional lecturer in English at the University of Alberta. At the same time he delved seriously into French literature, sitting in on courses and preparing himself in his "hobby" field.

In the process of finishing his master's degree in 1963, Ellenwood first realized that continuing to focus exclusively on English literature went against the grain. As he was preparing to embark on his PhD, he was wary of the trap of "stifling coverage" encountered by many people who did their doctorate in English. Knowing a lot about one field of endeavour—English literature—could mean that there was little opportunity to be open to other forms of learning. A French professor at the University of Alberta suggested to him the emerging field of comparative literature, where he could use his knowledge of English literature and his newly acquired mastery of French. This seemed to have more exciting and challenging possibilities. However, as very little was offered in this field at the doctoral level in Canadian universities, Ellenwood decided to do his PhD in Comparative Literature at Rutgers University. In the summer of 1967, he and Brenda, with two children in diapers, set out on the long drive (it took two weeks) to New Brunswick, New Jersey, and the next stage of his unusual journey.

Over the next five years, supported by a Canada Council doctoral fellowship, he studied French literature and undertook a more serious study of art history. Combining both interests, he chose to write his thesis on French surrealism, as approached through visual art. "André Breton and Freud" was the result. Ellenwood used an historical approach to examine different translations of Freud in France, and his reception among the surrealist painters and poets, especially André Breton.[3] The goal of this group was to shake up French society, a subversive enterprise that had its appeal for Ellenwood. He was interested in their leftist approach and in their disastrous flirtation with communism.

Equally importantly for the future translator, it was at Rutgers that Ellenwood started "fooling around" with translation, after a talk given by one of his professors, John McCormick, on the difficulties of rendering the lyrics of Georges Brassens into English. Intrigued by the challenge, Ellenwood worked on the songs for a paper he gave in the context of McCormick's course on the Methodology of Comparative Literature. Over the intervening years, Ellenwood has completed a couple of these lyrics "almost to [his] satisfaction." While this was done purely for his own amusement, he also undertook to translate about thirty pages of *Les vases communicants* by André Breton, with a view to doing the whole piece for publication. He approached Gallimard about this possibility, but was told that it had already been assigned to a translator.

A series of subsequent, fortuitous encounters would confirm Ellenwood's entry into translation. In the spring of 1970, while still at Rutgers, he and Brenda took a "scouting trip" to several Canadian universities to see about the possibility of his getting a teaching job after he had completed his doctorate. They were invited to dinner by Doug Jones, who was chair of the Comparative Canadian Literature department at the Université de Sherbrooke. There was no job available, but at one fateful moment, knowing he was interested in French surrealism, Jones asked Ellenwood whether he knew about *Refus global*, the manifesto of the Québec Automatists, and about the playwright Claude Gauvreau, who had helped to prepare the *Refus*. It was his first introduction to the group around Borduas, and his interest was piqued. The names mentioned that evening would change the course of his career both as scholar and translator. At the time of their meeting Doug Jones was married to Sheila Fischman. Both would later become Ellenwood's friends and colleagues in the Canadian world of translation.

In the meantime, there was a thesis to finish. The Ellenwoods spent the fall, winter and spring of 1970–71 in France living in the small town of Cordes, near Toulouse in the southwest. Intrigued by the idea of a Canadian working on French surrealism, a local newspaperwoman wrote an article on the Ellenwoods and introduced them to a teacher and amateur archaeologist named Francis Meunier. It was a fortuitous encounter, for Meunier had been associated with the surrealists after the war and had amassed an amazing collection of books, pamphlets, and memorabilia relating to this group of artists. He made his library available to Ellenwood, who dedicated his thesis to Meunier, in gratitude for his inestimable assistance.

Refus Global, Claude Gauvreau, and Jacques Ferron

The 1970s and early 1980s were a time of feverish translation activity in Canada. Undoubtedly as a result of the FLQ crisis and the invoking of the War Measures Act in 1970, people in English Canada were curious about Québec writing and culture. Small publishing houses such as Coach House, Anansi, Simon and Pierre, and Exile Editions, and magazines like *Exile*, *Brick*, *Impulse*, and *Canadian Fiction Magazine* were stimulating this interest by publishing translations of Québec literature.

At York University in Toronto where he began teaching in the summer of 1972, Ellenwood found himself surrounded by colleagues, including Barry Callaghan, Barbara Godard, and Frank Davey, who were very much a part of this literary ferment. Davey[4] and Godard, also profiled in this volume for her avant-garde feminist approach to translation, were instrumental in publishing a number of Québec translations at Coach House Press. Ellenwood attributes the beginning of his career as a translator to the encouragement, intellectual stimulation, and publishing opportunities afforded to him by being part of this group of energetic, outward-looking, and establishment-challenging young colleagues.

More particularly, Barry Callaghan, who was also in the English department at Atkinson College, and who edited the literary journal *Exile*, was looking for Québec literature in translation. Callaghan had many connections in the Québec literary world, and he showed Ellenwood the translation of a play by Claude Gauvreau, *Bien-Être*, he had received for publication in his magazine. The play was one of the pieces included in the *Refus global* pamphlet. Ellenwood was critical of the translation, and felt it was not a good English rendering. His own version was published in *Exile* in 1972.

Callaghan became the pipeline, encouraging Ellenwood to select and translate Québec authors and have his work published in *Exile*. Through this acquaintance with the Automatists (as the Québec authors and artists who had signed *Refus global* were called), Ellenwood was introduced to another writer whom Callaghan had met in the late 1960s, social and political activist Jacques Ferron. Originally an ally—his sister, visual artist Marcelle Ferron, was a signatory of *Refus global*—Ferron later opposed the group. A colourful figure, Ferron was arrested in 1949 for "participating in a demonstration against NATO" and ran in 1955 "unsuccessfully as a candidate for the 'Parti social démocratique.'" In 1963, he "founded the Rhinoceros Party, a nonsense Federalist party whose motto was 'From one pond to another,'"[5] before devoting his energy to his writing and his medical practice in Longueuil. Ferron's numerous texts are a mixture of social satire and surrealist fantasy. Ellenwood's translation of his novella *Papa Boss* appeared in *Exile* in 1973. These two first published translations pointed to a developing interest in the Automatists (Claude Gauvreau in particular) on the one hand, and in Jacques Ferron on the other, which would provide Ellenwood with motivation for translations and critical articles for the next twenty-five years.

From a historical perspective, the most important work Ellenwood translated was *Refus global*. The manifesto of the members of the Québec Automatist movement first appeared in Montréal in 1948, "in a mimeographed edition of 400 copies," and "caused an uproar in the press."[6] Paul-Émile Borduas, an instructor at the École du Meuble, was fired as a result by the Duplessis government. As Ellenwood points out, Borduas "starts with a sweeping history of a Quebec nation born under the sign of fear, ripe for revolt against a society based on moribund Christianity. It was this anti-Christian message which caused such a furor at the time." The group is now viewed as "forerunners in the Canadian avant-garde, not only in the visual arts, where they were pioneers of non-figurative painting and among the first Canadian painters to gain world recognition, but also in literature, dance, design and architecture."[7]

In 1985, Ellenwood translated the entire pamphlet, containing not only the title essay by Paul-Emile Borduas, which had previously been translated,[8] but also eight other pieces by Borduas, Claude Gauvreau, Françoise Sullivan, Fernand Leduc, and Bruno Cormier. This was the first complete English translation of this important document, accompanied by historical notes, a brief analysis of the components of the work, and a biography of each of the signatories. In preparing his edition, Ellenwood brought to bear his knowledge of the European roots of the Automatist movement as well as his strong impulse to illuminate for his fellow English Canadians the cultural climate of Montréal in 1948.

Ellenwood's relationship with Ferron has been equally enduring. With the encouragement and collaboration of Barry Callaghan, he translated Ferron's shorter works, and a collection of some of these stories was published under the title *Quince Jam* in 1977. This led to translations of two of Ferron's novels, *The Cart* (*La Charrette*) in 1981, and *The Penniless Redeemer* (*Le Ciel de Québec*) in 1984, both published by Exile Editions. During Ferron's lifetime and after his death in 1985, Ellenwood did everything he could to draw attention in English Canada to this pivotal writer. He gave lectures and wrote articles in literary and academic journals and in newspapers. In 1982, he was guest editor for a special issue of *Brick* dedicated to the work of Ferron. His lengthy and informative correspondence with Jacques Ferron was published in French in 1995.

Ellenwood's attitude to Ferron, scholarly, yet at the same time affectionate and admiring, is illustrated by the following anecdote. In October 2002, he was invited to Montréal with other translators, to take part in a National Film Board (NFB) documentary about the life of the Montréal doctor, wit, and author, arranged by Ferron's niece, Babalou Hamelin. The film, directed by Jean-Daniel Lafond, was to be part reminiscence and part scenes from his novels, brought to life by actors. This all took place in the aptly-named "Brasserie des Patriotes," where locals and casual visitors were welcomed with free drinks provided by the NFB crew. Ellenwood gave an interview about Ferron (in French) and then a reading from *La*

Charrette that was somewhat stiff and stilted. It was then that two young men, apparently unrelated to the proceedings, made a quick entrance and exit, lobbing a firecracker that landed between Ellenwood's feet. Needless to say, his second reading of *La Charrette* was much livelier. Ellenwood and the director interpreted this as one of Ferron's practical jokes from beyond the grave to help his friend relax.

Challenging the Two Solitudes

Ellenwood's work as an active promoter of translation in Canada took on a new dimension in 1974, when he was invited by Philip Stratford to attend a preliminary meeting of other Canadian literary translators at Stanley House, in Richmond, Québec,[9] with a view to forming a national association. Ellenwood was in France when that meeting was held, but he attended the founding meeting of the Literary Translators' Association of Canada (LTAC) held in Montréal in May 1975. From then until 1985 he served on the LTAC executive. In 1979 he became the third president of the association, and during his four-year term made every effort to create links with other writers' and translators' groups. In March 1983 he organized a colloquium in Kingston entitled "La Diffusion à l'étranger des littératures du Canada / Canadian Literature beyond the Borders." Representatives from writers' and translators' groups, External Affairs, the Canada Council, the Secretary of State, publishers, and literary agents were all invited to participate. The connections with other translators' groups have continued, but Ellenwood admits he found the short-lived response from writers' groups "disappointing."

Along with other LTAC members such as Patricia Claxton, also profiled in this book, Ellenwood was actively involved in the struggle to ensure copyright protection for literary translators, so that they would be remunerated when their texts were copied. From 1983 to 1987, he was the association's official representative on the Canadian Copyright Commission, and from 1986 to 1987 and again from 1995 to 1997, on the Public Lending Right Commission. All of these endeavours took a great deal of time and energy, but Ellenwood felt that they were worthwhile. By these efforts more opportunities were created for publishing translations and expanding the opportunities of readership for the translated texts.

During this time Ellenwood was also busy writing articles, giving lectures, and taking part in panel discussions and literary forums, with a view to gaining recognition for literary translators and creating a wider audience for translations. Like some of the authors he translated, he shared a taste and a talent for polemics. Several issues engaged him deeply, and he carried on arguments and correspondences with various people, including Canadian writers Robert Fulford and Rudy Wiebe. Their disagreements transcended personal animosity, becoming a passionate challenge. Gaining recognition for translators was a primary motif; he was fighting for support for translators as language artists in their own right. That was closely followed by attempts to persuade funding bodies to create opportunities for Canadians to translate literature from other countries.

The Politics of Translation

Ellenwood was also much concerned with the politics of translating Québec authors into English, especially the ticklish question of how to deal with *joual*. In his view it should not be ignored or glossed over. When he is faced with a text full of place names or phrases peculiar to Québec, with cultural overtones not immediately obvious to anglophone readers, he feels compelled to honour that quality and retain the cultural flavour of the original. It is his contention that translation should not be a tool for assimilation. At the same time he wants his text to be comprehensible and enjoyable in English.

In an article entitled "Les chians de la traduction," he explains how he dealt with two place names in his translation of Ferron's *Le Ciel de Québec*. He seizes the opportunity to add a few words of explanation for the name of a creek "des Chians" and "le village des Chiquettes": "What if some Anglo from Ontario got wind of that? Supposing he wanted to know what the names mean? Can't you just hear me saying, 'Well, there's a lot o' dawg in that creek, but then there's some shit too; and 'bout all you can do with a chique is chaw 'n spit.'"[10] The first line is from Ferron's original text, but the rest is simply worked into the flow of the situation. This allows Ellenwood to keep the names in French. Yet through a bit of "remake" (suggested to him by Ferron in a more general context), he can let his readers in on the humour, while at the same time educating them about Ferron and the importance of giving *joual* its due.

For someone who by his own admission has "no credentials in French," Ellenwood regularly chose to translate works that presented considerable difficulty, including poetry, plays, polemics, and dense and many-layered novels. His insistence on translating texts that he found fascinating and provocative is supported by his continuing research on the artistic, social, and political context in Québec and France. Through his own reading and study, Ellenwood found Québec authors and works he felt were important for anglophone Canadians to know about. As a teacher and a "shower and teller," translation became his preferred cultural and educational tool.

Besides Borduas and Ferron, Ellenwood's other choices of authors to translate, such as Marie-Claire Blais and Gilles Hénault, reflect his eclectic taste for works that challenge social or political conventions. Through Callaghan, he found out that General Publishing was looking for a translator for Blais's novel, *Les nuits de l'underground*, one of her first books as a declared lesbian writer, and he offered to work on it. She felt his translation did her text justice; *Nights in the Underground* continues to sell very well for both author and translator, a fact of which Ellenwood is proud. A writer in the surrealist tradition, influenced by the French poet Paul Éluard, Gilles Hénault was a supporter of the Automatists. Ellenwood knew him as a friend of Marcelle Ferron. He was intrigued by Hénault's leftist politics and liked him as a person and a poet. Of all the translations he has done, his version of Hénault's poetry is the work with which Ellenwood is the most satisfied.

Co-operation as Process

In an article entitled "Bouncing Ideas: Co-operation as Process in Literary Translation," Ellenwood describes the importance he attributes to arriving at a target language text that can stand on its own. Sometimes the translator needs to stand back from the work, to enable the new text to come to the surface in the translation process:

> All translation exists as a tension between fidelity to the source text and fidelity to the target language and, in literary translation especially the translation of poetry, this tension can be acute....In the final analysis, we have to ask ourselves if literary translation has really taken place if it does not result in an acceptable literary text in the target language....Concerning fidelity to the target language, the major problem is avoiding what I call the tyranny of the source language, where the French of the original will come to occupy my consciousness to such an extent that I lose track of my own tongue. If I can lay aside a first draft of a translation for some time and come back to it afresh, confronting it as an English text, all sorts of tainted, unidiomatic words and phrases leap off the page, and, quite often, the "correct" expression comes to mind immediately.[11]

In the same article, Ellenwood also reflects on how he has benefitted from his collaboration with Callaghan, developing a form of co-operative reading: "For some years now, I have had a mutual assistance arrangement with Barry Callaghan (an academic colleague, poet and translator) of a kind I would highly recommend. We exchange work. I check his work against the French (my knowledge of the language being greater than his)...; he reads mine exclusively as an English text, since he has a fine ear for the colloquial language and wide experience as a writer. We discuss each other's suggestions, accept or reject them, and often come up with a word or expression which we both recognize, instantly, as what is needed."[12]

Barry Callaghan considers Ellenwood's chief strengths[13] as a translator to be stamina and tenacity, qualities that help him overcome the difficulties and challenges of the source text, and even thrive on this adversity. In addition, he sees Ellenwood as a sensualist who is able to tap into his sensuality, to live in the author's world and reveal it to the readers of his translation. These two long-time friends and literary collaborators share the same view of what makes for good literary translation: "If it reads like a translation, better not to print it." The trick, in Callaghan's view, is to manipulate the literal meaning until you arrive at a line that sounds natural in English.

Sometimes Ellenwood's strong instinct for accuracy has created conflict. In his translation of Françoise Sullivan's essay on dance in the *Refus global* in 1985, for instance, he had to contend with her desire to rewrite her contribution, deleting statements that were now embarrassing to her. Ellenwood's aim to reproduce the original historical document was sometimes in direct opposition to Sullivan's determination to leave her mature viewpoint to posterity. The final result was a compromise that left historical accuracy intact.

Accuracy and Readability

Ellenwood's translation of Jacques Ferron's novel *Le Ciel de Québec* offers many examples of how he manages both to respect the meaning of the text and arrive at a translation that sounds natural in English. The book is a fanciful historical tale that mixes allusions to real Québec personages, such as Monsignor Camille Roy, rector of Université Laval, and Dugald Scott, archdeacon of the Anglican Church, with various fictitious characters in a ruthless political and social satire. The following passage is taken from chapter 5, where the action takes place around an entirely fictitious small hamlet, Chiquettes, outside Québec City.

In the first passage, Aurèle, a visiting cardinal's driver, has set off for Chiquettes, to get the villagers' help in moving the cardinal's limousine out of Chians Creek, where it has landed:

> Le bout des pieds réduit aux quatre doigts, car il avait perdu les orteils en même temps que les oreilles sur la grand'banquise des Oblats, dans les parages de la Terre Aurélie, Aurèle s'en allait en zigzagant, clopinant deçà, delà, biaisant vers ce côté-là puis vers ce côté-ci; c'est en clochant du pied qu'il se le reposait, en marchant bien qu'il se le fatiguait, de sorte qu'à toutes les deux minutes il devait passer le bon au mauvais, le mauvais au bon, et il parvenait en alternant ainsi à marcher presque aussi vite qu'un homme de son âge qui aurait eu ses huit doigts, deux orteils. Seulement celui-ci serait allé plus droit.[14]

Here is Ellenwood's version of the same passage from *The Penniless Redeemer*:

> Both his feet were reduced to four toes because the big ones had been lost at the same time as his ears on the great Oblate ice floes somewhere off in the Land of Aurélie. So Aurèle zigzagged as he walked, hobbling from side to side, leaning first one way, then the other. Limping was restful for him, but walking correctly tired him out, so every two minutes he had to change from walking well to walking badly, from badly to well, and in that way he was able to go almost as fast as a man his age with all ten toes, though a ten-toed man would have gone straighter.[15]

In French Ferron makes the parallel between "orteils" and "oreilles," both of them starting with the same two letters and rhyming with each other, as well as "Aurélie" and "Aurèle," which begin with the same sounds—"or," the word for "gold." Although this technique cannot be repeated in English, because the words "toes" and "ears" are quite different, Ellenwood makes "toes" rhyme with "floes" and later in the passage uses alliteration, as in "a man his age with all ten toes" and "a ten-toed man." Like Ferron, Ellenwood loves to play on and with words. Because of the sense of rhythm evident in "from walking well to walking badly, from badly to well," readers can hear and feel the unevenness in the way Aurèle walks. Having lost his toes and ears, Aurèle has difficulty balancing and hearing: he cannot walk a straight line.

No translation is ever a straight line, just putting in English words for French ones. Ellenwood has worked hard to recreate the twist of French humour, but the fun he has had disguises the difficulties encountered. The entire chapter is hilarious in its original language, and is equally comical in English. The translator must have a Québécois sense of humour, and he must make his English readers feel that humour as well. Although, as Ellenwood says of translators, "We are never up to it," he has succeeded in translating not just the words, but the funny bone, in *Le Ciel de Québec*, a book into which Ferron says "he put everything he knew."[16]

Claude Gauvreau's surrealistic play, *La charge de l'orignal épormyable*, offers different translation challenges. Ellenwood has had to capture the intensity behind the seemingly banal, and at times nonsensical, dialogue. To keep the tension that must exist between the viewers' desire to laugh and their horror at what they see on stage, his translation also needed to be tight and economical, allowing for ambiguity while bringing out the humour in this situation. At the same time, the lines had to keep the rhythm of the spoken language and a certain ordinariness underlying the surrealist effect. Ellenwood wrote a translator's note on Gauvreau, introducing him to anglophone readers as an important surrealist writer, well-known as a defender of the Automatist movement. As translator, Ellenwood wanted to communicate the eccentricity and love of avant-garde verbal and theatrical ideas that are now making Gauvreau's work interesting to theatre directors in Québec.[17]

Ellenwood himself feels that his translations of Hénault's poetry were among the "best writing" he did (revealing by his choice of words his conception of the creative, writerly, nature of translation). He could let his imagination roam more freely, having fun while still respecting the French text he was working from, as the following example illustrates. Hénault's original reads as follows:

> Signes mués en sigles
> Quel paléographe saura lire la toundra dénudée?
> Grand alphabet de glace parcouru par les loups
> qui tentent d'en formuler le sens en longs hurlements lunaires
> Faim froid paroles venteuses plus légères que balle de mil
> toute la douceur de vivre est passée au crible des forêts
> C'est alors que se love l'amour aux paumes
> des maisons luisantes
> Un couple à la barre du jour se penche sur un avenir de jardins
> Dont la dernière brindille était garante[18]

This poem is rendered into English in *Signals for Seers*:

> Signs stripped to acronyms
> What paleographer can read bare tundra?
> Wandering wolves howl and howl at the moon

trying to decode the great ice alphabet
Hunger cold windswept words lighter than drifting chaff
All the sweetness of life has been sifted through forest screens
That is when love curls up in the palms of glittering houses
At daybreak a couple leans over a future
of gardens
certified by the last twig[19]

Ellenwood has made a number of adjustments in his translation, changing "parcouru par des loups" into "wandering wolves," an alliteration, at the beginning of the line, whereas Hénault had put "les loups" at the end. "Trying to decode the great ice alphabet" arrives a line later in the translation. The inversion of the subject and verb can be switched, as in "love curls up" or as in "At daybreak a couple"; in either case their new position makes a more balanced poem in English. The new version of the poem is slightly shorter than the original, but still recognizably that of Gilles Hénault. Ellenwood's diction is crisp, and the poem's power passes unimpeded through the linguistic change. One can see why he feels the translator's presence should be acknowledged, and his or her name printed on the title page.

What It Means to Be a Translator

Translation has always been a part of Ellenwood's research, aesthetic, and critical interests, but in the last several years it has been superseded by academic obligations and his own writing and editing projects. For instance, he has written an account of the Montréal Automatist movement from an art history perspective, entitled *Égrégore*.[20] To mark the fiftieth anniversary of *Refus global*, with the help of his graduate students at York University, Ellenwood organized a conference/exhibition/performance event about Gauvreau, Borduas, and others, called Make Way for Magic. He does not look on translation as a full-time career, but prefers interspersing this activity with writing critical articles and essays about the authors he has translated. He has been able to do so because of the security of his career as an academic.

When asked if he considers himself an activist, Ellenwood's reply is that "an Activist (with a capital A) is probably a different animal." However, he does see what he has done as a political choice. Translating Gauvreau and the Automatist writers, as well as Ferron's political satires and *joual*, in particular, was not the easiest road for him to follow, but the same may be said, to a lesser degree, of many of his other choices of Québec writers to translate, including Victor-Lévy Beaulieu, Marie-Claire Blais, Gilles Hénault, Fernand Ouellette, Guillaume Charette, Yves Thériault, and François Charron.

Undoubtedly, his deliberate choice of what was most difficult to translate reflected his desire to learn more, to test himself: his love of the challenge. In his view, the translator is a visible creator, a cultural advocate, and deserves to be given credit for his or her work; all his labour on behalf of literary translation has been to that end. Through his efforts, Ellenwood has made many culturally significant works accessible to anglophone readers, assisted them in understanding the difficult works he has translated, and perhaps more importantly, passed on his own enthusiasm for the writers whose thought-provoking words he has made into English.

NOTES

1 These concerns are expressed clearly in a paper presented at the University of Ottawa's Symposium on Canadian literature in 1982, and published subsequently in an article entitled "Some Actualities of Canadian Literary Translation," in *Translation in Canadian Literature*, ed. Camille La Bossière (Ottawa: University of Ottawa Press, 1983), pp. 61–71.
2 Interviews with Ray Ellenwood, Toronto, May 2001–February 2004. Unless otherwise indicated, all quotations from Ray Ellenwood are from these interviews.
3 Ray Ellenwood. "André Breton and Freud," PhD diss., Rutgers University, 1972.
4 For more on this period of Coach House Press history, see Frank Davey, "The Beginnings of an End to Coach House Press," *Open Letter*, 9th ser., no. 8 (spring 1997): 40–77.
5 Donald Smith, "Jacques Ferron," in the *Oxford Companion to Canadian Literature*, ed. Eugene Benson and William Toye (Toronto: Oxford University Press, 1997), p. 397.
6 Ray Ellenwood, introduction to *Refus global/Total Refusal*, by Paul-Emile Borduas et al., trans. Ray Ellenwood (Toronto: Exile Editions, 1985), p. 7.
7 Ellenwood, introduction to *Refus global/Total Refusal*, by Paul-Émile Borduas, pp. 7, 14–15.
8 The best translation was an anonymous one, published in Ramsay Cook, *French-Canadian Nationalism: An Anthology* (Toronto: Macmillan, 1969), 9. For further information on this initial meeting, see the portraits of Philip Stratford and Patricia Claxton in this volume, as well as Patricia Claxton, "Looking Back," *Méta* 45, no. 1 (April 2000): 7–12.
9 See the portrait of Patricia Claxton for her involvement with other translators' groups. Ellenwood was briefly a member of ALTA, the American Literary Translators' Association.
10 Ray Ellenwood, "Les chians de la traduction," "Présence de Jacques Ferron," special issue, *Littératures*, nos. 9–10 (1982): 157. For another description of the

difficulties of translating joual, see Ray Ellenwood, "Translating 'québécisme' in Jacques Ferron's *Le Ciel de Québec,*" in *Culture in Transit: Translating the Literature of Quebec,* ed. Sherry Simon (Montréal: Véhicule Press, 1995), pp. 101–109.
11 Ray Ellenwood, "Bouncing Ideas: Co-operation as Process in Literary Translation," in *The Translation Process,* ed. C. Séguinot (Toronto: HG Publications), pp. 55, 56, 57.
12 Ellenwood, "Bouncing Ideas," p. 57.
13 Interview with Barry Callaghan in October 2001. Unless otherwise indicated, all quotations from Barry Callaghan are from this interview.
14 Jacques Ferron, *Le Ciel de Québec* (Montréal: Éditions du Jour, 1969), p. 43.
15 Jacques Ferron, *The Penniless Redeemer,* trans. Ray Ellenwood (Toronto: Exile Editions, 1984), pp. 34–40.
16 From a note Ellenwood wrote in the copy of *Le Ciel de Québec* given to him by Ferron in 1973. The note was written in May 1977.
17 See Ray Ellenwood, translator's note, in *The Charge of the Expormidable Moose,* by Claude Gavreau, trans. Ray Ellenwood (Toronto: Exile Editions, 1996), pp. 154–58.
18 Gilles Hénault, *Signaux pour les voyants* (Montréal: Éditions de l'Hexagone, 1972), p. 129.
19 Gilles Hénault, *Signals for Seers,* trans. Ray Ellenwood (Toronto: Exile Editions, 1996), p. 37.
20 See Ray Ellenwood, *Égrégore: A History of the Montréal Automatist Movement* (Toronto: Exile Editions, 1996).

BIBLIOGRAPHY

I. Primary Sources

Literary Translations (Books)

Borduas, Paul-Émile, et al. *Refus global/Total Refusal.* Trans. and Introd. Ray Ellenwood Toronto: Exile Editions, 1985. Translation of *Refus global.* Saint-Hilaire: ed. Mithia-Mythe, 1948.

Blais, Marie-Claire. *Nights in the Underground.* Trans. Ray Ellenwood. Toronto: General Publishing, 1979. Translation of *Les Nuits de l'Underground.* Montréal: Stanké, 1978.

Charette, Guillaume. *Vanishing Spaces.* Trans. and Afterword Ray Ellenwood. Winnipeg: Éditions Bois-Brûlés, 1980. Translation of *L'espace de Louis Goulet.* Winnipeg: Éditions Bois-Brûlés, 1976.

Ferron, Jacques. *Quince Jam.* Trans. Ray Ellenwood Toronto: Coach House Press, 1977. Translation of *Les Confitures de coings, Papa Boss, La Créance,* and Appendice aux *Confitures de coings.*

———. *The Cart.* Trans. Ray Ellenwood. Toronto: Exile Editions, 1981. Translation of *La charrette.* Montréal: Éditions HMV, 1968.

———. *The Penniless Redeemer*. Trans. and Afterword Ray Ellenwood. Toronto: Exile Editions, 1984. Translation of *Le Ciel de Québec*. Montréal: Éditions du Jour, 1969.

Gauvreau, Claude. *The Charge of the Expormidable Moose*. Trans. Ray Ellenwood. Toronto: Exile Editions, 1996. Translation of *La charge de l'orignal épormyable*. Montréal: Éditions de l'Hexagone, 1992.

———. *Entrails*. Trans. Ray Ellenwood with Introduction and Translator's Note. Toronto: Coach House Press, 1981. Translation of *Entrailles*.

Hénault, Gilles. *Signals for Seers*. Trans. Ray Ellenwood. Toronto: Exile Editions, 1988. Translation of *Signaux pour les voyants*. Montréal: Éditions de l'Hexagone, 1972.

Ouellette, Fernand. *Wells of Light*. Trans. Ray Ellenwood and Barry Callaghan. Toronto: Exile Editions, 1990. Translation of selected poems from *Ici ailleurs, la lumière*. Montréal: Éditions de l'Hexagone, 1977.

Literary Translations (in Journals and Edited Volumes)

Blais, Marie-Claire. "The Testament of Jean-Le-Maigre to His Brothers." Trans. Ray Ellenwood. *Exile* 3, no. 1 (1975): 5–13.

———. "Nights in the Underground." *Exile* 5, no. 3–4 (1978): 208–23. Translation of a section of *Les nuits de l'Underground*.

———. "An Intimate Death. " *Toronto Life*, Aug. 1989, 122–24. Translation of "Mort intime."

Charette, Guillaume. "From *L'espace de Louis Goulet*." *Brick*, no. 5 (winter 1979): 55–60. Translation of chapter 14 of *L'espace*.

Charron, François. "Victory." In *Les stratégies du réel / The Story So Far*, ed. Nicole Brossard. Montréal and Toronto: La Nouvelle Barre du Jour and Coach House Press, 1979. 174–93.

Ferron, Jacques. "Papa Boss, novella." *Exile* 1, no. 3 (1973): 27–84.

———. "Little William." *Impulse* 3, no. 2 (1974): 11–12. Translation of "Petit William."

———. "Quince Jam." *Exile* 2, no. 1 (1974): 17–88. Translation of *Les Confitures de coings*.

———. "Claude Gauvreau." Trans. R. Ellenwood. *Exile* 3, no. 2 (1976): 20–57. Translation of a section of *Du fond de mon arrière cuisine*.

———. "The Cart." *Exile* 4, no. 2 (1977): 23–46. Translation of a section of *La Charrette*.

———. "La Sorgne." *Exile* 5, nos. 3–4 (1978): 78–86. Translation of a chapter from an unpublished novel. Rpt. in *Brick*, no. 16 (fall 1982): 36–39.

———. "The Dragon, the Maiden and the Child." Trans. R. Ellenwood. *Brick*, no. 16 (fall 1982): 19-20. Translation of "Le Dragon, la pucelle et l'enfant."

———. "The Execution of Maski." Trans. R. Ellenwood. *Brick*, no. 16 (fall 1982): 41-46. Translation of "L'Exécution de Maski."

———. "God and His Scribes." Trans. R. Ellenwood. *Brick*, no. 16 (fall 1982): 18-19. Translation of "Dieu et ses scribes."

———. "One Death Too Many," Trans. R. Ellenwood. *Brick*, no. 16 (fall 1982): 21-25. Translation of "Une mort de trop."
———. "Purple Loosestrife." Trans. R. Ellenwood. *Brick*, no. 16 (fall 1982): 25-30. Translation of "Les Salicaires."
Gauvreau, Claude. "The Good Life" and "Reflections of a Novice Playwright." Trans. R. Ellenwood. *Exile* 1, no. 2 (1972): 32–52. Translation of "Bien-être" and "Réflexions d'un dramaturge débutant."
———. Translation of four short poems. *ellipse*, no. 17 (1975): 8–11.
———. "Prayer for Indulgence." Trans. R. Ellenwood. *Exile* 3, no. 2 (1976): 61–63.
———. "Glints of Night." Trans. R. Ellenwood. *Exile* 3, no. 2 (1976): 64–70.
———. "The Dream of the Bridge." Trans. R. Ellenwood. *Exile* 3, no. 2 (1976): 71–76.
———. "The Dream of the Bridge" and "The Prophet in the Sea." Trans. R. Ellenwood. In *Invisible Fictions: Contemporary Stories from Québec*, ed. G. Hancock. Toronto: Anansi, 1987. 241–56.
———. "Trustful Fatigue and Reality" and "The Leg of Mutton Créateur." Trans. R. Ellenwood. In *Poems for the Millenium*, ed. Jerome Rothenberg and Pierre Joris. Berkeley: University of California Press, 1998.
Lévy-Beaulieu, Victor. "The Rubber Ball." Trans. R. Ellenwood. In *Intimate Strangers: New Stories from Québec*, ed. Wayne Grady and Matt Cohen. Markham: Penguin, 1986. 77–91. Translation of "La boule de caoutchouc."
Mansour, Joyce. "*Jules César*, translation of a tale." Trans. R. Ellenwood. *Exile* 2, nos. 3–4 (1975): 5–25.
Thériault, Yves. "Missus Anna." Trans. R. Ellenwood. *Exile* 12, no. 4 (1988): 5–17. Translation of "La Femme Anna."

Reviews, Articles and Works on Translation

Ellenwood, Ray. Review of *Les belles-soeurs*. *Les Belles Soeurs* by Michel Tremblay, Vancouver: Talon Books. *Canadian Theatre Review*, no. 9 (Winter 1976): 181–82.
———. "How Not to Quince Words: A Translator Reflects on Jacques Ferron, the Political Doctor Who Writes with a Scalpel." *Books in Canada* 5, no. 5 (Mar. 1976): 8–11.
———. Review of *Enchanted Summer*, by Gabrielle Roy, trans. J. Marshall. *Books in Canada*, Nov. 1976, 12.
———. "Et in Arcadio Ego: Translation in Canada." *Brick*, no. 1 (1977): 69–71.
———. Review of *St. Lawrence Blues*, by Marie-Claire Blais, trans. R. Manheim. *Brick*, no. 1 (1977): 13–16.
———. Review of *Blackout*, by Hubert Aquin, and *Turns*, by Richard Outram, trans. A. Brown. *Brick*, no. 2 (1978): 56–57.
———. Review of *The Complete Poems of Saint-Denys Garneau*, trans. J. Glassco and *Poems by Anne Hébert*, trans. A. Brown. *Brick*, no. 2 (1978): 52–54.
———. "Avee-voo loo Victor Levy Bowlyoo?" *Brick*, no. 9 (spring 1980): 36–46.
———. Review of *Écrits/Writings 1942–1958*, by Paul-Émile Borduas. *Brick*, no. 13 (fall 1981): 5–7.

———. "Literary Translation in Canada." *Newsletter of the Academy of Canadian Writers* 3, no. 1 (Oct. 1981): 5.
———. "Giving Credit Where Credit's Due." *Globe and Mail*, May 2, 1983.
———. "Some Actualities of Literary Translation." In *Translation in Canadian Literature*, ed. Camille La Bossière. Ottawa: University of Ottawa Press, 1983. 61–71.
———. "Traduire le non-traduisible: Faisant front à Claude Gauvreau." *La Traduction: L'universitaire et le praticien*, ed. Rhoda Roberts. Ottawa: Éditions de l'Université d'Ottawa, 1984. 173–78.
———. "Welcome to Broke City. " Introduction to *Broke City*, by Jacques Renaud, trans. David Homel. Montréal: Guernica Editions, 1984. 7–11.
———. "Some Notes on the Politics of Translation." *Atkinson Review of Canadian Studies* 2, no. 1 (fall-winter 1984): 25–28.
———. "Jacques Ferron." *Globe and Mail*, May 2, 1985, E1.
———. "Death and Dr. Ferron." *Brick*, no. 13 (Spring 1985): 6–9.
———. "Paying the Piper." *Books in Canada*, Aug./Sept. 1986, 3–4.
———. "Bouncing Ideas: Co-operation as Process in Literary Translation." In *The Translation Process*, ed. Candace Séguinot. Toronto: HG Publications, 1989. 55–71.
———. "Government Funding: The Effect on Writers, Translators, and Their Associations." In *Towards a History of the Literary Institutions in Canada: Questions of Funding, Publishing and Distribution*, ed. I.S. McClaren and C. Potvin. Edmonton: University of Alberta Press, 1989. 77–84.
———. "Les chians de la traduction." "Présence de Jacques Ferron," ed. Jean-Pierre Duquette, Jane Everett, and Marcel Olscamp. Special issue, *Littératures*, nos. 9–10 (1992): 151–58.
———. "Translating 'québécisme' in Jacques Ferron's *Le Ciel de Québec*." In *Culture in Transit: Translating the Literature of Quebec*, ed. S. Simon. Montréal: Véhicule Press, 1995. 101–109.
———. "Qui est Joyce Marshall?" Trans. Suzanne Saint-Jacques Mineau. In *Blood and Bone / En chair et en os* by Joyce Marshall. Oakville: Mosaic Press, 1995. xii–xvii.
———. *Égrégore: A History of the Montréal Automatist Movement*. Toronto: Exile Editions, 1996.
———. "The Genius of the Absurd." *Literary Review of Canada* 4, no.10 (Nov. 1995): 19–20.
———. "Reclaiming Gauvreau." *Literary Review of Canada* 6, no. 2 (May 1997): 21–22.
———. "Pierre Gauvreau, provocateur." "L'Automatisme en mouvement," ed. Gilles Lapointe and Ginette Michaud. Special issue, *Études françaises* 34, nos. 2/3 (1998): 31–39.
———. "Influence et dépassement du surréalisme chez Claude Gauvreau." In *Les automatistes à Paris*, ed. Lise Gauvin. Saint-Laurent: Les 400 coups, 2000. 67–77.

———. "Jacques Ferron et les automatistes." In *Jacques Ferron: autour des commencements*, ed. Patrick Pourier. Montréal: Lanctôt Éditeur, 2000. 151–61.

———. "Some Activities and Publications around the Fiftieth Anniversary of *Refus global.*" *Journal of Canadian Art History* 22 (2001): 92–108.

———. "Lettres de Jacques Ferron à Ray Ellenwood." In *L'autre Ferron*, ed. Ginette Michaud and Patrick Poirier. Montréal: Fides, 1995.

II. Secondary Sources

Claxton, Patricia. "Looking Back." *Méta* 45, no. 1 (April 2000): 7–12.

Cook, Ramsay, ed. *French Canadian Nationalism: An Anthology*. Toronto: Macmillan, 1969.

La Bossière, Camille, ed. *Translation in Canadian Literature*. Ottawa: University of Ottawa Press, 1983.

Davey, Frank. "The Beginnings of an End to Coach House Press." *Open Letter*, 9th ser., no. 8 (spring 1997): 40–77.

Hancock, Geoff, ed. *Invisible Fictions: Contemporary Stories from Québec*. Toronto: Anansi, 1987.

MacLaren, I.S., and Claudine Potvin, eds. *Towards a History of the Literary Institutions in Canada: Questions of Funding, Publishing and Distribution*. Edmonton: University of Alberta Press, 1989.

Smith, Donald. "Ferron, Jacques." In the *Oxford Companion to Canadian Literature*, ed. Eugene Benson and William Toye. Toronto: Oxford University Press, 1997. 397–99.

10

Susanne de Lotbinière-Harwood
Totally Between

AGNÈS CONACHER

Recipient of such distinguished awards as the Literary Translators' Association of Canada's John Glassco Prize (1981) and Columbia University's Felix-Antoine Savard Prize (1991), Susanne de Lotbinière-Harwood came to translation almost by accident. In 1979, when working as a journalist for the *Montreal Star*, she was asked to translate some lyrics by the Québécois rock singer and poet Lucien Francoeur. Since then, her career as a translator has flourished. She has often collaborated with Québec feminist Nicole Brossard, translating, among other works, Brossard's *Le désert mauve*, a much-celebrated novel highlighting the complex task of translation. She has translated several other well-known Québécois women writers into English, including Louise Cotnoir, Lise Gauvin, Denise Desautels, Anne-Marie Alonzo, and Claudine Bertrand, and penned into French works by English-Canadian writers Gail Scott, Sharon Thesen, and Daphne Marlatt.

De Lotbinière-Harwood holds an unusual position among translators in that she translates in two directions. To date, her translations from French to English outnumber the ones from English to French. Living in Montréal, she observes, she is more likely to be approached by francophone writers. Through her bilingualism, she can interpret her francophone culture effectively into English: "French language writers I've translated enjoy my English versions because they retain a French 'accent,' making the new text foreign and familiar at the same time."[1]

In contrast to the generally accepted idea in Canada that one should translate into one's first language,[2] de Lotbinière-Harwood feels that translating from French into English creates more opportunity for active interpretation. A reflection of her love for both languages, her innovative and creative strategies are consciously geared to making the activity of translation visible. At the forefront of the development of a Canadian and international feminist practice of translation, she has given priority to translating women's writing. By explicitly feminizing the target text, de Lotbinière-Harwood enhances the understanding of translation. At the same time, she also contributes to making women visible in the textual world and to creating new space for women's expression in the real world. Some of her neologisms in both French and English, such as "auteure-ité" and "auther-ity,"[3] deconstructions of the words "autorité" and "authority," have already been incorporated into the international feminist lexicon.

De Lotbinière-Harwood has developed her co-active approach to translation in an important theoretical work, the deliberately bilingual text *Rebelle et infidèle: La traduction comme pratique de réécriture au féminin / The Body Bilingual: Translation as a Rewriting in the Feminine* (1991). Fun and pleasure are key words for this feminist translator. She takes pleasure in establishing connections, nourishing exchange with others, and trying to find just the right word that "will not only respect the meaning of her auther but also succeed in creating an aesthetic object."[4] Currently, de Lotbinière-Harwood, who lives and works in Montreal, combines her love of translating with her love of teaching.

Lucky to Be Bilingual[5]

"How to translate this body bilingual into a text when my *sans cesse* shifting word bodies...I mean, which one to speak in? You, dear reader, determine my choice today. And there's the ache of it: *devoir choisir*, something, necessarily, will be not-chosen."⁶ Bittersweet, the ambivalence of choice and the yoke of bilingualism run like two interwoven threads through the life and work of Lotbinière-Harwood. People have often told her that she was "lucky to be so bilingual"⁷; yet one can also ask what it actually means to be bilingual. "Sometimes you feel Other/sometimes you feel superior, being so 'rare,' so perfectly bi," reflects de Lotbinière-Harwood, "mostly you just feel *lâchée lousse*, footloose. but sometimes identity seems distressingly *indécidable*."⁸

For de Lotbinière-Harwood, to truly express herself would mean weaving her two languages together. To a certain degree, her work as translator enables her to explore and nourish this sense of duality. In this, her aut*her*s are lucky. Allowing for the transport/export of meaning in both directions, her work as a translator helps foster their writing, conveying it to a new readership, generating fruitful exchange, enriching and widening the feminist "we." Her translations could be described as "bridging both sides" of the linguistic and cultural divide "like a *main amoureuse*."⁹ As she observes, "allowing myself to switch voices is a political and poetic act that makes me feel less trapped in the structures of language"; but at times, her unusual position can be uncomfortable, even marginalizing. Inhabiting the space between the two languages, she is like a nomad, an "outsid(h)er," someone without a settled home. "For a *Québécoise*," says de Lotbinière-Harwood, "the place from where I speak is a politically, ethically and emotionally charged one. Solitary, risky."¹⁰ In many ways, her bilingualism is less a question of being lucky than a complex component of her own particular story as a Québécoise.

Hyphenating the Gap

Even before she was born on July 22, 1947, de Lotbinière-Harwood already belonged to a bilingual world. Her family name was the result of the marriage, in 1823 in Montreal, of her French Catholic ancestress, Louise-Josephte de Lotbinière, with a newly arrived Yorkshire businessman, Robert Unwin Harwood. At birth, her doubleness was reaffirmed when she was baptized with an English name (Susan) endowed with a French ending (e), Susanne, neither one nor the other, but both.

However, it was only at the age of four that English became a major part of her life. Her family had moved to Notre-Dame-de-Grâce, just west of Westmount, in Montréal. "Playing dolls on the cool concrete porch of the family's new home," she was surprised by a little neighbourhood girl who, proffering a "shiny green *pomme*," asked her in English, "Do you want an apple?"[11] As de Lotbinière-Harwood recounts the incident in *Matrix*, it was through the offer of an apple from this "little Eve"[12] that she was invited to betake both literally and symbolically of the other tongue, English: "The skin of self had been breached, the flesh of mothertongue irrigated with possibilities."[13]

De Lotbinière-Harwood rapidly started learning English and soon acquired a precocious sophistication in her new vocabulary. Always schooled in French, she found herself "correcting" her often-francophone teachers of English as a second language and leaving her classmates "struggling with the basics." It was not long before de Lotbinière-Harwood inhabited simultaneously both languages. In one, she went to mass with the nuns, learned the *p'tit catéchisme*, worked her way up "through the grades called *syntaxe, versification, rhétorique*" or tried to win an argument with her father, a businessman whom she would always call Daddy. In the other, she read *Vogue* magazine, fantasized about Brit pop-star Marianne Faithfull, and went wild for the Rolling Stones. She even fell in love with an English boy who introduced her to Dylan and taught her that "the 'b' in subtle is silent."[14]

Moving freely within one's different parts is not the same as being whole. While in Basil-Moreau College, where she was completing her *cours classique*, she was told by some militant indépendantistes that she should "drop the Harwood" from her name. It was the end of the 1960s, the memory of the FLQ bombings was still fresh; the 1970 October Crisis was in the making, and intercultural tensions in Québec were high. "*Traître*"! she was called. "But traitor to whom," she asks during my interview in March 2003: "Did my hyphenated name, a family name since 1823, make me less *Québécois(e)*? Was this about language or class? Hadn't Louise-Josephte fought the British during the Patriots Rebellion in 1837? Would dropping the 'Harwood' betray or confirm my origins?" For de Lotbinière-Harwood, abandoning her double name would also mean denying an important link with her Québécois "hystory." At the time of her ancestress,[15] daughters of the landed French nobility were entitled by the king to keep their patronym when there were no male heirs to pass on their father's name. Since 1837, the descendants of the de Lotbinière-Harwood family have all carried the hyphenated name.

A few years later, she was enjoying the festivities on Québec's national holiday, "la fête de la Saint-Jean," in Parc Lafontaine, in the heart of French-speaking East-end Montreal where she was then living, when she was approached by a young man asking her to sign a petition "*pour l'indépendance du Québec.*" She refused. By saying "No to the political dream," she once again chose not to choose, that is, she chose to remain true to her "body bilingual." Besides, she told the young man, *"Pis, j'suis pas moins Québécoise que toi pour ça."*[16] As she observes, she spoke English or "white" and she also spoke French, "fatherspeak," the language of her "patriarchal superego"; did this make her doubly colonized, "assimilée" by the English colonizer, but colonized as well by French, the patriarchal language of socialization?[17]

Once again, by choosing not to choose—that is, by refusing to drop the "Harwood" and by refusing to be what others thought she ought to be— de Lotbinière-Harwood chose not to split into two. It was for her a consciously subversive act of rebellion. Though she did not realize this at the time, de Lotbinière-Harwood's refusal to drop the "Harwood" meant that, like her ancestress who fought the English despite being married to one because she felt totally *canadienne-française*, she too would come to feel "Québécoise, whole, the *e muet* no longer silent."[18]

However, it would take some time for the *e* in *Québécoise* to cease to being silent. Hurt, lonely, feeling guilty and politically inexperienced, Susanne de Lotbinière-Harwood went into exile: she dropped out of McGill University where she was studying linguistics. Stepping off the bourgeois road, treading the path of rock and roll and Janis Joplin, she got a job at Eaton's, where she met new English-language friends, and with them she moved west of Boulevard Saint-Laurent, the Main that divides the two solitudes, to "anglo Montreal."

Establishing a Corpus or "Threading" Texts

De Lotbinière-Harwood supported her love affair with words and music by working as a freelance writer for the Entertainment section of the now defunct *Montreal Star*. Her editor, aware of cultural issues and astutely sensitive to cultural divides, used her as "a sort of foreign correspondent," having her write about Québécois culture for the paper's anglophone readership. And so it was as a "journalist for an English-language newspaper" that de Lotbinière-Harwood first became a literary translator. Fascinated by rock poet/singer Lucien Francoeur's ability to fit French to the beat of rock, she wrote a lengthy article about him and translated some of his lyrics for the assignment. Francoeur then asked her to translate a volume of his poems into English. The resulting publication, *Neons in the Night* (Véhicule Press, 1980), earned her the John Glassco Translation Prize (1981). However, this would be the last time she translated a major literary work by a male writer.

In the early 1980s, she became a member and co-ordinator (1980–83) of Powerhouse Gallery, run by and for women artists, and read her first feminist book, Mary Daly's *Beyond God the Father*. From then on, de Lotbinière-Harwood, who considers herself a feminist translator, chose to translate only women writers, and more often than not feminists. Stripping off the veil of invisibility draped over women in a patriarchal world was an opportunity for subversion. For de Lotbinière-Harwood "making the feminine subject visible is an important way of putting feminist politics into practice."[19] It would also enable her to make the feminine subject reciprocally visible in two cultures. An intense period of bidirectional translation followed, focussed on the reappropriation of text for gender-based purposes. As well as becoming a translator specializing in the visual arts and feminist literature, de Lotbinière-Hardwood was pioneering and experimenting with making visible the task of translation.

By the end of the 1980s, de Lotbinière-Harwood was doing translations in diverse genres, more often than not at the invitation of the auther. She translated theoretical texts such as "L'écriture des femmes au Québec: Un battement entre théorie et fiction" by Louise Cotnoir, which she titled, "Quebec Women's Writing: Space-in-Between Theory and Fiction" (1988). She translated poetry, including Nicole Brossard's text *Sous la langue* (*Under the Tongue*, 1988), which she declares was one of her greatest translation challenges. She was also involved in theatrical translation, and won Le prix du *Journal de Montréal* in 1986 for her translation of Jovette Marchessault's play, *Anaïs dans la queue de la comète* (*Anaïs in the Comet's Wake*, 1985).

To de Lotbinière-Harwood's growing list of translated works should be added numerous art texts and catalogues. These include the translation in 1985 of a review of the latest exhibition by Québec feminist artist Lise Nantel, which illustrates the importance of context for feminist translators. De Lotbinière-Harwood recalls that her translation of the male critic's "l'histoire des femmes" as "Women's hystory (*sic*)" was picked up by the editor, who erroneously "corrected" the translation as "Women's history (*sic*)," completely missing the point of the translation. De Lotbinière-Harwood admits that it was "naïve to try to force a radical strategy into a mainstream context,"[20] and that she should have explained her strategy. After this experience, de Lotbinière-Harwood decided to clarify her choice of words or puns in translator's notes at the end of the article or book.

Translator's notes are often used by feminist translators (this is the case for Barbara Godard, also profiled in this volume) to highlight the presence of the translator and her choices. For de Lotbinière-Harwood, notes, endnotes, or footnotes are also a way of "setting up a 'polyvocal composition, an arrangement of various voices,' not so much to direct the readership (exert auther-ity) as to give target culture readers added pleasure."[21] However, not all readers appreciate the strategy. A reaction to *Letters from an Other* (1989), her translation of Lise Gauvin's *Lettres d'une autre* (1984), is especially revealing. De Lotbinière-Harwood was criticized by Montréal writer David Homel, himself a translator, for having "hijacked" the source text, explaining too much "what Gauvin really meant," giving too many footnotes, and feminizing the book "beyond the author's original intention."[22] The salient point missed by the critic was that the intent of the original work was indeed feminist and subversive, and that the innovative translation carried the auther's approval. De Lotbinière-Harwood's creativity, her playfulness with language, and her own visibility as a translator were validated when she was awarded Columbia University's Félix-Antoine Savard Award for her translation of Gauvin's book.

For de Lotbinière-Harwood, feminism "over arches national(-ist) language(s) issues."[23] In 1988, she took on *Heroine* (1987), an important book by Montréal anglophone writer Gail Scott, which she translated into French under the title, *Héroïne*. It was a way for her to introduce to francophone readers a novel whose influence continues to be felt today in the literature of Québec. By highlighting "a you part of a them you could feel as a we," feminism offered her a "political grid that included, served and empowered [her]."[24] Hence her decision to translate only texts written by feminist writers, and in particular writers grounded in the North American continent, like Nicole Brossard, who encourage their translators to be creative and give them the freedom to view translation as "re-creation."[25]

In 1991, Lotbinière-Harwood brought together her experience defining feminist strategies and translation tactics in an innovative bilingual book, *Re-belle et infidèle: La traduction comme pratique de réécriture au féminin / The Body Bilingual: Translation as a Rewriting in the Feminine*, published simultaneously in Montréal and Toronto by Les Éditions du remue-ménage and Women's Press. Pure "jouissance" to write, the book is a celebration of the spontaneous flow of words unconfined by language of origin, a euphony of self-expression. Bilingual, it meant that she did "not have to choose." In one text, using two languages, de Lotbinière-Harwood outlines her translation practices. Packed with concrete examples of the different strategies required for each language, along with more theoretical reflections on developing a feminist ethic of translation, *Re-belle et Infidèle* is particularly seductive because it "reads like a story."[26]

Walking the Write

Seeing Geneviève Letarte, a young writer/musician, present her work with costume, music, and staging in a club setting one night in Montréal was a revelation to de Lotbinière-Harwood. For the first time, she saw and heard "language spatialized, off the page," in a way that confirmed her feeling that words were not just text but also an activity in language. This inspired her first to invite performance artists to perform at Powerhouse, and then to give performances herself. Her first, *Grafitti, ou L'envie d'écrire grand*, took place at Powerhouse in May 1984, and was followed by several other events involving part dance, part poetry.

Titled "Nos vieux papiers / Transformation Papers" and held at La Centrale/ Galerie Powerhouse, de Lotbinière-Harwood's first (and last, she insists) exhibition (May–June 2001) made the untold, unseen story of translation practice visible. In the gallery's small room, de Lotbinière-Harwood had assembled artists' handwritten original texts, computer printouts, post-its, word counts, and a slide projection of a translation-in-progress, as well as a videotaped conversation between her and an artist whose texts she often translated. The exhibition also featured an installation representing a translator's workspace, with table and chair, lamp, dictionaries, paper, and pens.

There, every Saturday afternoon during the show, de Lotbinière-Harwood performed the translator, the woman, *celle qui aime le rouge à lèvres*: "Back at my performative work table....I have given myself a stage, brought the translator out of the performance metaphor so beloved of postmodernism (due to its fascination with the body and representation) into real space and time. I have given her a physical stage, a live [typoed: love] audience. This matters because, contrary to all other interpretive performers, the translator's consummate achievement is to be invisible! So: out of the metaphor, out of the solitude, but still—no one can see the difficult language performance: I look just like a writer."[27]

By staging the act of translation, de Lotbinière-Harwood shows that translation, like performance, involves the body. Commenting on her experience of translating Brossard's *Le désert mauve*, she writes, "travelling through this complex source text, the translator's whole body is necessary and necessarily in constant e-motion between novels and languages, hoisting dictionaries, scanning the intertext, turning the pages of her memory, questioning the author, thinking of her readers."[28] By "performing" the act of translation, de Lotbinière-Harwood is also pointing out that translation, like performance, is an ephemeral art: always a story of becoming, of potentiality, always open to change, never final.

De Lotbinière-Harwood takes on texts to translate only very occasionally now, and when she does they tend to be art texts. These include the recent translation of Karen Spencer's text "Blanc cassé au bourgogne vert jaune" ("egg-shell white to burgundy to lime"), which accompanied Catherine Bodmer's exhibition, *Échantillons*, held in Longueil in February and March 2003. An important part of de Lotbinière-Harwood's corpus, such translations contribute to enlarging "the semantic space shared by women and others whose voices have been covered up by the dominant discourse/language/cultural conditions of the given society."[29] In 2004, she undertook a translation of another novel by Nicole Brossard, *Hier*.

The new millennium has confirmed her reputation as a feminist translator. In *Contemporary Translation Theories*, American translation specialist Edwin Gentzler cites her work as an example of what it means to use translation to go beyond "the traditional dichotomies of source/target, primary/secondary, high/low, writing/rewriting, coloniser/colonised that characterize translation theory historically."[30] She has been invited on two occasions to sit on the Canada Council jury for the prestigious Governor General's Literary Award for Translation (1991 and 2001). Her own work has been included in French- and English-language anthologies, such as *Trajectoire au féminin dans la littérature québécoise* and *Cultural Activism: Poetic Voices, Political Voices*. Her renown in English and in French is a good indicator of the impact of her work and how it has contributed to the Canadian production of women's culture and the emotive but fertile exchange between Québec and English Canada.

"Writing the Sub-Version"[31]

For de Lotbinière-Harwood, translation and politics are inseparable: "I consider translation a political activity. I'm a feminist, and through my work on language I'm putting my politics into practice via translation. The subject, or 'I,' is not neutral, has never been, contrary to popular belief. There is a quote I like by Henri Van Hoof: 'Translation has served to discover a culture, a body of knowledge…to defend or disseminate religious, philosophical, or political ideas, to struggle against an oppressor…to reveal a literature.' Feminist translation is all of these things."[32] Clearly, Lotbinière-Harwood sees her work as a feminist translator as "an active involvement in radical social change, an on-going struggle to shape a reality in which [women] can live more fully."[33] But what makes her contribution particularly significant is that by translating in both directions, she doubly subverts the patriarchal code. Although she welcomes "this source language / target language switch,"[34] she admits that "when four voices—English, French, masculine, feminine—are talking to your ear, creating the dissonance I call quadrophenia, who are you going to be faithful to? And to what degree?"[35]

Keeping in mind these last two questions can help pinpoint why, in order to remain faithful to herself, de Lotbinière-Harwood translates in both directions and why the passage from translating Francoeur to feminist writers such as Nicole Brossard may be better described in terms of a shift rather than a break. Francoeur's innovative and challenging language was engaging for someone who, like de Lotbinière-Harwood, has always been fascinated with the creative and subversive possibilities of breaking the conventions of language. Moreover, in the nationalist upsurge following Québec's not-always-Quiet Revolution of the 1960s, Francoeur used language to inscribe his *américanité*, to affirm his identity as a francophone North American, against the undermining effects of a colonial past and an uncertain cultural present.

De Lotbinière-Harwood describes poetically her identification with that same territory and urgent sense of being *Québécois(e)*: "i transgress in words & action to rid myself of this alienating hereditary fear. gotto run to keep from hiding. hands full of poetry! down geronimo's thunder road— the land of peace, love, justice & NO MERCY—american landscape in the **québécois** sense of the world."[36] These lines highlight de Lotbinière-Harwood's sense of rhythm—a talent that had not gone unnoticed by Francoeur when he asked her to translate his poems. They also indicate that, in translating the Québécois poet, Susanne de Lotbinière-Harwood was already a political translator "acting with a cause," wanting to communicate Québec-specific cultural issues to English Canada.

However, *Neons in the Night*, an anthology of five books of poetry Francoeur published between 1972 and 1975, was also a harrowing translation experience. Wanting to remain as true as she could to Francoeur's voice, de Lotbinière-Harwood had to distort her own writing style. The project lasted over three years, and she found herself beginning to feel like a male voyeur, struggling to reproduce the author's male gaze in an authentic male voice. The first lines of "Angel Iceberg, ange frigorifé" whose title is already sexually coded, offer an example of Francoeur's style: "sa jupe tellement courte son / vagin me fait des clins-d'oeil," which de Lotbinière-Harwood translated as: "her skirt so short her / vagina gives me the eye."[37] No wonder "I wound up lost in translation," says de Lotbinière-Harwood. Although she identified with Francoeur in terms of cultural identity, as a woman she felt cut off from herself. Her language-centred faculty exhausted, she was rescued by the work of feminist writers and their analyses of women's relationship to language.

In turning to feminist writers, de Lotbinière-Harwood was drawn to women whose writings, like those of Francoeur, were viscerally grounded in a North American sensibility. She responded particularly to the work of the eminent Québec feminist Nicole Brossard. In *Le désert mauve*, she encountered "a Québec-positive voice whose literary image-reservoir is geographically and culturally rooted in North America." Unlike Francoeur's poetry, whose target audience was male-bodied, Brossard's *Le désert mauve* allowed de Lotbinière-Harwood to engage with a novel written "with women readers in mind about close relationships between women";[38] she was able to escape the alienation induced by translating from the masculine. Furthermore, Brossard does not view translation as a subordinate or derivative practice, and she encourages her translators to intervene. This approach is especially visible in the bilingual edition of Brossard's *Elle serait la première phrase de mon prochain roman / She Would Be the First Sentence of My Next Novel*, where the two languages face each other across the pages of one book.

Carrying into another language the rhythm of the first requires a sensibility to rhythm in both languages. De Lotbinière-Harwood usually reads aloud both the text to be translated and her own translation. In *Le désert mauve*, one can see how she proceeds to keep the same effects of rhythm in her translation. In Brossard's text, the rhythm of French does not translate easily into English: "Aujourd'hui, elle avouait cependant que très jeune fille elle avait pris la mauvaise habitude."[39] De Lotbinière-Harwood translates the passage: "Today, however, she admitted that very young she had gotten in the bad habit."[40] A small change in the order of the words—"however" is placed before the verb—is enough to keep the same beat as the French text. Paying attention to the rhythm of language is also the reason why she prefers to describe her move from Francoeur to Brossard and other feminist writers not as a rupture but as a shift from "the spirit of rock 'n' roll to the spirit of sisterhood."[41] However, the move did affect her translation style. By taking on "the self-consciously transgressive feminist writers," de Lotbinière-Harwood was to feel "increasingly authorized (or in her own vocabulary, auth*e*rized) to valorise the signs of the feminine in the translated text."[42]

What does "auth*e*rization" mean for a feminist translator and how does it manifest itself? What strategies does it involve? It should be clear that for de Lotbinière-Harwood, auth*e*rizing oneself means working in close collaboration with the auth*e*r. Because the auth*e*rs she translates tend to be feminist, the strategies she uses to make women visible will, in many cases, be those used by the auth*e*r herself. Neither language is unbiased, de

Lotbinière-Harwood emphasizes. Whether one translates from French to English or vice versa, it is necessary to actively re-gender the text. This means finding strategies that go beyond just "desexization" through expressions like "he/she; man/woman." It also means going beyond placing the feminine before the masculine, as in "she/he" or "s/he," or using neutralizing expressions ("flight attendant" instead of a "stewardess").[43]

Highlighting the overly marked gender (French) or the seeming absence of gender (English), de Lotbinière-Harwood makes visible how both languages serve as instruments through which patriarchy maintains control over the female subject. Re-sexing the language requires paying close attention to words that have pejorative connotations, like "stewardess" or "actress," as well as reclaiming certain words by reversing their patriarchal meanings. In feminist contexts, words like "witch" are being recharged with positive meaning. Consequently, when translating "nous sommes toutes des métèques" for the Third International Feminist Book Fair Programme (Montréal, 1988), a word with negative connotations, de Lotbinière-Harwood wrote, "we are all outsid(h)ers."[44] As she points out, the "(h)" strategy, inspired by *Lovhers*, the title of Barbara Godard's translation of Nicole Brossard's *Amantes*, and which she has also used elsewhere, offered a graphic opportunity to reverse women's textual invisibility and marginalization.

The Bold e

Typography is another way of marking gender, especially when translating from French into English, because the English language lacks the capacity to celebrate gender in the same way as French. Where *autre* ("other") meant the female other in Michèle Causse's *L'Interloquée*, Lotbinière-Harwood put **her** in bold as in "the degradation of ot**her**."[45] The strategy engages the reader's curiosity and desire to turn to the note to find out what is happening. Since Michèle Causse was herself doing "revolutionizing" things to and with language, and the editor was also open to innovation and subversive opportunity, her **bold** tactic was accepted.

Valorizing the feminine implies using imagination as well as taking risks—and what is more risky and potentially subversive than creating new words? Working on *Le désert mauve* by Nicole Brossard, de Lotbinière-Harwood coined several new expressions. Almost by chance, through a typo, she discovered a way to translate the feminized word "auteure,"[46] by "auther."[47] Widely used by Québec feminists, the word "auteure" was based on an existing linguistic model ("prieure," the feminine form of prieur, for example). While "auther" may be criticized on etymological grounds, it has nonetheless become part of the feminist intertext, thus contributing to the growing visibility of women's culture and language.

The translation of *amoure* in the same novel also required creativity. Here is the passage in Brossard's words:

> – Les autres qui? Pauvre kathy, mon amoure. Pauvre moi, ton amoure. Qu'allons-nous devenir si tu ne m'aimes point comme je suis, si je te veux comme tu n'es point? Combien de caresses, combien de fois les mains sur nos bouches, combien de fois l'ardeur du ventre pour que nous devenions avec exactitude ce que nous sommes ? Ou cela n'a-t-il rien à voir?[48]

The translation conveys the gendered "amoure" with a neologism:

> – Others, who? Poor Kathy, my love. Poor me, your shelove. What will we become if you don't love me as I am, if I want you as you are not? How many caresses, how many times hands over our mouths, how many times the belly's fire before we become exactly what we are? Or is that irrelevant?[49]

In some respects, "shelove" is more daring than the French *amoure*, a word that until the end of the seventeenth century was always used in the feminine and so appears less subversive, or at least less explicitly so, than its English neologism. Yet if these rewriting strategies can be described as subversive, they all point to the responsibility of the translator to remain as faithful as possible to the subversive dimension of the auther's own writing. It was in keeping with these considerations that de Lotbinière-Harwood felt authorized, as translator, to use "shelove."

Although de Lotbinière-Harwood's decision to retain the *accent aigu* on "Mélanie," the name of one of the protagonists in *Mauve Desert*, may appear conventional now, at the time it was considered transgressive. As de Lotbinière-Harwood explains, translation was expected to be "idiomatic in the target language" in order to create the effect that the text was an original. By keeping *l'accent aigu*, she chose to be faithful to the source text, to her auther. The strategic mark helps retain "the small culture's presence in a text translated into the large culture's language." It is also a sign of a francophone practice of *américanité*, demonstrating how "non-dominant voices inscribe their sounds and visions into the larger picture to redraw the map."[50] In this way, her innovative strategies speak as well to male translators, encouraging them to reflect on the social and political implications of language use.

When translating Jovette Marchessault's play *La terre est trop courte, Violette Leduc*, which uses extensive excerpts from Leduc's books, de Lotbinière-Harwood came across Derek Coltman's translation of Violette Leduc's autobiography *La Bâtarde* (1964). She felt she could not use the published version of the translated excerpts. For example, the sentence "Je suis née brisée. Je suis le malheur d'une autre. Une bâtarde, quoi!"[51] had become "I was born broken. I am someone else's misfortune, a bastard!"[52] By translating "une autre" as "someone else," Coltman had totally erased the woman-centred meaning and rendered invisible "the bond between mother and daughter"[53] central to Leduc's tragic life story. To respect Leduc's text, de Lotbinière-Harwood retranslated the sentence as: "I was born broken, I am another woman's sorrow, a bastard!"[54]

Going the Other Way

What then are de Lotbinière-Harwood's strategies to validate the feminine when the source language is English (her other tongue)—whose "grammatical system does not mark gender overtly compared to the highly gender-marked French"[55]—and the target language is French (her mother tongue)? De Lotbinière-Harwood emphasizes that French, too, can benefit from being re-sexed, and for this, an understanding of the way words are used is crucial to help make the right choices. As de Lotbinière-Harwood explains, translating "woman/women," "female," "feminine," and "feminist" is complicated by the fact that these terms differ slightly in French.

This can be illustrated by the word "female" in the following sentence from Gail Scott's *Heroine:* "Maybe it is possible to have a set of female (non-patriarchal) standards to judge the world by."[56] It cannot be translated by "femelle," as de Lotbinière-Harwood observes in *Re-belle et Infidèle / The Body Bilingual*, because in English "female" is used not just in a biological sense but also to signify "woman."[57] French possesses only one word, *féminin*, to designate both female sex and feminine gender. Moreover, in this sentence, by adding "non-patriarchal," the auther had politicized the word "female." For this reason, de Lotbinière-Harwood decided not to use the word "feminine," whose meaning always includes a social (as opposed to biological) dimension. Instead, she translated the sentence as follows: "Peut-être est-il possible d'avoir un système de pensée, non patriarcal, qui permette de juger le monde au féminin."[58] She explains that "au féminin" is an expression often used by postmodern Québéc feminists of which the novel's heroine is one. In placing *au féminin* "at the end of the sentence,"[59] she was also guided by her sense of rhythm.

Creativity is a process extending over many hours of work, research, and reflection. Wanting to translate positively "the small point" that in

Heroine refers to the woman's organ of pleasure, de Lotbinière-Harwood went through *Le dictionnaire de l'argot moderne* and found the word *gousse*, which is defined as "lesbienne."[60] Using *gousse* for clitoris helped her rename and reinvest positively the female sexual organ while at the same time adding an interior rhythm to the French sentence. "Oh froth, your warm faucet's spurting warmly over my uh small point"[61] becomes in French "ton chaud robinet laisse couler la mousse blanche sur la petite gousse au fond du bain."[62] Patriarchal appropriation is particularly blatant where the naming of women's sexuality is at stake, and feminist translation informed by an intimate knowledge of both languages provides special opportunities for subversion.

For de Lotbinière-Harwood, the collaborative process of translation becomes most fruitful when she is working with auth*e*rs who are shaping a woman-centered language space. Auth*e*r-ization to feminize the language and to advance women's culture also includes the opportunity to inscribe one's own presence through the translator's notes, preface, and signature in the translated text. Highlighted as the translator's "personal reading," the translated work cannot be confused with the original. However, de Lotbinière-Harwood is careful, in her interventions, to balance her fidelity to the auth*e*r's meaning with her fidelity to her own ethics and the particular context of the translation.

Text and Context

Context, writes Susanne de Lotbinière-Harwood, "is composed of all determinants specific to each and every translation situation, all the strands and factors we must weave to make appropriate translation decisions."[63] This includes the auth*e*r, but also the publisher's wishes, and those readers to whom the text is addressed. The position she assumes as a feminist translator is not simple, nor without risk: she has had to turn down work, editors have sometimes mangled her innovative shifts, and some readers have been angered by the liberties she takes. At the same time, de Lotbinière-Harwood is often invited to translate by auth*e*rs, such as Scott and Brossard, who add to the complexities of language usage by writing texts that include both French and English.

De Lotbinière-Harwood's bidirectional translation career leads to a better understanding of how the subtleties of each language can be used to advantage in order to arrive at precision of meaning rather than mutual incomprehension. By intervening in both languages, she achieves her subversive goal of opening up a space for the feminine voice. She also contributes to the creation of an international feminist community, cutting across barriers of national identity. Nicole Brossard admits in *Elle serait la première phrase de mon prochain roman / She Would Be the Next Sentence of My Next Novel* that she never travels without de Lotbinière-Harwood's translation; she has read from it around the world. Aesthetic objects in their own right, de Lotbinière-Harwood's finished works are often described by her authers as "more beautiful than the original."[64]

What singles out de Lotbinière-Harwood as a translator is not just her attention to the rhythm or the beat of language, since this can characterize any translator. Nor is it her goal to subvert patriarchy, as this too is shared territory. De Lotbinière-Harwood's special claim to recognition may well lie in her very duality, her ability to play in a subversive way, in more than one direction, with her relationship with both languages.

NOTES

1 Susanne de Lotbinière-Harwood, *Re-belle et infidèle: La traduction comme pratique de réécriture au feminin / The Body Bilingual: Translation as a Rewriting in the Feminine* (Montréal: Éditions du remue-ménage; Toronto: Women's Press, 1991), p. 150. Following de Lotbinière-Harwood's practice, words or sentences in French will be left in italics.
2 This is the basic principle used in all Canadian university translation training programs.
3 See de Lotbinière-Harwood, *Re-belle et Infidèle*, p. 22.
4 Sherry Simon, *Gender in Translation: Cultural Identity and the Politics of Transmission* (London and New York: Routledge, 1996), p. 36.
5 This expression is borrowed from de Lotbinière-Harwood.
6 Susanne de Lotbinière-Harwood, "How She Might Tongue Me," *Matrix*, no. 60 (winter 2001): 42–44.
7 From notes taken during an interview with Susanne de Lotbinière-Harwood on March 22, 2003, in Montréal. Unless otherwise indicated, all subsequent quotations are from this interview.
8 de Lotbinière-Harwood, *Re-belle et infidèle*, p. 83.
9 de Lotbinière-Harwood, *Re-belle et infidèle*, p. 81.
10 de Lotbinière-Harwood, *Re-belle et infidèle*, p. 93.
11 de Lotbinière-Harwood, "How She Might Tongue Me," p. 42.
12 de Lotbinière-Harwood, "How She Might Tongue Me," p. 42.
13 de Lotbinière-Harwood, "How She Might Tongue Me," p. 42.
14 de Lotbinière-Harwood, "How She Might Tongue Me," p. 43.
15 To call or not to call Susanne de Lotbinière-Harwood a "translatress"—a word that Sherry Simon uses (*Gender in Translation*, p. 39)—that was the question. When I first proposed it to de Lotbinière-Harwood, she pointed out that

words ending in "ess" like "actress" and so on are not positively connoted. From that point of view, she could be criticized for using the word "ancestress." However, it could be argued that translatress, though a word that dates back to 1638, was never incorporated in the dictionary, whereas ancestress was.

16 de Lotbinière-Harwood, *Re-belle et infidèle*, p. 80.
17 de Lotbinière-Harwood, *Re-belle et infidèle*, p. 85.
18 de Lotbinière-Harwood, *Re-belle et infidèle*, p. 84.
19 See David Homel and Sherry Simon, eds., *Mapping Literature: The Art and Politics of Translation* (Montréal: Véhicule Press, 1988), p. 43.
20 de Lotbinière-Harwood, *Re-belle et infidèle*, p. 121.
21 de Lotbinière-Harwood, *Re-belle et infidèle*, p. 157, quoting Robert Majzels, "Feminist Fiction/Theory: Writings from the Margin," (PhD diss., Concordia University, 1987).
22 Quoted by Luise Von Flotow, "Feminist Translation: Contexts, Practices and Theories," *TTR: Traduction, terminologie, rédaction* 4, no. 2 (1991): 78–79.
23 de Lotbinière-Harwood, "How She Might Tongue Me," p. 43.
24 de Lotbinière-Harwood, *Re-belle et infidèle*, p. 84.
25 Simon, *Gender in Translation*, p. 160.
26 de Lotbinière-Harwood, "How She Might Tongue Me," p. 43.
27 de Lotbinière-Harwood, *Pink Link, ou La proposition rose*, p. 53.
28 Quoted by Simon, *Gender in Translation*, p. 160.
29 Edwin Gentzler, "Translation, Postcolonial Studies, and the Americas," *Entertext* 2, no. 2 (summer 2003) <www.brunel.ac.uk/4020/entertext2.2//gentzler.pdf>.
30 Gentzler, "Translation, Postcolonial Studies, and the Americas."
31 This is a subtitle from de Lotbinière-Harwood, *Re-belle et infidèle*, p. 107.
32 See David Homel and Sherry Simon, *Mapping Literature*, p. 44.
33 Lotbinière-Harwood, *Re-belle et infidèle*, p. 168.
34 Susanne de Lotbinière-Harwood, "Geo-graphies of Why," in *Culture in Transit*, ed. S. Simon (Montréal: Véhicule Press, 1995), p. 67.
35 See the excerpts from *Re-belle et infidèle* in *Semiotext(e) Canadas*, special issue of *Semiotext(e)* 4, no.2 (1994): 284.
36 de Lotbinière-Harwood, "Geo-graphies of Why," p. 56.
37 Lucien Francoeur, "Angel Iceberg, ange frigorifié," in Lucien Francoeur, *Neons in the Night*, trans. Susanne de Lotbinière-Harwood (Montréal: Véhicule, 1980), pp. 40-41.
38 de Lotbinière-Harwood, "Geo-graphies of Why," p. 65.
39 Nicole Brossard, *Le désert mauve* (Montréal: Hexagone, 1987), p. 18.
40 Nicole Brossard, *Mauve Desert*, trans. Susanne de Lotbinière-Harwood (Toronto: Coach House, 1990), p. 19.
41 de Lotbinière-Harwood, "Geo-graphies of Why," p. 64.
42 Simon, *Gender in Translation*, p. 32.
43 de Lotbinière-Harwood, *Re-belle et infidèle*, p. 113.
44 de Lotbinière-Harwood, *Re-belle et infidèle*, p. 130.

45 Michèle Causse, "L'Interloquée," trans. Susanne de Lotbinière-Harwood, *Trivia*, no. 13 (1998): 81.
46 Brossard, *Le désert mauve*, p. 570.
47 Brossard, *Mauve Desert*, trans. Susanne de Lotbinière-Harwood, p. 53.
48 Brossard, *Le désert mauve*, p. 132.
49 Nicole Brossard, *Mauve Desert*, trans. Susanne de Lotbinière-Harwood, p. 124.
50 Susanne de Lotbinière-Harwood, "Geo-graphies of Why," p. 67. Lawrence Venuti also speaks of a foreignizing strategy. See Lawrence Venuti, introduction to *Rethinking Translation* (New York: Routledge, 1992), pp. 1–7.
51 Violette Leduc, *La Bâtarde* (Paris: Gallimard, 1964), p. 465.
52 Violette Leduc, *The Bastard*, trans. Derek Coltman (Frogmore: Panther Books, 1967), p. 361.
53 de Lotbinière-Harwood, *Re-belle et infidèle*, p. 107.
54 de Lotbinière-Harwood's translation of Marchessault's play is unpublished. Her translation is given in *Re-belle et infidèle*, where she also indicates that "permission was obtained from the Violette Leduc estate to use [her] translation instead of Coltman's." de Lotbinière-Harwood, *Re-belle et infidèle*, 108.
55 de Lotbinière-Harwood, *Re-belle et infidèle*, p. 113.
56 Gail Scott, *Heroine* (Toronto: Coach House Press, 1987), p. 141.
57 de Lotbinière-Harwood, *Re-belle et infidèle*, p. 64.
58 Gail Scott, *Héroïne*, trans. Susanne de Lotbinière-Harwood, p. 192.
59 de Lotbinière-Harwood, *Re-belle et infidèle*, p. 63.
60 de Lotbinière-Harwood, *Re-belle et infidèle*, p. 65.
61 Scott, *Heroine*, p. 36
62 Scott, *Héroïne*, trans. Susanne de Lotbinière-Harwood, p. 11.
63 de Lotbinière-Harwood, *Re-belle et infidèle*, p. 120.
64 Simon, *Gender in Translation*, p. 53.

BIBLIOGRAPHY

This bibliography does not include Susanne de Lotbinière-Harwood's art text translations.

I Primary Sources

Literary Translations (Books)

Brossard, Nicole. *Sous la Langue / Under Tongue*. Trans. Susanne de Lotbinière-Harwood. Montréal and Charlottetown: L'Essentielle. Editrices / Gynergy Press, 1987.

———. *Mauve Desert*. Trans. Susanne de Lotbinière-Harwood. Toronto: Coach House Press, 1990. Translation of *Le désert mauve*. Montréal: Éditions de l'Hexagone, 1987.

———. *She Would Be the First Sentence of My Next Novel / Elle serait la première phrase de mon prochain roman*. Trans. Susanne de Lotbinière-Harwood. Toronto: Mercury Press, 1999.

———. *Yesterday at the Hotel Clarendon*. Trans. Suzanne de Lotbinière-Harwood. Toronto: Coach House Press, 2005. Translation of *Hier*. Montréal: Québec/Amérique, 2001.

Burgess, Marilyn, and Gail Valaskakis. *Indian Princesses and Cowgirls : Stereotypes from the Frontier / Princesses indiennes et cowgirls: Stéréotypes de la frontière*. Trans. Susanne de Lotbinière-Harwood. Montréal: Galerie Oboro, 1995.

Francoeur, Lucien. *Neons in the Night*. Trans. Susanne de Lotbinière-Harwood. Montréal: Véhicule Press, 1980. Translation of *Les néons las*. Montréal: Éditions de l'Hexagone, 1978.

Gauvin, Lise. *Letters from an Other*. Trans. Susanne de Lotbinière-Harwood. Toronto: Women's Press, 1989. Translation of *Lettres d'une autre*. Montréal: Éditions de l'Hexagone, 1984.

Scott, Gail. *Héroïne*. Trans. Susanne de Lotbinière-Harwood. Montréal: Éditions du remue-ménage, 1988. Translation of *Heroine*. Toronto: Coach House Press, 1987.

Literary Translations (in Journals and Edited Volumes)

Alonzo, Anne-Marie. "Ritual." Trans. Susanne de Lotbinière-Harwood. *Tessera*, no. 57 (1987): 50–52. Rpt in *Collaboration in the Feminine: Writings on Women and Culture from* Tessera, ed. Barbara Godard. Toronto: Second Story Press, 1994. 78–80.

Bertrand, Claudine. "Fiction in Lunar Black." Trans. Susanne de Lotbinière-Harwood. *Montréal Now!* 2, no. 4 (winter 1985): n.p.

Brossard, Nicole. "Certain Words." Trans. Susanne de Lotbinière-Harwood. *Mattoid* (Australia), Canadian supplement, (1986).

———. "Her Hand on a Book Resting While Our Bodies Obliquely." Trans. Susanne de Lotbinière-Harwood. *Writing*, no.16 (1986): 36–41.

———. "Autobiography Series." Trans. Susanne de Lotbinière-Harwood. In *Contemporary Authors*, vol. 16, ed. Joyce Nakamura. Detroit and London: Gale Research, 1992. 39–59.

———. "Tendons, Paragraphs and Milky Way." Trans. Susanne de Lotbinière-Harwood. *Yefief*, no. 1 (winter 1994).

Causse, Michèle. "L'Interloquée." Trans. Susanne de Lotbinière-Harwood. *Trivia*, no.13 (1988): 79–90.

Cotnoir, Louise. "A Space-in-Between Theory and Fiction." Trans. Susanne de Lotbinière-Harwood. *Trivia*, no. 13 (1988): 13–16.

Desautels, Denise. "The Archeologist." Trans. Susanne de Lotbinière-Harwood. *Tessera*, no. 57 (1987): 112–16.

Desjardins, Louise. "Sheltering Realities." Trans. Susanne de Lotbinière-Harwood. *Tessera*, no. 57 (1987): 70–77.

Hryniuk, Angela. *Luxton Avenue* (poèmes). Trans. Susanne de Lotbinière-Harwood. *Estuaire*, no. 75 (Nov. 1994): 9–18.

Marchessault, Jovette. "The Edge of Earth Is Too Near, Violette Leduc." Trans. Susanne de Lotbinière-Harwood. Unpublished.

Marlatt, Daphne. "S'écrire au travers le labyrinthe." Trans. Susanne de Lotbinière-Harwood. *Tessera / NBJ*, no. 157 (1985): 50–53.

Thesen, Sharon. "L'Écriture, la lecture et le lecteur / amant imaginaire." Trans. Susanne de Lotbinière-Harwood. *Tessera / NBJ*, no.157 (1985): 71–74.

Books and Articles on Translation

de Lotbinière-Harwood, Susanne. "Skin for Arts Sake." *Weekend*, no. 26 (1976): 10–12.

———. "Etat d'esprit New-York." *La nouvelle barre du jour*, no. 102 (1981): 87–95.

———. "Long jeu" and "Échappées belles." *Hobo-Québec*, no. 46/47 (1981): 32–41.

———. "Nourritures solaires." *La vie en rose*, no. 20 (1984): 46–47.

———. "Stella Vision: Une biographie lunaire (passage)." *La nouvelle barre du jour*, no. 136/137 (1984): 15–21.

———. "Extrême centre." *La nouvelle barre du jour*, no. 157 (1985): 75–82.

———. "Contre-plongée." *Montréal Now!* 2, no. 3 (fall,1985): n.p.

———. "L'ambiguïté d'un concept." Dossier "Traduire au Québec." *Spirale*, no. 62 (1986): 11–15.

———. "Les belles infidèles: La traduction comme pratique de ré-écriture au féminin." *Arcade*, no. 11 (1986): 22–25.

———. "La grammaire intérieure." *La vie en rose*, no. 38 (1986): 34–35.

———. "Post-mortem pour le journal d'une vie (1965–1985)." *Arcade*, no. 12 (1986): 8–11.

———. "Turning to Woman." *Canadian Journal of Feminist Ethics* 1, no. 3 (1986): 17–25.

———. "I Write *le* Body Bilingual," *Border/Lines*, no. 6 (1986–87): 1–33.

———. "Fire Words: The Politics of Subtitling." *Lip* 1, no. 2 (1987): 28–30.

———. "Deux mots pour chaque chose." *Tessera*, no. 5 (1989): 24–26.

———. "I Write *le* Body Bilingual: A Love Affair-e in Nomad's Land." *Trivia*, no. 14 (1989): 13–20.

———. "Translating through the Body." *Gasp* 2, no. 1 (1990): 24–27.

———. "La voir, sa voix," *Harbour* 1, no. 3 (1991): 23–27.

———. *Re-belle et infidèle: La traduction comme pratique de réécriture au féminin / The Body Bilingual: Translation as a Rewriting in the Feminine*. Montréal: Les Éditions du remue-ménage; Toronto: Women's Press, 1991. Excerpted in *Semiotext(e) Canadas*, no. 2, New York: Marginal Editions, 1994. 279–85. Extracts in *L'autre lecture: La critique au féminin et les textes québécois* vol. 2, ed. Tome II. Lori Saint-Martin. Montréal: XYZ éditeur, 1994. 59–66.

———. "Manu Opera: Fragments d'un parcours d'amoureuses / Fragments of a Lovers' Dis-course." *Trivia*, no. 20 (1993): 11–25. Revised version in *Trajectoires au féminin dans la littérature québécoise (1960–1990)*, ed. Lucie Joubert. Québec: Éditions Nota Bene, 2000.11–15.

———. "A Brillant Disguise." *Circuit*, no. 45 (1994): 13.

———. "Acting the (Re)Writer: A Feminist Translator's Practice of Space." *Fireweed*, no. 44/45 (1994): 101–10.

———. "Geo-graphies of Why." in *Culture in Transit: Translating The Literature of Quebec*, ed. S. Simon. Montréal: Véhicule Press, 1995. 55–68.

———. "Rachel Echenberg: The Water Nymph Project." *Agenda des femmes 1999*. Montréal: Éditions du Remue-ménage, 1999.

———. "I'm Not an Artist but..." In *Pink Link, ou La proposition rose*. Montréal: La Centrale / Powerhouse, 2001. 52–54.

———. "How She Might Tongue Me." *Matrix*, no. 60 (winter 2001): 42–44.

———, with Sheena Gourlay. Introduction to *Textura: L'artiste écrivant / The Artist Writing*. Montréal: La Centrale / Powerhouse, 2000. 5–9.

II. Secondary Sources

Brossard, Nicole. "Sous la langue / Under the Tongue." In *Deep Down: The New Sensual Writing by Women*, ed. Laura Chester. Boston: Faber and Faber, 1988. 182–83. Excerpt in *The Zenith of Desire*, ed. Gerry Gomez Pearlberg. New York: Crown, 1996.

Dodge, Bill, ed. *A Quebec Reader*. Toronto: Lester, 1992.

Gentzler, Edwin. "Translation, Postcolonial Studies, and the Americas." *Entertext* 2, no. 2 (summer 2003), <www.brunel.ac.uk/4020/entertext2.2//gentzler.pdf>.

Gonzalez James, Gertrude M., and Anne J.M. Mamary, eds. *Cultural Activisms: Poetic Voices, Political Voices*. New York: SUNY Press, 1999.

Homel, David, and Sherry Simon, eds. *Mapping Literature: The Art and Politics of Translation*. Montréal: Véhicule Press, 1988.

Joubert, Lucie, ed. *Trajectoires au féminin dans la littérature québécoise 1960–1990*. Québec: Editions Nota Bene, 2000.

Leduc, Violette. *La Bâtarde*. Paris: Gallimard, 1964.

———. *The Bastard*. Trans. Derek Coltman. London: Peter Owen, 1965. Frogmore: Panther Books, 1967.

Koski, R., K. Kells, and L. Forsyth, eds. *Les discours féminins dans l'écriture postmoderne au Québec*. New York: Mellen, 1993.

Simon, Sherry, ed. *Culture in Transit: Translating the Literature of Quebec*. Montréal: Véhicule Press, 1995.

———. *Gender in Translation: Cultural Identity and the Politics of Transmission*. London and New York: Routledge, 1996.

Venuti, Lawrence, ed. *Rethinking Translation: Discourse, Subjectivity, Ideology*. London and New York: Routledge, 1992.

Von Flotow, Luise. "Feminist Translation: Contexts, Practices and Theories," *TTR: Traduction, terminologie, rédaction* 4, no. 2 (1991): 69–83.

———. "Translating Women of the Eighties: Eroticism, Anger, Ethnicity." in *Culture in Transit: Translating the Literature of Quebec*, ed. S. Simon. Montréal: Véhicule Press, 1995. 31–46.

John Van Burek
Bringing Tremblay to Toronto

JANE KOUSTAS

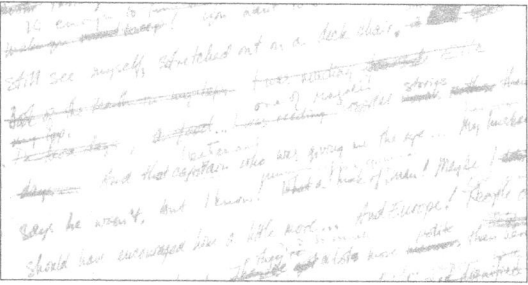

John Van Burek has earned national and international recognition for his work in the theatre as a director, teacher, and translator. In collaboration with Bill Glassco,[1] he has been instrumental in introducing and maintaining a French-language and Québec presence in the Toronto theatre scene. Over the last thirty years, he has produced and translated more than ten plays by renowned Québec playwright Michel Tremblay. Many of these translations have been reprinted and revised; they have also marked the debut, at the Canadian press Talonbooks, of the publication of an important series of Québec plays in translation. Yet Van Burek's initial goal was not so much to translate Tremblay, as to introduce him to Toronto and make him accessible to the Toronto theatre audience. Van Burek readily admits to being "first a theatre director,"[2] and a translator only by necessity. Nonetheless, through his desire to bring vibrant Québec theatre to Toronto and his decision to become a translator in order to do so, Van

Burek merits a place in a volume dedicated to people whose achievements have changed the face of translation practice in Canada.

Born in Toronto, Van Burek moved to the United States when he was ten. He attended college in New Hampshire and obtained a graduate degree from the University of New Brunswick in Fredericton. It was while travelling in France, after graduate school, that he learned French. In 1971, upon his return to Canada, his love of French language and culture led him to found Toronto's first French-language theatre, Le théâtre français de Toronto. Van Burek served as the artistic director from 1971 to 1978 and again from 1981 to 1992.

Van Burek's connection with Bill Glassco goes back to the early 1970s, a veritable boom period for Toronto theatre. Glassco had founded the Tarragon Theatre in 1970 with his wife, Jane. Interested in producing Québec theatre in English, he approached Van Burek, who was well-acquainted with the Québec theatre scene through his involvement with the Toronto francophone community. This initial contact led to over three decades of Tremblay plays in Toronto and, arguably, to a greatly transformed Toronto theatre scene.

Van Burek has mounted over eighty productions from opera to new Canadian plays, including, most notably, his own translations of Michel Tremblay. He has directed theatre in the United Kingdom and in France, and also led an international theatre exchange program in Bangladesh in 1996. In 1999, BRAVO! broadcast Van Burek's series of six television documentaries on new plays in Canada. Through his own theatre company, the Pleiades, founded in 1975, he has translated, produced, and directed Marivaux's *The Game of Love and Chance* (May 2000), *The Triumph of Love* (May 2001), and *Counterfeit Secrets* (May 2002). Marivaux had been previously translated, notably by the American director Stephen Wadsworth. Van Burek created versions better suited to the Canadian audience and can be credited with having translated and directed the only major Marivaux English-language productions in Canada. He has also translated theatre for young audiences, including *A Winter's Tale* (*Conte d'hiver*), by Anne Legault, and *Crying to Laugh* (*Pleurer pour rire*), by Marcel Sabourin.

Van Burek has developed other première productions including *Les Fridolinades*, by Gratien Gélinas, and an English dramatic adaptation of Mikhaïl Bulgakov's *Heart of a Dog* and *The Master and Margarita*. He has also taught drama at the École nationale de théâtre du Canada, and he continues to instruct at the Ryerson Theatre School and York University. A recipient of numerous awards and distinctions, including the Toronto Drama Bench's Award for Distinguished Contributions to Canadian Theatre, Van Burek was decorated by the l'Ordre de la Pléiade of the Assemblée parlementaire de la francophonie in 2001.

Bringing Québec Playwrights to Toronto

Michel Tremblay was by no means the first Québec playwright translated and produced for the Toronto stage. The Toronto audience had already "throw[n] out the red carpet"[3] to Gratien Gélinas and his production of *Tit-Coq* at the Royal Alexandra Theatre in 1951. Gélinas, author and director, was honoured with a doctorate and a sensational opening night, "a theatrical event about as rare as a blizzard in July,"[4] which concluded with "one of the most gala events of the winter season."[5] From then until the arrival of Michel Tremblay on the Toronto English theatre circuit in 1972, however, on average only one Québec play in translation was staged each year, Gélinas and Jacques Languirand being the most popular playwrights. In contrast, from 1972 to 1980, Toronto audiences had the opportunity every season to see usually two, if not three, professional productions of Québec plays, including at least one by Tremblay. Although not all of Tremblay's plays received the same enthusiastic reviews, the number of his plays professionally staged has proven the writer's popularity and Van Burek's ability to make Tremblay work in Toronto.

After his first production in Toronto, *Forever Yours, Marie-Lou* (Tarragon Theatre, November 14–December 10, 1972), Tremblay was recognized as a "writer of apparent power and tremendous drive,"[6] and through Van Burek's translations, he was soon "the darling of the critics and the chosen one of the Toronto theatre scene."[7] However, as Paula Dancy points out in her study of Tremblay at the Tarragon, the initial decision to produce Tremblay was a "daring" one, "because of his newness to the audience, his political affiliation, which always leaked through (intentionally) into the theme and structure of his plays, his subject matter and the questionable quality of the translation of his plays."[8]

Indeed, it was precisely the emotional rawness of Tremblay's work that attracted Van Burek. He was drawn by the "risky" elements, particularly the author's political agenda and the very grittiness of the language. Having grown up in the United States, observes Van Burek, he approached the French language, and French Canada and Québec, differently than the anglophone Canadians of his entourage. Ambivalent beneficiaries or victims of bilingual and bicultural politics and policies, their attitude towards Québec and particularly Québec French was frequently negative as a consequence of studying French in school. Seeing himself as more American than Canadian, and having learned, and learned to love, French in France,

Van Burek had a different viewpoint on the Québec cause. This is particularly evident in his remarks to Don Rubin on the negative image of *joual*: "I don't like the word 'joual.' It's like saying 'nigger-talk.' It seems degrading to me. It is simply a way that French is spoken in Quebec. Like American English. Tremblay's language isn't even 'joual,' it's more an evocation of the quality of the language...spoken by the people he writes about."[9] His mother being an Irish Catholic sensitive to religious strife in Northern Ireland, Van Burek also identified with Tremblay's forceful representation of the oppression of a minority group and the dominating influence of the Catholic Church.

In spite of his familiarity with and passion for Tremblay's message and language, however, the director-turned-translator readily admits that his first Tremblay translation in collaboration with Bill Glassco, *Forever Yours, Marie-Lou*, "took forever." Glassco, who spoke no French at the time, was a "stickler for precision." He aimed for a refined text and had a "good sense of what would work on stage." Van Burek, in contrast, was ruled more by "emotional impulse." As a result, the two directors made, in fact, a perfect team. As Van Burek notes, had he done it alone, the play would have been "all over the walls" whereas a solo effort by Glassco would have produced a "bloodless text." In the initial stages of the translation of *Forever Yours, Marie-Lou*, Van Burek telephoned Michel Tremblay, whom he had never met and with whom he had never spoken, to ask about producing an English version. Tremblay was in agreement, but suggested that the team first submit a partial draft of their translation. Zelda Heller, a Montréal arts critic, read the trial script and approved, so the show went on with Tremblay's consent. Indeed, he attended this and all subsequent Tarragon productions of his plays.

Les belles-soeurs: The Challenge of Translating *Joual*

After the resounding success of *Marie-Lou*, Van Burek was invited by Leon Major, then-director of Toronto Arts Productions, to collaborate on a production of *Les belles-soeurs*. Three weeks before opening night, Van Burek began working, once again with Bill Glassco, to produce a suitable script.

The problem of translating Tremblay's trademark *joual*[10] remains central to any discussion of Tremblay in Toronto, and this is particularly true, as Vivien Bosley points out, with respect to *Les belles-soeurs*. In addition to finding an English slang equivalent, the translation must convey the social, political, and religious connotations of *joual* and their repercussions throughout the play. For Bosley, it was a challenge Van Burek's text failed to meet:

As we look at a page of Tremblay in the original and in the translation what strikes us immediately is the fact that the English text looks like a drawing room version of the French....The elements that we recognize immediately in the French text as being very specific to a relatively small linguistic group fade away and the language is diluted as it is standardized into generic North American. What this also means is that the linguistic specifics that we have come to associate with valorization of Quebec's identity disappear, so that the overtones of nationalism which are inherent in the attempt to represent in a phonetic way the speech associations with the movement of emancipation from the linguistic hegemony of the French of France are completely lost.[11]

Bosley supports this critique with examples of the "dilution" of "sacres" (swear words based on religious imagery) and "anglicisms" (English structures in French), including an analysis of the following passage from the published text of Tremblay's play:

Germaine: C'est ça, méprise-moé! Bon, c'est correc, sors, fais à ta tête, c'est pas ben ben mêlant! Maudite vie! J'peux même pas avoir une p'tite joie y faut toujours que quelqu'un vienne toute gâter! Vas-y aux vues, Linda, vas-y, sors à soir, fait à ta tête! Maudit verrat de bâtard que chus donc tannée.[12]

Van Burek's published translation reads:

That's right. You've always said so. I'm dumb. Okay, Linda, go ahead. Do what you like. That's all you ever do anyway. It's nothing new. Christ. I can't have a bit of pleasure for myself. Someone's always got to spoil it for me. It's okay, Linda, if that's what you want. Go ahead. Go to your goddamn show![13]

Bosley identifies six assumptions revealed by linguistic markers in the original passage:

1. We know that the speakers belong to a specific and limited linguistic group.
2. We know that his group is situated in Quebec.
3. We know that the speakers are from a working class level of society.
4. We know that there is authorial identification with this group.
5. We know the *terminus a quo* of the composition of the piece.
6. We know that the language is being used as a metaphor for a state of oppression and that those who use it are being used as instruments to sound the call of assertion.[14]

In contrast, Bosley claims, the translation, unlike the original, gives no hint of the group's location, of the authorial attitude towards the group, or of the original's use of linguistic metaphor; nor does it indicate "the *terminus a quo* of the composition of the piece." Indeed, the only linguistic marker remaining is the one suggesting that "the speakers are from a working class level of society."

From discussions with Van Burek, Glassco was aware of the translation problem posed by *joual:* "He [Van Burek] warned me that it would be difficult to translate because of the *joual*, a peculiarly vibrant Québécois French which had become the language of the Quiet Revolution."[15] Van Burek himself readily admits that a great deal was lost in the translation, in the effort to convey the vulgarity of the original while at the same time achieving the musicality of language appropriate to a stage performance. Of importance as well was the need to reproduce Tremblay's tight, compact writing.

A study of the various versions of the translation, including an original handwritten manuscript, attests to the extent of these efforts and reveals the multiple changes and rewritings to which the script was subjected before arriving at the above passage. An earlier version reads,

> That's right, you've always said so. I'm dumb. Okay Linda, by all means go out. Do whatever you please. That's all you ever do anyway, it's nothing new. I can't have a bit of pleasure for myself. Someone's always got to spoil it for me. It's okay, Linda, if that's what you want, then go ahead. Go to your goddamned show![16]

Similarly, in other passages, one can trace Van Burek's attempts to render the grittiness of the original. Marie-Ange's claim "j'mange d'la marde, pis j'vas en manger toute ma vie" was first translated as "I live in pigsty" and finally "I live in shit."[17] Her lament, "j'les torche, mes enfants," first read "running after my kids, wiping their smelly noses" and then "wiping their asses all day long."[18] In the same passage, "J'veux pas crever dans la crasse pendant qu'elle, la grosse madame, a va se prélasser dans la soie et le velours," was first rendered as "I've got to live in garbage while her majesty struts around like a peacock," and, in the first published version, as "Believe me, I'm not gonna spend my life in this shit while Madame Fatso here goes swimming in velvet."[19] Pierrette, labelled in the published version as "nothing but a whore" was first described as having "turned out so badly," while "Goddamn Johnny" was previously "No good Johnny."[20]

The strategy behind these changes appears to be to liberally spice a fairly standard level of language with swear words and gallicisms as indications of the Québécois context. As Louise Ladouceur points out in an insightful article in which she analyzes the evolution and various revisions of the published text *Les belles-soeurs*, "Confrontés à l'extrême difficulté de traduire le joual en anglais..., les traducteurs ont adopté des stratégies qui ont eu pour effet de promouvoir auprès du public anglophone une représentation du texte de Tremblay qui fait appel à une langue anglaise de niveau courant, généreusement assaisonnée de sacres pour en rehausser la verdeur et de gallicismes chargés de révéler l'inhérente 'québécitude' du propos de la pièce."[21] However, even after what could be described as a reverse makeover to render the play less genteel, the dilution remains significant and can be held responsible, at least in part, for some loss of meaning. After noting "better off with a translation of Tremblay rather than no Tremblay at all," Bosley concludes, "What is lost in the translation, however, is the mirror effect noted by Alain Pontaut in his introduction to the Leméac edition of *LBS* [*Les belles-soeurs*]. For those of us who are foreigners to this world, the mirror becomes the optical lens of the scientific observer. We remain outside a world to which we do not possess the linguistic passport; for, as Tremblay himself said: *LBS* is unthinkable except in joual!"[22]

The translation was unthinkable, perhaps, but mercifully, thanks to Van Burek, not impossible and certainly not unsatisfactory in terms of critical response and box office sales. The production of Van Burek's translation of *Les belles-soeurs* by the St. Lawrence Centre Repertory Theatre Company (March 31–April 28, 1973) was heralded as a "milestone play, a high point for the St. Lawrence Centre."[23] Theatre critic Urjo Kareda urged the crowds lined up at *Move over Mrs. Markham*, "a shoddy British import," to cross the physical and cultural intersection and "go next door" to see the "10,000 times more entertaining Tremblay play."[24]

However, even in his enthusiasm, the same critic questioned the Toronto audience's ability to "jump across the (cultural) intersection." *Globe and Mail* critic H. Whittaker referred as well to "a kind of mute edged condescension indelibly WASP,"[25] while David McCaughna of the *Toronto Citizen* observed that it was not clear whether the audience who "stood and cheered at the end of the play did so to show their praise for the production or their respect for the national anthem with which it ends."[26] Noting that the audience's support was ambiguous, he confirmed Kareda's concern that the political angle could be lost in the translation. Myron Galloway, who described the Toronto production as a "massacre," was even more adamant, claiming, like Bosley, that "the play has nothing to say if the French-Canadian flavour is missing."[27] The St. Lawrence Centre production, he concluded in the review, "had nothing more to do with

Montreal than it [did] with Hong Kong," and the play "in no way came across."

Hosanna: Translation and Québec Politics

Similarly, due in part to a translation that diluted its "québécitude,'" the political message central to *Hosanna* may have been largely lost on the Toronto audience, although the play was wildly successful.[28] Described by Whittaker as a "heart-pounding tour de force"[29] and by Kareda as a "shimmering production,"[30] it was Tarragon Theatre's production of *Hosanna* that earned Tremblay his reputation as "the darling of the critics and the chosen one of the Toronto theatre scene."[31] A resounding success when it first opened at the Tarragon, *Hosanna* continued to draw Toronto crowds to three subsequent productions, at the Global Village Theatre (September 6–October 4, 1974), Toronto Workshop Productions (January 13–February 14, 1977) and the NDWT Theatre (March 11–22, 1980). It also ran at the Bijou Theatre on Broadway. Undoubtedly "Tremblay's most successful play to date,"[32] *Hosanna* has been considered "one of the most popular plays ever to be written by a Canadian playwright."[33] Nonetheless, it is arguable whether the English-language theatre audience was flocking to see the same *Hosanna* that had delighted the playwright's fellow *Montréalais* the previous year at the Théâtre de Quat'Sous (from May 10, 1973).

Tremblay himself claimed that the "folkloric aspect of the language" was missing and that his plays will never be as good in English as in French.[34] When asked for his opinion of the English translations of Tremblay, André Brassard, the author's friend and colleague, replied, "Fatal. With a text whose main asset is the language, you lose at least a third of it."[35] Theatre critics described the translation as a "repetition of the same four letter words,"[36] as "too awkward and poetic,"[37] even "too shrill."[38] However, decidedly more important than the flow of English version was its apparent lack of attention to the political and social connotation of Tremblay's work.

Like all of Tremblay's plays, *Hosanna* contains a political message. As Tremblay himself has stated,

> I do not mean that they [the main characters, Hosanna and Cuirette] are Québec or symbols or images of Québec. But their problems with the wider society are political problems. Because they are the fringe group in society, this society in a way hates them. But they want to be happy and they want to be somebody. Hosanna is a man who always wanted to be Elizabeth Taylor in *Cleopatra*. In other words, this

Québécois always wanted to be an English actress in an American movie about an Egyptian myth in a movie shot in Spain. In a way, that is a typically Québec problem. For the past 300 years we were taught that we were not a people, so we are dreaming about somebody else instead of ourselves. So *Hosanna* is a political play.[39]

As demonstrated by the critics' comments, this political aspect was largely missed by the Toronto audience. The play was seen as an exploration of the "poetics of love,"[40] a study of "the pain of deception and humiliation and the loss of dreams,"[41] "a sensitive delineation of a homosexual relationship,"[42] or "a classic study of homosexual revenge"[43] by "the Canadian theatre's most compassionate poet of individual isolation."[44] According to Whittaker, Tremblay was talking about "deceptions and the need for them, and the loss of them and comfort in misery. About any life, in fact."[45] Those critics who did make reference to the political question downplayed the possibility, claiming that such an allegory was "far-fetched"[46] or that "there was no inkling of such an idea to be found in the play no matter how hard one looked for signs."[47] Even more significantly, McCaughna, one of the first to acknowledge the political implications of *Les Belles-soeurs*, observed that although Tremblay is "a very political writer and all of his plays have dealt in one way or another with the condition of Québec society, it does not hit home that this is a play which has a great deal to do with Québec."[48]

Undoubtedly, the loss of political meaning is partially due to the "dilution" of "joual" to "drawing-room," or perhaps more accurately, poolroom English. The translation contains many four-letter words as well as slang expressions, such as "we all got plastered,"[49] but it fails to compensate for anglicisms. Such words as "cheap," which Tremblay used in English in the original, with, as Bosley points out, certain political connotations, were simply left as "cheap." The "sacres" often used in the published version were given an approximate, and frequently diluted, English equivalent: "Maudit que t'es bête" published as "Sacrement are you stupid" was read as "Christ are you stupid."[50]

Furthermore, as the following examples illustrate, in the prompt script, as opposed to the published translation, structures reminiscent of the French were eliminated. In some cases, vocabulary was changed:

> Original: Maudite kétaine! Maudite kétaine! Maudite kétaine!
> Published translation: Stupid bitch! Cheap stupid bitch! Stupide, stupide stupide.
> Prompt script: Stupid bitch. Cheap stupid bitch! Stupid bitch.[51]

In other cases, syntax as well as word choice was anglicized:

> Original: Ah oui! Chus la coiffeuse la plus drôle en ville.
> Published translation : Ah oui...me, I'm the funniest hairdresser in town.
> Prompt script: Oh sure. I'm the funniest hairdresser in town.[52]
> Original: Ah! Pis, j'ai pas le coeur à ça ce soir...Les pauses voluptueuses et provocantes, ça s'ra pour une autre fois. Aie...
> Published translation: Me, I'm not up to it tonight. "Les pauses voluptueuses et provocantes" will have to wait. Aie...
> Prompt script: Oh no, tonight I'm just not up to it. The voluptuous, provocative pauses will have to wait.[53]

It should be noted, however, that Richard Monette, who played Hosanna, adopted a heavy French-Canadian accent perhaps to compensate for this dilution. Described as both "ludicrous" and "helpful and endearing,"[54] it was also judged to be "distracting."[55] Furthermore, Hosanna's partner, Cuirette, played by Richard Donat, did not adopt an accent, thus possibly introducing another conflict, English (dominant/male) versus French (passive/female) into their relationship.

Despite, or perhaps because of the dilution of Québec slang, which to an informed, competent audience carries political connotations, Tremblay nonetheless flourished on the Toronto stage in translation. Indeed, he conquered the very bastions of Canadian English-language theatre: in 1991, *Les Belles Soeurs* was staged at Stratford. From the first production of *Forever Yours, Marie-Lou* (Tarragon Theatre, November 14–December 10, 1972) to the end of *Les belles-soeurs* cycle, including, along the way, *Bonjour là Bonjour* (Tarragon Theatre, February 1–March 16, 1975), *Sainte-Carmen of the Main* (Tarragon Theatre January 11–February 26, 1978), *La Duchesse de Langeais* (Tarragon Theatre, May 22–June 28, 1980), and *The Impromptu of Outremont* (Tarragon Theatre, May 22–June 28, 1980), from "landmark"[56] productions such as *Hosanna* to the somewhat ignored like *Surprise! Surprise!* (Toronto Arts Productions, St. Lawrence Centre, October 22–November 8, 1975), Van Burek's translations of Tremblay, however flawed, continued to draw crowds and critical attention, earning Tremblay the reputation of "Toronto's favourite Canadian playwright."[57]

New Québec Voices

The 1980s saw the arrival of new Québec voices on the Toronto stage. Robert Lepage, Gilles Maheu, René-Daniel Dubois, Normand Chaurette, and Jovette Marchessault introduced the audience to different directions in Québec theatre. As Alain Filewood notes, "This was the period when English Canadians discovered the new wave of imagistic performances in Québec; at the same time, québécois audiences discovered the audience beyond their borders."[58] In addition to experimenting with new forms of theatre resulting from the integration of various media such as dance and video into performance, Québec playwrights steered theatre in entirely new directions. As Diane Pavlovic states, the nationalist issue so central to Tremblay's earlier works was replaced by a greatly diversified response to broader, universal questions of the human condition: "Dans les années 1970, le projet théâtral coïncidait avec un projet de société: les artistes semblaient investis d'une mission et servaient volontiers la cause du nationalisme, de l'indépendance....Avec la fin des grandes causes, la fonction proprement politique du théâtre a connu un recul certain...N'étant plus réunies dans un même projet, les démarches artistiques sont éparpillées et proposent, chacune de son côté, des métaphores plus générales sur la condition humaine."[59]

The popularity of Québec's new voices, whose path to Toronto, it could be argued, had been paved by Tremblay, did not diminish Torontonians' loyalty to old favourites: Michel Tremblay, thanks to Van Burek's translations, once again wooed and won the Toronto audience with *Albertine in Five Times* (Tarragon Theatre April 9–May 11, 1985). Significantly, it was a "new style play, symptomatic of the Québec writer's increased introspection."[60] The play earned mixed reviews, being described as both "pure theatrical magic,"[61] "soporific,"[62] and "hard to grasp."[63] Seeking to "speak to all women in all times of their lives," this play introduced Toronto to a far less political Tremblay. The playwright himself acknowledged his change of direction stating "instead of judging society I was beginning to ask myself questions."[64]

It is Van Burek's favourite play, it is worth noting, and the one that, judging by a study of the various versions, presented the fewest translation difficulties. There remains a discrepancy between the decidedly countrified language of the original and the somewhat more refined register of the translation. However, the loss is considerably less than in earlier translations, primarily because of the very absence in the original of the politicized language so central to *Les belles-soeurs*, for example. Of the six markers identified by Bosley with respect to the latter play, only two, the geographical and social identity of the speakers, are important in *Albertine*. Consequently the loss through translation of the politically charged *joual*, at the core of the previous productions, is not an issue.

Similarly, Tremblay and Van Burek's subsequent production and critical success, *The Real World* (Tarragon Theatre, May 15–June 26, 1988) was acclaimed as "a gripping look at parallel realities"[65] by "a master craftsman now exploring an intensely personal phase in his artistic career,"[66] in short, "a far cry" from his earlier, more political productions.[67] Critical response to revivals of *Bonjour là, Bonjour* (Toronto Centre Stage, November 25–December 20, 1986) and *Hosanna* (Tarragon Theatre, May 17–June 28, 1987), both considered classics, revealed a greater appreciation for and understanding of his earlier work.

Controversial and comparatively unsuccessful when it first opened, *Bonjour là, Bonjour* was welcomed in the 1986 revival as a "highlight."[68] One critic praised it as a "modest masterpiece."[69] Overcoming their "sensitivity" to the incest issue on which the first "production's failure had been blamed," as Dancy observes,[70] theatregoers had "realized in spite of their Toronto reserve that they had been given something unexpectedly fine."[71] *Hosanna*'s political message, no longer such a sensitive point in post-referendum Canada, was now more readily acknowledged by the theatre community. Richard Monette, the star of the previous production, now turned director, noted, "The central metaphor is about being yourself, with the political implication that Québec should be what she is."[72] Toronto's understanding of Tremblay, who admitted that he felt before that he was being treated as "a nice neighbour," had clearly evolved.

New Directions

The 1990s brought an increasingly varied selection of Québec theatre to Toronto, including plays by Daniel Danis and Carole Frechette, and the public embarked on an entirely new enthusiasm for Robert Lepage. Nonetheless, Van Burek continued to translate and produce Tremblay, from the comparatively unsuccessful *Counter Service* (Tarragon Theatre, April 8–30, 1995) to the very popular *Marcel Pursued by the Hounds* (Pleiades and Factory Theatre, March 1997).

While both Tremblay and Van Burek have since moved into different areas, it is important to celebrate over a quarter century of Tremblay in Toronto. Much of the credit that Tremblay made it to, and at, the Tarragon, and elsewhere in English Canada, is due to Van Burek's knowledge of Québec theatre, his recognition of the value and possibility of bringing it to Toronto, and his diligent translations and theatrical direction. The significance of the translation issues raised and, as this study has endeavoured to show, the difficulties in meeting these challenges, should also be acknowledged. At the same time, over the years, the Toronto theatre-going public's appreciation of Tremblay clearly evolved.[73] Thanks to Van Burek's translations, the city found itself better prepared to understand new, complex, and diverse theatre from Québec.

In his professional biographical statement, Van Burek lists "translator" as the third of several occupations. Self-avowedly a director and teacher of theatre first, he, like many other translators who do not enjoy the "luxury of monoprofessionalism,"[74] has nonetheless made a significant contribution to literary translation in Canada. While translating Tremblay was clearly a means to an end, Van Burek brought to his translations, and hence to the English Canadian theatre audience, a sensitivity to, and awareness of, Tremblay and Québec theatre. Tremblay has himself recognized that his plays would necessarily take on new and different meanings outside Québec:

> When a play is presented in translation, the audience doesn't have the same relationship to the way the characters speak, to the language of the work. That's inevitable. I always say that I hope and assume that Tchekov was "better" in Russian. The key to good translations seems to lie with the translator's ability to capture the music and the rhythms of spoken language."[75]

Thus, while critics can, and indeed have, identified significant concerns, Van Burek's ability to capture "the music and rhythms of spoken language" has made Tremblay "the darling" of the Toronto theatre audience for almost three decades and has earned the translator a place of merit in the history of literary translation in Canada.

NOTES

1 It is important to recognize that, while Glassco's name is always included, the translations are primarily Van Burek's work. Bill Glassco comes from the Ontario branch of the same family as John Glassco, also profiled in this book, although the family link is quite removed.
2 Interviews with the author Dec. 27, 2000 and Mar. 15, 2001. All subsequent quotations are based on these interviews. The author wishes to acknowledge with sincere gratitude the assistance of John Van Burek as well as of Urjo Kareda, deceased and greatly missed. Thanks are due as well to the obliging staff of the MacDonald Stewart Room at the McLaughlin Library, University of Guelph.
3 Jack Karr, "Showplace," *Toronto Star*, Jan. 9, 1951. Sections of this discussion appeared previously in Jane Koustas, "From 'Awesome' to 'Homespun': Translated Quebec Theatre in Toronto," in *Essays on Modern Quebec Theatre*, ed. J.I. Donohue Jr. and J.M. Weiss (Lansing, MI: Michigan State University Press), pp. 81–109.
4 J. Karr, "Showplace."

5   H. Whittaker, "Showbusiness," *Globe and Mail*, Jan. 9, 1951.
6   H. Whittaker, "Les Belles-soeurs a milestone play," *Globe and Mail*, Mar. 4, 1973.
7   Ed Bean, "Hosanna!, Hosanna," *Varsity*, Sept. 20, 1974.
8   Paula Dancy, "Tremblay at the Tarragon 1972–1981," (MA thesis, University of Guelph, 1985), abstract.
9   Don Rubin, "John Van Burek: Tremblay in Translation," *Canadian Theatre Review*, no. 24 (1979) p. 45.
10 See David Homel and Sherry Simon, eds. *Mapping Literature*. Montréal: Véhicule Press, 1988, p. 83–86.
11 Vivien Bosley, "Diluting the Mixture," *TTR: Traduction, terminologie, rédaction* 1, no. 1 (1988): 140–41.
12 Michel Tremblay, *Les belles-soeurs* (Montréal: Leméac, 1972), p. 17.
13 Michel Tremblay, *Les Belles Soeurs*, trans. John Van Burek and Bill Glassco (Vancouver: Talonbooks, 1974), p. 9.
14 Bosley, "Diluting the Mixture," p. 141–42.
15 Bill Glassco, "Michel Tremblay: A Unique Vision," *Toronto Daily Star*, Jan. 16, 1978.
16 Michel Tremblay, *Les Belles Soeurs*. Trans. J. Van Burek and B. Glassco. Draft, Tarragon Theatre Archives, XZIMSA565008 Archival and Special Collections, McLaughlin Library, University of Guelph, Guelph, ON, p. 3.
17 Tremblay, *Les belles-soeurs*, p. 21.
18 Tremblay, *Les Belles Soeurs*, trans. John Van Burek and Bill Glassco, p. 14.
19 Tremblay, *Les belles-soeurs*, p. 22; Michel Tremblay, "Les Belles Soeurs," draft, Tarragon Theatre Archives, XZIMSA565008, Archival and Special Collections, McLaughlin Library, University of Guelph, p. 12; Tremblay, *Les Belles Soeurs*, trans. John Van Burek and Bill Glassco, p. 14.
20 Tremblay, *Les Belles Soeurs*, trans. John Van Burek and Bill Glassco, p. 68; Tremblay, "Les Belles Soeurs," draft, p. 22; Tremblay, *Les Belles Soeurs*, trans. John Van Burek and Bill Glassco, p. 69; Tremblay, "Les Belles Soeurs," draft, p. 69.
21 Louise Ladouceur, "Canada's Michel Tremblay: Des *Belles Soeurs* à *From the Pleasure of Seeing Her Again*," *TTR: Traduction, terminologie, rédaction* 15, no. 1 (2002), p. 138.
22 Bosley, "Diluting the Mixture," p. 145.
23 Whittaker, "Les Belles-soeurs a milestone play."
24 Urjo Kareda, "O'Keefe Crowd should go next door," *Toronto Star*, April 7, 1973.
25 Whittaker, "Les Belles-soeurs a milestone play."
26 David McCaughna, "Les Belles Soeurs," *Toronto Citizen*, Apr. 20, 1973.
27 Myron Gallaway, "Tremblay in English a Disaster," *Montreal Star*, Apr. 4, 1973.
28 Sections of this discussion appeared in Jane Koustas, "*Hosanna* in Toronto: Tour de force or Détour de traduction?" *TTR: Traduction, terminologie, rédaction* 1, no. 4 (1989), pp. 129–39.

29 H. Whittaker, "Hosanna a heart pounding tour de force," *Globe and Mail*, May 16, 1974.
30 Urjo Kareda, "Shimmering Production at Tarragon Theatre," *Toronto Daily Star*, May 16, 1974.
31 Bean, "Hosanna! Hosanna!"
32 D. McCaughna, "Tremblay Scores Again," *Motion*, July/Aug. 1974.
33 D. Ossea, "Hosanna," *Varsity*, 2 Jan. 2, 1977.
34 Renate Usmiani, "Where to Begin the Accusation," *Canadian Theatre Review*, no. 24 (fall 1979), p. 34.
35 Andre Brassard, "Discovering the Nuance," interview with R. Usmani, *Canadian Theatre Review*, no. 24 (fall 1979), p. 41.
36 A. Ashley, "Strong acting in weak Tremblay play," *Ottawa Citizen*, Oct. 7, 1974.
37 McCaughna, "Tremblay Scores Again."
38 Jack Kapica, " Hosanna Triumphs again," *Globe and Mail*, Jan. 14, 1977.
39 "Michel Tremblay," interviewed by Geraldine Anthony in *Stage Voices: Twelve Canadian Playwrights Talk about Their Lives and Work*, ed. G. Anthony (Toronto: Doubleday, 1978), p. 283.
40 Agnes Kruchio, "Review of Hosanna," *Excalibur*, Sept. 19, 1974.
41 Kareda, "Shimmering Production."
42 McCaughna, "Tremblay Scores Again."
43 G. Anthony, "Hosanna's magic is still there," *The Toronto Sun*, Sept. 13, 1974.
44 Urjo Kareda, "O'Keefe Crowd."
45 Whittaker, "Hosanna."
46 Charles Pope, "In Review," *Scene Changes*, January 1977.
47 John Hebert, "Hosanna," *Onion*, Feb. 15, 1977.
48 McCaughna, "Tremblay Scores Again."
49 Michel Tremblay, *Hosanna*, revised reading script, Tarragon Theatre Archives, XZIMASA181076, McLaughlin Library, University of Guelph, 1974, p. 57.
50 Michel Tremblay, *Hosanna* (Montréal: Leméac, 1973), p. 28; Michel Tremblay, *Hosanna*, trans. John Van Burek and Bill Glassco (Vancouver: Talonbooks, 1974), p. 35; Tremblay, *Hosanna*, revised reading script, p. 25.
51 Tremblay, *Hosanna*, p. 13; Tremblay, *Hosanna*, trans. John Van Burek and Bill Glassco, p. 10; Tremblay, *Hosanna*, revised reading script, p. 3.
52 Tremblay, *Hosanna*, p. 18; Tremblay, *Hosanna*, trans. John Van Burek and Bill Glassco, p. 18; Tremblay, *Hosanna*, revised reading script, p. 11.
53 Tremblay, *Hosanna*, p. 24; Tremblay, *Hosanna*, trans. John Van Burek and Bill Glassco, p. 29; Tremblay, *Hosanna*, revised reading script, p. 20.
54 McCaughna, "Tremblay Scores Again."
55 Myron Galloway, "Tremblay's Hosanna sold out in Toronto," *Montreal Gazette*, Jan. 11, 1974.
56 Gina Mallet, "Hosannas in order for actor Monette," *Toronto Star*, Jan. 14, 1977.
57 Urjo Kareda, "Theatre Plus makes a minus of Tremblay," *Toronto Star*, June 5, 1975.

58 Alain Filewood, "Diversity in Deficits: Theatre in Canada 1986–1988," in *Canada on Stage* (Toronto: Professional Association of Canadian Theatres Communication Centre, 1991), p. xv.
59 Diane Pavlovic and Lorraine Camerlain, "Le Québec des années 1980s: Éclecisme et exotisme," in *Canada on Stage* (Toronto: Professional Association of Canadian Theatres Communication Centre, 1991), p. xxxii.
60 Ray Conologue, "Poem-like Albertine is sophomoric in expression," *Globe and Mail*, Apr. 10, 1985.
61 Robert Crew, "New Tremblay play awesome and blessed with superb cast," *Toronto Star*, Apr. 10, 1985.
62 Ray Conologue, "Poem-like Albertine."
63 Ray Conologue, "Albertine's choral poetry hard to grasp," *Globe and Mail*, May 20, 1985.
64 Quoted in Robert Crew, "The Real World of Michel Tremblay," *Toronto Star*, May 31, 1988.
65 Ray Conologue, "A Gripping look at parallel realities," *Globe and Mail*, Apr. 26, 1988.
66 Robert Crew, "Michel Tremblay's new play a virtuoso piece of writing," *Toronto Star*, May 25, 1988.
67 Crew, "The Real World of Michel Tremblay."
68 Robert Crew, "Revival a highlight of the theatre season," *Toronto Star*, March 11, 1986.
69 Ray Conologue, "Modest masterpiece," *Globe and Mail*, Nov. 28, 1986.
70 Dancy, "Tremblay at the Tarragon," p. 93.
71 Conologue, "Modest masterpiece."
72 Robert Crew, "Hosanna on high to the queen," *Toronto Star*, May 27, 1987.
73 Suzanne Dansereau, review of *The Dragon's Trilogy*, *La Presse*, Nov. 5, 1995.
74 As Louise Ladouceur observes, the success of Linda Gaboriau's translation of *For the Pleasure of Seeing Her Again* suggests an evolution in both the Toronto audience's reception of Tremblay and the strategies used to translate his work. Ladouceur concludes, "C'est donc moins pour répondre aux besoins d'une dramaturgie naissante que pour célébrer un auteur devenu canonique qu'on traduit et produit cette pièce, dont on ne manque pas de souligner son «universal appeal». Plutôt que d'insister sur l'altérité d'une œuvre dont le propos universel mais peu flatteur est censé représenter une réalité autre que celle du public visé, comme c'était le cas pour *Les Belles-Sœurs* vingt-cinq ans plus tôt, on l'invite ici à se reconnaître dans une des voix les plus célébrées d'un répertoire canadien." Ladouceur, "Canada's Michel Tremblay," p. 150.
75 Michel Tremblay, "Interview: Michel Tremblay," interview by Linda Gaboriau, *Théâtre Québec* 8, no. 1 (spring 1992).

BIBLIOGRAPHY

I. Primary Sources
Literary Translations

Tremblay, Michel. *Forever Yours, Marie-Lou.* Trans. J. Van Burek and B. Glassco. Tarragon Theatre, Toronto, 1972. Vancouver: Talonbooks, 1975; rev. ed., 1994. Translation of *À toi pour toujours ta Marie-Lou.* Montréal: Leméac, 1972.

———. *Les Belles Sœurs.* Trans. J. Van Burek and B. Glassco. Draft, Tarragon Theatre Archives. XZIMSA565008. Archival and Special Collections, McLaughlin Library, University of Guelph, Guelph, ON. St. Lawrence Centre Repertory Theatre, Toronto, 1973. Vancouver: Talonbooks, 1974; rev. ed., 1992. Translation of *Les belles-soeurs.* Montréal: Leméac, 1972.

———. *Hosanna.* Trans. J. Van Burek and B. Glassco. Revised Reading Script. Tarragon Theatre Archives, XZIMASA181076. McLaughlin Library, University of Guelph, 1974. Tarragon Theatre, Toronto, 1974, 1987. Vancouver: Talonbooks, 1974; rev. ed., 1991. Translation of *Hosanna.* In *Hosanna* suivi de *La Duchesse de Langeais.* Montréal: Leméac, 1973.

———. *Bonjour là, Bonjour,* Trans. J. Van Burek and B. Glassco. Tarragon Theatre, Toronto, 1975. Toronto Centre Stage, 1986. Talonbooks, 1975; rev. ed., 1988. Translation of *Bonjour là, bonjour.* Montréal: Leméac, 1974.

———. *Surprise! Surprise!* Trans. J. Van Burek and B. Glassco. St. Lawrence Centre Repertory Theatre, Toronto, 1975; Canadian Stage, 1995. Vancouver: Talonbooks, 1975; rev. ed., *La Duchesse de Langeais and Other Plays.* Vancouver: Talonbooks, 1976. Translation of *Surprise, Surprise.* Montréal: Leméac, 1977.

———. *Trois Petits Tours* (*Berthe, Johnny Mangano and His Astonishing Dogs,* and *Gloria Star*) Trans. J. Van Burek and B. Glassco. In *La Duchesse de Langeais and Other Plays.* Vancouver: Talonbooks, 1976. 31–125. Translation of *Trois Petits Tours.* Montréal: Leméac, 1971.

———. *La Duchesse de Langeais.* Trans. J. Van Burek and B. Glassco. Black Cat Cabaret, Toronto, 1976; Tarragon, Toronto, 1980. *La Duchesse de Langeais and Other Plays.* Vancouver: Talonbooks, 1976. 7–30. Translation of *La Duchesse de Langeais.* In *Hosanna* suivi de *La Duchesse de Langeais.* Montréal: Leméac, 1973.

———. *Sainte-Carmen of the Main.* Trans. J. Van Burek and B. Glassco. Tarragon Theatre, Toronto, 1978. Vancouver: Talonbooks, 1981. Translation of *Sainte-Carmen de la Main.* Montréal: Leméac, 1976.

———. *Damnée Manon, Sacrée Sandra.* Trans. J. Van Burek and B. Glassco. Arts Club Theatre, Vancouver, 1979. Vancouver: Talonbooks, 1981. Translation of *Damnée Manon, Sacrée Sandra.* In *Damnée Manon, Sacrée Sandra* suivi de *Surprise, surprise.* Montréal: Leméac, 1977.

———. *The Impromptu of Outremont.* Trans. J. Van Burek and B. Glassco. Arts Club Theatre, Vancouver, 1980. Vancouver: Talonbooks, 1981. Translation of *L'impromptu d'Outremont.* Montréal: Leméac, 1980.

———. *Albertine in Five Times*. Trans. J. Van Burek and B. Glassco. Tarragon Theatre, Toronto, 1985. Vancouver: Talonbooks, 1986. Translation of *Albertine en cinq temps*. Montréal: Leméac, 1984.

———. *The Real World?* Trans. J. Van Burek and B. Glassco. Tarragon Theatre, Toronto, 1988. Vancouver Talonbooks, 1988. Translation of *Le vrai monde?* Montréal: Leméac, 1987.

———. *La Maison Suspendue*. Trans. J. Van Burek and B. Glassco. Canadian Stage Company, Toronto, 1990. Vancouver: Talonbooks, 1991. Translation of *La Maison suspendue*. Montréal: Leméac, 1990.

———. *Counter Service*. Trans. J. Van Burek and B. Glassco. Tarragon Theatre, Toronto, 1995. Translation of *En pièces detachées*. Montréal: Leméac, 1994.

———. *Marcel Pursued by the Hounds*. Trans. J. Van Burek and B. Glassco. Pleiades Theatre and Factory Theatre, 1997. Vancouver: Talonbooks, 1996. Translation of *Marcel poursuivi par les chiens*. Montréal: Leméac, 1992.

———. *Le gars de Québec*. Trans. J. Van Burek and B. Glassco. Tarragon, Toronto, 1998. Translation of *Le gars de Québec*. Montréal: Leméac, 1985.

Other (Published) Translations by John Van Burek
Lebeau, Suzanne. *A Tale of Day and Night*. Trans. John Van Burek. Toronto: Playwrights Union of Canada, 2000. Translation of *Conte du jour et de la nuit*. Montréal: Leméac, 1991.

II. Secondary Sources
Reviews
Anthony, Geraldine. "Hosanna's magic is still there," *Toronto Sun*, Sept. 13, 1974.
Ashley, A. "Strong acting in weak Tremblay play," *Ottawa Citizen*, Oct. 7, 1974.
Bean, Ed. "Hosanna!, Hosanna!," *Varsity*, Sept. 20, 1974.
Conologue, Ray. "Poem-like Albertine is sophomoric in expression," *Globe and Mail*, Apr. 10, 1985.
———. "Albertine's choral poetry hard to grasp," *Globe and Mail*, May 20, 1985.
———. "Modest masterpiece," *Globe and Mail*, Nov. 28, 1986.
———. "A Gripping look at parallel realities," *Globe and Mail*, May 26, 1988.
Crew, Robert. "New Tremblay play awesome and blessed with superb cast," *Toronto Star*, Apr. 10, 1985.
———. "Revival a highlight of the theatre season," *Toronto Star*, Mar. 11, 1986.
———. "Hosanna on high to the queen," *Toronto Star*, May 27, 1987.
———. "Michel Tremblay's new play a virtuoso piece of writing," *Toronto Star*, May 25, 1988.
———. The Real World of Michel Tremblay," *Toronto Star*, May 31, 1988.
Dansereau, Suzanne. Review of *The Dragon's Trilogy*, *La Presse*, Nov. 5, 1995.
Gallaway, Myron. "Tremblay in English a Disaster," *Montreal Star*, Apr. 4, 1973.
———. "Tremblay's Hosanna sold out in Toronto," *Montreal Gazette*, June 11, 1974.
Glassco, Bill. "Michel Tremblay: A Unique Vision," *Toronto Daily Star*, Jan. 16, 1973.

Hebert, John. "Hosanna," *Onion*, Feb. 15, 1977.
Kapica, Jack. "Hosanna Triumphs again," *Globe and Mail*, Jan. 14, 1977.
Kareda, Urjo. "O'Keefe Crowd should go next door," *Toronto Star*, April 7, 1973.
———. "Shimmering Production at Tarragon Theatre," *Toronto Daily Star*, May 16, 1974.
———. "Theatre Plus makes a minus of Tremblay," *Toronto Star*, June 5, 1975.
Karr, J. "Showplace," *Toronto Star*, Jan. 9, 1951.
Kruchio, Agnes. *Excalibur*, Sept. 19, 1974.
Mallet, Gina. *Toronto Star*, Jan. 14, 1977.
McCaughna, David. *Toronto Citizen*, Apr. 20, 1973.
———. *Motion*, July/Aug. 1974.
Ossea, D. *Varsity*, Jan. 2, 1977.
Pope, Charles. *Scene Changes*, January 1977.
Whittaker, H. "Showbusiness," *Globe and Mail*, Jan. 9, 1951.
———. Review of *Forever Yours, Marie-Lou*. *Globe and Mail*, Mar. 4, 1972.
———. "Les Belles-soeurs a milestone play," *Globe and Mail*, Mar. 4, 1973.
———. *Globe and Mail*, May 15, 1974.
———. *Globe and Mail*, May 16, 1974.

General Reference Works

Anthony, Geraldine, ed. *Stage Voices: Twelve Canadian Playwrights Talk about Their Lives and Work*. Toronto: Doubleday, 1978. 275–90.
Bosley, Vivien. "Diluting the Mixture: Translating Tremblay's *Les belles-soeurs*," *TTR: Traduction, terminologie, rédaction* 1, no. 1 (1988): 139–45.
Brassard, André. "Discovering the Nuance." Interview with Renate Usmiani in *Canadian Theatre Review*, no. 24 (1979): 38–41.
Dancy, Paula. "Tremblay at the Tarragon 1972–1981: The Plays, the Productions and the Critics." MA thesis, University of Guelph, 1985.
Filewood, Alain. "Diversity in Deficits: Theatre in Canada 1986–1988." In *Canada on Stage*. Toronto: Professional Association of Canadian Theatres Communication Centre, 1991. xi–xxi.
Homel, David, and Sherry Simon, eds. *Mapping Literature*. Montreal: Véhicule Press, 1988.
Koustas, Jane. "*Hosanna* in Toronto: Tour de force or Détour de traduction?" *TTR: Traduction, terminilogie, rédaction* 1, no. 4 (1989): 129–39.
———. "From 'Awesome' to 'Homespun': Translated Quebec Theatre in Toronto." *Essays on Modern Quebec Theatre*, ed. J.I. Donohue Jr. and J.M. Weiss. Lansing, MI: Michigan University Press, 1995. 81–109.
Ladouceur, Louise. "From Other Tongue to Mother Tongue in the Drama of Quebec and Canada." In *Changing the Terms: Translating in the Postcolonial Era*, ed. Sherry Simon and Paul St-Pierre. Ottawa: University of Ottawa Press, 2000. 207–26.
———. "Canada's Michel Tremblay: des *Belles Soeurs* à *From the Pleasure of Seeing Her Again*." *TTR: Traduction, terminologie, rédaction* 15, no. 1 (2002): 131–55.

Pavlovic, Diane, and Lorraine Camerlain. "Le Québec des années 1980: Éclectisme et exotisme." *Canada on Stage*. Toronto: PACTS Communication Centre, 1991. xxxi–vx.
Rubin, Don. "John Van Burek: Tremblay in Translation." *Canadian Theatre Review*, no. 24 (1979): 42–46.
Tremblay, Michel. *Les belles-sœurs*. Montreal: Leméac, 1972.
———. *Hosanna* suivi de *La Duchesse de Langeais*. Montreal: Leméac, 1973.
———. "Interview: Michel Tremblay." Interview by Linda Gaboriau. *Théâtre Québec* 8, no. 1 (Spring 1992): 83–90.
Usmiani, Renate. "Tremblay Opus: Unity in Diversity." *Canadian Theatre Review*, no. 24 (fall 1979): 12–25.
———. "Where to Begin the Accusation." *Canadian Theatre Review*, no. 24 (fall 1979): 26–38.

12

Linda Gaboriau
Playing with Performance

ROBERT WALLACE

In an interview published in a special issue of *Canadian Theatre Review* devoted to theatre and translation, Linda Gaboriau observes that many Canadians are surprised to learn that the mother of Michel Tremblay, the "quintessentially Québécois playwright," was "part Indian, and that *her* mother grew up in Saskatchewan."[1] Many Canadians might also be surprised to learn that Gaboriau herself, a prolific translator who has built an enviable reputation for translating Québécois plays into English, was born and raised in the United States.

What she discovered in Québec, when she moved to Montréal from Boston in 1963 to study French at McGill University, would change her life and provide Québécois playwrights with one of their most eloquent advocates. Today, with more than sixty translations to her credit, Gaboriau ranks as the pre-eminent translator of Québécois drama into English. Her translations have won three Chalmers Awards for drama[2] and three Dora Mavor Moore Awards for best new play produced in Toronto;[3] she has been nominated four times for the Governor General's Literary Award for Translation.⁴ Winning this last award in 1996 for her translation of Daniel Danis's *Stone and Ashes*, Gaboriau distinguished herself as the first translator to receive the honour for translating a play.

Gaboriau's decision to attend McGill during the 1960s was primarily practical: it provided her with easy access to French-speaking cultures, a bonus she found attractive. She was also "quite disillusioned about the country [she] was born in"; American involvement in the Vietnam War was "flat out" at the time, "so that sense of all of the ugly things about America was very real." Disappointed with American foreign and domestic policies, disenchanted, in particular, with one of its "main myths...the notion of the melting pot," she avidly embraced life in Montreal, happy "to find this incredible culture that was totally intact and totally distinct."⁵

Gaboriau's interest in Québécois culture quickly led her to appreciate francophone theatre, which had begun a period of remarkable growth and change during the mid-1960s. Although this experience deepened her estimation of Québec's "incredibly vibrant culture," it did not inspire her to pursue translation as a vocation. In fact, she enrolled in only one translation course at McGill, favouring French literature instead. Setting her sights on a career in journalism, Gaboriau hoped to share what she perceived as the "great cultural and political significance" of Québec with the rest of North America.⁶

After graduating from McGill in 1967, Gaboriau worked for a year and a half as a theatre critic for the *Gazette*, Montréal's English-language daily newspaper, and as a cultural journalist for *Quebec Now*, a CBC Radio program broadcast on the national network. In 1968, she wrote her first translation for this program, an excerpt from Michel Tremblay's ground-breaking play, *Les belles-soeurs* which had premiered that same year at Montreal's Le Théâtre du Rideau Vert (John Van Burek and Bill Glassco would eventually translate it into English in its entirety). In 1975, after working as a theatre officer for the Canada Council for the Arts, where she was responsible for both Québécois Theatre and Theatre for Young Audiences (TYA) across Canada, Gaboriau accepted her first full-length translation project. It was another play, *La nef des sorcières*, collectively created by six Québécoise theatre artists, that had premiered at Le Théâtre du Nouveau Monde to celebrate International Women's Year.⁷

In "The Cultures of Theatre," Gaboriau remarks that "It was my involvement in the cultural and political life of Québec that led to my work as a translator."⁸ Her comment underplays her active engagement with the women's movement during the 1970s, as well as her increased appreciation of Québécois theatre through her work as a journalist and theatre officer. In her interview with Beauchamp and Knowles, Gaboriau is more forthright about her first major translation contract: "I was asked to translate [*La nef des sorcières*] because people knew of my interest in Québec theatre, knew I was bilingual and knew that I was very concerned and tuned into women's issues."[9]

Gaboriau's American background, like her reasons for emigrating to Québec (she became a Canadian citizen in 1992), inform her work as a translator. With some embarrassment, she typifies herself and Hervé de Fontenay, her French-born husband, as "expatriates" who have become "citizens of the world." While the couple is definitely at home in contemporary Québec, Gaboriau feels that, "from a strictly Québécois point of view, every so often, even though we're fluently involved, both linguistically and in our work, in French-speaking Québec, every so often there are situations when we're reminded that we're not 100 percent '*pure laine.*'"[10]

This sense of exile facilitates her work. Not only does it allow her to perceive francophone culture in Québec as distinct but it also leads her to view herself as a mediator between Québec and the English-speaking world as well, one who "can understand what the stakes are [in Québec] and what the goals are and how they fit into a larger picture. Where those stakes have to be respected, and those goals can be considered absolutely admirable, respectable, important, understandable." At the same time, her work as a journalist has led her to travel throughout Québec (she has visited every region except Abitibi), and she has come to "know the characters that I am asked to translate. In an imaginary way, I have some sense of their world."[11]

For Gaboriau, Québécois theatre "is a statement of cultural survival, aspiration and communion,"[12] a point of view that partially accounts for her passionate devotion to its translation. She considers herself "lucky" to be living "in a world where people have named their concerns about the survival of French in North America." Her "luck" is, of course, as much a choice as her decision to vote *oui* in the two referendums on Québec sovereignty. "Within the paradox of being born outside [Québec] and feeling very committed to this society," Gaboriau translates plays with a belief that they "are remarkable records of our times."[13] For her, all writers are "voices in the wilderness, people who are daring to stand up and try to name the very peculiar angst or joy of this decade, this century, this place." The characters in the plays that she translates "are the chorus of [a] writer's voice;" her job is "to deliver it in a way that sounds most natural and alive on stage."[14]

Playing with Position: Locating the Translator's Role

Recognizing that she is "a servant of two masters: the writer and the audience," and perhaps sensing the potential conflict between the original language of a text and the language of her target audience, she quickly adds that her "first allegiance is definitely to the writer." For Gaboriau, translation is "a literary craft" that follows naturally from her interest in literature: "I made that choice thirty-odd years ago to study French literature,...because I was most deeply attracted to writers, and to the craft of writing, and to writers from another culture."[15]

In fact, her "reason for loving translation," she explains, "is the encounter with the most intimate and, often, most creative and original *inner* voices: it's the privilege of working with writers who have made significant contributions to theatre."[16] Gaboriau is unequivocal about feeling a stronger sense of responsibility to the playwrights she translates than to the audience she addresses: "Students of literary translations are urged to give a great deal of thought to bridging that distance between the original language and the target language, the target audience, and to somehow tailor-make translations to fit the size, the needs, the expectations of the target audience. I don't approach my work as a translator that way, for better or for worse, theatrically speaking."

Gaboriau's loyalty to the writer's "voice" has won her widespread respect amongst Québécois playwrights; concomitantly, it has led her to translate a great variety of their plays. Because of this, she is adamant that "there is no single 'Québécois dialect.'" There are as many variations on the theme of spoken Québécois as there are playwrights that I have translated." Her chief challenge when translating a play is "to understand which particular brand of Québécois is being spoken. To do that I have to sense the variety of words which the writer could have used but did not." Invariably, this leads her to read works "that might be related to what I'm translating"—which takes her through a variety of genres in addition to a range of dialects.

When she was translating *Les Feluettes* by Michel Marc Bouchard, for example, she unearthed a "copy of Gabriel D'Annunzio's original French version of *The Martyrdom of Saint Sebastien* in the rare books library at McGill University."[17] While translating *Being at Home with Claude*, a play by René-Daniel Dubois, she started to read all of Dashiell Hammet's work "because the play is a detective story and consciously American (Dubois calls it his 'American' play). When I was translating *La Déposition* by Hélène Pedneault, I was reading mystery fiction...by Ruth Rendell and

Dorothy Sayers. With Garneau [*Émilie ne sera plus jamais cueillie par l'anémone*], of course, I read Emily Dickinson."[18]

The recognition that languages are as multi-layered as the cultural contexts that produce them leads to the understanding that translation is always incomplete: if translation is a bridge, then it undergoes perpetual (re)construction. And languages, like cultures, are never equal. The translator, "particularly when translating into the language of a dominant culture," as Beauchamp and Knowles explain, "must always carefully toe the line between the target language's either exoticizing or appropriating the 'other'—or, inversely, excluding it."[19]

"All translators have to face the issue of divided loyalties," concurs Gaboriau. "I'm trying to capture the originality of this work, and to convey not only *what* these artists are talking about but *how* they are talking about it."[20] However, in serving the playwright, she does not feel obliged to become "a slave to his or her exact syntax, choice of words and so on. When I say that I am faithful, as my option, it comes up in different types of choice."[21] Ultimately, as she observes in a statement whose brevity belies its complexity, "My translations have to *play;* they have to get on their feet."

Playing with Process: Negotiating the Production of Meaning

Although Gaboriau has never targeted the reader or addressee in her translation process, such an orientation is nevertheless unavoidable, at least to some degree, if only for one practical reason: Gaboriau translates for the theatre where the active reception of speech is literally concretized in the bodies of speaking actors. She comes close to acknowledging this fact in "The Cultures of Theatre" when she observes that "the translated text will be filtered through intermediaries—the actors—whose style may be different from those in the original setting."[22] Only more recently, however, does she address the impact of this understanding on her translating process. In her interview with me, she explained that, in part, the vocal "concretization" of text evolves because of her own "filtering" of language, which she describes as physical: "As I filter my own draft before I have the benefit of the actors filtering the translation, at least around a table in a workshop situation, I filter it physically. I hear it through my ears....I'm a muttering person. I don't filter it though my own voice by reading my finished draft from beginning to end but, as I'm working on it, I'll say the lines and I'm listening to them, I'm trying to feel whether you can breathe them."

In trying to "breathe" the lines of her translations, Gaboriau practices an activity akin to performance, the importance of which she has learned from both playwrights and actors. She recounts how, while collaborating with Gratien Gélinas on *The Passion of Narcisse Mondoux* in 1988, the playwright insisted that "I stamp my foot *there* when I do this in French, and I want to stamp my foot there in English as well!" In this instance, Gélinas's demands as an actor dictated not only his approach to writing but those of the translator as well. For Gaboriau, the experience was "very telling about how the words not only have to roll off the tongue, but how a dramatic text is *embodied*." Working with Gélinas, she learned that "an actor really has to be there and really put body and soul into a line,"[23] and how this affects translation: "If the actor has to be lethargic to render the character's mood in a certain scene, then the lines have to wind down in a kind of way. If he or she has to be emphatic, you have to give them the raw material to do it. So I'm very body conscious. Certain scenes, certain lines, have to build in a certain way: and the high note has to come where the body language, whatever it is—the stamp of a foot or whatever—can support the delivery of the script."

With such remarks, Gaboriau indicates her awareness of the specific nature of theatrical translation. More importantly, she acknowledges a primary addressee of her texts. In her interview with Beauchamp and Knowles in 2000, she suggests that translation, like drama itself, can be compared to "a score written for an instrument, the actors."[24] This represents a significant change in Gaboriau's discourse about translation during the last decade, one that finds some stylistic expression in her work. Barbara Godard, for instance, contends that "With later translations, Gaboriau has adopted a target language approach, changing the names of people and places, as well as the cultural references, to meet the demands of performance in the target culture."[25]

Although Godard tends to draw this conclusion on the basis of too few examples, Gaboriau does lend some credibility to her claim: "When [the source text] gets alienating because it's too 'other,'" she tells Beauchamp and Knowles, "I don't think I'm doing the best service to the playwright." When Beauchamp pushes her to expand on this idea, Gaboriau supplies the fullest account to date of the choices she faces as a translator whose work literally functions as "a complex *interplay*" between cultures: "I don't think underscoring the otherness in a self-conscious way, or even allowing it to be to apparent, is a necessarily good choice. But I also do not think that we have to pander to audience identification, you know, by always transplanting it to Ontario, or the eastern seaboard of the United States."[26]

As Don Druick points out, "The intention of theatre text—and therefore of translations of theatre texts—is primarily in its utterance."[27] Considerations of the target audience enter Gaboriau's translating process regardless of her loyalty to a playwright's text because theatre is a social art. These considerations include not only the actors who speak the text in the target language but also the myriad of spectators—the theatre-going public—that both hears *and sees* them spoken on the stage. The physicality of theatre, like its temporality, contributes to a complex semiotic—the performance (con)text—that reconfigures the translator's words in yet another act of translation.[28] While the idea of a "performance text" is not new, theorizing how it conditions the processes of meaning-making is relatively recent. Primarily, in performance studies, the focus of examination shifts from words on the page to words in performance—or, more accurately, to the physical and temporal contexts in which words are, or are not, spoken.[29] Gaboriau implies her concurrence with this idea in discussing her decision not to use *"tourtière"* in her translation of Bouchard's *Down Dangerous Passes Road*. She explains that "we left [the word] for the first couple of productions, thinking that people would sort of understand:...But we finally, the last time, decided to translate it generically.... Because we felt that it tripped up the actor, and that for people who are not familiar with [it], you don't get it."[30]

Gaboriau may have hoped to avoid an embarrassment similar to the one she experienced almost a decade earlier while watching a production of her translation of Jovette Marchessault's *The Magnificent Voyage of Emily Carr*: "Faithful to my option to convey the feeling of the author's original style," she recounts, "I had not made Jovette's dialogue any more conversational than it is in French. It is often very lyrical, sometimes philosophical, especially when Emily muses on the nature of painting and art." Gaboriau details the consequence of her choice by discussing the performance text: "What happened is that the delivery, the acting style, especially from the actors playing the other characters [than Emily], had the feeling of psychological drama, and the text sounded as if it were coming from somewhere else...I sat in the audience and squirmed."[31]

Perhaps because of other experiences of this kind, Gaboriau is prone to generalize about differences between the styles and approaches of Québécois theatre and its English-Canadian counterpart to the detriment of the latter. For her, actors in English-Canadian theatre are not comfortable "with flights of language, with poetry, or lyrical, rhetorical material." Given her perception that "these are precisely the elements which have been most characteristic of Québec theatre during the last two decades," the "limitations" of English-Canadian actors obviously present her with problems.[32] Reconsidering her translation of *The Magnificent Voyage of Emily Carr*, she muses that perhaps "it might have been more appropriate for me to have written the dialogue in a more conversational tone. But then the audience would not have heard how Jovette Marchesault chooses to write for the theatre in Québec today."[33]

Gaboriau links the experience of translating *The Magnificent Voyage of Emily Carr* to one of her earliest translations, Marchessault's *Saga of the Wet Hens*, as well as to recent translations of plays by Daniel Danis—all of which "read like poetry or overly lyrical dialogue compared to most North American English-language drama." Gaboriau explains that

> many people in the theatre community sometimes say to me "maybe you should water [the translation] down a bit, maybe you should make it a little less excessively infatuated with language, less rhetorical, less lyrical, because the actors who will be performing it and the directors who will be staging it don't work with that sort of clay most of the time." I've heard that and I've taken it seriously, and I can't do it....To not deliver into the English-speaking world the idiosyncrasies, the so-called excessive aspects perhaps, the very personal (because writing is all about sharing your very personal view of the world we live in)...I can't.

Playing with Performance: Incorporating the Effects of Production

Gaboriau follows many of her translations through their premiere productions in English; more significantly, she regularly views their original French productions as well: "I've seen the original production of at least ninety percent of the plays that I have translated." She has acknowledged that viewing the production of a play in its source language has an important impact on her translating process: "Seeing it in the source production [in Québec] gives me the basis for knowing what its theatrical signature is, as opposed to content, voice and so on....what is the theatrical shape of this play." In addition, Gaboriau "often talk[s] with the playwrights about those productions" and learns their reactions to them.[34] This also has practical consequences for her work. When the play has found "an appropriate shape" in performance, "it helps me to define the theatrical shape and potential of the piece in the translation through the theatricality I inject into the approach to dialogue and the way the characters speak."

Arguably, Linda Gaboriau translates not only playwrights' scripts but, in many cases, "traces" of their source productions as well—the performance texts that allow her to perceive the "differences" between Québécois and English-Canadian theatre that she regularly mentions in conversation. Gaboriau considers that the original production of Marchessault's *La saga des poules mouillées* at Montréal's Le Théâtre du Nouveau Monde in 1981 "was so spectacularly theatrical that it's a perfect example of one of the challenges of translating Québec theatre." She recalls, "Having seen it work on stage, having seen it be spectacular, magical and everything, of course that informed the fact that I could proceed and not dilute that text in translation." Moreover, knowing that Michelle Rossignol, the director of the source production, would direct the play's English premiere at Toronto's Tarragon Theatre the following year "was liberating" for Gaboriau as she wrote her translation. She was convinced that Rossignol "would urge the actors to take flight, to let their fancy flow and to go with the passion of the four women writers that Jovette had chosen to bring together in that imaginary encounter."[35]

Gaboriau's understanding of the relation of script to performance, along with her access to the performance and reception of her source texts, also leads her to collaborate with playwrights on changes to the original script that sometimes only emerge in her translations. Using Michel Marc Bouchard and Daniel Danis as her examples, she explains, "I often have discussions [with playwrights] as I try to zero in on something that is eluding me in a character or a scene in which they realize that I have put my finger on a murky area of their own writing. Sometimes that will lead them to rewrite the section, but only because my questions touch on things that resonate for them." A note that she includes in the initial publication of *Lilies*, her translation of *Les Feluettes* by Michel Marc Bouchard, confirms this practice as early as 1990: "For the benefit of readers who might wish to compare this translation with the original as published by Leméac Éditeur, it is important to note that, at the playwright's request, the translation is based on the script as it was revised for production. Certain lines were rewritten and others cut."[36]

Gaboriau's work with Michel Marc Bouchard on a more recent play, *The Coronation Voyage*, illustrates this idea more completely. After watching the premiere of the source text, *Le voyage du Couronnement*, in a co-production between Le Théâtre du Nouveau Monde (Montréal) and Le Théâtre du Trident (Québec City) in 1995, Bouchard "felt he had not sustained the metaphor that was the through-line." As a result, he decided to rewrite the script for its premiere production in English, another co-production, this one between the Belfry Theatre (Victoria) and Alberta Theatre Projects (Calgary). Bouchard, Gaboriau, and Roy Surette, the director of the English-language production, cloistered themselves for three weeks at the Banff Playwrights Colony where they had been invited to workshop the translation.

In this case, Gaboriau actively collaborated on the playwright's new text by translating his rewrites as he developed them with his director and the actors employed by the colony. As a consequence, Gaboriau confirms, "What people saw in English was a rewritten play." To put this another way: the source text, originally published in 1995, differs significantly from its English translation, published in 1999. In helping Bouchard achieve this difference, Gaboriau, as translator, literally affects the traffic in languages by "playing" with the writer and director to create a script that both conditions a new performance text and realizes the playwright's vision more completely. Her translation, in other words, rather than being a mimetic re-enaction of the source text, rewrites it anew.

While Gaboriau continues to assert that "The translator should simply be an invisible channel for the very personal style of the playwright to come to life in English," she has obviously had to realign her priorities during her career, not out of disregard for the source text, but rather to respect its ultimate goal, intrinsic to both versions—*performance*: "But sometimes the translator's job involves that kind of creative process where you have to get away from the words on the page—the characters' lines—and back to the essence of what's driving the play, what the forces of destiny at work on the lives of those characters are." Invariably, this leads Gaboriau to investigate "the subliminal forces at work, the currents, the moods and so on" in order "to find the words that will translate some of the untranslatable things—a phrase, title, or series of images that the playwright has woven throughout" his or her text.

Today, this approach increasingly guides Gaboriau's work as a translator, primarily because the texts that most interest her include "untranslatable things"—physical and vocal *coups de théâtre* as well as words and utterances that defy rational, let alone literal, translation. In her interview with Beauchamp and Knowles, Gaboriau cites *"les feluettes"* as an obvious example of an untranslatable word. Discussing her choices for this word in English, she documents the process by which she adapted the title of the source play of the same name into *Lilies*. Her English title draws upon tropes and images that Michel Marc Bouchard uses throughout the French version. What Gaboriau does not say is that, because the new title conveys such a striking image, she felt that the original subtitle of the play—*La répétition d'un drame romantique*—also required adapting.

She explains her choice of *The Revival of a Romantic Drama* for the English subtitle, and her decision to forego the word *"répétition"* in English: "[The English subtitle] could be read as simply the rehearsal of a romantic drama, it could be the repetition of the drama because it is being relived, or it could be a revival which has the dramatic pain of an open wound being revived—you know, the painful memories....But it's also a theatrical term, as is *'répétition'*; you can have the revival of a Williams' play, whatever. So, I explained to Michel Marc, we retain a theatrical allusion, but there's more bite for me and more drama to the 'revival' of this drama because it revives such painful passion in the characters."

Other recent translations have presented Gaboriau with more complex challenges. "Untranslatable things" have increased exponentially with her movement to new playwrights such as Daniel Danis, whose plays use idiosyncratic French constructions to blend storytelling, poetry, and unusual dialects into passionate displays of longing and despair. In meeting these challenges, Gaboriau reveals a sophisticated understanding of the relationship between script and performance text by gesturing beyond the words on the page to the languages of the stage in which these words achieve embodiment in production. The short but detailed notes that she provides for the performer and director of *Song of the Say-Sayer* are all the more remarkable given that, as a translator, her ostensible concern is the written word: "At two or three moments in the performance, it would be appropriate to hear the three brothers produce throat music akin to the act of breathing, like certain types of African and Inuit chanting. Not a single recognizable word or onomatopoeia should be used. This chanting would represent a form of human voice from before or after language."[37]

Gaboriau stresses that this direction follows Danis's instruction; but she also acknowledges that it does not exist in the source text. Rather, she explains, "[it] developed through Daniel's experience of the [play's] productions and my asking him how we can help people reading this script know how to render it." Ultimately, she acknowledges that the direction is "a slight addition that came both through my working on the translation with him but also through his own experience of what, in his mind, were mistakes in productions that resulted when people approached [the characters' speeches] in ways that he didn't intend."

Discussing the difficulty of translating a play like *Le chant du Dire-Dire* in which, Gaboriau confesses, "I felt I'd met my Waterloo," she is led once again to invoke the musical metaphor:

For those playwrights who demand in French an interpretation—a performance of lines—that is unusual in its rhythms, its musicality, its pace, I have to get down on paper something that will make it clear to an actor in a city I've never been to, that there's something about what is required to perform this script that involves an investigation of pace and rhythm. So I have to create a score in addition to the words—to the choice of vocabulary that helps us identify the world of the characters or their mood.... I have to create a score that dictates, if not the exact pace or tempo or rhythm, then the need to explore and investigate the notion of rhythm.

With *Le chant du Dire-Dire*, Gaboriau felt required not only to score the rhythm of the source text's musical phrasing but, in addition, to create neologisms that would convey a sense of the characters' bizarre ideolects similar to the one that Danis effects in French. Invariably, this led her to rely on what she terms "the translator's poetic stance"—the kind of creative process that a "good actor will have to go through to render that character as well." Gaboriau illustrates this process of "figuring out how to make a word out of not-a-word" by discussing the title of the play itself, first explaining that the "dire-dire" to which it refers is a rehabilitative toy created by the parents of the play's characters—four adopted children whose probable abuse has caused them to retreat into silence. The parents use the "dire-dire" to induce their children's speaking; Danis, in turn, uses the children's speech to create the play's twenty-one scenes that he calls "Les dires."

Translated literally, "dire-dire" means "to say-to say"; but, as Gaboriau explains, "although it's the infinitive 'to say' repeated twice, the resonance reminds you of another childhood object, the 'tirelire' which means 'piggy-bank.'" As a result, Gaboriau felt that "whatever word I came up with had to have a sound that could be part of a child's world, [and] it had to be about speech because the children spoke into it—it was the facilitator in the story of their finally being able to say things." Her choice is inspired, for, as she acknowledges, "say-sayer" has "that kind of singsong quality" that is both typical of children's speech and appropriate to "Les dires," which she translates in the text as "The Sayings." While Gaboriau respects "Danis's poetic style, with its striking images and the alternating long monologues in verse more abstract and wordy even than Marchessault's line,"[38] her neologisms in this text—and there are many—exercise her option to find creative ways of expressing the characters' evocative speech.

While Gaboriau does not pander to the target audience with such choices (indeed, I would argue, she does the opposite), she illustrates an engagement with the performance text that goes beyond mere loyalty to a playwright: "How am I going to come up with a way of speaking that...doesn't sound falsely child-like or innocent or inventive?" Gaboriau's question about the source language of *Le chant du Dire-Dire* led her to rely on her own "poetic stance" and, as a consequence, to begin "to see the linguistic patterns of how [the characters] very simplistically constructed their language." Her concern with "speaking," as opposed to writing, in other words, led her to address the ways by which an actor plays a role, and to consider how his or her performance will be received by an audience. Her concern, like her process, illustrates her understanding that, in theatre, the materiality of sound contributes as much to the meaning of language as the written word itself.

Playing with Texts: Differentiating between Performance and Publication

Traditional approaches to the study of drama and theatre "have considered the collaborative art of actor, director and designer to be one of 'translating' a dramatic text in order to bring it to life on the stage, communicating 'the playwright's meanings' more or less 'accurately' to audiences in the theatre."[39] The actors, directors, scenographers, and others charged to translate a play from the page to the stage construct sets of meanings that are specific both to their collaboration and to the cultural contexts in which it takes place. Noting that plays are often published *after* they have been produced (a practice more common in English-speaking Canada than in Québec), Beauchamp and Knowles suggest that play publication "is itself an art of translating the various performed languages of the stage—spoken language, of course, but also the languages of gesture, movement, light, colour, shape and sound—for the benefit of the solitary reader for whom the source text—the performance text—was not originally intended."[40]

Their comments help to explain Linda Gaboriau's regard for production in her approach to theatrical translation. For many of her readers, access to productions of her texts is infrequent, if it is available at all. As Lucie Robert, a specialist in Québec theatre notes, "Plays are still published nowadays, not so much for actors as for readers; they are studied as a component of the literary canon. They are often all that is left of theatre or all that is made available to those who do not live in cities or close to an active theatrical milieu."[41] While this possibly influences Gaboriau's translation choices, production, not publication, is the prime target of her texts. She has written large number of translations for productions that have not been published. Publication, to the degree that it remains important to her, allows greater dissemination of the work she values—and, hopefully, further production; for it is only in performance that Gaboriau can test the ability of her translations to achieve their fullest potential. Ultimately, this draws her even closer to the playwrights with whom she collaborates, inasmuch as it gives her a stake in her work similar to theirs—that is, having a text produced which, arguably, is the goal of all working playwrights.

Other, economic reasons also influence Gaboriau's stake in the production of her translations: "Translating a play is even less lucrative than translating a novel unless it goes into a real [full] production because a Canada Council translation grant ranges between $1,500–2,200 (it's 12 cents a word) whereas, with a novel, it's more like $12,000–18,000 because there are more words to translate." While the translation program of the Canada Council for the Arts can be seen as contributing to "the increasingly politicized, *institutionalization* of translation"[42] in Canada, the institution of theatrical translation to which Gaboriau contributes nonetheless remains underpaid and poorly recognized. It is also, as she notes, "very labour-intensive because, to get [the translation] right, you have to put it though the final filter of a workshop with actors or even a rehearsal period before production."

Gaboriau rarely receives a fee from a publisher for her translated text, and she never receives royalties from its publication—which adds an ironic dimension to her notion of being the playwright's servant. However, she always receives royalties for her translations when they are produced: in fact, she is paid every time her translations are produced. Thus, the question of how a translated text *plays* in its target language is paramount to her for practical as well as aesthetic reasons; indeed, it is synonymous with the traffic between cultures to which it contributes.

The complexities of mediating source texts and the production components that influence their translation during and after her work with a playwright now appear to engage Gaboriau's interest as much as her desire to communicate "the vision and style of exceptional writers from Québec."[43] While in 1995 Gaboriau seemed limited to this latter goal, her recent comments demonstrate greater concern for the actors who perform her translations, as well as keener interest in the theatres that produce them. One of the things Gaboriau enjoys about theatrical translation is that "it is less solitary than the literary translation of other genres," primarily because she, along with the playwrights whose work she translates, "do our final finishing touches when we finally hear the play. So we really count on—it's our polishing—the generous help and intuitions of actors."[44]

Godard finds Gaboriau's shift in orientation "in keeping with what appears to be a changing attitude towards language and a new trend in theatre translation in English Canada favouring versions speakable by actors in Canadian English."[45] A point missed by Godard is that Gaboriau has helped facilitate this shift, as well as participate in it, by organizing and administering programs in intercultural and multidisciplinary exchange through Montréal's Le Centre d'essai des auteurs dramatiques (CEAD) since the early 1980s. It was here, after being employed to develop outreach programs to theatres in Canada and abroad, that Gaboriau introduced the first workshop and play-development program for Québécois playwrights—a highly successful initiative that continues today.

In her work with CEAD, as well as in subsequent programs such as Inter-Act with Toronto's Factory Theatre and the playRite's Colony at the Banff Centre for the Arts, Gaboriau has honed her skills as a dramaturge as well as a translator, becoming one of the most sought-after in Canada today. She has added administrative responsibilities to her roster by overseeing international exchange projects for both the Banff Centre and CEAD. In 1999, she organized a highly successful residency project for playwrights and translators at Tadoussac, Québec, that has become an annual affair. Such initiatives help Gaboriau expand her ability to introduce Québécois theatre to North American audiences by giving her opportunities to pair playwrights with other translators and, in some cases, with playwrights from other cultures.

Discussing the Tadoussac residency program, where four playwrights from English-Canada join four of their Québécois counterparts for an intensive period of work, Gaboriau notes that the "experience has been with playwrights who were willing, as John Murrell with Carole Frechette's play *The Four Lives of Marie*, to play that chameleon role, and to slip into the colours of the other writer."[46] This program is particularly important to her because it helps her promote the translation of Québécois playwrights by other translators which, she recognizes, is increasingly necessary: "I haven't done any of the plays by the new wave of Québécois writers— very interesting writers that have emerged in the last few years." Quite simply, she doesn't have time, especially since Michel Tremblay has joined the group of Québécois playwrights that regularly rely on her services.

Gaboriau is proud of the Tadoussac program for another reason as well: she recognizes that besides providing playwrights with time to translate each other's work, it also facilitates "a cultural exchange experience...a forum for eight writers to talk about how they're approaching the stage today."[47] For all her interest in words, Linda Gaboriau's abiding regard for the stage emerges in everything she says. Recalling her early years at CEAD, she suggests that she "was very lucky...that my work developed beyond just the exchange in translation workshops and that I became involved, as well, in creating the dramaturgical programme." Indeed, her work in this and other dramaturgical projects has provided her with some of her most useful resources. It has allowed her "to understand better the workings of the playwright's mind, and the challenges a playwright has to face, the problems a playwright has to solve, to create individual voices, to create *drama*, movement, variety of action and rhythm in a play."

Evaluating the impact of dramaturgical work on her translation process, Gaboriau inadvertently summarizes the reasons for her success as a translator: "I really know what goes into making a play come to life in the original language—what a playwright is striving to achieve and what the ingredients are—so I'm sure that having that knowledge helps me make sure that some of that same dynamic is present in the English translation." To use the word on which she so consistently relies, Linda Gaboriau knows how to make a translation *play*.

NOTES

1. Linda Gaboriau, "A Servant of Two Masters: An Interview with Linda Gaboriau," interview by Hélène Beauchamp and Ric Knowles, *Canadian Theatre Review*, no. 102 (spring 2000): 42.
2. Translations by Linda Gaboriau that won the Chalmers New Canadian Play Award are Michel Marc Bouchard's *Lilies, or the Revival of a Romantic Drama* (1991), Normand Chaurette's *The Queens* (1993), and Michel Tremblay's *For the Pleasure of Seeing Her Again* (2000).
3. Translations by Linda Gaboriau that won Toronto's Dora Mavor Moore for best new play are Michel Marc Bouchard's *Lilies, or the Revival of a Romantic Drama* (1991), Normand Chaurette's *The Queens* (1993), and Michel Tremblay's *For the Pleasure of Seeing Her Again* (2000).
4. Translations by Linda Gaboriau that have been nominated for the Governor General's Literary Award for Translation are Michel Marc Bouchard's *Lilies, or the Revival of a Romantic Drama* (1991), Pierre Morency's *The Eye Is an Eagle* (1994), Daniel Danis's *Stone and Ashes* (1996), Michel Marc Bouchard's *Down Dangerous Passes Road* (2000), and Michel Tremblay's *Impromptu on Nun's Island* (2002).
5. Gaboriau, "A Servant of Two Masters," p. 43.
6. Gaboriau, "A Servant of Two Masters," pp. 42, 43.
7. The six co-creators of *La nef des sorcières* are Marthe Blackburn, Marie-Claire Blais, Nicole Brossard, Odette Gagnon, Luce Guilbeault, Pol Pelletier, and France Théoret. The original text was published by Les Quinze (Montréal) in 1976.

8 Linda Gaboriau, "The Cultures of Theatre," in *Cultures in Transit: Translating the Literature of Québec*, ed. Sherry Siman (Montréal: Véhicule Press, 1995), p. 89.
9 Gaboriau, "A Servant of Two Masters," p. 42.
10 Gaboriau, "A Servant of Two Masters," p. 43.
11 Gaboriau, "A Servant of Two Masters," p. 43.
12 Gaboriau, "The Cultures of Theatre," p. 87.
13 Gaboriau, "A Servant of Two Masters," p. 43.
14 Gaboriau, "A Servant of Two Masters," p. 44.
15 Gaboriau, "A Servant of Two Masters," p. 42.
16 Personal interview with Linda Gaboriau conducted in her home in Montreal on Aug. 20, 2001. All subsequent quotations are from this interview, unless otherwise identified.
17 Gaboriau, "A Servant of Two Masters," p. 46.
18 Gaboriau, "The Cultures of Theatre," p. 90.
19 Hélène Beauchamp and Ric Knowles, "Theatre and Translation," *Canadian Theatre Review*, no. 102 (spring 2000): 3.
20 Gaboriau, "The Cultures of Theatre," p. 83.
21 Gaboriau, "A Servant of Two Masters," p. 42.
22 Gaboriau, "The Cultures of Theatre," p. 85.
23 Gaboriau, "A Servant of Two Masters," p. 46.
24 Gaboriau, "A Servant of Two Masters," p. 47.
25 Barbara Godard, "Between Performative and Performance: Translation and Theatre in the Canadian/Québec Context," *Modern Drama* 42 (fall 2000): 346.
26 Gaboriau, "A Servant of Two Masters," pp. 45, 46.
27 Don Druick, "The Tender Translations of Tadoussac," *Canadian Theatre Review*, no. 102 (spring 2000): 40.
28 Lucie Robert notes this fact with apparent frustration: "The [published] text is not theatre; it is related to it in many obvious ways, but the two constitute distinct realities. Although a literary reading of drama is still possible, it has to be seen in the context of the study of theatre as an autonomous form of expression." See Lucie Robert, "The Language of Theatre," in *Essays on Modern Quebec Theatre*, ed. Joseph L. Donohue Jr. and Jonathan W. Weiss (East Lansing: Michigan State University Press, 1995), p. 110.
29 In *Theory/Theatre*, Mark Fortier explains that, in its narrowest sense, "performance" "refers to certain para- theatrical activities—happenings, demonstrations, museum exhibits involving human participants and so forth—which are related to theatre in the traditional sense." When it is more widely conceived, the term also "refers to any perfomative human activity—everything from murder trials and elections to religious and social rituals, to everyday acts, such as high school English class or shaving in front of a mirror." One way of thinking of drama, theatre, and performance, he suggests, "is to see drama as part of theatre and theatre as part of performance." While, for him, "a full study of theatre must be open to words on the page," even more importantly, "a study of theatre which does not see its relation to performance in general has made

an artificial and limiting distinction." Mark Fortier, *Theory/Theatre: An Introduction* (London and New York: Routledge 1997), pp. 12–13.
30 Gaboriau, "A Servant of Two Masters," p. 45.
31 Gaboriau, "'The Cultures of Theatre," p. 85.
32 Gaboriau, "The Cultures of Theatre," p. 84.
33 Gaboriau, "The Cultures of Theatre," p. 85.
34 Gaboriau, "A Servant of Two Masters," p. 47.
35 In Barbara Godard's estimation, Rossignol staged "an extraordinarily dynamic ritualized performance with exaggerated movement in which Marchessault's lyric flights functioned as speech in action, creating effects of spectacle through their rhythm and duration as stylized ritual rather than through any oppositional conflict among psychological characters." Godard, "Between Performative and Performance," p. 344.
36 Linda Gaboriau, translator's note in *Lilies, or the Revival of a Romantic Drama*, by Michel Marc Bouchard, trans. L. Gaboriau (Toronto: Coach House Press, 1990), p. 4.
37 Godard, "Between Performative and Performance," p. 344.
38 Godard, "Between Performative and Performance," p. 347.
39 The presence of quotation marks in these comments by Beauchamp and Knowles implies their recognition that fidelity to the playwright's "voice" in such instances frequently equals a search for authorial intent—an approach to interpretation that, since the 1960s, has been devalued by literary and critical theorists to the point of dismissal. In the variety of theories floating in its wake, those that privilege the response of readers or, as Stanley Fish calls them, "interpretative communities," hold the most relevance to contemporary theatrical practice (witness Susan Bennett's useful study, *Theatre Audiences: A Theory of Production and Reception*). In most of these theories (collectively deemed reader-response theory), authorial intent is replaced by readers' reactions, which, in turn, are determined by "competencies"—the capacities for interpretation that allow different groups of people to construct different sets of meanings, even of the same text. Fish's notion that "interpretative communities are made up of those who share interpretative strategies not for reading (in the conventional sense) but for writing texts, for constituting their properties and assigning their intentions" illuminates the theatrical practice that Beauchamp and Knowles detail in their introduction. See Stanley Fish, *Is There a Text in This Class?* (Cambridge: Harvard University Press, 1980), p. 35; and Hélène Beauchamp and Ric Knowles, "Theatre and Translation," p. 3.
40 Beauchamp and Knowles, "Theatre and Translation," p. 4.
41 Robert, "The Language of Theatre," p. 110.
42 Beauchamp and Knowles, "Theatre and Translation," p. 4; emphasis in original.
43 Gaboriau, "The Cultures of Theatre," p. 83.
44 Gaboriau, "A Servant of Two Masters," p. 47.
45 Godard, "Between Performative and Performance," p. 346.
46 Gaboriau, "A Servant of Two Masters," p. 44.
47 Gaboriau, "A Servant of Two Masters," p. 44.

BIBLIOGRAPHY

I. Primary Sources

Unpublished Translations (for Production)

Barbeau, Jean. *The Guys*. Trans. Linda Gaboriau. Vancouver: Vancouver Playhouse, 1984.

Bernard, Marielle. *The White Raven*. Trans. Linda Gaboriau. Montréal: Théâtre Sans Fil, 1979.

Bombardier, Louise. *Hippopotamus Tea*. Trans. Linda Gaboriau. Toronto: Factory Theatre / Theatre Direct, 1992.

Bouchard, Michel Marc. *Desire*. Trans. Linda Gaboriau. Knowlton: Théâtre Lac Brome, 1996.

Canac-Marquis, Normand. *Children of Urantia*. Trans. Linda Gaboriau. Toronto: Interact 91, CEAD, and Factory Theatre, 1991.

Dubois, René-Daniel. *But It's Springtime, Mr. Deslauriers*. Trans. Linda Gaboriau. Toronto: Theatre Plus, 1989.

———. *But Laura Didn't Answer*. Trans. Linda Gaboriau. Vancouver: CBC Radio, 1990.

Garneau, Michel. *Emilie*. Trans. Linda Gaboriau. Montréal: CEAD, 1987.

———. *Miss Red and the Wolves*. Trans. Linda Gaboriau. Toronto: Factory Theatre, 1992.

Gauthier, Gilles. *I Am a Bear*. Trans. Linda Gaboriau. Beloeil: Théâtre l'Arrière-Scene, 1984.

Hebert, Marie-Francine. *Yes or No*. Trans. Linda Gaboriau. Montréal: Théâtre de Carton, 1990.

Herbiet, Hedwige. *The Dandelion Days Are Over*. Trans. Linda Gaboriau. Ottawa: Page to Stage, National Arts Centre, 1991.

Lavigne, Louis-Dominique, and Daniel Meilleur. *Parasols*. Trans. Linda Gaboriau. Montréal: Théâtre de la Marmaille, 1998.

Lepage, Robert. *Vinci*. Trans. Linda Gaboriau. Montréal: Théâtre de Quat'Sous, 1987–88.

Major, Henriette. *Dream Catchers*. Trans. Linda Gaboriau. Montréal: Théâtre Sans Fil, 1992.

———. *The Crown of Destiny*. Trans. Linda Gaboriau. Montréal: Théâtre Sans Fil, 1995; Edinburgh: Edinburgh Children's Festival, 1995.

Pelletier, Pol. *Joy*. Trans. Linda Gaboriau. Toronto: Productions Pol Pelletier / Theatre Passe-Muraille, 1995.

Theatre de l'Œil. *Follow the Sun*. Trans. Linda Gaboriau. Montréal: Théâtre de l'Œil, 1980.

———. *See What You Can See*. Trans. Linda Gaboriau. Montréal: Théâtre de l'Œil,1984.

Vaillancourt, Lise. *Friends Forever*. Trans. Linda Gaboriau. Canadian Tour: Théâtre des Confettis, 1996.

Voyer, Pierre. *The Hobbit*. Trans. Linda Gaboriau. Montréal: Théâtre Sans Fil, 1980–82.

———. *The Lord of the Rings*. Trans. Linda Gaboriau. Montréal: Théâtre Sans Fil, 1986–88.

———. *The Night Fantastic*. Trans. Linda Gaboriau. Montréal: Théâtre Sans Fil, 1992.

Published Translations

Anfousse, Ginette. *My Friend Pichou, The Fight School, The Party, A Baby Sister, I'm Sulking*. Trans. Linda Gaboriau. Montréal: Éditions de la Courte échelle, 1988.

———. *Rosalie's Catastrophes*. Trans. Linda Gaboriau. Charlottetown: Ragweed Press, 1994.

———. *Rosalie's Battles*. Trans. Linda Gaboriau. Charlottetown: Ragweed Press, 1995.

———. *Rosalie's Big Dream*. Trans. Linda Gaboriau. Charlottetown: Ragweed Press, 1995.

Blackburn, Marthe, Marie-Claire Blais, Nicole Brossard, Odette Gagnon, Luce Guilbeault, Pol Pelletier, and France Theoret. *A Clash of Symbols*. Trans. Linda Gaboriau. Toronto: Coach House Press, 1979.

Blais, Marie-Claire. *American Notebooks: A Writer's Journey*. Trans. Linda Gaboriau. Vancouver: Talonbooks, 1996.

Bouchard, Michel Marc. *Lilies, or the Revival of a Romantic Drama*. Trans. Linda Gaboriau. Toronto: Coach House Press, 1990.

———. *The Orphan Muses*. Trans. Linda Gaboriau. Winnipeg: Scirocco Drama, 1995.

———. *The Coronation Voyage*. Trans. Linda Gaboriau. Vancouver: Talonbooks, 1999.

———. *The Tale of Teeka*. Trans. Linda Gaboriau. Vancouver: Talonbooks, 1999.

———. *Down Dangerous Passes Road*. Trans. Linda Gaboriau. Vancouver: Talonbooks, 2000.

Brouillet, Chrystine. *The Chinese Puzzle*. Trans. Linda Gaboriau. Charlottetown: Ragweed Press, 1996.

———. *The Enchanted Horses*. Trans. Linda Gaboriau. Charlottetown: Ragweed Press, 1996.

———. *No Orchids for Andrea!* Trans. Linda Gaboriau. Charlottetown: Ragweed Press, 1996.

Chaurette, Normand. *The Queens*. Trans. L. Gaboriau. Toronto: Coach House Press, 1992.

———. *Fragments of a Farewell Letter Read by Geologists*. Trans. L. Gaboriau. Vancouver: Talonbooks, 1998.

———. *All the Verdis of Venice*. Trans. L. Gaboriau. Vancouver: Talonbooks, 2000.

Danis, Daniel. *Stone and Ashes*. Trans. L. Gaboriau. Toronto: Coach House Press, 1995.

———. *That Woman*. Trans. L. Gaboriau. Vancouver: Talonbooks, 1998.

———. *The Song of the Say-Sayer*. Vancouver: Talonbooks, 1999.
Dubois, René-Daniel. *Being at Home with Claude*. Trans. L. Gaboriau. *Canadian Theatre Review*, no. 5 (spring 1987): 37–58.
Flores Patiño, Gilberto. *Estaban*. Trans. L. Gaboriau. Dunvegan: Cormorant Books, 1995.
Les Folles Alliées. *Miss Autobody*. Trans. L. Gaboriau. Charlottetown: Gynergy Books / Ragweed Press, 1993.
Garneau, Michel. *Warriors*. Trans. L. Gaboriau. Vancouver: Talonbooks, 1990.
Gélinas, Gratien. *The Passion of Narcisse Mondoux*. Trans. L. Gaboriau. Toronto: House of Anansi Press, 1991.
Gingras, René. "Breaks." Trans. L. Gaboriau. In *Québec Voices*, ed. Robert Wallace. Toronto: Coach House Press, 1986. 53–106.
Hebert, Marie-Francine. *My Body Inside Out*. Trans. L. Gaboriau. Montréal: Éditions de la Courte échelle, 1989.
Marchessault, Jovette. *Saga of the Wet Hens*. Trans. L. Gaboriau. Vancouver: Talonbooks, 1983.
———. *The Magnificent Voyage of Emily Carr*. Trans. L. Gaboriau. Vancouver: Talonbooks, 1992.
Morency, Pierre. *The Eye Is an Eagle*. Trans. L. Gaboriau. Toronto: Exile Editions, 1992.
Pedneault, Hélène. *Evidence to the Contrary*. Trans. L. Gaboriau. Montréal: NuAge Editions, 1993.
Tremblay, Michel. *For the Pleasure of Seeing Her Again*. Trans. L. Gaboriau. Vancouver: Talonbooks, 2000.
———. *Impromptu on Nun's Island*. Trans. L. Gaboriau. Vancouver: Talonbooks, 2002.

Published Works on Translation

Gaboriau, Linda. "A Luminous Wake in Space." *Canadian Theatre Review*, no. 43 (summer 1985).
———. "The Cultures of Theatre." In *Cultures in Transit: Translating the Literature of Québec*, ed. Sherry Simon. Montréal: Véhicule Press, 1995. 83–90.
———. "Traduire le génie l'auteur." *Jeu*, no. 56 (1996): 43–48.
———. "A Servant of Two Masters: An Interview with Linda Gaboriau." Interview by Hélène Beauchamp and Ric Knowles. *Canadian Theatre Review*, no. 102 (spring 2000): 41–47.

II. Secondary Sources

Bassnett, Susan. "The Problems of Translating Theatre Texts." *Theatre Quarterly* 10, no. 38 (1980): 47–55.
Beauchamp, Hélène, and Ric Knowles. "Theatre and Translation." *Canadian Theatre Review* no. 102 (spring 2000): 3–4.
Bennett, Susan. *Theatre Audiences: A Theory of Production and Reception*. 2nd ed. London and New York: Routledge, 1997.

Druick, Don. "The Tender Translations of Tadoussac." *Canadian Theatre Review*, no. 102 (spring 2000): 38–40.
Fish, Stanley. *Is There a Text in This Class?* Cambridge: Harvard University Press, 1980.
Fortier, Mark. *Theory/Theatre: An Introduction.* London and New York: Routledge, 1997.
Godard, Barbara. "Between Performative and Performance: Translation and Theatre in the Canadian/Québec Context." *Modern Drama* 42 (fall 2000): 327–58.
Robert, Lucie. "The Language of Theatre." In *Essays on Modern Quebec Theatre*, ed. Joseph L. Donohue Jr. and Jonathan W. Weiss. East Lansing: Michigan State University Press, 1995. 109–29.

List of Contributors

Agnès Conacher is an assistant professor in the French Department at Queen's University. She has published studies on Agrippa d'Aubigné, her area of specialization, and the nouveau roman (Claude Simon, Butor). She has also translated Mireille Calle Gruber's article for *The Hélène Cixous Reader* and essays by Derrida for the journal *Trois*. Her current research focusses on mysticism, seventeenth-century women philosophers, and Cyrano de Bergerac.

Jane Everett is an associate professor in the Department of French Language and Literature at McGill University, where she teaches Québec francophone literature and translation. Her edition of the Gabrielle Roy–Joyce Marshall correspondence was published by the University of Toronto Press in 2005. Recent publications include "Réécrire," in Jane Everett and François Ricard, ed., *Gabrielle Roy réécrite* and "Le devenir-anglais du texte et le rapport à l'écriture: Gabrielle Roy et Jacques Ferron," in Brigitte Faivre-Duboz and Patrick Poirier, eds., *Jacques Ferron: Le palimpseste infini*.

Patricia Godbout is an associate professor of translation at the Université de Sherbrooke and a member of the Literary Translators' Association of Canada. From 1986 to 1992, she was co-editor of *ellipse*, a literary magazine devoted to the translation of Canadian poetry. She is the author of *Traduction littéraire et sociabilité interculturelle au Canada (1950–1960)*.

Pamela Grant is a professor and former director of the Département des lettres et communications at the Université de Sherbrooke, where she teaches courses in professional writing, editing, translation, and translation theory. She holds a PhD in linguistics from the Université de Montréal. A certified translator (OTTIAQ), she is a co-author of the *Bibliography of Comparative Studies in Canadian, Québec, and Foreign Literatures / Bibliographie d'études comparées des littératures canadienne, québécoise et étrangères 1930–1995*. The Québec English specialist for the *Canadian Oxford Dictionary*, she has published her work in a variety of scholarly publications in Canada, the United States, and Europe.

Barbara Kerslake holds a PhD from the University of Chicago. Her career as a translator began in 1979 with Harlequin Books. A freelance translator with the Secretary of State since 1983, she has also worked for the Canada Council and various academic publishers, translating from French to English. Her interests include Québec culture and literature, especially theatre, since she is also a playwright. Since 1986, she has taught translation at York University.

Jane Koustas is an associate professor in the Department of Modern Languages, Literatures, and Cultures at Brock University. Her articles on Québec theatre and translation have appeared in *French Literature and Society, Québec Studies, Essays on Parody, Méta, TTR*, and the *University of Toronto Quarterly*. A contributor to the *Dictionary of Literary Biography*, she is the co-author (with J. Donohoe) of *Robert Lepage: Théâtre sans frontières*. In 2002, she edited a special issue of *TTR, Translation in Canada: Trends and Traditions*.

Gillian Lane-Mercier is an associate professor in the Department of French Language and Literature at McGill University, where she teaches critical theory and twentieth-century French literature. Her current areas of research include translation studies, literary theory, reception theory, the contemporary French novel, and literary translation in Québec and Canada since 1960. Author of *La parole romanesque* and co-author of *Faulkner: Une experience de retraduction*, she has published numerous articles on the theory of the novel and in the field of translation studies. She is currently working on a book on contemporary Anglo-Québécois and Canadian novelist-translators.

Kathy Mezei teaches in the Department of Humanities at Simon Fraser University; she has published several articles on literary translation and the *Bibliography of Criticism on French and English Literary Translations* *in Canada*; she was one of the founding editors of *Tessera*, a feminist journal. She is part of the team, based at the Université de Sherbrooke, producing a database on Comparative Canadian Literatures and Translation Studies. *Domestic Modernism, the Inter-War Novel, and E.H. Young*, co-authored with Chiara Briganti, is forthcoming from Ashgate Press.

Stephanie Nutting is an associate professor in the Department of French Studies at the University of Guelph. Her main area of research is Québec theatre and poetry. She has published *Le tragique dans le théâtre québécois et canadien-français, 1950–1989* and numerous articles in *Voix et Images*, the *French Review*, *Spirale*, the *University of Toronto Quarterly*, and other journals. She is president of the Association des professeur(e)s de français des universités et collèges canadiens.

Sherry Simon taught for many years at Concordia University. She is Canada Research Chair in Translation and Cultural History at Glendon College, York University. A member of the editorial board of the cultural magazine *Spirale* for more than ten years, she is the author or editor of numerous publications on feminist and postcolonial theories of translation, including (with David Homel), *Mapping Literature: The Art and Politics of Translation, Le Trafic des langues, Culture in Transit: Translating the Literature of Quebec*, and *Gender in Translation: Cultural Identity and the Politics of Transmission*.

Robert Wallace is Professor Emeritus of English and Drama Studies at York University. His books include *Producing Marginality: Theatre and Criticism in Canada, The Work: Conversations with English-Canadian Playwrights* (with Cynthia Zimmerman), *Quebec Voices, Making Out: Plays by Gay Men, Theatre and Transformation in Contemporary Canada*, and *Staging a Nation: Evolutions in Contemporary Canadian Theatre*. He has written and produced ten documentaries for CBC radio about twentieth-century performance and edited more than twenty volumes of Canadian plays for Coach House Press.

Agnes Whitfield co-ordinated the translation program at Queen's University for ten years, and is now a professor and the former director of the School of Translation at York University. She has published ten books and over fifty articles on Québec literature and translation, including *Le Métier du double: Portraits de traducteurs et traductrices francophones*. Her most recent articles have appeared in *Méta*, the *University of Toronto Quarterly*, and international conference proceedings in Porto and Prague.

Shortlisted for the Governor-General's Award for *Divine D*iva, her translation of *Venite a cantare* by Québec writer Daniel Gagnon, she is a certified translator (ATIO). President of the Canadian Association for Translation Studies for two mandates (1995–99), she was Seagram Visiting Chair at the McGill Institute for the Study of Canada (2003–2004).

www.ingramcontent.com/pod-product-compliance
Lightning Source LLC
Chambersburg PA
CBHW071149070526
44584CB00019B/2726